GREEK ORATORS II

Dinarchus and Hyperides

For
Oliver Edward Worthington
Born 23 January, 1998

Advisory Editor: M.M. Willcock

Greek Orators II

Dinarchus and Hyperides

edited and translated by
Ian Worthington

ARIS & PHILLIPS LTD – WARMINSTER – ENGLAND

ISBN   limp   0 85668 306 X
          cloth   0 85668 307 8

British Library Cataloguing-in-Publication Data
A catalogue record of this book is available from the British Library

Published and printed in England by Aris & Phillips Ltd, Teddington House, Warminster, Wiltshire BA12 8PQ

CONTENTS

PREFACE

It is a pleasure to contribute this volume to this series on the Greek orators. The original idea was that Volume 2 in the series would feature Hyperides; when that volume was delayed and I became involved in the series, I was delighted that Professor Willcock agreed to include a speech of Dinarchus as well.

Hyperides has been neglected in modern scholarship on the orators, and it is hoped that the two speeches here will help to remedy that. Dinarchus also has received little treatment, at least until the publication of my commentary on his three extant speeches in 1992 (see under abbreviations below). The inclusion of Dinarchus' speech *Against Demosthenes* in this volume gave me the chance to include a Greek text (which could not be included in my other commentary) and to revise the translation of that speech from my earlier book. The three orations in this volume are selected for two major reasons: they are the last speeches we have by classical Greek orators, and they were delivered in 323 and 322 at a time when Athens, and indeed Greece, was controlled by Macedon and attempting to regain its autonomy one last time in the classical period. Thus, the three speeches stand nicely together not least for the contemporary information which they impart on this important and complex period; the historical background is discussed in the Introduction of this volume.

This book took longer to write than it should have since shortly after I started it I moved from the Department of Classics at the University of Tasmania, Australia, to the Department of History at the University of Missouri-Columbia, U.S.A. It is a pleasure to be a member of a remarkable scholarly department with stimulating and convivial colleagues (in both the History and Classical Studies departments), who are committed to the highest quality of teaching and research. I would like to acknowledge Columbia's timely generosity in coming to my aid in what for Classics in Australia is a period of departmental and institutional deterioration, brought on not only because of government cutbacks in the humanities.

I have several people to thank, without whose support this book would not have seen the light of day. To Professor Malcolm Willcock I owe the greatest academic debt. Despite his other commitments, he was always willing to help me on numerous points of detail, especially in the preparation of the text and translation, and responded patiently to my many pestering questions with lengthy letters. He has read the entire book in at least two draft stages, and many of his suggestions are incorporated into it (although I have not always followed his advice, which is likely to be to my own detriment). I am also very grateful to Professors Jenny Strauss Clay (Virginia) and Peter Toohey (now Calgary – a substantial loss to Australia) for responding to questions and acting as sounding boards for my ideas. Professor Marianne McDonald (UC San Diego) is someone I particularly want to single out. Her support and belief in my research mean more than she knows: many have learned much from her own valuable work, and many can learn much from her as a person. I also wish to thank the staff at Aris and Phillips, especially Janet Davis, not only for their hard work in producing my book but also for overcoming many technical problems with the Greek text in this volume. Finally, to my wife Tracy: I am grateful as always for her encouragement through good and bad times. I especially thank her for all she did and is doing for our son Oliver: the best thing that ever happened to me.

Ian Worthington
Department of History
University of Missouri-Columbia
April 1999

SPECIAL NOTES

(1) The translation of the speeches of Dinarchus and of Hyperides is my own, although I have referred to that of J.O. Burtt (*Minor Attic Orators*, Vol. 2, Loeb Classical Library) in cases where I feel his translation cannot be bettered. The extent of my reliance will be obvious.

(2) Translations of other speeches and of other ancient authors are taken from the relevant Loeb Classical Library editions.

(3) Speeches of Hyperides follow the numbering of the Oxford and Loeb texts; thus the *Against Demosthenes* is Speech 5, not Speech 1 as in Jensen's Teubner text.

(4) The commentaries on the three speeches in this volume are historical, although some literary and philological points are discussed where relevant.

(5) In the commentaries, arabic numerals appearing by themselves refer to the sections of the speech in question. References to speeches by the same or by other orators are preceded by the relevant numeral so as to avoid confusion.

(6) The commentary on Dinarchus' speech *Against Demosthenes* is taken largely from my bigger commentary on Dinarchus (see abbreviations below). I have adapted this to the needs and readership of the present volume, but for more detailed discussion readers should consult my other work. The translation of Dinarchus' speech is new, and readers are asked in future to use the version in this volume and not that in my bigger commentary.

(7) I am a firm believer in giving the anglicised forms of Greek names. I have tried to be as consistent as possible in this practice; however, certain words of a technical nature have not been anglicised – for example *logographos* – and these will be evident when they appear.

(8) All dates are B.C. unless otherwise indicated.

ABBREVIATIONS

Ancient Authors:

Aes.	Aeschines
AP	*Athenaion Politeia* (attributed to Aristotle)
Arr.	Arrian, *Anabasis Alexandri*
Curt.	Quintus Curtius Rufus
Dem.	Demosthenes
[Dem.]	Pseudo-Demosthenes
Din.	Dinarchus
Diod.	Diodorus
Dion. Hal.	Dionysius of Halicarnassus
Hyp.	Hyperides
Plut.	Plutarch
[Plut.]	Pseudo-Plutarch

The following abbreviations for modern works are used:

Berve, *Alexander*	H. Berve, *Das Alexanderreich auf prosopographischer Grundlage*, 2 vols. (Munich: 1926)
Blass	F. Blass, *Dinarchus Orationes*, Teubner text (Leipzig: 1888)
Bosworth, *Conquest and Empire*	A.B. Bosworth, *Conquest and Empire. The Reign of Alexander the Great* (Cambridge: 1988)
Burtt	J.O. Burtt, *Minor Attic Orators*, Vol. 2, Loeb Classical Library (London: 1954)
Colin	G. Colin, *Hypéride, Discours*, Budé text (Paris: 1946)
Conomis	N.C. Conomis, *Dinarchi Orationes*, Teubner text (Leipzig: 1975)
Davies, *APF*	J.K. Davies, *Athenian Propertied Families* (Oxford: 1971)
FGrH	F. Jacoby, *Die Fragmente der griechischen Historiker* several vols. (Berlin: 1926-30/ Leiden: 1940-58)
Hammond & Griffith, *HM* 2	N.G.L. Hammond and G.T. Griffith, *A History of Macedonia*, Vol. 2 (Oxford: 1979)
Hammond & Walbank, *HM* 3	N.G.L. Hammond and F.W. Walbank, *A History of Macedonia*, Vol. 3 (Oxford: 1988)
IG	*Inscriptiones Graecae*
Jensen	C. Jensen, *Hyperidis Orationes*, Teubner text (Leipzig: 1917, repr. 1963)

Kenyon   F.G. Kenyon, *Hyperidis Orationes et Fragmenta*, Oxford Classical text (Oxford: 1906)

Nouhaud and Dors-Méary   M. Nouhaud and L. Dors-Méary, *Dinarque Discours*, Budé text (Paris: 1990)

PA   J.E. Kirchner, *Prosopographia Attika*, 2 vols. (Berlin: 1901-03)

Worthington, *Dinarchus*   Ian Worthington, *A Historical Commentary on Dinarchus. Rhetoric and Conspiracy in Later Fourth-Century Athens* (Ann Arbor: 1992)

SELECT BIBLIOGRAPHY

Adams, C.D. 'The Harpalos Case', *TAPhA* 32 (1901), 121-153

Adcock, F. and D.J. Mosley, *Diplomacy in Ancient Greece* (London: 1975)

Ashton, N.G. 'The Lamian War – a False Start?', *Antichthon* 17 (1983), 47-63

——— 'The Lamian War – stat magni nominis umbra', *JHS* 104 (1984), 152-157

Atkinson, J.E. *A Commentary on Q. Curtius Rufus' Historiae Alexandri Magni Books 3 and 4* (Amsterdam: 1980)

Atkinson, K.M.T. 'Demosthenes, Alexander and Asebeia', *Athenaeum* 51 (1973), 310-335

Aymard, A. 'Un Ordre d'Alexandre', *REA* 39 (1937), 5-28

Badian, E. 'Harpalus', *JHS* 81 (1961), 16-43

——— 'The Deification of Alexander the Great', *Ancient Macedonian Studies in Honour of C.F. Edson*, ed. H.J. Dell, Institute for Balkan Studies (Thessaloniki: 1981), 27-71

——— 'Alexander the Great between Two Thrones and Heaven: Variations on an Old Theme', *Subject and Ruler: The Cult of the Ruling Power in Classical Antiquity*, ed. A. Small [Ann Arbor: 1996), 11-26

Balsdon, J.P.V.D. 'The 'Divinity' of Alexander', *Historia* 1 (1950), 363-388

Bickerman, E.J. 'La lettre d'Alexandre le Grand aux bannis Grecs', *REA* 42 (1940), 25-35

——— 'Sur un passage d'Hypéride', *Athenaeum* 41 (1963), 70-85

Blass, F. *Die attische Beredsamkeit²*, 3 vols (Leipzig: 1887-98)

Bosworth, A.B. *A Historical Commentary on Arrian's* History of Alexander, 1 (Oxford: 1980) and 2 (Oxford: 1995)

Burke, E.M. 'Lycurgan Finances', *GRBS* 26 (1985), 251-264

Carawan, E.M. '*Apophasis* and *Eisangelia*: The Rôle of the Areopagus in Athenian Political Trials', *GRBS* 26 (1985), 115-140

Cargill, J. *The Second Athenian League* (Berkeley: 1981)

——— *Athenian Settlements of the Fourth Century BC* (Leiden: 1995)

Cawkwell, G.L. 'Demosthenes' Policy after the Peace of Philocrates I and II', *CQ²* 13 (1963), 120-138 and 200-213

—— 'The Crowning of Demosthenes', *CQ²* 19 (1969), 163-180

—— 'The End of Greek Liberty', *Transitions to Empire, Essays in Honor of E. Badian*, edd. R. W. Wallace and E.M. Harris (Norman: 1996), 98-121

Cloché, P. *Démosthène et la fin de la démocratie Athénienne* (Paris: 1937)

Colin, G. 'Démosthène et l'affaire d'Harpale', *REG* 38 (1925), 306-349 and 39 (1926), 31-89

—— 'Le discours d'Hypéride contre Démosthène sur l'argent d'Harpale', *Annales de l'Est, Mémoires* 4 (Nancy: 1934), 6-32

Denniston, J.D. *Greek Prose Style* (Oxford: 1952)

Dobson, J.F. *The Greek Orators* (London: 1919)

Dover, K.J. *Lysias and the Corpus Lysiacum* (Berkeley: 1968)

—— *Greek Popular Morality in the Time of Plato and Aristotle* (Oxford: 1974)

Ellis, J.R. *Philip II and Macedonian Imperialism* (London: 1976)

Fredricksmeyer, E. 'Alexander and Philip: Emulation and Resentment', *CJ* 85 (1990), 3-15

Goldstein, J.A. *The Letters of Demosthenes* (New York and London: 1968)

Griffith, G.T. (ed.) *Alexander the Great, The Main Problems* (Cambridge: 1966)

Gunderson, L.L. 'Alexander and the Attic Orators', *Ancient Macedonian Studies in Honour of C.F. Edson*, ed. H.J. Dell, Institute for Balkan Studies (Thessaloniki: 1981), 183-192

Hamilton, J.R. *Plutarch, Alexander. A Commentary* (Oxford: 1969)

Hammond, N.G.L. *Alexander the Great, King, Commander and Statesman* (Park Ridge: 1980)

—— *The Genius of Alexander* (London: 1996)

Hansen, M.H. *The Athenian Ecclesia*, Vol. 1, *A Collection of Articles 1976-83* (Copenhagen: 1983)

—— *The Athenian Assembly in the Age of Demosthenes* (Oxford: 1987)

—— *The Athenian Ecclesia*, Vol. 2, *A Collection of Articles 1983-89* (Copenhagen: 1989)

Harding, P. 'Athenian Foreign Policy in the Fourth Century', *Klio* 77 (1995), 105-125

Harrison, A.R.W. *The Law of Athens*, 2 vols. (Oxford: 1968–1971)

Heckel, W. *The Marshals of Alexander's Empire* (London: 1992)

Heisserer, A.J. *Alexander the Great and the Greeks, the Epigraphic Evidence* (Norman: 1980)

Jaschinski, S. *Alexander und Griechenland unter dem Eindruck der Flucht des Harpalos* (Bonn: 1981)

Jebb, R.C. *The Attic Orators from Antiphon to Isaeus²* 2 vols. (London: 1883)

Kennedy, G. *The Art of Persuasion in Greece* (Princeton: 1963)

—— *A New History of Classical Rhetoric* (Princeton: 1994)

Loraux, L. *The Invention of Athens. The Funeral Oration in the Classical City* (Cambridge, Mass.: 1986)

MacDowell, D.M. *The Law in Classical Athens* (London: 1978)

Mikalson, J.D. *Religion in Hellenistic Athens* (Berkeley and Los Angeles: 1998)

Mitchel, F.W. 'Athens in the Age of Alexander', *G&R*[2] 12 (1965), 189-204

—— 'Lykourgan Athens: 338-322', *Lectures in Memory of L.T. Semple* 2 (Cincinnati: 1970)

Nouhard, M. *L'Utilisation de l'Histoire par les Orateurs Attiques* (Paris: 1982)

Ober, J. *Mass and Elite in Democratic Athens. Rhetoric, Ideology and the Power of the People* (Princeton: 1989)

Pearson, L. 'Historical Allusions in the Attic Orators', *CPh* 36 (1941), 209-229

Perlman, S. 'The Historical Example, Its Use and Importance as Political Propaganda in the Attic Orators', *SH* 7 (1961), 150-166

—— 'Political Leadership in Athens in the Fourth Century B.C.', *PP* 22 (1967), 161-176

—— (ed.) *Philip and Athens* (Cambridge: 1973)

Pickard-Cambridge, A.W. *Demosthenes and the Last Days of Greek Freedom, 384-322 B.C.* (London: 1914)

Rhodes, P.J. *The Athenian Boule* (Oxford: 1972)

—— *A Commentary on the Aristotelian* Athenaion Politeia (Oxford: 1981)

—— 'Political Activity in Classical Athens', *JHS* 106 (1986), 132-144

Roebuck, C. 'The Settlement of Philip II with the Greek States in 338 B.C.', *CPh* 43 (1948), 73-92

Rosen, K. 'Der 'Göttliche' Alexander, Athen und Samos', *Historia* 27 (1978), 20-39

Ryder, T.T.B. *Koine Eirene* (Oxford: 1965)

Sawada, N. 'Athenian Politics in the Age of Alexander the Great: A Reconsideration of the Trial of Ctesiphon', *Chiron* 26 (1996), 57-84

Schäfer, A. *Demosthenes und seine Zeit*[2], 3 vols. (Leipzig: 1885-1887)

Schwenk, C.J. *Athens in the Age of Alexander. The Dated Laws and Decrees of 'the Lykourgan Era,'* 338-322 B.C. (Chicago: 1985)

Sealey, R. *Demosthenes and his Time* (Oxford: 1993)

Seibert, J. *Alexander der Grosse* (Darmstadt: 1972)

Shoemaker, G. 'Dinarchus. Traditions of His Life and Speeches with a Commentary on the Fragments of the Speeches', unpub. Ph.D. dissertation (Columbia University: 1968)

Stewart, A. *Faces of Power. Alexander's Image and Hellenistic Politics* (Berkeley and Los Angeles: 1993)

Tod, M.N. *Greek Historical Inscriptions* 2 (Oxford: 1948)

Usher, S. *Demosthenes On The Crown* (Warminster: 1993)

Wallace, R.W. *The Areopagos Council, to 307 B.C.* (Baltimore and London: 1989)

Worthington, Ian 'The Chronology of the Harpalus Affair', *SO* 61 (1986), 63-76

—— (ed.) *Persuasion: Greek Rhetoric In Action* (London: 1994)

—— (ed.) *Ventures Into Greek History. Essays in Honour of N.G.L. Hammond* (Oxford: 1994)

Introduction

(1) The Historical Background

The Beginning of the End of Greek Autonomy

The years from the mid-340's to the late fourth century were not glorious ones for the Athenians (or for the Greek states in general), a stark contrast to their exploits and indeed reputation in the fifth and earlier fourth centuries. During this time, Greece's autonomy was steadily eroded and then lost forever, in 337, to the might of Macedon, and eventually, in 146, to the power of Rome. Although Athens later attempted to throw off the Macedonian yoke, combining with Sparta, certain other states and Ptolemy II Philadelphus in the Chremonidean War (268-262), this too ended in failure. Antigonus II Gonatas' enforced rule which followed firmly established the Antigonid dynasty in Greece, and showed the total control of Macedon. To all intents and purposes, however, Greek autonomy had been lost on the field at Chaeronea in 338 before the army of Philip II, who had ruled Macedon from 359 to 336 and established that state as the most powerful in the Greek world.

In reality of course it was the Greeks themselves who were to blame for their demise, not Macedonian superiority in battle. While Demosthenes, one of the most influential Athenian statesmen of the fourth century, was certainly right in his oratory to harangue his fellow-countrymen for their apathy and sloth in resisting Philip II, or while the apparent inconsistency of Athenian foreign policy as well as a system of direct democracy were factors in Athens' downfall, no one realised – or at least was prepared to argue – that the real problem lay in the obsolete *polis* system of Greece.[1] Another Athenian, Isocrates, in his *Philip* of 346 (cf. *Epistle* 3) rightly saw that the civil distress that existed in so many *poleis* and the inter-*polis* strife would never allow any common unity and would prove the undoing of the various Greek states. Over the course of forty years, in his treatises the *Panegyricus* and the *Philip*, he called for the invasion of Persia by a union of the Greek *poleis* – in the first (written c. 380) under the leadership of Athens, and in the second (in 346) under Philip II. His calls came to nothing, if indeed they had been real political policy calls in the first place – imagine a union of Athens and Sparta in 380, or the Athenians voluntarily turning themselves over to Philip's lead and authority in 346!

That Isocrates' treatises were unsuccessful had nothing to do with the impracticality of an invasion of Persia of course. A country composed of independent and xenophobic *poleis*, all too often at war with each other, for the most

---

[1] Note the criticisms of N.G.L. Hammond, *Philip of Macedon* (London: 1994), 64-78, and see too G. Cawkwell, 'The End of Greek Liberty', in *Transitions to Empire, Essays in Honor of E. Badian*, edd. R. W. Wallace and E.M. Harris (Norman: 1996), 98-121. For a very different view of the abilities of the Athenian people and for a consistent foreign policy see P. Harding, 'Athenian Foreign Policy in the Fourth Century', *Klio* 77 (1995), 105-125.

part able to unite only when faced by a common foe (and then not always with ease, as is evident in 481/80 when the threat of Persian invasion under Xerxes became known), proved no obstacle to the concentrated power of a state dominated by a single king, under whom served a superbly trained army willing to fight. Nor could a direct democracy, such as the Athenian, run a war. Athenian direct democracy was the principal reason why Athens had lost the Peloponnesian War (431-404), and in the fourth century the interminable meetings of the Assembly, which had to ratify military as well as political policies, and the ease with which the people were swayed by the rhetoric of a few, brought Athens again to its knees. This is a stark contrast to the potential of a state in which power lay in the hands of one man, one undisputed king. That state, after 359, was Macedon, and the man was its king, Philip II.

Although the Athenians headed a powerful naval empire (the Second Athenian Confederacy), founded in 378/7, in reality Macedon had been dominating Greek politics since 346, the Peace of Philocrates.[2] In that year the Sacred War waged by the Greek *poleis* and Philip against the state of Phocis (Diod. 16.23 ff.), which had sacrilegiously occupied Delphi, came to an end.[3] The bloodthirsty mood of the Amphictyonic Council, which was responsible for administering the oracle of Apollo at Delphi, was tempered by Philip himself (Diod. 16.60). Of course, our oratorical sources do not properly represent Philip on this matter (cf. Dem. 19.64 ff., Hyp. 6.13), but there is no question that Philip was able to save the Phocians from a terrible fate. The king was made a formal member of the Amphictyonic Council with two votes, and even more significant he, a 'barbarian' in Greek eyes,[4] was to preside at the Pythian games in September of that year. The Peace of Philocrates also brought to an end the warfare between Philip and the Athenians, which had broken out in 357 over the king's retention of Amphipolis (Diod. 16.8.2).[5] The Athenians lost heavily in the conditions of the peace, and at first neither they nor the Spartans would participate in the Games (Dem. 19.128). Philip simply demanded their presence, along with their acknowledgement of his membership of the Amphictyonic Council and his presidency of the games (Dem. 19.111 ff.). The writing was on the wall, and faced with the king's ultimatum Demosthenes delivered his speech *On The Peace* (5), and the Athenians capitulated. At the same time, it is important to note that in his speech Demosthenes merely saw the peace as a breathing space before further hostilities.

Over the next ten years Macedon would come to dominate Greek affairs. In 340, when Philip II seized the Athenian corn fleet, Demosthenes persuaded the Athenians

---

[2]   On the establishment and nature of the Second Athenian Confederacy see R. Sealey, *Demosthenes and his Time* (Oxford: 1993), 50-73; cf. commentary on Dinarchus 1.28. On the peace see Hammond & Griffith, *HM* 2, 329-347; on the historical background here discussed see especially J.R. Ellis, *Philip II and Macedonian Imperialism* (London: 1976), 125 ff., Hammond & Griffith, *HM* 2, 329 ff. and Hammond, *Philip of Macedon*, 98 ff., quoting ancient sources and modern bibliography.

[3]   Diod. 16.59.2-4, Dem. 6.13, 19.126 and Aes. 2.137 ff.

[4]   Even as late as 323 we have references to the Macedonians as 'barbarians' (Din. 1.24).

[5]   See commentary on Dinarchus 1.28.

to declare war on him.[6] This second war would not last long, and the only real setback for Philip in the course of it was Athens' alliance with its old enemies the Thebans, effected by Demosthenes, in 339.[7] In 338 Athens and Thebes, helped by Achaea, Megara, Corinth and several islands (Dem. 18.237), staked a last-ditch effort against Philip at Chaeronea in Boeotia, but to no avail. The battle of Chaeronea, fought on 2 August 338, saw the total defeat of the Greek force at the hands of Philip, ably helped by the heir to the throne, the eighteen year old Alexander.[8] Philip treated the Thebans harshly (*inter alia*, establishing a Macedonian garrison on the Cadmea), and then turned to Athens. In the city, there was panic and confusion (Lycurgus 1.39-45). Hyperides proposed to enfranchise the *atimoi* (those who had lost their civic rights for offences) and metics (non-citizen residents of Athens) and to manumit the slaves, so that they could fight, and to send the women, children, and sacred objects to the Piraeus for safety.[9] An understandably anxious Demosthenes then took his leave of Athens by securing a commission to acquire corn supplies,[10] for which Dinarchus (1.80-82) later condemned him. Demosthenes, though, was chosen by the Athenians to deliver the *epitaphios* (funeral oration) over those who had died in battle at Chaeronea, and that signal public honour shows his influence in Athens (Dem. 18.285, Plut. *Demosthenes* 21.2). Speech 60 in the Demosthenic corpus is the funeral oration. However, it is possible that what survives today is a poor imitation, for in antiquity it was regarded as spurious (Dion. Hal. *Demosthenes* 44).

Philip, to everyone's surprise, contented himself with having the Athenians merely dismantle their naval empire. He had no need to march on Athens for the battle of Chaeronea had made him master of Greece, and besides he needed the Athenians' naval expertise and strength for his planned invasion of Persia. The Athenian prisoners from Chaeronea were returned unransomed to Athens, and the ashes of those who died at the battle were escorted to the city by no less than Alexander, the heir apparent, and Antipater themselves.[11] Thus, in the winter of 338/7 deputations from the Greek states had been summoned by Philip to meet at Corinth, and all but the Spartans attended.[12] At this congress Philip announced a Common Peace, headed by a leader with a council of the allies, and with each state having a number of votes, which would discuss policy, maintain peace, and be loyal to Philip and — significantly — his descendants. Philip's dynasty was here to stay, and along with it the subservience of Greece. Philip was duly elected leader of the League — what choice did the Greeks have? He promised that the autonomy of the

---

6   Dem. 18.72, 87 ff., 139, 240-243, Diod. 16.77.2-3.
7   Dem. 18.168-188, 211, Aes. 3.140-141; cf. Din. 1.12 (with commentary), Diod. 16.84 ff., Plut. *Demosthenes* 18.1, and see Ellis, *Philip II and Macedonian Imperialism*, 191-193.
8   Diod. 16.85.5 ff., Plut. *Alexander* 9.2, Polyaenus 4.2.2 and 4.2.7. See in detail Hammond & Griffith, *HM* 2, 596-603; cf. commentary on Dinarchus 1.78.
9   Lycurgus 1.16, 41, [Dem.] 26.11, [Plut.] *Moralia* 849a.
10 Aes. 3.159, 259, Dem. 18.248, Lycurgus 1.42.
11 Diod. 18.56.6-7, Plut. *Alexander* 28.1-2, Pausanias 1.25.3, 1.34.1.
12 *IG* ii² 236, Diod. 16.89.1-3, [Dem.] 17. 1 ff., Justin 9.5.1-6. See further Hammond & Griffith, *HM* 2, 623-646 and Hammond, *Philip of Macedon*, 158-164.

Greek states would be assured and then presented a proposal for the invasion of
Persia, a variation on the panhellenic plan as put forward by Isocrates in the *Philip*
of 346.[13] Given Philip's power, the League could only meekly accept the proposal
of its leader, and the Athenians followed up this endorsement with an embassy to
Philip offering him a golden crown and their guarantee not to harbour any of his
enemies (Diod. 16.92.1-2).

Then in July 336 Philip II was murdered, cut down at his niece's wedding in the
theatre of Aegae by the assassin's sword (Diod. 16.93-95, Arr. 1.1.1). The motives
for his murder do not concern us here,[14] but one thing can be said: Philip's manner
of death was not fitting for the most exciting and dynamic man of the fourth century.
Greece rejoiced at the news of Philip's death and, backed by Persia, immediately
revolted from Macedon and the League of Corinth. In Athens, the story goes,
Demosthenes danced around the town, literally, in festal clothes and persuaded the
Boule to make a public sacrifice of thanksgiving even though his daughter had died
less than a week earlier (Aes. 3.77, 160, cf. Plut. *Phocion* 16.6). Both rejoicing and
revolting were to be short-lived: Alexander 'the Great', Philip's heir, would see to
that. It is under Alexander's rule that we see the total reduction of Greece as a
political and military power, and we move more fully now to the historical
background against which the speeches of Dinarchus and Hyperides were set.

The Alexander Years

Supported unanimously by the Macedonian army, Alexander III ('the Great')[15]
assumed the throne of Macedon in 336 and stormed into Greece with such
unexpected speed (Diod. 17.4.4) that the Greeks were quickly overwhelmed. In a
matter of months he had subdued them by force and alliances, and then he
reimposed the Common Peace of the League of Corinth. At a meeting of the League
Alexander was proclaimed leader of the Greeks and the Persian invasion was again
endorsed (Diod. 17.4.9). Only Sparta once again remained aloof.[16]

At least one Greek state did not yet have its spirit broken. In 335 Thebes
revolted, and received support from some other states (including initially Athens)
and also money from the Persian king, who evidently took Alexander's invasion
threat seriously. The Thebans' hope of overthrowing Macedonian power proved
vain: Alexander swept against them with some 30,000 infantry and 300 cavalry and
ordered their surrender (Diod. 17.9.ff., Arr. 1.7.1-3, Plut. *Demosthenes* 23.1). They
defied him, but there would be no second chances. After forcing the city to
surrender he had it razed to the ground, cynically operating through the League of

---

[13]   Diod. 16.89.2. For the decree, see M.N. Tod, *Greek Historical Inscriptions* 2 (Oxford:
       1948), no. 177; cf. T.T.B. Ryder, *Koine Eirene* (Oxford: 1965), 102-105 and 150-162.
[14]   Cf. Hammond, *Philip of Macedon*, 170-176.
[15]   On the appropriateness of Alexander's epithet see my 'How Great was Alexander?', *AHB*
       13 (1999), 39-55.
[16]   On the following historical background see Hammond & Walbank, *HM* 3, 72 ff. and
       Bosworth, *Conquest and Empire*, 25 ff., citing ancient sources and modern bibliography.

Corinth (Diod. 17.14.1, Arr. 1.7.7-8.8, Justin 11.3.8); 6,000 Thebans were killed and 30,000 were taken prisoner.[17]

This catastrophic event sent shock-waves throughout the Greek world, and the Athenians, fearing retribution for their early support of the Thebans, sent an embassy to the king which contemptibly congratulated him for his punishment of the Theban revolt. Although Alexander demanded the surrender of several leading orators, including Demosthenes, Lycurgus and apparently Hyperides (although the latter's inclusion is suspect: see below, Section 4.), he later relented. In 334 Alexander left for Persia, never to return to Greece, leaving behind the tried and trusted old general Antipater as guardian (*epitropos*) of a stable Greece and Macedon (Arr. 1.11.3) and to act as deputy leader in the League of Corinth.

For the Greeks, Alexander's departure and Antipater's tight control gave them a period of sufficient peace to enable some prosperity. Nowhere was this prosperity more evident than in Athens, thanks to the administration of Lycurgus,[18] who had near total control of Athenian finances for a dozen years (Diod. 16.88.1). By careful manipulation of the Athenian tax system, Lycurgus was able to save Athens from the financial straits of recent years, even to the extent of putting into action a building programme (including a naval arsenal, the Panathenaic Stadium and the Theatre of Dionysus) aimed at fortifying and beautifying the city, and the introduction of the ephebic system, a form of military conscription. All of this is in keeping with a new, grander, phase of Athenian history after the darkness of recent decades. Lycurgus died in 324, an old and sick man, although just before he died the story goes that he was indicted by the Athenians and tried for corruption and that he was carried into court on his death bed ([Plut.] *Moralia* 842e). After his death his children were prosecuted, although they were acquitted thanks to Demosthenes' epistolary intervention (*Epistle* 3; cf. [Plut.] *Moralia* 842e).

The punishment meted out by Alexander to the Thebans in 335 was intended as a lesson to be learned by all: rejection of the League of Corinth – in other words, rebellion against Macedonian control – would be met with no mercy. The lesson was well learned, especially by the Athenians, who in the 330s and 320s prudently maintained a low profile in international affairs compared to the decades before then. Caution was the order of the day in dealings with Macedon, as is proved by the lack of support given in 331 to the Spartan king Agis III, who attempted to unite the Greeks against Macedon. Only a few states rallied to him, most in the Peloponnese, and Antipater quickly terminated Agis' war the following year (Diod. 17.63.1-3, Curt. 6.1).[19]

---

[17]   See further, commentary on Dinarchus 1.10 and 18-21.

[18]   Diod. 16.88.1, [Plut.] *Moralia* 841b-844a, and see E.M. Burke, 'Lycurgan finances', *GRBS* 26 (1985), 251-264 with F.W. Mitchel, 'Lykourgan Athens: 338-322', *Semple Lectures* 2 (Cincinnati: 1970), Bosworth, *Conquest and Empire*, 204-215, and on religion J.D. Mikalson, *Religion in Hellenistic Athens* (Berkeley and Los Angeles), 11-45 (I owe this reference to L.T. Brown III).

[19]   On the war see commentary on Dinarchus 1.34 with bibliography cited, to which add E. Badian, 'Agis III: Revisions and Reflections', *Ventures Into Greek History. Essays in Honour of N.G.L. Hammond*, ed. Ian Worthington (Oxford: 1994), 258-292.

Appearance, though, is not always reality. The Common Peace of 337 had been an enforced one, and even worse the Greeks were forced to unite under a Macedonian master. But then time passed. Greece enjoyed a period of peace and prosperity, and we must try to consider what was the Greek attitude to the Macedonian hegemony (see below). Perhaps clues may be seen in the events in Athens in 330 and in 324/3.

In 330 Athens was the venue for two trials of no small interest: the prosecution of a certain Leocrates by Lycurgus and the great *Crown* trial involving the statesmen and arch-rivals Demosthenes and Aeschines. Leocrates had fled Athens in the chaotic aftermath of the Battle of Chaeronea, first to Rhodes, then to Megara (Lycurgus 1.21), even though the Athenians may have decreed that no one should flee the city. Later, perhaps even in 330, he had returned to the city, and Lycurgus prosecuted him on the grounds of treason. The speech is Lycurgus' only extant oration. Leocrates' defence, that he had not fled Athens but merely gone to visit people overseas, was poor, and there is no question that he was guilty. Surprisingly, he was acquitted, though only by one vote (Aes. 3.252).

The trial of Leocrates was closely followed by the so-called 'Crown' trial, in which Aeschines attempted to discredit and destroy Demosthenes by attacking one of his political supporters, Ctesiphon. In 336 Ctesiphon had proposed a gold crown for Demosthenes as a reward for Demosthenes' service to the state. Demosthenes was not crowned in the Theatre of Dionysus for Aeschines at the time attacked the motion as illegal, but the case did not come to court until 330. Although Aeschines properly states that it was illegal for a magistrate to be honoured in this way while still in office (Aes. 3.24), the basis of his indictment was that Demosthenes had not advised the best policy for the people as Ctesiphon had maintained in his original proposal (Aes. 3.49-50).[20] Though Ctesiphon delivered a short speech of defence, the proper reply to Aeschines' prosecution speech came from Demosthenes. We have both speeches, Aeschines, *Against Ctesiphon* (Speech 3) and Demosthenes, *On The Crown* (Speech 18), both invaluable sources for the period, though riddled with rhetorical embellishment and falsehood. We might expect Demosthenes to have been defeated given the stranglehold which the Macedonians had over the Greeks and the enforced League of Corinth. Yet Ctesiphon/Demosthenes were vindicated, and Aeschines was defeated, even failing to win one-fifth of the votes cast (Plut. *Demosthenes* 24.2). He retired to Rhodes in exile to set up a school of rhetoric there – and eventually to disappear from history. The story goes that Aeschines would recite his speech to his students, who would express surprise at the fact that he lost his case. Aeschines' reply was that they would not react like this if they had heard Demosthenes' speech (Plut.] *Moralia* 840d-e).

The results of both trials show that the issue of Macedonian hegemony was not a burning one in 330, and are further grounds for accepting that the Athenians, and the

---

[20] See S. Usher's discussion of the trial in *Demosthenes On The Crown*, Volume 5 in the Aris & Phillips *Greek Orators* series (Warminster: 1993), 13-17, with bibliography cited. On both trials and the background see too N. Sawada, 'Athenian Politics in the Age of Alexander the Great: A Reconsideration of the Trial of Ctesiphon', *Chiron* 26 (1996), 57-84.

Greeks, benefitted from that rule because of the peace and prosperity it brought and accepted it (on the Greek attitude to the Macedonian hegemony see below).

For the next six years Athenian domestic politics remain settled until the notorious Harpalus affair of 324/3, which brought with it the opportunity for outright revolt against Macedon.[21] Harpalus, the imperial treasurer and a long-time personal friend of Alexander, absconded to Athens with considerable manpower and money to be deployed against the king (Diod. 17.108.6). His debauchery and corruption at his court in Babylon[22] were matched only by his ability to flee at a moment's notice, and as Alexander returned from exploits in the east punishing disloyal and corrupt satraps and generals (Diod. 17.108.6) Harpalus saw the writing on the wall. For Harpalus' personal security, revolt against Alexander was the only option, and since he was an Athenian citizen (Athenaeus 13.586d, 596a-b), and Athens represented the last place on the Greek mainland which could offer any real opposition to Macedon, he took a powerful force of six thousand mercenaries, five thousand talents of stolen money (Diod. 17.108.6) and thirty warships (Curt. 10.2.1), and sought asylum there.

The Athenians (and by extension the Greeks as a whole) had even more cause to welcome Harpalus' offer and revolt owing to the recent arrival of Nicanor of Stagira, who brought with him Alexander's Exiles Decree for proclamation at Olympia.[23] All Greek cites were to receive back their exiles (excluding the Thebans), and Antipater was empowered by Alexander to enforce the terms of the decree on any unwilling city (Diod. 18.8.4). The decree was technically illegal since it clearly flouted the autonomy of the Greek states as guaranteed in the League of Corinth. Though the Athenians refused to receive back their exiles (Curt. 10.2.6-7; cf. Din. 1.58 and 94), resistance was futile: Alexander was king, the Macedonians controlled Greece, and the final clause of the decree, baldly stating that Antipater would have authority to coerce any Greek city to receive back its exiles, would not be lost on the Greeks. The Athenians were hit especially hard by the decree, as under its terms they would also have to surrender the island of Samos, whose native owners they had forced into exile some time before.[24]

Also playing a factor on the political scene was the notion that Alexander III be worshipped as a god by the mainland Greeks. Whether such a notion took the form of a request or not, and indeed whether it even came from the king or not, our sources indicate that there certainly was some debate among the Greeks over his deification at this time, although many states including Athens resisted.[25]

---

[21] On Harpalus, see Berve, *Alexander* 2, no. 143; on the affair in detail, see Worthington, *Dinarchus*, 41-77 and bibliography cited.

[22] Diod. 17.108.4-6, Athenaeus 13.586c-d, 594e-596a, Curt. 10.1.45.

[23] On the Exiles Decree see Bosworth, *Conquest and Empire*, 220-228, citing sources and bibliography.

[24] Samos was important for Athens for military reasons as well as for its use as a granary: G. Shipley, *A History of Samos* (Oxford: 1987), 155-168; cf. commentary on Dinarchus 1.14.

[25] Athenaeus 12.538b; cf. Hyp. 5.18-19, Diod. 18.8.7, Curt. 10.2.5-7, Justin 13.5.1-6, Polybius 12.12b3, [Plut.] *Moralia* 804b, 842d, Aelian, *VH* 5.12. See further G.L.

Despite the resentment both the Exiles Decree and apparent deification request must have caused, coupled with the attraction of Harpalus' offer, Demosthenes advised the Athenians against using Harpalus' force in a revolt against the king. Accordingly, the Assembly ordered the *strategos* (general) Philocles to deny Harpalus entry ([Plut.] *Moralia* 846a), and he made for the mercenary base at Taenarum in southern Laconia. It appears that many ex-mercenaries had already collected there, having fled in the wake of Alexander's dissolution decree as he returned from the east, which ordered the mercenary generals and satraps to disband their armies.

Obstinately, and with a much reduced force and allegedly 700 talents, Harpalus returned to Athens, this time as a suppliant, and was admitted into the city by Philocles (whom he is likely to have bribed, hence his later prosecution: Dinarchus 3) in about June 324.[26] Perhaps it is now that we can detect a split between Demosthenes and the more militant Hyperides (cf. Hyp. 5. 17-19 and 31), who was anxious to seize the opportunity for revolt afforded by Harpalus and his force and money. A second Assembly meeting was held, after Harpalus had entered Athens, at which envoys from Antipater, Alexander's regent in Greece, the king's mother Olympias and apparently also Philoxenus, Alexander's financial governor of Sardis, demanded his extradition.[27] It is safe to assume that he would have been transported to Alexander and executed for his misdeeds. Again, however, Demosthenes won the day. Harpalus was to be imprisoned and his money impounded on the Acropolis (Din. 1.70, 89, [Plut.] *Moralia* 846b). When asked the amount in the Assembly, Harpalus replied that it was seven hundred talents (Hyp. 5.9-10; cf. [Plut.] *Moralia* 846b), and according to Hyperides (5.9) the money was taken to the Acropolis on the next day.[28] Demosthenes' course was no doubt influenced by the fact that the Athenians were about to send an embassy to Alexander over the Exiles Decree (specifically, the non-return of the Athenian exiles and the retention of Samos) – as other states were doing – and so refused Harpalus' offer of revolt in case this jeopardised its chances of success.

The importance attached to this embassy is seen in the reaction to the deification issue. While Harpalus was in prison Demosthenes went to Olympia as *architheoros* (leader of a religious delegation) in order to discuss the terms of the Exiles Decree with the king's royal messenger Nicanor. It was only after he returned from this meeting that he advocated acquiescence in Alexander's superhuman status, a *volte face* that was seen as the result of his accepting a bribe (presumably from Nicanor) and duly criticised (Din. 1.94, 103, Hyp. 5.31-32). It would appear from Hyperides (5.21, 6.21) that statues of Alexander and also shrines and altars to him were erected in Athens, though this is highly doubtful. Therefore, it is plausible that he supported

---

Cawkwell, 'The Deification of Alexander the Great: A Note', *Ventures Into Greek History*, ed. Ian Worthington (Oxford: 1994), 293-306.

[26]   On chronology see Ian Worthington, 'The Chronology of the Harpalus Affair', *SO* 61 (1986), 63-76.

[27]   Hyp. 5.8, Diod. 17.108.7, [Plut.] *Moralia* 846b.

[28]   Harpalus probably lied about the figure and had with him about 450 talents: see in detail Worthington, *Dinarchus*, 65-69.

the proposed apotheosis simply to placate Alexander and to bolster the chances of success of the Athenian embassy to Alexander.[29] What did it matter to call Alexander a god if he ruled in the Athenians' favour? Demades hit the nail on the head with his remark, if it may be connected to the Samian issue, that the Athenians were so concerned about heaven that they stood to lose the earth (Valerius Maximus 7.2.13).

Ultimately Demosthenes' strategy did not pay off. After Demosthenes returned from Olympia Harpalus escaped (Diod. 17.108.7), causing an uproar in the city. He fled to Taenarum, and then to Crete where he was murdered.[30] His death did not, however, signal an end to the affair. Accusations were brought out that Demosthenes and others had taken bribes from Harpalus to facilitate his escape, hence bribes to the detriment of the city given the importance with which Alexander viewed Harpalus (Diod. 17.108.8). These allegations gained credence when only half of Harpalus' alleged 700 talents were actually found deposited on the Acropolis. At a meeting of the Assembly Demosthenes proposed that the Areopagus investigate the matter by means of the judicial procedure known as *apophasis* (Din. 1.1). Under this, the Areopagus held an enquiry (*zetesis*) into those suspected of treason and delivered a preliminary verdict (*apophasis* or 'report'). If found guilty, then the accused was brought to trial for a final verdict in an ordinary law court. Furthermore, Demosthenes also offered to submit to the death penalty if it found him guilty of accepting a bribe from Harpalus (Din. 3.2, 5, 16, 21). During its enquiry he issued a *proklesis*, a challenge, to the Assembly to present the Areopagus with evidence for its accusation (Din. 1.5, Hyp. 5.2), but stating that he had taken money from Harpalus not as a bribe but on behalf of the city, as a loan for the Theoric Fund (Hyp. 5.12-13).[31]

After six months (Din. 1.45) the Areopagus issued its report accusing Demosthenes and several others of receiving bribes against the best interests of the state (*dorodokia*).[32] Significantly it cited no evidence, but only the names of those suspected of receiving a bribe, together with the amounts supposedly taken.[33] Around the same time news came that Alexander had rejected the Athenian embassy's pleas over the Exiles Decree. The coincidence is too much, and presumably the Areopagites hoped that by including Demosthenes' name in their findings Alexander might have been favourably swayed should the Athenians appeal again. Demosthenes himself pleaded that he had been sacrificed to please the king (Hyp. 5.14) and resorted to a second *proklesis*, aimed this time at the Areopagites, to

---

[29] Cf. A. Schäfer, *Demosthenes und seine Zeit*[2] 3 (Leipzig: 1887), 318-319. The contempt in Demosthenes' comment that Alexander could call himself the son of Zeus and Poseidon if he so wished is clear: Hyperides 5.31 – see commentary *ad loc.*

[30] Diod. 17.108.18, 18.9.2, [Plut.] *Moralia* 846c, Curt. 10.2.3.

[31] The Theoric Fund was probably introduced by Pericles in the 450's, and consisted of money used to enable the poor to attend the festivals: see further, commentary on Hyperides 5.13.

[32] Phocion was apparently implicated in the affair (cf. Plut. *Phocion* 21.3-4), but was not brought to trial.

[33] Din. 2.21, Hyp. 5.6, Dem. *Epistle* 2.1, 15 and 3.42.

produce the evidence on which their findings had been based (Din. 1.6, 61, Hyp. 5.3).

Despite Demosthenes' protestations of innocence, he was brought to trial in about March 323 on the serious charge of *dorodokia*, with its penalty of either a fine ten times the amount of bribe taken (with disenfranchisement until it was paid) or death.[34] He was prosecuted by ten men, including Hyperides ([Plut.] *Moralia* 846c) and Stratocles (Din. 1.1, 21), who came first in the prosecution line, followed by the unknown person for whom Dinarchus wrote his prosecution speech. Demosthenes was condemned; he was fined fifty talents and imprisoned, but after one week he fled into self-imposed exile, continuing his protestations of innocence.[35]

The prosecution speeches against him (of which we have only Dinarchus 1 and Hyperides 5) rested on the premise that the reputation of the Areopagus alone should be sufficient for accepting its report against Demosthenes. However, others indicted in the affair, against whom no proof of complicity was given, were acquitted, such as Aristogeiton (Dem. *Epistle* 3.37, 42), Hagnonides and Polyeuctus of Sphettus (cf. Plut. *Phocion* 29.3, [Plut.] *Moralia* 846c-d); Demades was probably fined (Din. 2.14; see commentary on Dinarchus 1.29), and only the *strategos* Philocles was probably condemned (Dem. *Epistle* 3.31). Since no evidence was cited for the allegations of bribery, all of the accused should either have been condemned or acquitted – a fact also recognised by the prosecution (Din. 1.113, 2.21, Hyp. 5.5-7). That even one of those accused was exculpated on the same lack of evidence on which all were brought to trial shows the weakness of both the Areopagus' findings and the hidden agenda that governed Demosthenes' trial. We are led plausibly to the belief that the verdict of Demosthenes' guilt was political, designed to remove him from active participation in politics, and Wilcken's comment is particularly apt: '[the trial] vividly exhibits the absolute rottenness of Attic democracy at the time.'[36]

Demosthenes' guilt or innocence cannot, however, be fully resolved. He claimed that he did take money from Harpalus, but as a loan for the Theoric Fund (Hyp. 5.13).[37] That he may well have been innocent of the charge of *dorodokia* and be a victim of the political background of the Exiles Decree is however very likely.

There is no question that the Athenians wanted to resist the Exiles Decree and especially to retain Samos, possession of which had even been reconfirmed by Philip II after the battle of Chaeronea (Diod. 18.56.7). Pride was at issue here. Demosthenes' mission to Olympia was unsuccessful (other than perhaps achieving a stay of execution thanks to his diplomatic prowess), and in view of this, his surprising acquiescence in Alexander's deification, and then Harpalus' sudden flight from Athens, the Athenians directed their disfavour and suspicion on him. Demosthenes claimed that he was being sacrificed in order to please Alexander

---

[34] *AP* 54.2, Din. 1.60, Hyp. 5.24; cf. Andocides 1.73-79, Dem. 21.113, Aes. 3.232.

[35] *Epistle* 2.2, 14-16, 21, 26, 3.37-38 and 43.

[36] U. Wilcken, *Alexander the Great* (New York: 1967), 217.

[37] E. Badian, 'Harpalus', *JHS* 81 (1961), 37-40, believes that the money was secretly used to support a group of mercenaries at Taenarum in the event of a revolt against Alexander, which Demosthenes, for obvious reasons, did not wish to divulge. This is highly implausible: see in detail Worthington, *Dinarchus*, 66-68.

(Hyp. 5.14), and the circumstances indicate that Hyperides may not be wholly rhetorical here. Demosthenes had talked to the royal messenger Nicanor and must have received advice on what would please the king and what would not. Hence the removal of Harpalus from the scene and the call to recognise Alexander's divinity. Harpalus' escape was not so much for his own well-being but for that of the city (Diod. 17.108.7, Plut. *Demosthenes* 25.6), and the fact that he was no longer harboured in Athens, coupled with the Athenians' recognising Alexander as a god, would surely help the Athenian embassy to Alexander over Samos and the non return of the city's exiles.

However, Alexander ruled against Athens in its claim to Samos, and the publication of the Areopagus' findings after six months ties in with the news of Athens' diplomatic failure. Hyperides now seized the opportunity to bring about Demosthenes' downfall, and thus control what had been up to then a moderate and cautious policy towards Macedon. While politics certainly played a role in the Areopagus' decision, this does not prove Demosthenes' innocence (of bribery), but the conspiracy factor is very strong.

The same is true in the case of Demosthenes' trial, where, as was noted above, no proof of guilt was given against those accused, yet Demosthenes was condemned and others were not. The trial was a façade, for on what grounds did the jurors declare who was guilty and who innocent? Demosthenes' guilt was political in order to remove him from political life.

What of Demosthenes' claim that he did take money, but for the Theoric Fund (Hyp. 5.13)? First, we should note that Dinarchus does not refer to it, so perhaps Hyperides added a false claim to the revised version of his speech after the trial. If Demosthenes had taken the money for this purpose it should have been demonstrable and not open to suggestion in this way. Moreover, Hyperides uses the phrase ὡς ἔοικεν ('as it seems'), which would indicate hearsay or at least an amount of uncertainty. Thus, he may simply be distorting facts to create bias against Demosthenes by illustrating his ability to switch from one thing to another, a strategy also used by Dinarchus (1.91 and 94).

However, if there is any truth in Hyperides' allegation, then a possible explanation is that in 324/3 there was a shortage in Athenian finances which led to a deficit in the Theoric Fund. The Athenian state often ran short of money until the taxes were collected (Dem. 20.115, 24.98) in the ninth prytany (*AP* 47.4; cf. Dem. 24.96-99).[38] The Theoric Fund derived its income from surplus taxation, and since the surplus was calculated only at the end of the year, it follows that the Athenians would not have been aware until the ninth prytany whether there would be any surplus in that particular year. Athenian finances were often in dire straits, and voluntary contributions of ships and loans were sometimes made.[39] Lycurgus'

---

[38] M.H. Hansen, 'The Theoric Fund and the *Graphe Paranomon* against Apollodorus', *GRBS* 17 (1976), 214-243.
[39] [Plut.] *Moralia* 852b; cf. *SIG*³ 289, 29.

administration had seen the completion of several large-scale works,[40] and so if there were no surplus in taxes (as was the case at times), then this would lead to a shortage in the Fund. Perhaps, then, this situation arose in 324/3 and Demosthenes, in an attempt to combat it, borrowed (stupidly, as it turned out) twenty talents from Harpalus. If so, then his action certainly backfired on him later.

We would surely expect that the Harpalus affair and the Exiles Decree, perhaps also Alexander's proposed apotheosis if it came from him, would have tested the subservience of the Greeks to the Macedonian hegemony. In Harpalus and his force lay a very real chance to throw off the Macedonian yoke, yet there was no rebellion, nor even any planned military mobilisation by any Greek state at this stage. A far cry from the mood of the Greeks to the Macedonians in the days of Philip II. These factors, plus the diplomatic reaction to the Exiles Decree, have implications for the Greek attitude to the Macedonian hegemony, which will be discussed below.

Just as Athens was recovering from the Harpalus scandal came the news that no one at this time could have predicted: Alexander the Great had died. This was so unexpected that at first it was not believed – as Demades put it, 'if Alexander were really dead, the whole world would smell from his corpse' (Plut. *Phocion* 22.3). The king breathed his last on 10 June 323,[41] and news of his death was greeted by the immediate disregard of the Exiles Decree by the Greek states, apart from Tegea, where inscriptional evidence proves their return.[42] Also in connection with the backlash against the decree we find the Athenians waging war against the Samians, who seem already to have been returning to their island.[43] More significantly, the Greek states, with the exception of the Boeotian and the Euboean Leagues, revolted against Macedon: while Alexander was alive, rebellion was out of the question; Alexander dead – and the bulk of his army so far away in Babylonia – was quite another matter. And with Alexander died the League of Corinth. Although in Athens the general Phocion spoke against going to war (Plut. *Phocion* 23.1-2, *Timoleon* 6.5), Hyperides defeated his caution.

The Lamian War
The Greek revolt against Macedon in 323 is commonly called the Lamian War, and broke out in probably September 323.[44] With Demosthenes and the other

---

[40]   E.M. Burke, 'Lycurgan Finances', *GRBS* 26 (1985), 251-264 with F.W. Mitchel, 'Lykourgan Athens: 338-322', *Semple Lectures* 2 (Cincinnati: 1970) and Bosworth, *Conquest and Empire*, 204-215, citing sources and bibliography.

[41]   On the date see J.R. Hamilton, *Plutarch, Alexander. A Commentary* (Oxford: 1969), 152.

[42]   See further Ian Worthington, 'The Date of the Tegea decree (Tod ii 202): A Response to the *Diagramma* of Alexander III or of Polyperchon?', *Ancient History Bulletin* 7 (1993), 59-64.

[43]   Shipley, *History of Samos*, 166-168.

[44]   On the historical background see especially Hammond & Walbank, *HM* 3, 108 ff., citing ancient sources and modern bibliography. On the name, which postdates the actual war (contemporaries called it 'The Greek War' until about 301 when Lamian War became the norm), see N.G. Ashton, 'The Lamian War – stat magni nominis umbra', *JHS* 94 (1984), 152-157.

'moderates' disgraced after the Harpalus affair, Hyperides came to the fore in Athenian public life and politics took on a more militant bent. Hyperides and the 'radicals' held secret negotiations with the powerful Athenian *strategos* Leosthenes, sending him some of Harpalus' money which was still on the Acropolis to hire mercenaries (Diod. 18.9.2-4). This action was followed by his visits to several states to raise troops (Diod. 18.9.5). It was Leosthenes who already had contacts with the ex-mercenaries at the mercenary base of Taenarum, whose numbers had been swelled by Alexander's dissolution decree as he returned from the east, and also by Harpalus' force. Despite the caution of Phocion, the militants, presumably led by Hyperides, were able to rouse the Athenians to war in probably September 323 (Diod. 18.10), and many states followed suit (Diod. 18.11.1-2). A huge fleet of 240 vessels was deployed to use against Macedon and those up to the age of forty had been enlisted in an Athenian army (Diod. 18.10.2).

Although in 337 the Greeks had sworn loyalty to Philip II and his descendants, Alexander left behind no undisputed successor, and this is of key importance in tracing why the Greeks rebelled at this time. Alexander's wife Roxanne was still pregnant when her husband died; the only other male candidate was Alexander's half-brother, the youthful but apparently incompetent Philip Arrhidaeus (later Philip III), son of Philip II; and a number of Alexander's key generals wanted their own share of power. They would embark on a lengthy power-struggle from the time of Alexander's death in 323 until 301 (battle of Ipsus), in the process splitting apart Alexander's empire – not that it would have survived for very long anyway with no undisputed heir and the personal ambitions of the generals now coming to the fore. Certainly the Greeks were not prepared to accept one of the generals as leader of the League of Corinth: Alexander might have given his signet ring to Perdiccas,[45] the commander of the companion cavalry, perhaps designating him as his heir, but this action did not mean anything to the Greeks (nor to the other generals for that matter). Even when Roxanne gave birth to a boy, the future Alexander IV, the Greeks remained set on rebellion.

The Greek revolt which faced Antipater was a significant one, even though it took him only about a year to crush it. There was the huge Greek fleet of over 240 vessels which must have been double what the Macedonians could muster (Diod. 18.9.2), and an ever-increasing number of soldiers. Leosthenes himself took 8,000 mercenaries from Taenarum to Aetolia to join the combined Greek force, and then invaded Boeotia (which, with Euboea apart from Carystus, remained loyal to Macedon) to link up with an Athenian force of about 7,000 (5,000 citizens and 2,000 mercenaries) and 500 cavalry. This large force defeated a Boeotian/Euboean army, and then moved on to threaten the key strategic town of Thermopylae (Diod. 18.11.3-5). By this time, the Greek force had swelled to around 30,000 compared to the Macedonian one of 13,000 soldiers and 600 cavalry (Diod. 18.12.2), supplemented by 2,000 Thessalian cavalry. More importantly, the Greeks were led by the great general Leosthenes, whose battle strategy and military abilities severely tested Antipater.

---

[45] Diod. 17.117.3, 18.2.4, Curt. 10.5.4, Justin 12.15.12.

Antipater immediately sent word to two other Macedonian generals, Craterus and Leonnatus, as well as Philotas, satrap of Hellespontine Phrygia, that they should bring their armies to him (Diod. 18.12.1). Whether Antipater was short of men as a result of Alexander's repeated demands for reinforcements when the king was involved in his costly Asian campaigns is open to debate. Diodorus 18.12.2 says that Antipater lacked 'citizen soldiers', that is Macedonians proper, but whether or not Antipater needed fighting manpower urgently there is no question that he was hard-pressed by the revolt.[46] Perhaps he expected that in any pitched battle he would have the upper hand, supported as he was by the superb Thessalian cavalry, and reinforcements from Craterus and Leonnatus were en route. If so, he was mistaken. At Thermopylae the two sides met in battle, but the Thessalian cavalry almost immediately deserted to the Greek side, and victory went to the Greeks (Diod. 18.12.3-4). Antipater managed to struggle to the little town of Lamia for refuge, where he remained for the winter of 323/2.[47]

The fortifications of Lamia were such that Greek attempts to take the town failed, and in one of them, in late 323, Leosthenes was wounded and later died (Diod. 18.13.5, Justin 13.5.12). Antiphilus, a man 'outstanding in military genius and courage' according to Diodorus (18.13.6), succeeded him.[48] Antipater now offered to surrender on terms, but the Athenians refused. About this time Demosthenes, who had been touring other Greek states during his exile after the Harpalus affair in order to raise opposition against Macedon, returned in glory to Athens ([Lucian] *Enc. Dem.* 31).

Meanwhile Leonnatus had arrived in Macedon with more than 20,000 troops and · 1,500 cavalry (Diod. 18.14.5), and in early spring he marched to the aid of Antipater in Lamia. Though Leonnatus was defeated and killed in battle by Antiphilus, Antipater was able to escape and to make his way back to Macedon.[49] Antipater's return was a turning point in the war, and very probably many in Athenians realised this. Although Macedonian troops had been defeated in battle, and Antiphilus had even defeated and killed Leonnatus, the gloomy military and political situation must have been obvious. The astute Phocion, who had been against the revolt in the first place and openly clashed with Hyperides and Leosthenes over it (Plut. *Phocion* 23.1-2, *Timoleon* 6.5), must have been one who realised the gravity of the situation, and given his participation in political life he would have made his views known. The capture of Antipater, on the other hand, would have made a major difference, and in hindsight the Athenians would have been better to accept Antipater's earlier

---

[46] Scholars such as Hammond (Hammond & Walbank, *HM* 3, 109) and Bosworth ('Alexander the Great and the Decline of Macedon', *JHS* 106 [1986], 1-12) blame Alexander for his demands for reinforcements which depleted Antipater's fighting manpower, but see now E. Badian, 'Agis III: Revisions and Reflections', *Ventures Into Greek History*, 258-292.

[47] Hyp. 6.12, Diod. 18.12.4-13.5, Plut. *Demosthenes* 27.1, *Phocion* 23.4-5, Polyaenus 4.4.2.

[48] The eulogy to Leosthenes contained in Hyperides' *epitaphios* or funeral oration (6) attests his worth and reputation; see also L. Tritle, 'Leosthenes and Plutarch's View of the Athenian *Strategia*', *AHB* 1 (1987), 6-9.

[49] Diod. 18.15.1-7, Plut. *Phocion* 25; cf. Justin 13.5.14-16.

offer of surrender, even on terms. With this background in mind, Hyperides – 'foremost of the orators in eloquence and in hostility towards the Macedonians' (Diod. 18.13.5) – was now chosen by the Athenians to deliver the *epitaphios* or funeral oration over those Athenians who had died in the first year of the Lamian War (see Hyperides 6 in this volume; on the genre of the funeral oration see below, Section 5). This was no easy task. The chronology is uncertain, but in view of the eulogy to the Athenian commander Leosthenes contained in the speech and the lack of reference to the defeat of the Athenian fleet in the summer of 322 at the battle of Abydus, we may plausibly date the *epitaphios* to the spring of 322, and probably after Antipater escaped from Lamia.

A short while later, in the summer of 322, the powerful Greek fleet was destroyed. Parts of it had probably been operating in several areas, such as the Hellespont for the safety of the corn route, or close to Attica to act as protection should the Macedonian fleet attack Athens. However, splitting the combined fleet in this way was strategically unsound, as was proved by the ease with which the Macedonian admiral Cleitus was able to defeat each force of ships. In a series of four battles Cleitus destroyed the combined Greek fleet, including the Athenian fleet at the battle of Abydus which numbered 170 vessels (Diod. 18.15.8-9). Macedonian superiority at sea was thus established.

Cleitus' victories now allowed Craterus a safe route to bring his troops (about 10,000 infantry, 1,500 Persian archers and 1,500 cavalry) from Cilicia to Macedon and to link with Antipater and his force (Diod. 18.16.4-5). In August 322 (Plut. *Camillus* 19.8) at Crannon in central Thessaly, Antipater, in sole control of the Macedonian army, which now numbered around 48,000 soldiers including 5,000 cavalry, met the Greek force of around 25,000 soldiers and 3,500 cavalry (Diod. 18.17.1-2). Antipater was victorious: the Greeks lost over 500 men and the Macedonians 130 (Diod. 18.17.3-5), and Antipater then made a separate alliance with each state, apart from Aetolia and (significantly) Athens, which stood in non-splendid isolation (Diod. 18.17.6-8). Both of these states, says Diodorus, were 'most hostile to the Macedonians' (18.17.8). The Aetolian League fought on throughout the winter of 322/1, but only thanks to clashes between Antipater, Craterus and Perdiccas for personal power following Alexander's death was it saved from total annihilation (Diod. 18.24-25).

In Athens, Demades, Phocion and Demetrius of Phalerum were empowered by the people to seek peace terms from Antipater and Craterus.[50] They proved less merciful than Alexander III, or Philip II, towards Athens, and insisted on unconditional surrender.[51] The ambassadors returned home with these terms, and probably at this point Demosthenes and Hyperides, who had been the main opponents of Macedon, saw the writing on the wall and fled into exile. The Athenians had no choice but to agree to the Macedonians' terms, and a second embassy of Demades, Phocion and Xenocrates (the head of the Academy) returned to Antipater to hear the worst.

---

[50] Diod. 18.18.1-2, Plut. *Phocion* 26, Nepos, *Phocion* 2.
[51] Diod. 18.18.3, Plut. *Demosthenes* 28.1, *Phocion* 26-29.

Amongst other things, the Athenians were ordered to pay for the costs of the war (however, this heavy war reparation was deferred while they remained loyal to Macedon), and to surrender the anti-Macedonian leaders to Antipater; the Macedonians stationed a garrison at Munychia (a hill in the Piraeus, the port of Athens), and resolved that Athenian citizenship was henceforth to be based on wealth alone, *viz.*, 2,000 drachmas (Diod. 18.18.4). As a result, some 12,000 were disfranchised and fled to Thrace; only 9,000 'citizens' (i.e., those above the wealth limit) remained in the city (Diod. 18.18.5).[52] Athens became an oligarchy, one imposed by Macedon, and many Athenians fled to Thrace. Rubbing more salt into the wounds, Antipater then arranged to hand over Samos, that bone of contention between Athens and Macedon since the days of the Exiles Decree, to the Samians. The only concession Antipater was prepared to make was not to invade Attica himself (even though apparently Craterus was urging this: Plut. *Phocion* 26.5-7).

Hyperides was one of those whose surrender was ordered by Antipater. Despite his standing in Athens, as is shown by his being chosen to deliver the funeral oration over those who died in the first year of the war, on the motion of Demades both he and Demosthenes were condemned to death, and fled into exile. Demosthenes committed suicide (Plut. *Demosthenes* 29.7, [Plut.] *Moralia* 847b, ([Lucian] *Enc. Dem.* 28, 43-49), but Hyperides was captured and, along with others, surrendered to Antipater and was subsequently executed (see below, Section 4). Although Diodorus says that the Athenians were 'humanely treated beyond their hopes' by Antipater (18.18.6), this was the end of an era for Athens, an inglorious end to that city's proud history. Antipater's punishment was severe but understandable. Athens' reputation was formidable, and he could not afford another revolt – even less so now that the struggles between Alexander's successors were taking up more time and energy, struggles in which he was to play a premier role until his death in 319.

The Greek Attitude to the Macedonian Hegemony[53]

The Common Peace of 337 had been forced on the Greeks by Philip II through the medium of the League of Corinth, and had been reinforced by Alexander III when he took power (see above). We should expect that the Greeks, given their heritage and the concept of individual autonomy that was the basis of the *polis* system, would have taken steps to throw off Macedonian control at every opportunity. However,

---

52 The figure of 12,000 dispossessed citizens in Diodorus is perhaps over high, and he may have confused it with the total number of Athenian citizens, in which case, accepting 9,000 who retained citizenship, about 3,000 lost their citizenship. On the other hand, Plutarch, *Phocion* 28.4, says more than 12,000; cf. Hammond & Walbank, *HM* 3, 115 note 2 (who mistakenly refer to 22,000 displaced citizens). For the peace terms in full see Diodorus 18.8.3-6, 18.56 and 18.65, Plutarch, *Demosthenes* 28-30 and *Phocion* 29 and 33, Pseudo-Plutarch, *Moralia* 846e-847b, 847d, 849a-d, Pausanias 1.43.1 and 7.10.1.

53 The following points are argued in detail in my 'The Harpalus Affair and the Greek Response to the Macedonian Hegemony', *Ventures Into Greek History*, 307-330. On the end of Greek liberty see also now G. Cawkwell, 'The End of Greek Liberty', in *Transitions to Empire, Essays in Honor of E. Badian*, edd. R. W. Wallace and E.M. Harris (Norman: 1996), 98-121.

this is simply not the case – the Greeks were subservient to the Common Peace and hence to Macedon (the war of Agis III may be treated as a peculiarity since Sparta was not a member of the League and so few Greek states supported Agis). Support for this may be seen in the two trials in Athens in 330 of Leocrates and Ctesiphon/Demosthenes – Aeschines, the prosecutor, was really attacking Demosthenes and using Ctesiphon, who had proposed civic honours on Demosthenes in 338, as a pawn. Everyone knew this, and that is why the surviving defence speech from this trial is that of Demosthenes (18) and Ctesiphon seems only to have given a short opening speech before Demosthenes spoke. Leocrates had fled Athens when it appeared that Philip II would invade the city in 338; some time later he had returned, and he was charged with treason for deserting his city in a potential time of need.

Both trials may be linked to the Athenian – and Greek – attitude towards Macedon. If both Leocrates, who had fled in time of need, and Demosthenes, the staunch resistor of Macedonian imperialism, whose policies had brought Athens, indeed Greece, to its knees, were condemned, then this could be an indication of a hostile attitude towards Macedon. Indeed, the timing of their trials is significant since Agis III was probably still at war with Alexander (the battle of Megalopolis, at which Agis was defeated, was fought probably in spring 330), and so it is plausible to suspect a hidden agenda on the part of some in Athens of drumming up support for Agis. Yet the fact that both men were acquitted tells us that the Athenians at this time did not see the Macedonian issue as they might have done had these trials been held ten years earlier. Moreover, Leocrates' 'crime' was not that great. Lycurgus essentially was charging him with treason, but there is no anti-Macedonian propaganda or politics as such in the speech, and Lycurgus may well be using the opportunity to support his new policy of educating the youth and the duty of the ephebeia.[54] Aeschines' speech never stood a chance: the jurors recognised its legal weaknesses, and so overwhelmingly did they acquit Demosthenes that Aeschines failed to win one-fifth of the votes cast and so left Athens.[55] The Athenians, then, were enjoying the peace and prosperity which the Macedonian rule had brought to Greece, and had no wish to disrupt it.

The same mood seems to have prevailed in 324/3, when the Harpalus affair, Exiles Decree, and even Alexander's proposed apotheosis must have tested the subservience of the Greeks to the Macedonian hegemony. The Exiles Decree clearly flouted the individual autonomy of the states, and we would have expected this to be the final straw, especially when Harpalus appeared on the scene with the promise of men and money in a revolt. However, the fact that Demosthenes' counsel prevailed at the meeting of the Assembly held when Harpalus had been admitted into the city (see above) shows that the majority of the Athenians had no anti-Macedonian sentiment – or rather, not enough to wage war against Alexander. The Athenians sent a diplomatic envoy to the king about Harpalus, and joined in

---

[54] See N. Sawada, 'Athenian Politics in the Age of Alexander the Great: A Reconsideration of the Trial of Ctesiphon', *Chiron* 26 (1996), 78-79.

[55] On the weaknesses in Aeschines' case see E.M. Harris, 'Law and Oratory', in *Persuasion. Greek Rhetoric in Action*, ed. Ian Worthington (London: 1994), especially 142-148.

with the rest of the Greeks who resorted to diplomacy in order to counter the decree. Thus, at the time of the Harpalus affair the Athenians were not bent on military resistance, nor does it plausibly seem were the other states, which were largely quiet and which, despite a diversity of attitudes, would have looked to Athens for leadership.

The Greeks may well have expressed their dissatisfaction over the Exiles Decree, and no doubt over divine rights for Alexander, but dissatisfaction is very different from rebellion. The implications of the Harpalus affair and Exiles Decree for how the Macedonian hegemony was viewed by the Greeks are wide-sweeping: instead of our seeing the Greeks as ready to seize the first chance to revolt against their Macedonian masters, a different picture emerges, one which sees the Greeks as subservient and more willing to resort to diplomacy than to revolt. The picture thus indicates an acceptance of Macedonian rule, for life under it was not so harsh, and Alexander generally had been responsive to the Greeks, particularly the Athenians. The terms of the League of Corinth of 337 were not so unduly harmful for the Greeks, especially the Athenians, and certainly allowed them the right to make their own domestic decisions. Greece may thus have come to accept a Macedonian rule, which allowed it the chance for some peace and prosperity.[56] Hence when there were problems affecting the Greek states the first reaction to resolve them was by diplomacy, not revolt.

However, in 323 Greece did revolt from Macedonian rule in the Lamian War. Although the Macedonians had pretty soon and completely cowed the Greeks into military submission, especially after Agis' abortive war, Alexander's death was the turning-point. The Exiles Decree, which so blatantly disregarded the autonomy of the Greek states, together with Alexander's increasing megalomania, were obviously resented; however, once Alexander so unexpectedly died and left behind no strong successor, the Greeks realised that the time had come to do something about their situation, and they seized it. The key to the Lamian War lay not in Alexander's final deeds but his death.

Whilst Alexander may not have bequeathed his throne to an undisputed heir, he still left a powerful legacy to his people: the continuation of the Macedonian power established by his father. Though the Macedonian hegemony of Greece was formalised in the League of Corinth of 337, and was never severely jeopardised after this time, its origins may be traced to a decade earlier. However, it is in those crucial years from 324 down to 322 that we see the total power of Macedon in Greek affairs, and against these years we may view the last surviving speeches of true Attic oratory by Dinarchus and by Hyperides, which are the real subjects of this volume.

---

[56]   See, for example, E.M. Burke, 'Lycurgan Finances', *GRBS* 26 (1985), 261-264.

(2) Dinarchus' Life and Works

Apart from the two speeches of Hyperides in this volume, Dinarchus' speeches are the last extant ones of fourth century Attic oratory. Information on Dinarchus' life is scarce,[57] and comes from four later – and often contradictory – sources: Dionysius of Halicarnassus' essay on Dinarchus, Pseudo-Plutarch's brief life (*Moralia* 850b-e), Photius, and the *Suda* (s.v. Dinarchus). Dionysius' research, literary appreciation and critical methodology makes him the most important and reliable of these four.[58] Pseudo-Plutarch's life supplies fewer details and has some inaccuracies. Photius perhaps drew entirely on Pseudo-Plutarch since no difference between the two accounts is obvious, other than that he begins his biography with a description of Dinarchus' speeches and style, whereas Pseudo-Plutarch (and Dionysius too) ends with these descriptions. Finally, the *Suda* has only a brief mention of Dinarchus, and even this is problematic as it confuses Dinarchus the orator with his homonym, the Corinthian politician, and states that Dinarchus held political office. The latter is impossible since Dinarchus was a metic (non-citizen) in Athens, and only full Athenian citizens were eligible to hold any political office.[59]

Dinarchus, the son of Sostratus (Dion. Hal. *Dinarchus* 2), was born in Corinth into what must have been a wealthy family given that when he moved to Athens he attended the school of Theophrastus, the foremost teacher in Athens and Aristotle's successor as head of the Lyceum. The date of Dinarchus' birth is problematic, but it was probably in 361/0 (following Dionysius' chronology). He moved to Athens when he was relatively young, probably a little before 338 in time to fight at the battle of Chaeronea (the implication of Rutilius Lupus 2.16), and spent most of his professional life there. His knowledge of legal procedures was very wide, and he had expertise in many branches of the law, as is shown by the topics of his prosecution and defence speeches, which dealt with treasonable offences, impiety, and illegal citizenship, along with various economic cases: perjury, adoption, and private injury and damages (see the list of genuine public and private speeches supplied by Dionysius at the end of his essay).

Some time would have elapsed between Dinarchus' arrival and the commencement of his career as a professional speechwriter (*logographos*), and this is supported by Pseudo-Plutarch, who says that he became a pupil of Theophrastus and attended the lectures of the influential Demetrius of Phalerum (*Moralia* 850c; cf. Dion. Hal. *Dinarchus* 2). There may well be a political reason why Dinarchus chose to be taught by these two men. Membership of Theophrastus' school would not only have enhanced Dinarchus' own rhetorical reputation but also brought him into contact with some of the more powerful men in the city, such as Demetrius of

---

[57] On Dinarchus' life in detail see Worthington, *Dinarchus*, 3-10, citing and discussing previous scholarship.

[58] Dionysius' literary and biographical merits are well discussed by W.R. Roberts, *Dionysius of Halicarnassus on Literary Composition* (Cambridge: 1910); see also the introduction of W.K. Pritchett, *Dionysius of Halicarnassus: On Thucydides* (Berkeley: 1975).

[59] On the metics see A.R.W. Harrison, *The Law of Athens* 1 (Oxford: 1968), 187-199, and in detail D. Whitehead, *Ideology of the Athenian Metic* (Cambridge: 1977).

Phalerum. Dinarchus' career would have started properly by 336/5, and given his metic status he devoted himself entirely to it while he lived in Athens. The Harpalus affair of 324/3 was the turning-point in his career since his prosecution speech against Demosthenes established his reputation as one of the leading speechwriters.

Dinarchus made a lot of money in his career (Dion. Hal. *Dinarchus* 2) and reached his professional peak after the death of Alexander the Great in 323 when Cassander of Macedon controlled the city from 317 to 307 through his agent Demetrius of Phalerum (Dion. Hal. *Dinarchus* 2, [Plut.] *Moralia* 850c). In 323 Dinarchus was commissioned by the state to write speeches for one of the ten prosecutors selected by the people in the politically-charged Harpalus trials (see above, Section 1). The identity of his client is unknown.

Dinarchus' friendship with Antipater (before the latter's death in 319) and even more so with Cassander was the cause of his exile in 307/6. In that year Demetrius Poliorcetes, son of the Macedonian Antigonus Monophthalmus, ousted Demetrius of Phalerum (and thus Cassander) and restored a limited democracy to Athens, though still subject to his overall rule (Dion. Hal. *Dinarchus* 2, [Plut.] *Moralia* 850d). Dinarchus left the city before his trial and went to Chalcis, having sold most of his property for cash. He lived in exile there for fifteen years, during which time he amassed even greater wealth.

Dinarchus returned to the city in 292/1 (during the archonship of Philippus) with the consent of Demetrius Poliorcetes, who may have been persuaded to recall him by Theophrastus ([Plut.] *Moralia* 850d). While lodging in the city with his friend Proxenus, Dinarchus lost a considerable amount of money and brought a suit against his host, the first time, as Dionysius and Pseudo-Plutarch tell us, that Dinarchus himself delivered a speech. The indictment was preserved by Dionysius (*Dinarchus* 3) and is mentioned by Pseudo-Plutarch (*Moralia* 850e). Only a fragment of this speech remains.[60] Since Dinarchus was a metic, this prosecution must have taken place in the court of the *polemarchos* archon, which judged cases concerning metics (*AP* 58). The outcome of the trial is unknown.

We do not know when, how or where Dinarchus died. A move back to Corinth would, one might suspect, have prompted a reference in Dionysius' careful account, as indeed would a violent end to his life or disgrace in a trial, so Dinarchus may well have died of old age while still living in Athens.

Dinarchus was a prolific writer, and his knowledge of Athenian law was immense. Demetrius of Magnesia (quoted by Dion. Hal. *Dinarchus* 1) says that he wrote over 160 public and private speeches, Pseudo-Plutarch (and also Photius) 64, some of which he attributed to Aristogeiton (*Moralia* 850e), and the *Suda*'s figure is '160 or 60'. Absolute certainty will never be known but for a more accurate figure we should follow Dionysius' figure of 61. In the case of the genuine speeches, Dionysius mentions only the titles and opening words in his list (*Dinarchus* 10 and 12); of those which he considers spurious he cites title, opening words and then the criteria for rejection, often based on matter that he considers incompatible in content

---

[60] Dion. Hal. *Dinarchus* 12 = Conomis, fr. XLVIII, Burtt, fr. C.14 and Nouhaud and Dors-Méary, fr. B.IX.

with the known life of his subject. Dionysius' critical approach thus gives him the edge over other sources, hence his figure of 61 speeches (29 public and 32 private) should be accepted.[61]

Only three public speeches have survived in any extant form: those written against Demosthenes, Aristogeiton, and Philocles (1, 2 and 3), when brought to trial in 323 for their role in the Harpalus scandal. Of these, the latter two are incomplete, but that against Demosthenes survives virtually intact apart from minor *lacunae* at sections 33/34, 64, and 82 (cf. commentary *ad loc.*). Fragments exist of many others of Dinarchus' speeches (see Conomis, 73-151) including three against others prosecuted in the Harpalus trials: Aristonicus,[62] Hagnonides[63] and Polyeuctus of Sphettus.[64]

(3) Dinarchus' Style

Despite his inclusion in the so-called Canon of the Ten Attic Orators, a list of orators probably drawn up in Alexandrian times,[65] Dinarchus' rhetorical style and composition have been almost universally condemned since antiquity.[66] He does lack the stylistic grace and charm of Hyperides (see below), and indeed to Dionysius Dinarchus was stylistically, compositionally, and linguistically inferior to Demosthenes, Lysias and Hyperides (*Dinarchus* 1, 5-6), only attaining repute after Alexander's death because there was no one else left who was better (*Dinarchus* 2; cf. [Plut.] *Moralia* 850c). Dionysius characterised him as a 'rustic Demosthenes' on account of his inferiority to Demosthenes in his arrangement of material, choice of vocabulary, general diversity, and composition (*Dinarchus* 8). Others have been less harsh: Callimachus thought Dinarchus was one of the most notable orators (*Suda,* s.v. *Kallimachos*; cf. Athenaeus 15.669c), as did Cicero (*De oratore* 2.94; cf. *Brutus* 36), and in the second century A.D. both Harpocration and Pollux cited Dinarchus in complimentary terms for his style. However, modern opinion adheres to that of Dionysius.

---

[61] On the controversy of the number of speeches see in detail Worthington, *Dinarchus*, 10-12, citing previous work.

[62] Dion. Hal. *Dinarchus* 10, Conomis, fr. XXVII, Burtt, fr. A.10; cf. *P. Ant.* 2.62 (= Conomis, fr. 4 p. 146).

[63] Dion. Hal. *Dinarchus* 10, Conomis, fr. XXVI, Burtt, fr. A.9; cf. *P. Ant.* 2.62 (= Conomis, fr. 4 p. 146).

[64] Dionysius does not mention a speech against Polyeuctus for accepting a bribe, but see Dinarchus 1.100 (with commentary) and below, Section 7.

[65] The order of the canon is Antiphon, Andocides, Lysias, Isocrates, Isaeus, Demosthenes, Aeschines, Hyperides, Lycurgus, and Dinarchus; see further my 'The Canon of the Ten Attic Orators', in *Persuasion: Greek Rhetoric In Action*, ed. Ian Worthington (London: 1994), 244-263. For a succinct discussion of oratory and rhetoric see M. Edwards and S. Usher in *Antiphon & Lysias*, Volume 1 in the Aris & Phillips *Greek Orators* series (Warminster: 1985), 5-13.

[66] For a detailed discussion of Dinarchus' style see Worthington, *Dinarchus*, 13-39.

Blass believed that Dinarchus' speeches were disjointed,[67] Jebb dismissed Dinarchus in a mere page of his work on the Attic orators as being of no value because of his many plagiarisms,[68] and Dobson saw him as representing the decline in Attic oratory and that he was guilty of incoherent arrangement and long and formless sentences,[69] a view echoed by Kennedy and most recently by Nouhaud and Dors-Méary.[70] See further below on this issue.

However, the point must be made that Dinarchus' inclusion in the Canon of the Ten Attic Orators testifies to his literary reputation, given that so many orators must have been excluded from it. Moreover, although Dionysius condemned Dinarchus for unoriginality and for imitating the style of Demosthenes, Hyperides, and Lysias (*Dinarchus* 5-8), nevertheless Dinarchus was able to write in the different styles of these orators to such an extent that it was often hard to determine the authorship, and this is no mean feat.

There is a commendable varying of subject matter in Dinarchus' speeches by his quoting decrees, oracles, and other evidence (for example, 1.16, 47, 52, 78, 82, 83, 98), but Dinarchus is noteworthy also in his use of direct speech and appeals to the accused and to the jurors (all following examples are taken from Speech 1, *Against Demosthenes*):

> What did Demosthenes do at that time, who has the power to advise and make proposals, and who will soon tell us that he hates our current state of affairs? I will pass over the other dangers. Did you make any proposals concerning these ones? Did you offer advice? Did you contribute money? Were you of the least value to those working for the common safety? Not at all: you went around recruiting speechwriters. (35)

> Athenians, which one of you is so hopeful, which so reckless, which so ignorant of affairs past and present, that he expects that the man who has reduced the city from such prosperity to such disrepute, through whatever cause or fortune – and I disregard that – will now save us by serving as adviser and administrator? (93)

In the manner of Lysias and Hyperides, Dinarchus at times has a jocular tone to his style:

> By our Lady Athena and Zeus the Protector, if only the enemies of the city would be helped by such advisers and leaders, and never better ones! (36)

---

[67]   F. Blass, *Die attische Beredsamkeit*², 3.2 (Leipzig: 1898), 289-333.
[68]   R.C. Jebb, *The Attic Orators from Antiphon to Isaeus*² 2 (London: 1883), 374.
[69]   J.F. Dobson, *The Greek Orators* (London: 1919), 302-307.
[70]   G. Kennedy, *The Art of Persuasion in Greece* (Princeton: 1963), 256-257, Nouhaud and Dors-Méary, xvi.

He also enjoys using extemporaneous comments for a greater sense of immediacy:

> If the city must reap the rewards of Demosthenes' dishonesty and misfortune so that we are even more possessed by an evil spirit – I'm at a loss to describe it any other way – we should acquiesce in our current circumstances. (91)

And rhetorical tricks such as that involving the water-clock, which gives the impression he has a lot of evidence but time precludes him from detailing all of it:

> When he began to advise the people, and would he had never done so – I will pass over his private affairs, for time does not allow me to speak at length – is it not the case that absolutely no good has come to the city, and that not only the city but the whole of Greece has fallen into dangers, misfortunes, and disgrace? (31)

There are also picturesque details to bring scenes to life, such as the arrival of the Theban envoys at the Arcadian camp (18):

> The Arcadians, having come to the isthmus, had sent away the embassy from Antipater – it had no success – but they had welcomed that from the hard-pressed Thebans, which had reached them with difficulty by sea, bearing a suppliant's olive-branch and heralds' wands plaited, as they said, from young shoots.

Idiosyncrasies of Dinarchus include his love of repeating the opening pronoun or phrase for emphasis:

> Athenians, this man is a hireling; he is a hireling with a long history. (28)

> These men, Athenians, these men were worthy advisers and leaders for you and the people (40)

We also have the inclusion of much historical narrative (on historical narrative in oratory see below, Section 6), some of which is patriotic (the exploits of Timotheus at 14, or the Athenian help to Thebes against Sparta at 38-39), scandalous (Demosthenes' plot with Aristarchus against Nicodemus at 30, or Polyeuctus' subversive activities at 58-59), and emotional (the fall of Thebes at 18-24). Although the speech is not overly rich in the use of metaphor, on occasion it evokes a vivid picture, such as the destruction of Thebes at 24:

> But thanks to this traitor the children and wives of the Thebans were divided among the tents of the barbarians, a neighbouring and allied city has been ripped up from the middle of Greece – the city of the

Thebans, which shared the war against Philip with you, is being ploughed and sown. I repeat: it is being ploughed and sown!

All of these rhetorical tricks and the vivid use of imagery lend a dramatic and forceful weight to all of Dinarchus' speeches as we have them today.

While the characteristics of an individual author need to be described, it is important to avoid value judgements on the quality of the style and language used since ultimately that judgment is based on only a portion of Greek ever spoken or written, and today we often have no idea what were contemporary evaluations of the quality of the Greek. Moreover, given the sophisticated ring structures in Speech 1, which we will now consider, Dinarchus will have chosen his words and written his Greek after very careful consideration.

Indeed, criticism of Dinarchus' compositional abilities, and by extension his oratorical style, may be refuted by the presence of sophisticated ring composition in the *Against Demosthenes*. In a nutshell, ring composition is the complex arrangement of subject matter to achieve a structural symmetry within a work with echoes of language and themes; as one scholar put it, 'the technique of repeating at the end of a structural unit a word or phrase or theme with which the unit began'.[71] The device has been studied in a wide variety of Greek and Roman verse and prose authors, but has not hitherto been identified in the orators.[72] Dinarchus' speech takes on a new light; it demonstrates a structural symmetry, and his ability to compose in ring structures at extremely complex levels renders null his condemnation for incoherent arrangement of material. Where the speech appears to some scholars repetitious, for example, and thus monotonous, this is not the product of a mediocre writer but part of a general design where often reiteration of a theme tends to enclose a particular structural unit.

The speech against Demosthenes may be divided into eleven parts (the primary level). Each part of the primary level – the major framework of the speech – subdivides further into a secondary level, and parts of this divide into tertiary and post-tertiary levels; in other words, each ring composition often has a ring composition within it. From this construction we may also see how it was envisaged and how the material was structured to the arguments to be advanced. Only the primary level is given here in order to demonstrate Dinarchus' control of his subject matter and compositional ability: for the entire range of post-primary level structures with discussion see Worthington, *Dinarchus*, 27-39 with Appendix 2. The abbreviation A stands for the Areopagus/Areopagites and D for Demosthenes.

---

[71]   J.J. Keaney, 'Ring composition in Aristotle's *Athenaion Politeia*', *AJPh* 90 (1969), 407; on the ring structures of *AP* see ibid., 406-423 with P.J. Rhodes, *A Commentary on the Aristotelian Athenaion Politeia* (Oxford: 1981), 40-51.

[72]   See the bibliographical information in Worthington, *Dinarchus*, 28 with notes 43-45.

Dinarchus 1
Primary Level

A (1-4) INTRODUCTION: The A was ordered by D to investigate the charges of bribery. He imposed his own death penalty if found guilty of taking a bribe and the A decided against him. Exhortation made to convict D and not endanger the rights and safety of the city and country.

B (5-11) JUSTIFICATION OF REPORT: The trustworthy reputation of the A is emphasised in order to counteract D's accusation that it lied when accusing him and Demades.

C (11-28) PAST HISTORY I: Reference made to D and selected past exploits to demonstrate that his changes of policy and acceptance of bribes were detrimental to Athens and its allies but beneficial to the city's enemies.

D (29-47) PAST HISTORY II: Citation of noble deeds of Athens' ancestors, allowing a contrast to be drawn between past and present leaders, and a call to curtail D's continued leadership because of his past.

E (48-53) JUDICIAL PROCESS OF A: D's proposal that the A should investigate the affair is highlighted, and the machinery of the A in beginning an investigation is related.

F (54-60) JUDICIAL POWER OF A: When publishing the results of its investigations the A need only issue a report against someone, which should be automatically accepted.

E' (61-63) JUDICIAL AUTHORITY OF A: The sovereign power of the A, previously supported by D, is set in a context of its condemnation of previous men, but D now challenges its report against him.

D' (64-85) PAST HISTORY II: Contrast drawn between leaders' responsibilities for both good and bad fortunes affecting a city, allowing appeal against the continued leadership of D in view of his past inaction and policies.

C' (86-103) PAST HISTORY I: Specific exploits of D and his venality in ccepting a bribe are used in order to demonstrate that he has not worked for the good of Athens but for that of its foes.

B' (104) JUSTIFICATION OF REPORT: Further argument to discredit D's accusation that the A's report against him was false by the contrast with Demades.

A' (105-114) CONCLUSION: D, who proposed his own death sentence, must be condemned for the sake of the city and the country.

The commentary on Speech 1 is structured to each primary-level part of the speech, and the secondary level of each part is given in the introduction to each commentary section.

As the primary-level diagram reveals, the Areopagus and its findings play an important role in the speech (as in those others connected with the Harpalus trials), and this is hardly surprising given the dearth of evidence against Demosthenes. Since Demosthenes had made himself subject to the death penalty if the Areopagus found him guilty of taking a bribe from Harpalus, Dinarchus has to stress its infallibility as he exhorts the jurors to condemn Demosthenes. This emotional argument is found in the first part of the Introduction (1-4) and much of the second part (5-11), together with their corresponding parts (105-114 and 104, respectively). Moreover, it forms the core of the speech (both structural and argumentative): the Areopagus needs only to issue a report (*apophasis*) after its investigation (*zetesis*) and is not bound to cite evidence if it finds against its subject (55; cf. Hyp. 5.6). The central part (54-60) falls between two others dealing with the Areopagus (48-53 and 61-63), in which Dinarchus subtly and ironically uses various contexts to outline how the Areopagus was empowered to start an investigation (48-53) and to emphasise that it holds sovereign power over all Athenian citizens (61-63). To elaborate: since Demosthenes proposed the investigation into Harpalus' alleged missing money, and at the end of its investigation (*zetesis*) the Areopagus reported against him, and since the Areopagus had the right to punish any citizen accused of wrongdoing, then Demosthenes must now suffer condemnation.

Dinarchus also makes much use of Athens' past history against Demosthenes. He argues that the good and bad fortunes of a city stem from the policies of its leaders, and thus that thanks to Demosthenes Athens has declined in prosperity and power and will continue to do so unless his influence in the city is terminated. Demosthenes' corruption and worthlessness is thus demonstrated by a survey of past history, and this form of attack is another major theme of the speech, especially in the parts called Past History I and II.

The Areopagus and past history are the two major subjects of the first speech. It is obvious that there is a logical and ordered pattern into which the subject matter is fitted; instead of using a mere linear progression of events, Dinarchus employs ring composition for stylistic effect with each element naturally (and each major part of the speech) balancing its partner in subject or theme. Thus, what Blass and Dobson described as long, formless and disjointed sentences are, in fact, highly complex units, each containing a wide variety of subject-matter deliberately preplanned in its placement. Greater appreciation of Dinarchus' compositional ability and oratorical style must follow.

(4) Hyperides' Life and Works

Although Hyperides played an influential role in Athenian political life, unlike Dinarchus, our knowledge of his life and career is again not extensive and comes from three later sources: Pseudo-Plutarch's brief biography (*Moralia* 848d-850b), Hermippus, *The Pupils of Isocrates* 3, and the *Suda*, s.v. Hyperides, together with scattered references in other orators and writers. Of the three principal sources, Pseudo-Plutarch supplies the most details and is the most reliable.

Hyperides, son of Glaucippus, of the deme Collytus,[73] was born in about 389/8 into a fairly well-to-do Athenian family. He was living in Athens at a time when oratory had ceased to be a gentlemanly pursuit and was recognised as not only a literary art form but also the key to political and judicial ascendancy. He studied philosophy under Plato ([Plut.] *Moralia* 848d, Diogenes Laertius 3.46, *Suda*) and rhetoric under Isocrates ([Plut.] *Moralia* 837d, 848d, Athenaeus 8.342c, *Suda*), as had Isaeus before him and as a great contemporary orator of his, Lycurgus, also did. Like Isocrates Hyperides started a professional career as a *logographos* or speechwriter ([Plut.] *Moralia* 848e), but unlike his former teacher he continued in that profession after he entered political life, and indeed until close to the end of his political career – his third speech, *Against Athenogenes*, was composed for a litigant at some point in the 320s. Hyperides' son Glaucippus ([Plut.] *Moralia* 848d, Athenaeus 13.590c, *Suda*) also followed in the family tradition of logography as we know of a speech by him against Phocion (Plut. *Phocion* 4.2).

Hyperides also acted as a *synegoros* (a speaker or advocate for clients in court), in four known cases: (1) for Apollodorus in an *eisangelia* (impeachment) in 361 (Hyp. fr. 10), (2) for Chaerephilus in an *apophasis* (denunciation for treason) after 345 (Hyp. fr. 59), (3) for Euxenippus in an *eisangelia* between 330 and 324 (Hyp. 4.41), and (4) for an unknown person in a *graphe paranomon* (a prosecution for having made illegal proposals) in 336 (Hyp. 4).

Despite Hyperides' influential role in Athenian politics (see below), little is known of his personal life apart from his great partiality for eating fish (Athenaeus 8.341e), his sexual activity and his wealth. At one time he was able to keep three courtesans: Myrrhina, the most expensive in the city (in the process expelling his son from their house in Athens so she could live in it), Aristagora, whom he kept in his house in the Piraeus, and the ex-slave Phila of Thebes (whose ransom of 2,000 drachmas he paid himself), whom he kept on his estate at Eleusis ([Plut.] *Moralia* 849d; cf. Athenaeus 8.341e). He must also have known another courtesan, the famous Phryne, since tradition records that he defended her on a charge of impiety (see below). The three properties referred to by our sources, together with other evidence (for example, *IG* ii² 1585, 12: Hyperides the lessee of a silver mine at Besa) thus show him to be rich – certainly, one assumes, wealthy enough to have

---

[73] *PA* 13912, F. Blass, *Die attische Beredsamkeit²*, 3.2 (Leipzig: 1887-98), 1 ff., Berve, *Alexander* 2, no. 762, Davies, *APF*, 517-520, A. Schäfer, *Demosthenes und seine Zeit²* 2 (Leipzig: 1885), 324 ff. and 3 (Leipzig: 1887) *passim*, Blass, *Die attische Beredsamkeit²*, 3.2, 1 ff. and Colin, 5-51.

abandoned his career as a paid *logographos*, though he chose not to do so for some reason. He was also ruthless in whom he chose to prosecute, such as his ex-mistress Aristagora, and cared little about his clients' morals or the validity of their cases.[74]

Hyperides performed three liturgies (personal duties for the state paid from one's own funds) that we know of, all three in the same year (340/39): (1) a *trierarchia* (maintenance of a ship for one year) on his trireme called *Andreia Alkaiou* at the siege of Byzantium (*IG* ii² 1628, 436 ff., 1629, 957 ff., [Plut.] *Moralia* 848e), (2) responsibility for equipping forty triremes when Philip II sailed against Euboea, of which Hyperides donated the first two himself in his own name and that of his son ([Plut.] *Moralia* 849f), and (3) a *choregia* (provision of a chorus for a dramatic performance – [Plut.] *Moralia* 848e). Three liturgies falling within the same year suggest that Hyperides was exploiting them for political ends, and perhaps they could be undertaken from his receipt of Persian gold, which Pseudo-Plutarch (*Moralia* 848e) says he shared with a certain Ephialtes. This episode may be dated to 340 since Ephialtes served on an embassy to Persia in 341/0, and secretly returned with money for distribution among the politicians in order to provoke war against Philip II (Din. 1.33, [Plut.] *Moralia* 847f, 848e). Some of this apparently was given to Demosthenes and to Hyperides ([Plut.] *Moralia* 847f, 848e).

Hyperides probably entered the political arena on the completion of his rhetorical training.[75] The various embassies on which he served, his judicial activity and his decrees show him to have been an active and influential politician. Pseudo-Plutarch records an embassy to Delos, as well as embassies to Rhodes and Elis (*Moralia* 850a-b). The first embassy, to Delos, must be the one of 343 when the Assembly's first choice of ambassador – Aeschines – was over-ruled by the Areopagus in favour of Hyperides (Dem. 18.134), and the second, to Rhodes, may be dated to 342 (Hyp. fr. 48). Other embassies are known to Thasos in 361 (Hyp. fr. 23), Cythnus in 338 (Hyp. fr. 28), Elis in 332 (Hyp. fr. 25), and the Peloponnese in 323 (Justin 13.5.10).

The Athenian law courts were often as political an arena as the Assembly, and Hyperides also took part in cases of political interest. Perhaps most significant is his prosecution in 343 of Philocrates for the Peace of Philocrates of 346 between Athens and Philip II.[76] Although Philocrates fled into exile before the trial and was condemned to death *in absentia* (Dem. 19.114 ff., Aes. 2.6, 3.79 ff.), Hyperides was instrumental in the original prosecution. We know of other cases: *graphai paranomon* (prosecutions for having made illegal proposals) against Aristophon in 363/2 (Scholiast, Aes. 1.64), Demades of Paeania in 338-336 (Hyp. fr. 13), Meidias before 322 (Hyp. fr. 33), and an unknown other after 335 (Hyp. fr. 22), as well as *eisangeliai* (impeachments) against Aristophon between 361 and 343 (Hyp. 4.28), Diopeithes of Sphettus between 361 and 343 (Hyp. 4.29), and Philocrates in 344 (Hyp. 4.29, Dem. 19.116).

---

[74] See the remarks of Kennedy, *Art of Persuasion*, 253-254.

[75] See my '[Plutarch], *X.Or.* 848e: A Loeb Mistranslation and Its Effect on Hyperides' Entry Into Athenian Political Life', *Electronic Antiquity* 3.2 (September 1995).

[76] Hyp. 4.29, Burtt, fr. 16; see commentary on Dinarchus 1.28.

Hyperides would not escape litigation against himself: he was a defendant in several *graphai paranomon* brought against him in 339 (Hyp. fr. 18) and in 338, the latter for his panic decree after the battle of Chaeronea (Hyp. fr. 6; see below). Nor was he always successful in his cases: he opposed the grant of a gift for Phocion as proposed by Meidias of Anagyros in the archonship of Xenias, and failed ([Plut.] *Moralia* 850b).

It is after the battle of Chaeronea in 338 that Hyperides introduced his most radical legislation. At that battle Philip II led his Macedonian force to victory over the Athenians and Thebans, and when news of Philip's victory reached Athens and it was feared that the king would next march on the city, Hyperides, who had not fought in the battle (Lucian, *Parasit.* 42), made the radical proposal of enfranchising the *atimoi* (those who had lost their civic rights for offences) and metics (non-citizen residents of Athens), and manumitting the slaves in order that they might fight on behalf of the city, as well as sending the women, children, and sacred objects to the Piraeus for safety.[77] The fear of Macedonian attack proved unfounded, and for this proposal Hyperides was later – and unsuccessfully – prosecuted by Aristogeiton under the *graphe paranomon* procedure (Hyp. fr. 6). His defence was based on the famous remark that the shields of the Macedonians had cast a shadow over his eyes – i.e., the shadow of the shields at Chaeronea had made him unable to see the laws.

Hyperides' anti-Macedonian stance is further evidenced when in 335 he supported Demosthenes' opposition to Alexander the Great's demand for Athenian ships ([Plut.] *Moralia* 847c, 848e; cf. Plut. *Phocion* 21.1). He is also likely to have supported the revolt of Thebes in the same year, which was then systematically razed to the ground by Alexander. Apparently Alexander demanded Hyperides' surrender, along with several other Athenian statesmen, but his inclusion in this demand is suspect, and furthermore Pseudo-Plutarch (*Moralia* 848e) infers that Hyperides spoke against Alexander's demand.[78] Whatever the truth, he was certainly not handed over as Alexander eventually relented.

Although Hyperides and Demosthenes shared similar anti-Macedonian sympathies, and he had even proposed honours for Demosthenes in 339/8 (Dem. 18.222-223, [Plut.] *Moralia* 848f), Hyperides' opposition to Macedon by more overt military means eventually led to a split with Demosthenes. Perhaps the origins of military opposition may be seen even as early as 340, when, as was already noted (see above), he appears to have been in receipt of Persian gold following a mission by Ephialtes, which was to be used in order to provoke war against Philip II (Din. 1.33, [Plut.] *Moralia* 847f, 848e).

Such a split with Demosthenes and Phocion had certainly come about by 324/3 since in the notorious Harpalus affair (see above, Section 1) Hyperides successfully prosecuted Demosthenes (Speech 5, in this volume). There is a belief that Hyperides was implicated in the affair since Athenaeus preserves a fragment of

---

[77] Hyp. fr. 18, Burtt, fr. B.18, Lycurgus 1.16, 41, [Dem.] 26.11, [Plut.] *Moralia* 849a.

[78] Diod. 17.115, Arr. 1.10.4-6, Plut. *Demosthenes* 23.4, *Phocion* 17.2, [Plut.] *Moralia* 841e, 847c, 848e, Justin 11.4.10-11; cf. Aes. 3.161 and Din. 1.82, and on this episode cf. the discussion of A.B. Bosworth, *A Historical Commentary on Arrian's History of Alexander*, 1 (Oxford: 1980), 92-96.

Timocles' *Delos* (8.341e-342a), in which Hyperides is named amongst those
receiving bribes from Harpalus, but this is clearly incorrect. When a disgraced
Demosthenes fled into exile after his trial, Hyperides dominated the Athenian *demos*
and persuaded the city to revolt against the Macedonian hegemony on the death of
Alexander on 10 June 323. The Lamian War, as the revolt has become known (see
above, Section 1), saw victories in the first year for the Greeks, and at the end of the
first year the Athenians honoured their dead. Hyperides was chosen to deliver the
epitaphios or funeral oration ([Plut.] *Moralia* 849a): see Speech 6 in this volume
(and on the genre of the funeral oration see below, Section 5). However, the Lamian
War ended in disaster for the Athenians and the Greeks the following year, 322,
when Antipater defeated them at the battle of Crannon. Hyperides fled to Aegina
rather than surrender himself to Antipater, and the story goes that he made peace
with Demosthenes, who had also fled after Crannon, for his previous enmity.

Hyperides was captured at Hermione, and died in 322 ([Plut.] *Moralia* 849b).
Various versions of the manner of his death are known: (1) he was brought to
Antipater in Corinth and bit off his tongue and so died; (2) he was brought to
Macedon, had his tongue cut out, was left unburied, but a relative brought him back
to Athens for burial despite a decree forbidding him to be buried there (Pseudo-
Plutarch ascribes this tradition to Hermippus); and (3) he died at Cleonaea, where
his tongue was cut out, and his body was then brought back to Athens.[79]

Like Dinarchus Hyperides was a prolific writer, although his output was not as
considerable and this may be owing to his role in the political life of Athens.
Seventy-seven speeches were said to have been written by him, of which Pseudo-
Plutarch considered fifty-two genuine (*Moralia* 849d).[80] Today we have only six
speeches by him and several fragments. The speech *On The Treaty with Alexander*
in the Demosthenic corpus (17) was thought by Libanius to have been written by
Hyperides. Almost all of Hyperides' surviving speeches are fragmentary (only the
speech *In Defence of Euxenippus* is complete), which makes an assessment of his
style, not to mention establishing a context for a particular accusation, problematic.
Hyperides himself delivered the speech written against Demosthenes (5) for his part
in the Harpalus affair. Whereas Dinarchus' speech against Demosthenes (1) is
virtually intact, that of Hyperides is riddled with lacunae and restoration is often
impossible. Of his six extant speeches, the *Epitaphios* (6) is the last surviving
speech we have by an Attic orator.

(5) Hyperides' Style

Hyperides was also included in the so-called Canon of the Ten Attic Orators.[81]
However, unlike Dinarchus he has received widespread literary praise from ancient

---

[79]   Plut. *Demosthenes* 28.4, *Phocion* 29.1, [Plut.] *Moralia* 849b-c.
[80]   See the list of seventy-one thought to be by Hyperides at Blass, *Die attische
       Beredsamkeit*², 3.2, 19-22; cf. Colin, 51-73.
[81]   On the canon see above, note 65.

and modern critics. Dionysius of Halicarnassus, who intended to write an essay on him (*Isaeus* 20) – although if he did it has not survived – says that with Hyperides, Demosthenes and Aeschines, oratory reached a perfected form (*Isaeus* 20), and that he was a perfecter of styles (*Dinarchus* 1; cf. 6-8). Pseudo-Plutarch says that Hyperides excelled all in declamation (*Moralia* 849d), and Pseudo-Longinus thought he was a better orator than even Demosthenes (*On The Sublime* 34).[82] His style is described as 'charming' by Quintilian (10.1.77), and Cicero also speaks well of him (*de Oratore* 3.28; cf. *Brutus* 290, *Orator* 110). Other ancient critics such as Tacitus (*Dialogus* 25), Pliny (*Epistle* 1.10.4), Petronius (*Satyricon* 2), and Dio Chrysostom (18.11), are equally flattering.[83] There are a few negative comments: Dionysius believed Hyperides inferior to Lysias in his choice of words (*Dinarchus* 6), and his use of colloquial expression was criticised by Hermogenes.[84]

Modern critics also are laudatory. Blass, for example, talked highly of Hyperides' use of vocabulary, arrangement of material, and his ability to move from the grandeur of the Isocratean period (as in the *Epitaphios* or funeral oration) to the simplicity of the Lysianic style.[85] Dobson praised Hyperides' wit, irony, and verbal dexterity,[86] while to Jebb he was 'second to no one except Demosthenes',[87] and Kennedy says that he has a 'wonderful naturalness'.[88]

There is a grace to Hyperides' works which is lacking from what little we have of his great contemporary Lycurgus, with whom he is said to have engaged in oratorical contests (Dion. Hal. *ad Amm.* 1.2), or from Dinarchus. Certainly, Hyperides' prowess as an orator was undoubted, and other orators influenced him. In his use of metaphor and simile, humour and colloquialisms, we see the influence of Lysias,[89] and in his use of the periodic sentence his teacher Isocrates.

However, Hyperides was his own man: when using the periodic style (as in the *Epitaphios*) he wrote much shorter sentences, probably as an aid to understanding, and while he resembled Lysias in general simplicity his vocabulary was richer, often shocking, and his arrangement of material more subtle. Moreover, he was not afraid of innovation, and was prepared to tinge his speeches with unusual or audacious moves – there is the famous story that during his defence of the courtesan Phryne for impiety he bared her breasts in court in order to secure her acquittal.[90]

---

82   See Jebb, *Attic Orators* 2, 385-387, on the assessment (including a translation of it).
83   See further Blass, *Die attische Beredsamkeit*[2], 3.23-26.
84   Cf. Jebb's comment in *Attic Orators* 2, 384.
85   Blass, *Die attische Beredsamkeit*[2], 3.2, 26-61.
86   Dobson, *Greek Orators*, 289-301.
87   Jebb, *Attic Orators* 2, 381-392; the quotation is on p. 387.
88   Kennedy, *Art of Persuasion*, 252-255.
89   See especially Blass, *Die attische Beredsamkeit*[2], 3.2, 26 ff. with Dobson, *Greek Orators*, 289 ff. and 382-384 and Colin, 10 ff.
90   [Plut.] *Moralia* 849e; cf. Athenaeus 13.590d-e, Quintilian 2.15.9. So famous was this speech that it was translated into Latin by Messala Corvinus (Quintilian 2.15.9, 10.5.2). Poseidippus' comment in Athenaeus 13.590 is that Phryne was able to secure acquittal herself. On the trial see now C. Cooper, 'Hyperides and the Trial of Phryne', *Phoenix* 49 (1995), 303-318, who argues that the incident was apocryphal but became part of the Hyperides life story thanks to ancient biographers.

The wit, irony and sarcasm that are found in his speeches, showing a greater affinity to comedy than the speeches of Dinarchus do, make Hyperides pleasurable reading.[91] For example, when he discredits Demosthenes by drawing on the well-known numerous daily tides in the Euripus strait (which separates Euboea from the mainland):

> Demosthenes proposed these men for Athenian citizenship, and he consorts with them in particular more than anyone else. No need to be amazed at this! I think that since he is never able to hold to the same policy himself he has logically made friends with those from the Euripus! (5.20)

However, Hyperides' sarcasm can be very damning when he wants it to be:

> You were the one who decreed that a guard should be set up over Harpalus, but when it was found wanting you did not set it up again, nor when it was dismissed did you bring suit against those responsible, and you clearly did not take pay for the way you dealt with these circumstances. When Harpalus handed out gold to the lesser orators who can only raise a din and shout, did he overlook you who were in charge of our entire policy? Who can believe that? (5.12)

Hyperides' use of metaphor and simile can be striking. In the first example below (5.30), of a nation robbed of its crown, there is a near-pun on the crown, which was proposed for Demosthenes in 336 for his services to the state (see above, Section 1). In the second (6.5), Athens is compared to the sun, and by extension how dependent people are on both:

> the people so acted that, although owing to chance they were deprived of their crown of victory, they did not deprive us of the crown they had granted. (5.30)

> Just as the sun traverses the whole world, dividing up the seasons as is fitting and establishing everything for the best, and, for men who are wise and good, controlling their birth and nourishment and crops and all the other necessities of life, so our city continues to punish wrongdoers, helps the just, deals out fairness instead of injustice to all men, and at its own danger and cost provides a common freedom from fear for the Greeks. (6.5)

Hyperides also has direct speech and appeals to the accused and to the jurors in the speech against Demosthenes:

---

[91]   On the influence of comedy on oratory (focusing on Lysias, Isocrates, and Demosthenes) see P. Harding, 'Comedy and Rhetoric', *Persuasion: Greek Rhetoric In Action*, 196-221.

you yourself destroyed that friendship when you took gold against your country and changed your loyalties. You made yourself a laughing stock and you shamed those who in previous years shared in some aspects of your policy. When it was possible for us to become the most distinguished in the eyes of the people and to have enjoyed the best of reputations for the rest of our lives you upset all of this, and you are not ashamed now at your advanced age to be tried by young men for accepting bribes. And yet, the opposite should apply: the younger orators should be educated by people like you, and if they did something foolhardy they should be reprimanded and punished by you. (5.21)

Like Dinarchus, Hyperides make use of extemporaneous comments and tricks to bring an air of dramatic immediacy to his speech:

Gentlemen of the jury, as I was just saying to those sitting next to me, I am taken aback by this situation: that, by Zeus, everyone in the city is subject to the laws which enforce an arrangement proposed by someone against his own best interests apart from Demosthenes, and he is not subject to the decrees of the people, which you swore to uphold in your vote. (5.1)

Hyperides includes much historical narrative in his speeches. In the speech against Demosthenes (5), he writes in a fast-paced, staccato-like manner in order to convey the speed with which events took place in Athens in 324/3. The reader – and listener – is thus drawn into the drama and sense of urgency which must have prevailed in Athens then:

(8) Gentlemen of the jury, when Harpalus came to Attica, and at the same time the envoys from Philoxenus demanding him were brought into the Assembly, Demosthenes then stepped forward and delivered a long speech. He said that the city could not rightly hand over Harpalus to the envoys who had come from Philoxenus, but that it was essential that no blame be attached to the people by Alexander on account of him. (9) The safest course for the city, he said, was to guard both the money and Harpalus, and to carry up all of the money, which Harpalus had brought with him to Attica, to the Acropolis the next day, and that Harpalus should now make it known how much money there was. He did not do this, as it seems, so as to discover how big the sum was, but to determine from how large a sum he should claim his payment from him. Sitting down below in the niche, where he is accustomed to sit, he ordered Mnesitheus the dancer to ask Harpalus how much was the money that would be carried up to the Acropolis. And Harpalus replied seven hundred (10) talents.

The tone of the *Epitaphios* is naturally more sombre to fit the occasion, though of course the style of the Greek is still superb and the funeral oration is a real art-form. It was the custom of the Athenians to honour their dead in a solemn public ceremony, held in the Cerameicus district of Athens before the whole citizen body, and for a leading statesman to deliver the *epitaphios* or funeral oration (cf. Thucydides 2.34; quoted in the introduction to the commentary on Hyperides 6). This type of oration belonged to the genre of epideictic (demonstrative) oratory, where the aim was to awaken admiration in the listeners as opposed to persuading them to adopt a policy (as was the case with symbouleutic or political oratory) or to secure an acquittal or conviction (in the case of forensic or judicial oratory). An *epitaphios* was meant to honour the dead and at the same time glorify the city and the exploits of its ancestors and thus rally the spirits of the people. It was meant to praise good men by showing that they had died to preserve the freedom of the Greeks, and in the case of Athens democratic government. It had a conventional or solemn formula (see further below), and historical narrative was naturally patriotic, although the speaker had to tread a fine line in properly acknowledging the debt felt to those who had recently died without overly lauding ancestral valour. This kind of speech was highly rhetorical, and this is to expected given its nature. Hyperides' task when writing his funeral oration was made doubly difficult by his own intimate role in political affairs and by the military situation, for his speech was delivered in spring 322, probably after Antipater had escaped from Lamia and was regrouping his forces in Macedon (see above, Section 1).

In exhorting the people, the speaker of the *epitaphios* also had to show that those who had died for the city had done so for a purpose. In other words, that their deaths were not needless nor served only to enhance the city's and their own personal reputation, but that they had contributed to the very real continuation of the city, its autonomy, and especially Greek freedom or ἐλευθερία (cf. 6.10, 16). Though Hyperides makes Leosthenes the subject of his speech, there is no doubt that he anchors it on the ideal of ἐλευθερία, a word which he uses several times in the speech, thereby showing that those who fell in battle died for the noblest of causes. For example:

> For who would not rightly praise those citizens who died in this war, who gave their lives for the freedom of the Greeks, thinking this the clearest proof of their wish to confer freedom on Greece: to die fighting in battle on its behalf? (6.16)

Five other funeral orations have survived:

1) Pericles' *Epitaphios*: Thucydides says that at the end of the first year of the Peloponnesian War (431/30) Pericles delivered a funeral oration over those who had died in the war, and he quotes the speech at 2.35-46. However, it is highly unlikely that Thucydides quoted the speech verbatim.

2) Gorgias: A fragment of this speech survives, which refers to the Peace of Nicias of 421, which terminated the first ten years of the Peloponnesian War.

3) Lysias 2: This speech may be dated to 392. It is set in the context of the Corinthian War between Athens, Thebes, Corinth and Argos against Sparta (395-386). This speech was written for someone else (Lysias was a metic and so could

not have delivered it himself), but there is controversy about whether it was actually spoken or is merely a rhetorical exercise.

4) Socrates' speech: This is found in Plato, *Menexenus* 236d-249c, and is dated to about 386. Although in the dialogue Socrates delivers it himself to Menexenus, he ascribes it to a certain Aspasia of Miletus. However, the speech was obviously written by Plato, perhaps as an example of what a good speech should be, since Socrates was put to death in 399 and there are references to the Peace of Antalcidas of 386! If we can believe Cicero (*Orator* 151), the speech was read out in public annually in Athens.

5) Demosthenes 60: Demosthenes wrote and delivered a funeral oration in 338 in honour of those who had died in the battle of Chaeronea, when a force of Athenians and Thebans was defeated by Philip II of Macedon. Whether the speech we have today is genuine or a poor imitation is disputed, for in antiquity it was regarded as spurious (Dion. Hal. *Demosthenes* 44). It is certainly a very disjointed and rambling speech, and one unworthy of Demosthenes for such a sober and important occasion.

The funeral speeches which we have show a basic similarity in content and structure which we may say conforms to a pattern.[92] The speaker usually begins with an apologetic reference to his audience for what he is about to say and the fact that he will be repeating the exploits of the Athenians' ancestors again. Then he goes on to cite past history, sometimes stretching as far back as mythological times (cf. Thucydides 2.36-41, Lysias 2.4-60, Dem. 60.7-31, Hyp. 6.35-40, almost all of Socrates' speech in Plato, *Menexenus* 236d-249c). The deeds of the recently deceased are then lauded, and their deaths are linked to the defence of that great ideal the common freedom of the Greeks or ἐλευθερία (cf. Lysias 2.21-44, 55, 67-69, Dem. 60.23, Hyp. 6.5, 10-12, 16, 24-25, 37). Praise of Athens and of its democracy is also found (especially in Pericles' alleged *epitaphios*: Thucydides 37-43 – Athens is referred to as 'the School of Greece' at 2.41.1), but the emphasis is fixed firmly on glorifying both ancestors and those recently deceased for dying in the cause of freedom. Here, reference is most often made to the Greeks' defeat of the Persian threat to their freedom in the fifth century (Lysias 2.21-44, Plato, *Menexenus* 239d-241c, Hyp. 6.12). Thus in his speech Hyperides attempts to rally the Athenians with his analogy of the present war against Macedon to that fought against the Persians, another foreign foe, in the fifth century (6.12; see commentary *ad loc.*). They too endangered the freedom of the Greeks, but they were defeated by them. The speaker may then offer some words of condolence and even advice, often to the surviving children (cf. Thucydides 2.44.3, 46.1, Dem. 60.37, Plato, *Menexenus* 246d-248d, Hyp. 6.40), and then he brings his speech to a close by dismissing his audience.

Although Hyperides conforms to what may be said is the general pattern of an *epitaphios*, the point was made above that he was not afraid of innovation. This is

---

[92] See further on Hyperides 6 and the speeches cited above, Kennedy, *Art of Persuasion*, 152-203, Colin, 279-286 and 'L'oraison funèbre d'Hypéride: ses rapports avec les autres oraisons funèbres athéniennes', *REG* 51 (1938), 209-266 and 305-394 and especially N. Loraux, *The Invention of Athens. The Funeral Oration in the Classical City* (Cambridge, Mass.: 1986).

the case even with so sombre and formalised a genre as epideictic oratory. The injection of a personal element into the speech is seen in Hyperides' eulogy on Leosthenes, the Athenian general in the first year of the Lamian War and of course one of his political allies (see above, Section 1) – and it is bold and striking. Leosthenes becomes the hero of, and indeed central to, the speech:

> Leosthenes saw that the whole of Greece was humiliated and cowed, corrupted by those accepting bribes from Philip and Alexander to the detriment of their own countries. Realising that our city needed a man, and the whole of Greece a city, able to undertake the role of leader, he gave himself to his country and the city to the Greeks for the sake of freedom. (6.10)

At the same time, Hyperides has to take care not to downplay those others who lost their lives, as at 6.15:

> Let no one think that in making my speech I am ignoring the other citizens and eulogising Leosthenes alone. For the praise heaped on Leosthenes for these battles is also a eulogy for the other citizens. A general is responsible for the right battle strategy, but those willing to put their lives at risk ensure victory in the actual fighting. Consequently, when I praise the victory which was gained, I am paying tribute at the same time to the leadership of Leosthenes and the courage of his men.

Thus, Hyperides' personal treatment of Leosthenes gives this speech a vitality which might otherwise have been lacking, and at the same time is in keeping with the solemnity and patriotic appeal of an *epitaphios*.

(6) Oratory and History

The speeches of Dinarchus and Hyperides 5 and 6 are important contemporary sources for fourth century Greek history, and especially in the case of Dinarchus 1 and Hyperides 5 (despite its fragmentary nature) for the controversial Harpalus affair of 324/3 and the end of Greek autonomy. However, as historical sources they must be read and used extremely carefully, and here some mention must be made of the orators' use of history and the pitfalls associated with the historical veracity of oratory. The orators of the fifth and fourth centuries were not historians but rhetoricians. There is no such thing as an objective presentation of information in oratory since we are dealing with rhetoric, aimed at achieving conviction by painting the opposing party in the worst light possible. Bias is rampant. When dealing with past and even contemporary history in speeches facts, persons and events were exploited, manipulated and even, if necessary, created in order to persuade the audience, all causing us to doubt the accuracy of the historical information found in the Greek orators.[93]

Historical examples were often used by the orators as vehicles of propaganda, and were shaped by the political situation of the fourth century. When dealing with past history the orators are presumably alluding to a view of the Athenian past that they think will appeal to their audience, and so offer us the opportunity to gauge the current popular opinion on a particular issue. Thus, for propaganda and patriotic purposes the Athenians' role in defeating the Persians (the battle of Salamis is most frequently cited by the orators), their headship of the Delian League, and their eventual imperial hegemony in the fifth century, topics which become rhetorical topoi, suited well the imperialistic position and policies of their city in the fourth. Athens' role in Greek affairs by means of its empire was influential, and in the process of referring to the fifth century there is more than merely the propaganda element at work: by choosing examples from the fifth century empire, when Athenian power was at its zenith, the orators were advocating the Athenians' claim as leader of the Greeks in the fourth century by means of the Second Athenian Confederacy.

The orators have favourite historical examples, which soon established themselves as popular topoi ('stock' or popular events and deeds). The restoration of Athenian democracy after the despotic rule of the Thirty in 403 is one,[94] as is the treatment of the traitor and outlaw Arthmius of Zelea by the Athenians' ancestors in the 460's.[95] Rhetorical topoi about individuals or against opponents pose major problems when evaluating their historical accuracy. For example, the exploits of Conon and Timotheus formed a historical topos,[96] which is handled very differently by Lysias and – half a century later – by Dinarchus, in which Timotheus emerges as something of a popular hero (see commentary on Dinarchus 1.14). Both Aeschines (3. 239-240; cf. 133 and 156-157) and Dinarchus (1.18-21; cf. 10 and 24-26) accuse Demosthenes of responsibility for betraying Thebes to its destruction at the hands of Alexander in 335; however, this allegation is almost certainly untrue and was meant to discredit Demosthenes (see commentary on Dinarchus 1.10 and 21).[97]

Another problem concerning the historical veracity of Greek oratory is that speeches were revised after oral delivery. Here, the dilemma for ancient historians is highlighted, for it does not follow that information now present in speeches was orally delivered at the time of the trials. After oral delivery there is scope to add material omitted as a result of time constraints, or which simply had not occurred to

---

[93] On this topic see Ian Worthington, 'Greek Oratory, Revision of Speeches and the Problem of Historical Reliability', *Classica et Mediaevalia* 42 (1991), 55-74 and 'History and Oratorical Exploitation', in *Persuasion: Greek Rhetoric In Action*, 109-129, with bibliography cited, and M. Nouhaud, *L'Utilisation de L'Histoire par les Orateurs Attiques* (Paris: 1982).

[94] Lycurgus 1.61, Aes. 3.190-192, 195, 208, Din. 1.15.

[95] Dem. 9.41-45, 19.271-272, Aes. 3.258, Din. 2.24-26.

[96] Lysias 2.54 ff., Dem. 15.9-10, [Dem.] 13.22, Isocrates 7.12, 15.101 ff., Din. 1.14, 75, 3.17.

[97] See further on topoi in Dinarchus: Worthington, *Dinarchus*, 18-24.

orators at the time.[98] The complexity of ring composition is also a factor here. For the reading audience the composition and structure of the speech were more elaborate, while a simpler ring-structuring was probably used by the orators in the oral version of the speech, where ring composition was used essentially as a mnemonic device. In the revised version the emphasis was on the arrangement and handling of subject-matter for literary effect, and thus, with the outcome of an assembly debate or of a trial not hanging in the balance, it does not follow that the orator was bound to use material as he might have done in the oral version of a speech. Dinarchus, for example, is likely to have revised his speech in the light of Demosthenes' defence speech, and included material that either had not occurred to him at the time or against which the jurors may have adversely reacted.

How can we be certain what is factual in speeches and what is not? Sometimes we can corroborate information in oratory with independent historical sources; however, when these are lacking the tendency is to view the information in the speech with scepticism. However, a means of solving the dilemma, again drawing on the implications of ring composition, is by identifying 'complex' and 'simple' structures, for it is difficult to reconcile the sophistication of complex ring structures in some parts of speeches with historical accuracy.[99] If a structural sophistication is the aim of the revised speech, then it follows that the subject-matter is adapted and worked in to fit the pattern at the expense of accuracy.

(7) The Texts

Dinarchus

The major manuscript of Dinarchus[100] is the thirteenth-century *Codex Crippsianus, Brit. Mus. Burneianus* 95 (A). This was revised and corrected by the same scribe and later by others. The second manuscript is the thirteenth- or early-fourteenth-century *Codex Oxoniensis Bodleianus* misc. 208 (N). This also was corrected by the original scribe and later by others. From A five other manuscripts (from the fifteenth century) are ultimately derived (B, L, P, M and Z).[101] A contains many errors, but it is generally regarded as the more important manuscript. My tendency is to follow A more than N, especially for word order (as does Burtt, for example). Indeed, A's superiority for word order is supported to a very large extent by the recent discovery of *P. Oxy.* 49, 3436 and 3437 (see below).

Several papyrus fragments generally support the text of the above manuscripts or help to resolve textual difficulties. These are: (i) *P. Ant.* 2, 62 (= Conomis, fr. 4

---

[98] A trial lasted normally only for a day, although it is likely that some political trials, especially with multiple prosecutors (as in the Harpalus case), would stretch to two or three days: Ian Worthington, 'The Duration of an Athenian Political Trial', *JHS* 109 (1989), 204-207.

[99] See Worthington, 'History and Oratorical Exploitation', 119-126.

[100] The following is extracted from my discussion of Dinarchus' text at *Dinarchus*, 79-82.

[101] For further discussion see in particular Nouhaud and Dors-Méary, xxii-xxv; cf. Conomis, v-vii and xvii.

p. 146), which contains on one side part of a prosecution speech, perhaps against either Aristonicus or Hagnonides, against whom Dinarchus is said to have written speeches (Dion. Hal. *Dinarchus* 10);[102] (ii) *P. Ant.* 2, 81, the other side of the above leaf and containing part of sections 3-4 of Dinarchus 3 *Philocles*;[103] (iii) *P. Oxy.* 15, 1804 fr. 3, 7-8 (= Conomis, fr. IVb), which contains a reference to a speech by Dinarchus against Polyeuctus, perhaps indicating that he was tried in the Harpalus trials (cf. Din. 1.100);[104] (iv) *P. Oxy.* 35, 2744 col. ii lines 9-20 (= Conomis, fr. III), which quotes part of Dinarchus' speech against a certain Polyeuctus (Dion. Hal. *Dinarchus* 10);[105] (v) *P. Oxy.* 49, 3436 (Π¹), which contains most of Dinarchus 1.7 and the opening of 8 and 108-111;[106] (vi) *P. Oxy.* 49, 3437, containing the greater part of Dinarchus 3.17-22;[107] and (vii) Didymus, *Comm. ad Demosth.* Π 9780 (= Conomis, fr. LXXI), an extract from Dinarchus' defence speech for Docimus against Antiphanes set in the late 340s or 330s.

The *editio princeps* of Dinarchus was the Aldine in 1513. The most recent text is by Nouhaud and Dors-Méary (Budé) in 1990. For a list of editions of Dinarchus, linguistic discussions, and early commentaries, see Conomis, ix-xi, to which should be added the works listed by Nouhaud and Dors-Méary at p. xxvi.

The text of Dinarchus used in this volume is based on the Teubner edition of N.C. Conomis (Leipzig: 1975), which is cited by editor's name only: variations are listed after the text and translation. In an effort to provide as 'clean' and reader-friendly text as possible, the decision was made not to include the angled and other brackets which indicate alterations to the Greek and are very common in his edition. The discovery of the papyrus fragments cited in (v) above, which postdate his text, has obviously had an impact on the relevant sections, and I follow these readings. Other principal texts of Dinarchus referred to by editor's name only are the earlier Teubner edition of F. Blass (Leipzig: 1888), the Loeb Classical Library text of J.O. Burtt, *Minor Attic Orators* Vol. 2 (London: 1954) and the Budé text of M. Nouhaud and L. Dors-Méary, (Paris: 1990).

Hyperides

Hyperides' speeches did not survive in the normal manuscript tradition as was the case with Dinarchus and the other orators in the 'Canon of the Ten Attic Orators'.[108] Although Hyperides' speeches were apparently well-known for several centuries,

---

[102] *The Antinoopolis Papyri* 2, edited by J.W.B. Barns and H. Zilliacus (London: 1960), 42-43.
[103] *The Antinoopolis Papyri* 2, 70-71.
[104] *The Oxyrhynchus Papyri* 15, edited by B.P. Grenfell and A.S. Hunt (London: 1922), 168.
[105] *The Oxyrhynchus Papyri* 35, edited by. A. Lobel (London: 1968), 95, 98, 100-101.
[106] *The Oxyrhynchus Papyri* 49, edited by A. Bülow-Jacobsen and J.E.G. Whitehorne (London: 1982), 21-24.
[107] *The Oxyrhynchus Papyri* 49, 25-28.
[108] The titles and types of cases of Hyperides' speeches are collected by Blass, *Die attische Beredsamkeit*², 3.2, 19-22; individual speeches are discussed by him on 61 ff.; cf. Dobson, *Greek Orators*, 298-301.

they disappeared from circulation and view until 1847 when fragments only of some of them were found on papyri in Egypt. To date we have only six speeches by him, and four of these are incomplete (see below). However, we are fortunate to be able to read even fragments of Hyperides' speeches, for he was a great orator.

There are four major papyri: A, L, P and S, of which A is the earliest. Scribes later corrected A, L and P. A (= *Mus. Brit. Pap.* 108 and 115) was found in 1847 and contains *Against Demosthenes* and *In Defence of Lycophron.* Later in the same year, it was discovered that *In Defence of Euxenippus* (the only complete speech by Hyperides which we have) was also contained on the same papyrus. L (= *Mus. Brit. Pap.* 134) contains *Against Philippides*, P (= *Mus. Louvre* 9331 and 10438) contains *Against Athenogenes*, and finally S (= *Mus. Brit. Pap.* 98) contains the *Funeral Oration* or *Epitaphios*.[109]

The order in which Hyperides' speeches were delivered is unknown, which affects their numbering. Thus, Blass and Jensen numbered the speeches in the order in which they were discovered: *Against Demosthenes* (1), *In Defence of Lycophron* (2), *In Defence of Euxenippus* (3), *Against Philippides* (4), *Against Athenogenes* (5) and *Epitaphios* (6). On the other hand, Kenyon and Burtt follow the order in which they were thought to have been delivered: *In Defence of Lycophron* (1), *Against Philippides* (2), *Against Athenogenes* (3), *In Defence of Euxenippus* (4), *Against Demosthenes* (5) and *Epitaphios* (6). My own practice is to follow the latter order. Even the authorship of some speeches is not clear-cut. For example, the fragmentary *Against Philippides* (delivered between 338 and 336) has neither the title nor the author's name, but since Athenaeus (12.522d) tells us that Hyperides composed a speech against Philippides, we may accept that this is the speech in question.

The *editio princeps* of Hyperides was that of A.C. Harris, who published the speech *Against Demosthenes* in 1848. This was closely followed by C. Babington, who published the various speeches during the period 1850-1858. The most recent text is by J.O. Burtt (Loeb Classical Library, *Minor Attic Orators* Vol. 2) in 1954. For a list of editions of Hyperides, linguistic discussions, and early commentaries, see especially Jensen, XL-XLV.

Five of Hyperides' speeches are incomplete: *In Defence of Lycophron, Against Philippides, Against Athenogenes, Against Demosthenes* and the *Epitaphios.* The fragmentary nature of Hyperides' work poses enormous difficulties of interpretation and restoration, especially in the speech against Demosthenes (5). We do not even know how long this speech was in either its oral or written form, and trying to piece it together from the papyrus fragments which were found was a Herculean labour. Indeed, it is a tribute to the nineteenth century scholars, especially Blass, Sauppe and indeed Kenyon, who did so much to produce some order in the fragments we have of this speech.

The text of Hyperides used in this volume is based on the Teubner text of C. Jensen (Leipzig: 1963), which is cited by editor's name only: variations are listed after the text and translation. Jensen's edition is set out in two columns following

---

[109] For further discussion see Jensen, V-XXI and Colin, 51-65.

the papyrus. In an effort to provide as 'clean' and reader-friendly text as possible, the decision was made to reformat his text and print it as normal prose (as do other editors such as Kenyon, Colin and Burtt), and to exclude angled brackets and dots under letters (indicating broken or obscure letters). Square brackets (indicating that the papyrus is illegible) are included in the text <u>except</u> where a reading is virtually certain: in those cases, the square brackets also are omitted. Those who wish to be better informed of the readings of the papyrus should consult Jensen. I have changed the punctuation quite often to that in Colin's text since it seems more natural than that of Jensen. Other principal texts of Hyperides referred to by editor's name only are the Teubner texts of F. Blass (3rd edition, Leipzig: 1884), the Oxford Classical Text of F.G. Kenyon (Oxford: 1906), the Budé text of G. Colin (Paris: 1946) and the Loeb Classical Library text of J.O. Burtt, *Minor Attic Orators* Vol. 2 (London: 1954).

It should be noted also that whereas Dinarchus 1 and Hyperides 6 are divided numerically into sections (small paragraphs), Hyperides 5, being much more fragmentary, is presented according to the numbering of the fragments and the columns of the papyrus.

Finally, whilst the Greek text of Hyperides retains square brackets to show less certain modern supplements, square brackets are usually omitted in the translation so as to provide a more 'uncluttered' and cleaner reading.

TEXT AND TRANSLATION

ΔΕΙΝΑΡΧΟΥ

1. ΚΑΤΑ ΔΗΜΟΣΘΕΝΟΥΣ

1 Ὁ μὲν δημαγωγὸς ὑμῖν, ὦ Ἀθηναῖοι, καὶ θανάτου τετιμημένος ἑαυτῷ, ἐὰν ἐξελεγχθῇ ὁτιοῦν εἰληφὼς παρ' Ἁρπάλου, οὗτος φανερῶς ἐξελήλεγκται δῶρ' εἰληφὼς παρὰ τούτων, οἷς ἐναντία πράττειν ἔφη τὸν ἄλλον χρόνον. πολλῶν δ' ὑπὸ Στρατοκλέους εἰρημένων, καὶ τῶν πλείστων προκατειλημμένων κατηγορημάτων, καὶ περὶ μὲν αὐτῆς τῆς ἀποφάσεως τῆς ἐξ Ἀρείου πάγου βουλῆς δικαίας καὶ ἀληθεῖς ἀποδείξεις εἰρηκυίας, περὶ δὲ τῶν ἀκολούθων τούτοις Στρατοκλέους εἰρηκότος καὶ τὰ ψηφίσματ' ἀνεγνωκότος ἤδη

2 τὰ περὶ τούτων, ὑπόλοιπον ἡμῖν, ὦ Ἀθηναῖοι, καὶ ταῦτ' ἀγωνιζομένοις ἀγῶνα τηλικοῦτον, ἡλίκος οὐδὲ πώποτε γέγονεν ἐν τῇ πόλει, κοινῇ πᾶσιν ὑμῖν παρακελεύεσθαι, πρῶτον μὲν τοῖς λοιποῖς ἡμῖν συγγνώμην ἔχειν, ἂν τῶν αὐτῶν ἐνίοις περιπίπτωμεν – οὐ γὰρ ἵν' ἐνοχλῶμεν ὑμᾶς, ἀλλ' ἵνα μᾶλλον παροξύνωμεν, δὶς περὶ τῶν αὐτῶν ἐροῦμεν –, ἔπειτα μὴ προΐεσθαι τὰ κοινὰ τῆς πόλεως ἁπάσης δίκαια, μηδὲ τὴν κοινὴν σωτηρίαν ἀντικαταλλάξασθαι τῶν τοῦ κρινομένου

3 λόγων. ὁρᾶτε γάρ, ὦ Ἀθηναῖοι, ὅτι παρὰ μὲν ὑμῖν Δημοσθένης οὑτοσὶ κρίνεται, παρὰ δὲ τοῖς ἄλλοις ὑμεῖς· οἳ σκοποῦσι τίνα ποτὲ γνώμην ἕξετε περὶ τῶν τῇ πατρίδι συμφερόντων, καὶ πότερον τὰς ἰδίας τούτων δωροδοκίας καὶ πονηρίας ἀναδέξεσθ' εἰς ὑμᾶς αὐτούς, ἢ φανερὸν πᾶσιν ἀνθρώποις ποιήσετε, διότι μισεῖτε τοὺς κατὰ τῆς πολιτείας δῶρα λαμβάνοντας, καὶ οὐχ ἵν' ἀφῆτε ζητεῖν προσετάξατε τῇ ἐξ Ἀρείου πάγου βουλῇ, ἀλλ' ἵν' ἀποφηνάντων τούτων ὑμεῖς

4 τιμωρήσησθε τῶν ἀδικημάτων ἀξίως. νυνὶ τοίνυν τοῦτ' ἐφ' ὑμῖν ἐστι. ψηφισαμένου γὰρ τοῦ δήμου δίκαιον ψήφισμα, καὶ πάντων τῶν πολιτῶν βουλομένων εὑρεῖν, τίνες εἰσὶ τῶν ῥητόρων οἱ τολμήσαντες ἐπὶ διαβολῇ καὶ κινδύνῳ τῆς πόλεως χρήματα παρ' Ἁρπάλου λαβεῖν, καὶ πρὸς τούτοις ἐν τῷ ψηφίσματι γράψαντος, ὦ Δημόσθενες, σοῦ καὶ ἑτέρων πολλῶν, ζητεῖν τὴν βουλὴν περὶ αὐτῶν, ὡς αὐτῇ πάτριόν ἐστιν, εἴ

5 τινες εἰλήφασι παρ' Ἁρπάλου χρυσίον, ζητεῖ ἡ βουλή, οὐκ ἐκ τῶν σῶν προκλήσεων μαθοῦσα τὸ δίκαιον, οὐδὲ τὴν ἀλήθειαν καὶ τὴν πίστιν τὴν περὶ αὐτῆς ἐπὶ σοῦ καταλῦσαι βουλομένη,

Dinarchus 1, *Against Demosthenes*

(1) Athenians, your popular leader has pronounced a sentence of death on himself if it be proved that he took any sum from Harpalus. He has been unequivocally convicted of taking bribes from those whom in the past he claimed he opposed. Since Stratocles has said a great deal and the majority of the charges have already been detailed, and as for the actual report the Council of the Areopagus has published fair and true findings, and Stratocles has already outlined the consequences of this matter and has read out the pertinent decrees, (2) it remains for us, Athenians, especially when engaged in a case as important as this – the magnitude of which has never been encountered in the city – to make a common plea to all of you. Firstly, be sympathetic to those of us still to speak should we repeat points previously made. We will not do so to annoy you, but to whip up your anger by our repetition. Secondly, do not betray the common rights of the entire city, nor trade the public safety for the pleadings of the defendant. (3) You should consider, Athenians, that just as this man Demosthenes is on trial before you, so before your peers are you. These are the ones who are waiting to see what decision you will bring concerning the country's interests: whether you will surrender yourselves to the personal corruption and venality of these men, or whether you will make clear to all mankind that you detest those taking bribes to the detriment of the country. You did not order the Areopagus' investigation so that you could acquit them, but to exact suitable punishment for their crimes when its findings were declared. (4) This decision is now up to you. When the Assembly voted in favour of a lawful decree and when all of the citizens wanted to determine which of the politicians dared to take money from Harpalus to the disgrace and danger of the city, and, further, when you and many others, Demosthenes, proposed in the decree that the Areopagus should investigate these men – as is its traditional right – to see if any have taken gold from Harpalus, the Council of the Areopagus began its enquiry.

(5) Regardless of your challenges it made the right decision and it did not wish to subvert the truth and its own prestige because of you. Yet,

ἀλλ' ὅπερ καὶ αὐτοὶ οἱ Ἀρεοπαγῖται εἶπον, προορῶσα μὲν ἡ βουλή, ὦ ἄνδρες, τὴν τούτων ἰσχὺν καὶ τὴν ἐν τῷ λέγειν καὶ πράττειν δύναμιν, οὐκ οἰομένη δὲ δεῖν οὐδεμίαν ὑπολογίζεσθαι τῶν περὶ αὑτῆς ἐσομένων βλασφημιῶν, εἴ τις μέλλει τῇ πατρίδι αὑτῆς αἰτία μοχθηρὰ καὶ κίνδυνος ἔσεσθαι.

6 τούτων, ὡς ἐδόκει τῷ δήμῳ, καλῶς καὶ συμφερόντως πεπραγμένων, αἰτίαι νῦν καὶ προκλήσεις καὶ συκοφαντίαι παρὰ Δημοσθένους ἥκουσιν, ἐπειδὴ οὗτος ἀποπέφανται εἴκοσι τάλαντ' ἔχων χρυσίου· καὶ ἡ τῶν ἐκ προνοίας φόνων ἀξιόπιστος οὖσα βουλὴ τὸ δίκαιον καὶ τἀληθὲς εὑρεῖν, καὶ κυρία δικάσαι περί τε τοῦ σώματος καὶ τῆς ψυχῆς ἑκάστου τῶν πολιτῶν, καὶ τοῖς μὲν βιαίῳ θανάτῳ τετελευτηκόσι βοηθῆσαι, τοὺς δὲ παράνομόν τι τῶν ἐν τῇ πόλει διαπεπραγμένους ἐκβαλεῖν ἢ θανάτῳ ζημιῶσαι, νῦν ἐπὶ τοῖς κατὰ Δημοσθένους ἀποπεφασμένοις χρήμασιν ἄκυρος ἔσται τοῦ δικαίου;

7 Ναί· κατέψευσται γὰρ ἡ βουλὴ Δημοσθένους· τουτὶ γάρ ἐστιν ὑπερβολὴ τοῦ πράγματος. σοῦ κατέψευσται καὶ Δημάδου; καθ' ὧν οὐδὲ τἀληθὲς εἰπεῖν ὡς ἔοικεν ἀσφαλές ἐστιν; οἳ πολλὰ πρότερον τῶν κοινῶν ἐκείνῃ ζητεῖν προσετάξατε καὶ διὰ τὰς γενομένας ζητήσεις ἐπῃνέσατε; οὓς δ' ἡ πόλις ἅπασ' οὐ δύναται ἀναγκάσαι τὰ δίκαια ποιεῖν, κατὰ τούτων ἡ βουλὴ ψευδεῖς ἀποφάσεις πεποίηται; ὦ

8 Ἡράκλεις. διὰ τί οὖν ἐν τῷ δήμῳ συνεχώρεις, ὦ Δημόσθενες, ἐὰν ἀποφήνῃ κατὰ σοῦ ἡ βουλή, θάνατον ἑαυτῷ τὴν ζημίαν; καὶ διὰ τί πολλοὺς ἀνῄρηκας σὺ ταῖς τῆς βουλῆς ἰσχυριζόμενος ἀποφάσεσιν; ἢ ποῖ νῦν ἐλθὼν ὁ δῆμος ἢ τίσι προστάξας ζητεῖν περὶ τῶν ἀφανῶν καὶ μεγάλων ἀδικημάτων

9 εὕρῃ τὴν ἀλήθειαν; τὸ μὲν γὰρ συνέδριον τὸ πρότερον εἶναι δοκοῦν πιστὸν σὺ καταλύεις ὁ δημοτικὸς εἶναι φάσκων, ᾧ τὴν τῶν σωμάτων φυλακὴν ὁ δῆμος παρακαταθήκην ἔδωκεν, ᾧ τὴν πολιτείαν καὶ δημοκρατίαν πολλάκις ἐγκεχείρικεν, ὃ διαπεφύλαχε τὸ σὸν σῶμα τοῦ βλασφημεῖν περὶ αὑτοῦ μέλλοντος πολλάκις, ὡς σὺ φῄς, ἐπιβουλευθέν, ὃ φυλάττει τὰς ἀπορρήτους διαθήκας, ἐν αἷς τὰ τῆς πόλεως σωτήρια κεῖται.

10 Δίκαια μὲν οὖν, δίκαια τρόπον γέ τινα πάσχει τὸ συνέδριον· εἰρήσεται γὰρ ἃ γιγνώσκω. δυοῖν γὰρ θάτερον ἐχρῆν αὐτούς, ἢ καὶ τὴν προτέραν ζήτησιν τὴν ὑπὲρ τῶν τριακοσίων ταλάντων τῶν παρὰ τοῦ Περσῶν βασιλέως

gentlemen, as the Areopagites themselves said, the council well knew beforehand the power of these men and their influence as orators and as politicians. But if any harm or danger was threatening its country it did not think that it should pay attention to any slander that would be directed against it. (6) Although it seemed to the people that the investigation was conducted fairly and with expediency, accusations, challenges, and charges have come from Demosthenes since this man has been shown to have taken twenty talents of gold. Shall the Council, which is sufficiently trustworthy to establish justice and truth in cases of wilful murder, and which has the right to pass life and death judgments on each citizen, and to champion those who died a violent death, and to expel or punish by execution those who have transgressed any law in the city, shall it now be powerless to exact justice over the money shown to have been taken by Demosthenes?

(7) 'Yes! Because the council has lied against Demosthenes' – this is the over-riding argument in his defence. Has it lied against you and Demades? It is not safe even to speak the truth against you men, as it seems! Did you not order that body to investigate numerous public affairs in the past and because of its findings praise the way it enquired? Has the council made false declarations against these men whom the entire city cannot force to do right? Dear Heracles! (8) Why then, Demosthenes, did you agree in the Assembly to the death penalty on yourself if the council should report against you? Why have you yourself destroyed many others by steadfastly endorsing the reports of the Council? What body shall the people now approach or whom shall it order to probe puzzling and major crimes if it is to find out the truth? (9) Despite claiming to be the people's man you are dishonouring the Council, previously held in high repute, to which the people gave in trust the protection of their lives, to which they have often entrusted the constitution and democracy, which – although you are about to slander it – has protected your life, many times threatened so you allege, and it guards the sacred deposits on which the safety of the city depends.

(10) The Council is in one way suffering a just retribution – for I shall say what I think. It had two alternatives before it. Either to conduct the previous investigation over the three hundred talents which came from the Persian

ἀφικομένων ζητεῖν, καθάπερ συνέταξεν ὁ δῆμος, ἵνα τότε
δόντος δίκην τοῦ θηρίου τούτου, καὶ τῶν μερισαμένων ἐκεῖνα
τὰ χρήματα φανερῶν γενομένων, καὶ τῆς περὶ Θηβαίους
προδοσίας ἐξελεγχθείσης ἣν οὗτος προδέδωκεν, ἀπηλλάγμεθα
11 τούτου τοῦ δημαγωγοῦ δίκην ἀξίαν δόντος· ἢ εἰ ταῦθ' ὑμεῖς
ἐβούλεσθε Δημοσθένει συγχωρεῖν καὶ πολλοὺς ἐν τῇ πόλει
τοὺς καθ' ὑμῶν δωροδοκήσοντας εἶναι, τὴν περὶ τῶν νῦν
ἀποπεφασμένων ζήτησιν χρημάτων μὴ προσδέχεσθαι, πεῖραν
ὑμῶν ἐν τοῖς πρότερον εἰληφότας· ὅπου γ' οὕτω καλῶς καὶ
δικαίως τῶν ἀποφάσεων τῶν κατὰ τούτου καὶ τῶν ἄλλων νυνὶ
γεγενημένων, καὶ τῆς ἐξ Ἀρείου πάγου βουλῆς οὔτε τὴν
Δημοσθένους οὔτε τὴν Δημάδου δύναμιν ὑποστειλαμένης,
ἀλλὰ τὸ δίκαιον αὐτὸ καὶ τἀληθὲς προύργιαίτερον
12 πεποιημένης, οὐδὲν ἧττον περιέρχεται Δημοσθένης περί τε
τῆς βουλῆς βλασφημῶν, καὶ περὶ ἑαυτοῦ λέγων οἷσπερ ἴσως
καὶ πρὸς ὑμᾶς αὐτίκα χρήσεται λόγοις ἐξαπατῶν ὑμᾶς, ὡς
"ἐγὼ Θηβαίους ὑμῖν ἐποίησα συμμάχους." οὔκ, ἀλλὰ τὸ κοινῇ
συμφέρον ἀμφοτέραις ἐλυμήνω ταῖς πόλεσιν, ὦ Δημόσθενες.
"ἐγὼ παρέταξα πάντας εἰς Χαιρώνειαν." οὔκ, ἀλλ' ἔλιπες
μόνος αὐτὸς τὴν ἐκεῖ τάξιν. "ἐγὼ πολλὰς ὑπὲρ ὑμῶν
13 ἐπρέσβευσα πρεσβείας." ἐφ' οἷς οὐκ οἶδ' ὅ τί ποτ' ἂν
ἐποίησεν ἢ τίνας ἂν εἶπε λόγους, εἰ συνέβη κατορθῶσαι αὐτῷ
ἃ συνεβούλευσεν, ὃς ἐπὶ τοῖς τοιούτοις ἀτυχήμασι καὶ κακοῖς
ἅπασαν ἐπεληλυθὼς τὴν οἰκουμένην, ὅμως ἀξιοῖ δωρεὰς αὐτῷ
δίδοσθαι τὰς μεγίστας, λαμβάνειν δῶρα κατὰ τῆς πατρίδος
14 καὶ λέγειν καὶ πράττειν κατὰ τοῦ δήμου ἃ ἂν βούληται. καὶ
Τιμοθέῳ μέν, ὦ Ἀθηναῖοι, Πελοπόννησον περιπλεύσαντι καὶ
τὴν ἐν Κερκύρᾳ ναυμαχίαν νικήσαντι Λακεδαιμονίους καὶ
Κόνωνος υἱεῖ τοῦ τοὺς Ἕλληνας ἐλευθερώσαντος καὶ Σάμον
λαβόντι καὶ Μεθώνην καὶ Πύδναν καὶ Ποτείδαιαν καὶ πρὸς
ταύταις ἑτέρας εἴκοσι πόλεις, οὐκ ἐποιήσασθ' ὑπόλογον, οὐδὲ
τῆς τότ' ἐνεστώσης κρίσεως οὐδὲ τῶν ὅρκων, οὓς ὀμωμοκότες
ἐφέρετε τὴν ψῆφον, ἀντικατηλλάξασθε τὰς τοιαύτας
εὐεργεσίας, ἀλλ' ἑκατὸν ταλάντων ἐτιμήσατε, ὅτι χρήματ'
15 αὐτὸν Ἀριστοφῶν ἔφη παρὰ Χίων εἰληφέναι καὶ Ῥοδίων· τὸν
δὲ κατάπτυστον τοῦτον καὶ Σκύθην — ἐξάγομαι γάρ —, ὃν οὐχ
εἷς ἀνὴρ ἀλλὰ πᾶσ' ἡ ἐξ Ἀρείου πάγου βουλὴ ζητήσασ' ἀποπέφαγκεν χρήματ' ἔχειν καθ' ὑμῶν, καὶ ὃς ἀποπέφανται

king, as the Assembly ordered. Thus, by convicting this monster then, and exposing those who shared in that money and the treachery over Thebes – which this man betrayed – we would have been free of this demagogue, when he had received due punishment. (11) Or, if you wanted to pardon Demosthenes for these things, and have many in the city who will take bribes against you, the council should not have undertaken an investigation into the money now reported, having had experience of your wishes in the previous case.

Yet in spite of the excellence and justice of these recent reports against this man and the others, and in spite of the fact that the Council of the Areopagus has not been swayed by the influence of either Demosthenes or Demades, but has deemed justice itself and truth of more consequence, (12) Demosthenes nevertheless goes around both slandering the council and speaking about himself, tales that he will perhaps presently tell you in an effort to deceive you. Thus: 'I made the Thebans your allies.' No, Demosthenes, you harmed the common interests of both our states. 'I brought everyone into line at Chaeronea.' No again; on the contrary, you yourself and no one else fled from the line there. 'I was an ambassador on many embassies on your behalf.' (13) I do not know what he would have done or what he would have said if, in connection with these missions, what he had advocated had turned out to be successful! After touring the whole world arranging these misfortunes and disasters he nevertheless claims to be given the greatest privileges: to take bribes against the country and to say and do what he wishes against the people.

(14) Athenians, you did not take into account the actions of Timotheus, who sailed around the Peloponnese and defeated the Spartans in the naval battle off Corcyra. He was the son of Conon who freed the Greeks, and he took Samos, Methone, Pydna, Potidaea, and twenty other cities as well. You did not treat such services as a counterbalance to the trial then taking place or the oaths in accordance with which you cast your votes, but you fined him one hundred talents because Aristophon said he had taken money from the Chians and the Rhodians. (15) Will you not punish this despicable creature and Scythian – I'm almost speechless with rage – whom not one man but the entire Areopagus council at the end of its enquiry has shown to possess

μισθαρνῶν καὶ δωροδοκῶν κατὰ τῆς πόλεως καὶ ταῦτ'
ἐξελήλεγκται, τοῦτον οὐ τιμωρησάμενοι παράδειγμα ποιήσετε
τοῖς ἄλλοις; ὃς οὐκ ἐκ τῶν βασιλικῶν μόνον εἰληφὼς χρυσίον
φανερός ἐστιν, ἀλλὰ καὶ ἐξ αὐτῆς τῆς πόλεως κε-
χρηματισμένος· ὁ νῦν οὐδὲ τῶν ὑφ' Ἁρπάλου κομισθέντων
16 χρημάτων εἰς τὴν πόλιν ἀποσχόμενος. καίτοι τί μέρος ἐστὶ
τῶν ὑπὸ Τιμοθέου πεπραγμένων ἀγαθῶν ἃς Δημοσθένης
ἐπρέσβευσεν πρεσβείας; ἢ τίς οὐκ ἂν καταγελάσειεν ὑμῶν
τῶν τούτου τολμώντων ἀκούειν, ἀντιθεὶς ἐφ' αἷς οὗτος
σεμνύνεται πράξεσιν ἐκείνας ἃς Τιμόθεος ὑμᾶς καὶ Κόνων
εὐεργέτησαν; ἀλλὰ γὰρ οὐ πρὸς τοῦτο τὸ κάθαρμα
παραβάλλειν δεῖ τοὺς ἄξια καὶ τῆς πόλεως καὶ τῶν προγόνων
ὑπὲρ ὑμῶν πράξαντας. παρασχόμενος οὖν τὸ ψήφισμα τὸ
Τιμοθέῳ γενόμενον, πάλιν ἐπὶ τοὺς περὶ τούτου λόγους
βαδιοῦμαι. λέγε.

ΨΗΦΙΣΜΑ

17 Ὁ τοιοῦτος, ὦ Δημόσθενες, πολίτης, ὃς δικαίως ἂν καὶ
συγγνώμης καὶ χάριτος ἐτύγχανε παρὰ τῶν ἐν ἐκείνοις τοῖς
χρόνοις συμπεπολιτευμένων, οὐ λόγοις ἀλλ' ἔργοις μεγάλα
τὴν πόλιν ἀγαθὰ ποιήσας, καὶ διαμείνας ἐπὶ τῆς αὐτῆς
πολιτείας καὶ οὐκ ἄνω καὶ κάτω μεταβαλόμενος ὥσπερ σύ,
ἐτελεύτησεν οὐ τηλικαύτας τὸν δῆμον αἰτήσας δωρεάς, ὥστε
τῶν νόμων εἶναι κρείττων, οὐδ' οἰόμενος δεῖν τοὺς
ὀμωμοκότας κατὰ τοὺς νόμους οἴσειν τὴν ψῆφον ἄλλο τι
προὐργιαίτερον ποιεῖσθαι τῆς εὐσεβείας, ἀλλ' ὑπομένων καὶ
κρίνεσθαι, εἰ δόξειεν τοῖς δικασταῖς, καὶ οὐ καιροὺς λέγων,
οὐδ' ἕτερα φρονῶν καὶ δημηγορῶν.

18 Οὐκ ἀποκτενεῖτ', ἄνδρες Ἀθηναῖοι, τὸν μιαρὸν τοῦτον
ἄνθρωπον, ὃς πρὸς ἑτέροις πολλοῖς καὶ μεγάλοις ἁμαρτήμασι
καὶ τὴν Θηβαίων πόλιν περιεῖδεν ἀνάστατον γενομένην,
τριακόσια τάλαντα λαβὼν εἰς τὴν ἐκείνων σωτηρίαν παρὰ τοῦ
Περσῶν βασιλέως, καὶ Ἀρκάδων ἡκόντων εἰς Ἰσθμὸν καὶ τὴν
μὲν παρ' Ἀντιπάτρου πρεσβείαν ἄπρακτον ἀποστειλάντων,
τὴν δὲ παρὰ Θηβαίων τῶν ταλαιπώρων προσδεξαμένων, οἳ
κατὰ θάλατταν μόλις ἀφίκοντο πρὸς ἐκείνους, ἱκετηρίαν
ἔχοντες καὶ κηρύκεια συμπεπλεγμένα, ὡς ἔφασαν, ἐκ τῶν
19 θαλλῶν, ἐροῦντες τοῖς Ἀρκάσιν ὅτι οὐ τὴν πρὸς τοὺς

money against you, whose acceptance of bribes and venality against the city have been shown, who has accordingly been proved guilty, and make him an example to others? Not only is he known to have taken money from the Great King but also to have enriched himself at the city's own expense, and just recently he even helped himself to some of the money brought into Athens by Harpalus. (**16**) And yet, what fraction of the noble deeds performed by Timotheus are the embassies upon which Demosthenes served? Which one of you would not ridicule anyone presuming to listen to this man, who is proud of comparing his deeds with what Timotheus and Conon performed for you? You must not compare this outcast to those who acted worthily on your behalf for the city and your ancestors. I shall now produce the decree concerning Timotheus, and then return to my case against Demosthenes. Read it.

DECREE

(**17**) Such was the nature of this citizen, Demosthenes, who might rightly have gained the sympathy and gratitude of his fellow politicians at that time. He performed great deeds for the city by actions and not by words, and he stayed loyal to the same policy rather than switching back and forth like you. He did not die asking the people for any forms of benefit that would make him superior to the laws, nor did he think that those who have sworn to vote according to the laws should regard anything as more important than their vowed duty. But he was ready even to be condemned, if it was decided by the jurors, and did not plead circumstances or voice opinions in public that he did not hold.

(**18**) Gentlemen of Athens, will you not execute this accursed man? On top of many other great errors he ignored the destruction of the city of the Thebans, even though he had taken three hundred talents from the Persian king for its defence. The Arcadians, having come to the isthmus, had sent away the embassy from Antipater – it had no success – but they had welcomed that from the hard-pressed Thebans, which had reached them with difficulty by sea, bearing a suppliant's olive-branch and heralds' wands plaited, as they said, from young shoots. (**19**) The Thebans came to tell the Arcadians that they had revolted not from the desire to break their friendship

Ἕλληνας φιλίαν Θηβαῖοι διαλῦσαι βουλόμενοι τοῖς πράγμασιν
ἐπανέστησαν, οὐδ' ἐναντίον τῶν Ἑλλήνων οὐδὲν πράξοντες,
ἀλλὰ τὰ παρ' αὐτοῖς ὑπὸ τῶν Μακεδόνων ἐν τῇ πόλει
γιγνόμενα φέρειν οὐκέτι δυνάμενοι, οὐδὲ τὴν δουλείαν
ὑπομένειν, οὐδὲ τὰς ὕβρεις ὁρᾶν τὰς εἰς τὰ ἐλεύθερα
20 σώματα γιγνομένας, – οἷς ἑτοίμων γενομένων τῶν Ἀρκάδων
βοηθεῖν, καὶ ἐλεησάντων ἐν οἷς ἦσαν κακοῖς, καὶ φανερὸν
ποιησάντων, ὅτι τοῖς μὲν σώμασι μετ' Ἀλεξάνδρου διὰ τοὺς
καιροὺς ἀκολουθεῖν ἠναγκάζοντο, ταῖς δ' εὐνοίαις μετὰ
Θηβαίων καὶ τῆς τῶν Ἑλλήνων ἐλευθερίας ἦσαν, καὶ τοῦ
στρατηγοῦ αὐτῶν Ἀστύλου ὠνίου ὄντος, ὥσπερ καὶ
Στρατοκλῆς εἶπε, καὶ δέκα τάλαντ' αἰτοῦντος ὥστ' ἀγαγεῖν
τὴν βοήθειαν τοῖς Θηβαίοις, καὶ τῶν πρεσβευτῶν ὡς τοῦτον
ἐλθόντων, ὃν ᾔδεσαν ἔχοντα τὸ βασιλικὸν χρυσίον, καὶ
δεομένων καὶ ἱκετευόντων δοῦναι τὰ χρήματ' εἰς τὴν τῆς
21 πόλεως σωτηρίαν, οὐκ ἐτόλμησεν ὁ μιαρὸς οὗτος καὶ ἀσεβὴς
καὶ αἰσχροκερδὴς ἀπὸ τῶν πολλῶν χρημάτων ὧν εἶχε δέκα
μόνον τάλαντα δοῦναι, τοσαύτας ὁρῶν ἐλπίδας ὑποφαινούσας
εἰς τὴν Θηβαίων σωτηρίαν, ἀλλὰ περιεῖδεν ἑτέρους δόντας
τοῦτο τὸ ἀργύριον, ὥσπερ καὶ Στρατοκλῆς εἶπεν, ὑπὲρ τοῦ
πάλιν ἀπελθεῖν οἴκαδε τοὺς ἐξεληλυθότας Ἀρκάδων καὶ μὴ
22 βοηθῆσαι τοῖς Θηβαίοις. ἆρ' ὑμῖν δοκεῖ μικρῶν κακῶν ἢ τῶν
τυχόντων ὅλῃ τῇ Ἑλλάδι αἴτιος γεγενῆσθαι Δημοσθένης καὶ
ἡ τούτου φιλαργυρία; ἢ προσήκειν αὐτὸν ὑφ' ὑμῶν ἐλέου
τινὸς τυγχάνειν τοιαῦτα διαπεπραγμένον, ἀλλ' οὐ τῆς
ἐσχάτης τιμωρίας καὶ ὑπὲρ τῶν νῦν καὶ ὑπὲρ τῶν πρότερον
γεγενημένων ἀδικημάτων; ἀκούσονται τὴν κρίσιν, ὦ Ἀθηναῖοι,
τὴν ὑφ' ὑμῶν ἐν τῇ τήμερον ἡμέρᾳ γεγενημένην πάντες
ἄνθρωποι· θεωρήσουσιν ὑμᾶς τοὺς κρίνοντας, ὅπως χρῆσθε τῷ
23 τὰ τοιαῦτα διαπεπραγμένῳ. ὑμεῖς ἔσθ' οἱ διὰ πολλῷ τῶν ὑπὸ
τούτου πεπραγμένων ἀδικημάτων ἐλάττω μεγάλας καὶ
ἀπαραιτήτους ἐνίοις ἐπιτεθηκότες τιμωρίας. ὑμεῖς Μένωνα
μὲν τὸν μυλωθρὸν ἀπεκτείνατε, διότι παῖδ' ἐλεύθερον ἐκ
Πελλήνης ἔσχεν ἐν τῷ μυλῶνι· Θεμίστιον δὲ τὸν Ἀφιδναῖον,
διότι τὴν Ῥοδίαν κιθαρίστριαν ὕβρισεν Ἐλευσινίοις, θανάτῳ
ἐζημιώσατε, Εὐθύμαχον δέ, διότι τὴν Ὀλυνθίαν παιδίσκην
24 ἔστησεν ἐπ' οἰκήματος. διὰ δὲ τοῦτον τὸν προδότην παῖδες
καὶ γυναῖκες αἱ Θηβαίων ἐπὶ τὰς σκηνὰς τῶν βαρβάρων

with the Greeks, nor did they want to do anything in opposition to Greece, but they were no longer able to bear the conduct of the Macedonians among them in the city, nor to suffer slavery, nor to witness the abuses committed against the persons of free people. (20) The Arcadians were ready to help them and pitied them in their misfortunes, and they made it clear that although they were constrained because of circumstances to follow Alexander with their bodies, in spirit they were with the Thebans and the freedom of the Greeks. Since their general Astylus was open to bribery, as Stratocles also said, and demanded ten talents to bring the relief force to the Thebans, the envoys sought out this man, who they knew had the king's gold, and begged and beseeched him to give the money for the deliverance of their city. (21) But this miserable, impious, and mercenary man had no desire to part with a mere ten talents from the huge capital that he had, even though he saw such high hopes dawning for the safety of Thebes. Instead he allowed others to furnish this money, just as Stratocles said, so as to persuade the Arcadians who had marched out to go back home, and not help the Thebans.

(22) Do you think that Demosthenes and his venality have been responsible for minor evils or those of a trifling nature affecting the whole of Greece? Do you think that he should meet with any pity on your part for having committed such transgressions, rather than with the ultimate penalty for both his recent crimes and those of the past? Athenians, all mankind will hear the judgment meted out by you today: they will take note of you the judges, and how you deal with the man who has committed such iniquities. (23) You are those who, for crimes of much less import than those perpetrated by this man, have imposed extreme and inexorable penalties on certain men. You executed Menon the miller because he had a free boy from Pellene in his mill. You inflicted death on Themistius of Aphidna because he assaulted the Rhodian lyre-player at the Eleusinia, and on Euthymachus because he put the Olynthian girl in his brothel. (24) But thanks to this traitor the children and wives of the Thebans were divided among the tents

διενεμήθησαν, πόλις ἀστυγείτων καὶ σύμμαχος ἐκ μέσης τῆς Ἑλλάδος ἀνήρπασται, ἀροῦται καὶ σπείρεται τὸ Θηβαίων ἄστυ τῶν κοινωνησάντων ὑμῖν τοῦ πρὸς Φίλιππον πολέμου. ἀροῦταί φημι καὶ σπείρεται· καὶ οὐκ ἠλέησέ φημι ὁ μιαρὸς οὗτος πόλιν οὕτως οἰκτρῶς ἀπολλυμένην, εἰς ἣν ἐπρέσβευσεν ὑφ' ὑμῶν ἀποσταλείς, ἧς ὁμόσπονδος καὶ ὁμοτράπεζος πολλάκις γέγονεν, ἣν αὐτός φησι σύμμαχον ὑμῖν ποιῆσαι, ἀλλὰ πρὸς οὓς εὐτυχοῦντας πολλάκις ἦλθε, τούτους 25 ἀτυχοῦντας προδέδωκεν. κἀκεῖνοι μέν, ὡς οἱ πρεσβύτεροι λέγουσι, καταλελυμένης τῆς δημοκρατίας τῆς παρ' ἡμῖν καὶ συνάγοντος ἐν Θήβαις Θρασυβούλου τοὺς φυγάδας ἐπὶ τὴν Φυλῆς κατάληψιν, καὶ Λακεδαιμονίων ἰσχυόντων καὶ ἀπαγορευόντων μηδέν' Ἀθηναίων ὑποδέχεσθαι μηδ' ἐκπέμπειν, ὅμως συνέπραττον τῷ δήμῳ τὴν κάθοδον καὶ τὸ πολλάκις ἀνεγνωσμένον παρ' ὑμῖν ἐψηφίσαντο ψήφισμα, περιορᾶν ἐάν 26 τις Ἀθηναίων ὅπλα διὰ τῆς χώρας ἔχων πορεύηται· οὗτος δ' ὁ κοινὸν αὑτὸν τοῖς συμμάχοις, ὡς αὐτίκα φήσει, παρέχων οὐδὲν τοιοῦτον ἔπραξεν, οὐδὲ τῶν χρημάτων ὧν ἔλαβεν εἰς τὴν τούτων σωτηρίαν οὐδὲν ἠθέλησε προέσθαι. ὧν ὑμεῖς, ὦ ἄνδρες, μνησθέντες, καὶ τὰ ἀτυχήματα τὰ γιγνόμενα διὰ τοὺς προδότας θεωρήσαντες ἐν ταῖς Ὀλυνθίων καὶ Θηβαίων συμφοραῖς, ὑπὲρ ὑμῶν αὐτῶν ὀρθῶς νυνὶ βουλεύεσθε, καὶ τοὺς δωροδοκεῖν ἐθέλοντας κατὰ τῆς πατρίδος ἀνελόντες, ἐν ὑμῖν αὐτοῖς καὶ τοῖς θεοῖς τὰς ἐλπίδας τῆς σωτηρίας ἔχετε. 27 μόνως γὰρ οὕτως, ἄνδρες Ἀθηναῖοι, μόνως καὶ τοὺς ἄλλους ποιήσετε βελτίους, ἐὰν τοὺς ἐνδόξους τῶν πονηρῶν ἐξελέγξαντες κολάσητε τῶν ἀδικημάτων ἀξίως. τοὺς μὲν γὰρ τυχόντας τῶν κρινομένων, ὅταν ἁλῶσιν, οὐδεὶς οἶδεν οὐδὲ ζητεῖ πυθέσθαι τί πεπόνθασι· τοὺς δ' ἐνδόξους πάντες πυνθάνονται, καὶ τοὺς δικάζοντας ἐπαινοῦσιν, ὅταν τὸ δίκαιον μὴ πρόωνται ταῖς τῶν κρινομένων δόξαις. ἀνάγνωθι τὸ ψήφισμα τὸ Θηβαίων. λέγε τὰς μαρτυρίας. ἀναγίγνωσκε τὰς ἐπιστολάς.

ΨΗΦΙΣΜΑ. ΜΑΡΤΥΡΙΑΙ. ΕΠΙΣΤΟΛΑΙ

28 Μισθωτὸς οὗτος, ὦ Ἀθηναῖοι, μισθωτός ἐστι παλαιός. οὗτος ἦν ὁ τὴν πρεσβείαν τὴν παρὰ Φιλίππου πορευομένην ὡς ἡμᾶς ἐκ Θηβῶν καλέσας, καὶ τοῦ λυθῆναι τὸν πρῶτον

of the barbarians, a neighbouring and allied city has been ripped up from the middle of Greece – the city of the Thebans, which shared the war against Philip with you, is being ploughed and sown. I repeat: it is being ploughed and sown! I tell you this contemptible man was not moved by a city so piteously destroyed, to which he went as an envoy on your behalf, many times sharing the drink and eating at the table of its people, and which he claims he himself made your ally. But those to whom he has often turned when they were affluent he has betrayed when they were struck by misfortune. (25) When the democracy in our city had been overthrown and the exiles were being mustered in Thebes by Thrasybulus for the seizure of Phyle, those men, as our elders say, despite the strength of the Spartans and their prohibition to admit or let depart any Athenian, nevertheless aided the return of the democrats and passed the decree, so many times read out to you, that they should overlook any Athenian bearing arms passing through their territory. (26) But this man, who so intimately associates himself with our allies, as he will presently tell you, did no such thing in reciprocation, and did not want to part with any of the money that he received for their safety. Gentlemen, remember these things, and bear in mind the disasters that came about because of traitors in the ruin of Olynthus and Thebes. Decide wisely now for your own best interests: get rid of those wanting to take bribes against their country and fix your hopes of safety on yourselves and on the gods. (27) For only by one way, gentlemen of Athens, and one way alone will you make mankind better: if you expose those criminals who are famous men and punish them as befits their crimes. In the case of ordinary defendants no one knows – or even wants to find out – how they have been punished when they are convicted, but everyone will know this in the case of eminent men, and they praise the jurors when they have not sacrificed justice to the reputation of the defendants. Read the decree of the Thebans. Quote the evidence. Read the letters.

DECREE   EVIDENCE   LETTERS

(28) Athenians, this man is a hireling; he is a hireling with a long history. This was the man who summoned from Thebes the embassy coming to us

πόλεμον αἴτιος γενόμενος· οὗτος Φιλοκράτει συναπελογεῖτο
τῷ γράψαντι πρὸς Φίλιππον εἰρήνην, δι' ἣν ὑμεῖς ἐκεῖνον
ἐξεβάλετε, καὶ ζεύγη τοῖς πρέσβεσιν ἐμισθώσατο τοῖς μετ'
Ἀντιπάτρου δεῦρ' ἐλθοῦσιν, ἀναλαμβάνων αὐτοὺς καὶ τὸ
κολακεύειν τοὺς Μακεδόνας πρῶτος εἰς τὴν πόλιν εἰσάγων.

29 Μὴ ἀφῆτ', ἄνδρες Ἀθηναῖοι, μὴ ἀφῆτε τὸν ἐπὶ τοῖς τῆς
πόλεως καὶ τῶν ἄλλων Ἑλλήνων ἀτυχήμασιν ἐπιγεγραμμένον
ἀτιμώρητον, εἰλημμένον ἐπ' αὐτοφώρῳ δῶρ' ἔχοντα κατὰ τῆς
πόλεως, μηδὲ τῆς ἀγαθῆς τύχης ὑμᾶς ἐπὶ τὸ βέλτιον
ἀγούσης, καὶ τὸν μὲν ἕτερον τῶν τὴν πατρίδα λελυμασμένων
ἐκ τῆς πόλεως ἐκβεβληκυίας, τοῦτον δ' ὑμῖν ἀποκτεῖναι
παραδούσης, αὐτοὶ τοῖς πᾶσι συμφέρουσιν ἐναντιωθῆτε, ἀλλὰ
μετοιωνίσασθε τὰς τῆς πόλεως πράξεις, εἰς τούτους τοὺς
30 ἡγεμόνας τὰς ἀτυχίας τρέψαντες. εἰς ποῖον γὰρ καιρὸν
ἀποθήσεσθε τοῦτον ὑπολαβόντες χρήσιμον ὑμῖν αὐτοῖς
ἔσεσθαι; ἔχοι τις ἂν εἰπεῖν ἢ ὑμῶν ἢ τῶν περιεστηκότων,
εἰς ποῖ' οὗτος πράγματ' εἰσελθὼν ἢ ἴδια ἢ κοινὰ οὐκ
ἀνατέτραφεν; οὐκ εἰς μὲν τὴν Ἀριστάρχου οἰκίαν εἰσελθών,
βουλεύσας μετ' ἐκείνου τὸν Νικοδήμῳ θάνατον
κατασκευασθέντα, ὃν ἴστε πάντες, ἐξέβαλε τὸν Ἀρίσταρχον
ἐπὶ ταῖς αἰσχίσταις αἰτίαις; καὶ τοιούτῳ φίλῳ Δημοσθένει
ἐχρήσατο, ὥστε δαίμον' αὐτῷ τοῦτον καὶ τῶν γεγενημένων
31 συμφορῶν ἡγεμόνα νομίσαι προσελθεῖν; οὐκ ἐπειδὴ τῷ δήμῳ
συμβουλεύειν ἤρξατο, ὡς μήποτ' ὤφελεν – ἀφήσω γὰρ αὐτοῦ
τὰ ἴδια· ὁ γὰρ χρόνος οὐκ ἐπιδέχεται μακρολογεῖν –, ἀγαθὸν
μὲν ἁπλῶς εἰπεῖν οὐδὲν γέγονε τῇ πόλει, ἐν κινδύνοις δὲ καὶ
κακοῖς καὶ ἀδοξίᾳ πᾶσ' ἡ Ἑλλάς, οὐ μόνον ἡ πόλις,
καθέστηκε; καὶ πλείστοις καιροῖς ἐν ταῖς δημηγορίαις
χρώμενος, ἅπαντας ἀφῆκε τοὺς ὑπὲρ ὑμῶν καιρούς; καὶ ἐν
οἷς τις ἂν φιλόπολις ἀνὴρ καὶ κηδεμὼν τῆς πόλεως
προείλετό τι πρᾶξαι, τοσοῦτον ἐδέησεν ὁ δημαγωγὸς καὶ
χρήσιμος αὐτίκα φήσων ὑμῖν γεγενῆσθαι πρᾶξίν τινα
προφέρειν, ὥστε καὶ τοὺς πράττοντας ὑπὲρ ὑμῶν τι τῆς
32 αὐτοῦ τύχης ἀνέπλησεν. ἀπῆρε Χαρίδημος πρὸς τὸν Περσῶν
βασιλέα, χρήσιμος ὑμῖν οὐ λόγοις ἀλλ' ἔργοις βουλόμενος
γενέσθαι, καὶ τοῖς ἰδίοις τοῖς ἑαυτοῦ κινδύνοις ὑμῖν καὶ τοῖς
ἄλλοις Ἕλλησι βουλόμενος τὴν σωτηρίαν παρασκευάσαι·
περιιὼν οὗτος κατὰ τὴν ἀγορὰν ἐλογοποίει καὶ

from Philip and was responsible for the termination of the first war. This man helped to defend Philocrates, who proposed peace with Philip (because of which you exiled him), and he hired a carriage for the ambassadors who came here with Antipater, bringing them with him and first introducing into the city the habit of fawning on the Macedonians.

(29) Gentlemen of Athens, do not acquit him, do not let go unpunished the man who is responsible for the misfortunes of the city and the whole of Greece, when he has been caught red-handed with bribes against the city. Since good fortune is leading you to prosperity and has handed this one over to you for execution, and having expelled from the city one of the two who has defiled the country, do not yourselves oppose all our interests but procure happier omens for the affairs of state and divert our misfortunes onto these leaders. (30) For what occasion will you preserve this man thinking that he will be of value to you? Could any one of you or of the bystanders say with what private or public matters this man has come into contact and not ruined them? Did he not go to the home of Aristarchus and plan with him the death of Nicodemus, which they accomplished – you all know about this – and then expel Aristarchus on disgraceful charges? And did he not find Demosthenes such a friend as to make him consider this man was an evil spirit come to visit him and the source of his misfortunes? (31) When he began to advise the people, and would he had never done so – I will pass over his private affairs, for time does not allow me to speak at length – is it not the case that absolutely no good has come to the city, and that not only the city but the whole of Greece has fallen into dangers, misfortunes, and disgrace? Has he not let slip every opportunity for your betterment, despite having had many such opportunities in his speeches? On those occasions when some caring and patriotic man would have elected to do something for the city, this demagogue, who will soon say how useful he has been to you, so far from taking positive action has diverted his own bad fortune onto those doing something on your behalf. (32) Charidemus sailed to the Persian king, wanting to be of service to you with actions not with words, and at his own personal risk wanting to secure safety for you and the other Greeks. This man walked around the market place delivering speeches, and

τῶν πραττομένων εἰσεποίει κοινωνὸν αὐτόν· οὕτω
κατέστρεψεν ἡ τύχη ταῦτα, ὥστ' ἐναντία γενέσθαι τοῖς
33 προσδοκωμένοις. ἐξέπλευσεν Ἐφιάλτης μισῶν μὲν τοῦτον,
ἀναγκαζόμενος δὲ τῶν πραγμάτων κοινωνεῖν· ἀφείλετο καὶ
τοῦτον ἡ τύχη τῆς πόλεως. Εὐθύδικος προῃρεῖτο τὰς ὑπὲρ
τοῦ δήμου πράξεις· ἔφη τούτῳ Δημοσθένης φίλος εἶναι· καὶ
οὗτος ἀπώλετο. καὶ ταῦθ' ὑμεῖς ὁρῶντες καὶ ἐπιστάμενοι
πολὺ βέλτιον ἢ ἐγώ, οὐ λογίζεσθε, οὐ σκοπεῖσθε πρὸς ὑμᾶς
αὐτούς, τεκμαιρόμενοι τὰ μέλλοντ' ἐκ τῶν γεγενημένων, ὅτι
οὐδὲν οὗτος χρήσιμος ἀλλ' ἢ τοῖς ἐχθροῖς κατὰ τῆς πόλεως
34 ‹καταλύουσιν; δεῖ ὑμᾶς› συστῆσαι κατασκευὴν ἑτέραν οἵα
ἐπ' Ἄγιδος ἐγένετο, ὅτε Λακεδαιμόνιοι μὲν ἅπαντες
ἐξεστράτευσαν, Ἀχαιοὶ δὲ καὶ Ἠλεῖοι τῶν πραγμάτων
ἐκοινώνουν, ὑπῆρχον δὲ ξένοι μύριοι, Ἀλέξανδρος δ', ὡς οἱ
λέγοντες, ἐν Ἰνδοῖς ἦν, ἡ δ' Ἑλλὰς ἅπασα διὰ τοὺς ἐν
ἑκάστῃ τῶν πόλεων προδότας ἀχθομένη τοῖς παροῦσι
πράγμασιν ἡσμένει μεταβολήν τινα τῶν παρεστηκότων κακῶν;
35 τί οὖν; ἐν τούτοις τοῖς καιροῖς Δημοσθένης τίς ἦν, ὁ τοῦ
συμβουλεῦσαι καὶ γράψαι κύριος καὶ φήσων αὐτίκα δὴ μισεῖν
τὰ καθεστηκότα πράγματα; ἐῶ γὰρ τοὺς ἄλλους κινδύνους.
ἔγραψάς τι περὶ τούτων; συνεβούλευσας; ἐπόρισας χρήματα;
μικρόν τι χρήσιμος ἐγένου τοῖς ὑπὲρ τῆς κοινῆς σωτηρίας
πράττουσιν; οὐδ' ὁτιοῦν, ἀλλὰ περιήεις κατασκευάζων
λογοποιούς, καὶ παρ' αὐτῷ γράφων ἐπιστολὴν καὶ
καταισχύνων τὴν τῆς πόλεως δόξαν, ἐκ τῶν δακτύλων
36 ἀναψάμενος περιεπορεύετο, τρυφῶν ἐν τοῖς τῆς πόλεως
κακοῖς, καὶ ἐπὶ φορείου κατακομιζόμενος τὴν εἰς Πειραιᾶ
ὁδόν, καὶ τὰς τῶν πενήτων ἀπορίας ὀνειδίζων. εἶθ' οὗτος εἰς
τοὺς μέλλοντας ὑμῖν καιροὺς ἔσται χρήσιμος, παραβεβηκὼς
ἅπαντας τοὺς παρεληλυθότας; τοιούτων, ὦ δέσποιν' Ἀθηνᾶ
καὶ Ζεῦ σῶτερ, συμβούλων καὶ ἡγεμόνων ὤφελον τυχεῖν οἱ
πολεμήσαντες τῇ πόλει, καὶ μηδεπώποτε βελτιόνων.
37 Οὐκ ἀναμνήσεσθ', ὦ ἄνδρες, τὰς τῶν πρεσβυτέρων πράξεις,
οἳ μεγάλων καὶ πολλῶν κινδύνων καταλαμβανόντων τὴν πόλιν
ἀξίως τῆς πατρίδος καὶ τῆς ἑαυτῶν ἐλευθερίας καὶ τῆς
δόξης τῆς δικαίας ὑπὲρ τῶν τοῦ δήμου συμφερόντων
ἐκινδύνευσαν; ὧν τοὺς μὲν ἀρχαίους ἐκείνους μακρὸν ἂν εἴη

made himself a partner in the undertaking. Fortune so upset the plan that it turned out the opposite to what was anticipated. (33) Ephialtes, hating this man, sailed off, compelled to be a partner in the undertaking. Fortune also took this man from the city. Euthydicus promised beneficial deeds on behalf of the people. Demosthenes said he was this man's friend. This man also perished. Do you not think about these things, which you see and understand far better than I, or reflect in your own minds, weighing up future prospects in the light of the past, that this man is of no benefit except to enemies plotting against the city? (34) Is it not necessary for you to raise up another force such as we had in the time of Agis, when all the Spartans had taken the field and the Achaeans and Eleans were sharing in the campaign, as were ten thousand mercenaries, and Alexander, so they said, was in India, and the whole of Greece was bemoaning the current state of affairs because of traitors in each city, and was hoping for some change from the present misfortunes? (35) What then? What did Demosthenes do at that time, who has the power to advise and make proposals, and who will soon tell us that he hates our current state of affairs? I will pass over the other dangers. Did you make any proposals concerning these ones? Did you offer advice? Did you contribute money? Were you of the least value to those working for the common safety? Not at all: you went around recruiting speechwriters. He wrote a letter at home, shaming the dignity of the city, and strolled around dangling it from his fingertips, (36) living well in the midst of the city's hardships, and travelling in a sedan-chair on the road to Piraeus and abusing the needy for their poverty. Shall this man, then, be of benefit to you on future occasions when he has let slip all previous ones? By our Lady Athena and Zeus the Protector, if only the enemies of the city would be helped by such advisers and leaders, and never better ones!

(37) Gentlemen, will you not remember the deeds of your ancestors who, when great and numerous dangers were befalling the city, risked peril for the well-being of the people, honourably for the city, their own freedom, and just reputation? It would be a long task to tell of those great men of the past,

λέγειν, Ἀριστείδην καὶ Θεμιστοκλέα, ,οὺς ὀρθώσαντας τὰ
τείχη τῆς πόλεως καὶ τοὺς φόρους εἰς ἀκρόπολιν
ἀνενεγκόντας παρ' ἑκόντων καὶ βουλομένων τῶν Ἑλλήνων,
38 ἀλλὰ ταυτὶ τὰ μικρὸν πρὸ τῆς ἡμετέρας ἡλικίας γεγενημένα
ὑπὸ Κεφάλου τοῦ ῥήτορος καὶ Θράσωνος τοῦ Ἐρχιέως καὶ
Ἡλείου καὶ Φορμισίου καὶ ἑτέρων ἀνδρῶν ἀγαθῶν, ὧν ἐνίων
ἔτι καὶ νῦν ζῇ τὰ σώματα. τούτων γὰρ οἱ μὲν φρουρουμένης
ὑπὸ Λακεδαιμονίων τῆς Καδμείας βοηθήσαντες τοῖς εἰς
Θήβας κατιοῦσι τῶν φυγάδων, τοῖς ἰδίοις κινδύνοις
ἠλευθέρωσαν πόλιν ἀστυγείτονα καὶ πολὺν χρόνον
39 δουλεύουσαν, οἱ δὲ πείσαντος ἐξελθεῖν ὑμῶν τοὺς προγόνους
Κεφάλου τοῦ τὸ ψήφισμα γράψαντος, ὃς οὐ καταπλαγεὶς τὴν
Λακεδαιμονίων δύναμιν, οὐδὲ λογισάμενος ὅτι τὸ κινδυνεύειν
καὶ τὸ γράφειν ὑπὲρ τῆς πόλεως ἐπισφαλές ἐστιν, ἔγραψεν
ἐξιέναι βοηθήσοντας Ἀθηναίους τοῖς κατειληφόσι τῶν
φυγάδων Θήβας· καὶ ἐξελθόντων ἐκεῖσε τῶν ὑμετέρων
πατέρων ὀλίγαις ἡμέραις ἐξεβλήθη ὁ τῶν Λακεδαιμονίων
φρούραρχος, ἠλευθέρωντο Θηβαῖοι, διεπέπρακτο ἡ πόλις ἡ
40 ὑμετέρα ἄξια τῶν προγόνων. ἐκεῖνοι ἦσαν, ἐκεῖνοι, ὦ
Ἀθηναῖοι, ἄξιοι σύμβουλοι καὶ ἡγεμόνες ὑμῶν καὶ τοῦ δήμου,
μὰ Δί' οὐ τὰ τοιαῦτα κινάδη, οἳ πεποιήκασιν μὲν οὐδὲν οὐδὲ
πράξουσιν ἀγαθὸν ὑπὲρ τῆς πόλεως, τὴν δ' ἑαυτῶν ἀσφάλειαν
τηροῦντες καὶ πανταχόθεν ἀργυριζόμενοι καὶ πεποιηκότες τὴν
πόλιν ἀδοξοτέραν ἑαυτῶν, καὶ νῦν εἰλημμένοι δῶρα καθ' ὑμῶν
εἰληφότες, παρακρούονθ' ὑμᾶς, καὶ ἀξιοῦσι τοιοῦτοι
γεγενημένοι περὶ τῆς ἑαυτῶν πλεονεξίας παραγγέλλειν· οὓς
χρῆν τεθνάναι πάλαι κατὰ τὸ ἑαυτῶν ψήφισμα, τοιαῦτα
διαπεπραγμένους.
41 Οὐκ αἰσχύνεσθ', ἄνδρες Ἀθηναῖοι, τὴν κατὰ Δημοσθένους
τιμωρίαν ἐκ τῶν ἡμετέρων λόγων μόνων ἡγούμενοι δεῖν
κρίνειν; οὐκ ἴστε τοῦτον αὐτοὶ δωροδόκον ὄντα καὶ κλέπτην
καὶ προδότην τῶν φίλων, καὶ τῆς πόλεως ἀνάξιον καὶ αὐτὸν
καὶ τὴν περὶ τοῦτον τύχην γεγενημένην; ἀπὸ ποίων
42 ψηφισμάτων οὗτος ἢ ποίων νόμων οὐκ εἴληφεν ἀργύριον; εἰσί
τινες ἐν τῷ δικαστηρίῳ τῶν ἐν τοῖς τριακοσίοις
γεγενημένων, ὅθ' οὗτος ἐτίθει τὸν περὶ τῶν τριηράρχων
νόμον; οὐ φράσετε τοῖς πλησίον ὅτι τρία τάλαντα λαβὼν
μετέγραφε καὶ μετεσκεύαζε τὸν νόμον καθ' ἑκάστην
ἐκκλησίαν, καὶ τὰ μὲν ἐπώλει ὧν εἰλήφει τὴν τιμήν,

Aristeides and Themistocles, who built the walls of the city and carried the tribute freely and willingly paid by the Greeks up to the Acropolis; **(38)** but you will remember the deeds shortly before the present time performed by Cephalus the orator, Thrason of Herchia, Eleus, and Phormisius, and other fine men, some of whom even now are still alive. For some of these lent help to the exiles, when the Spartans had garrisoned the Cadmea, so that they could return to Thebes, and at their own peril freed a neighbouring city so long enslaved. **(39)** And others marched out when your ancestors were persuaded by the decree proposed by Cephalus, who was not swayed by the power of Sparta and did not take into account that taking risks and making proposals on behalf of the city is a risky business. He proposed that the Athenians should march out and lend support to the exiles who had seized Thebes. And when your fathers went there, within a few days the commander of the Spartan garrison was expelled and the Thebans were set free, and your city had acted in a manner worthy of your ancestors. **(40)** These men, Athenians, these men were worthy advisers and leaders for you and the people, not, by Zeus, rogues such as these, who have done nothing nor will do anything of value for the city, but look after their own safety and make money from all quarters. They have made the city more shameful than themselves, and now, convicted of accepting bribes against you, they deceive you and think it right after behaving in such a way to appeal to you about their own gain. For acts such as these they should have been put to death long ago, in accordance with their own decree.

(41) Gentlemen of Athens, are you not ashamed to think that the judgment against Demosthenes should be decided from only our speeches? Do you yourselves not know that this man is open to bribes and is a thief and a betrayer of his friends, and that he and the fortune associated with him are hardly good for the city? From what decrees or laws has this man not made money? **(42)** Are there any of you in the law court who were among the three hundred when this man introduced the law concerning trierarchs? Will you not say to those sitting next to you that he took three talents to change and redraft the law for each Assembly meeting, and that he resold measures for which he had taken payment, and that he did not make good those for

43 τὰ δ' ἀποδόμενος οὐκ ἐβεβαίου; εἴπατέ μοι πρὸς Διός, ὦ
ἄνδρες, προῖκα τοῦτον οἴεσθε γράψαι Διφίλῳ τὴν ἐν
πρυτανείῳ σίτησιν καὶ τὴν εἰς τὴν ἀγορὰν σταθησομένην
εἰκόνα; ἢ τὸ ποιῆσαι πολίτας ὑμετέρους Χαιρέφιλον καὶ
Φείδωνα καὶ Πάμφιλον καὶ Φείδιππον, ἢ πάλιν Ἐπιγένην καὶ
Κόνωνα τοὺς τραπεζίτας; ἢ τὸ χαλκοῦς ἐν ἀγορᾷ στῆσαι
Παιρισάδην καὶ Σάτυρον καὶ Γόργιππον τοὺς ἐκ τοῦ Πόντου
τυράννους, παρ' ὧν αὐτῷ χίλιοι μέδιμνοι τοῦ ἐνιαυτοῦ πυρῶν
ἀποστέλλονται, τῷ οὐδ' ὅποι καταφύγῃ αὐτίκα φήσοντι εἶναι;
44 ἢ τὸ γράψαι Ταυροσθένην Ἀθηναῖον εἶναι τὸν τοὺς μὲν
αὐτοῦ πολίτας καταδουλωσάμενον, τῆς δ' Εὐβοίας ὅλης μετὰ
τοῦ ἀδελφοῦ Καλλίου προδότην Φιλίππῳ γεγενημένον; ὃν οὐκ
ἐῶσιν οἱ νόμοι τῆς Ἀθηναίων χώρας ἐπιβαίνειν, εἰ δὲ μή,
τοῖς αὐτοῖς ἔνοχον εἶναι κελεύουσιν, οἷσπερ ἄν τις τῶν
φευγόντων ἐξ Ἀρείου πάγου κατίῃ. καὶ τοῦτον οὗτος ὁ
45 δημοτικὸς ὑμέτερον ἔγραψε πολίτην εἶναι. περὶ τούτων οὖν
μάρτυρας ὑμῖν δεῖ καλεῖν, ἢ περὶ τῶν ἄλλων ὅσους οὗτος
γέγραφε προξένους εἶναι καὶ Ἀθηναίους; εἶτα, πρὸς τῆς
Ἀθηνᾶς, οἴεσθ' αὐτὸν ἀργύριον μὲν χαίρειν λαμβάνοντα,
χρυσίου δ' εἴκοσι τάλαντ' οὐκ ἂν λαβεῖν; ἢ κατὰ μικρὸν μὲν
δωροδοκεῖν, ἀθρόον δ' οὐκ ἂν προσδέξασθαι τοσοῦτον λῆμμα;
ἢ τὴν ἐξ Ἀρείου πάγου βουλὴν Δημοσθένην καὶ Δημάδην καὶ
Κηφισοφῶντα ζητήσασαν ἓξ μῆνας ἀδίκως εἰς ὑμᾶς
πεποιῆσθαι τὰς ἀποφάσεις;
46   Πολλοί, ὦ ἄνδρες, πολλοὶ τῶν πολιτῶν καὶ τῶν ἄλλων
Ἑλλήνων, ὅπερ καὶ πρότερον εἶπον, θεωροῦσιν ὑμᾶς πῶς
τοῦτον δικάσετε τὸν ἀγῶνα, καὶ πότερον εἰσαγωγίμους καὶ
τὰς τῶν ἄλλων δωροδοκίας ποιήσετε, ἢ ἀνέδην ἐξέσται δῶρα
λαμβάνειν καθ' ὑμῶν, καὶ τὰ πρότερον δοκοῦντα πιστὰ καὶ
βέβαι' εἶναι νῦν ἄπιστα διὰ τὴν Δημοσθένους κρίσιν
γενήσεται, ὃν ἐκ τῶν ἄλλων προσῆκεν ἀπολωλέναι τῶν
πεπολιτευμένων αὐτῷ, ὃς ἁπάσαις ταῖς ἀραῖς ταῖς ἐν τῇ
47 πόλει γιγνομέναις ἔνοχος καθέστηκεν, ἐπιωρκηκὼς μὲν τὰς
σεμνὰς θεὰς ἐν Ἀρείῳ πάγῳ καὶ τοὺς ἄλλους θεοὺς οὓς ἐκεῖ
διόμνυσθαι νόμιμόν ἐστι, κατάρατος δὲ καθ' ἑκάστην
ἐκκλησίαν γιγνόμενος, ἐξεληλεγμένος μὲν δῶρα κατὰ τῆς
πόλεως εἰληφώς, ἐξηπατηκὼς δὲ καὶ τὸν δῆμον καὶ τὴν
βουλὴν παρὰ τὴν ἀράν, ἕτερα μὲν λέγων ἕτερα δὲ

which he had been paid? (43) Gentlemen, tell me, by Zeus, do you think this man proposed public maintenance in the Prytaneum for Diphilus and the statue to be erected in the market place as a free gift? Or the conferment of your citizenship on Chaerephilus, Pheidon, Pamphilus and Pheidippus, or again on Epigenes and Conon the bankers? Or the bronze statues in the market place of Paerisades, Satyrus, and Gorgippus, the tyrants of the Pontus, from whom one thousand medimni of corn per year are sent to him – this man who presently will tell you he may not take refuge anywhere? (44) Or did he introduce the proposal that Taurosthenes become an Athenian as a free gift, the man who enslaved his own countrymen and, with his brother Callias, was the betrayer of the whole of Euboea to Philip? The laws do not allow him to set foot on Athenian soil, otherwise they order him subject to the same penalties as those imposed if a man exiled by the Areopagus returns. And this democrat of yours proposed this man to be a citizen! (45) Is it necessary for me to summon witnesses for you about these men or the others whom this man proposed as *proxenoi* and citizens? By Athena, do you think that when he happily takes silver he would not take twenty talents of gold? Or when he receives bribes in small amounts he would not take such a large sum all at once? Or that the Council of the Areopagus, which investigated Demosthenes, Demades, and Cephisophon for six months, has unjustly made the reports to you?

(46) Gentlemen, there are many, as I've said before, many citizens and other Greeks watching you and how you will judge this case: whether you will make the acceptance of bribes by others subject to prosecution by law or allow bribes to be taken against your interests without restraint, and whether matters previously considered as trustworthy and assured will now become untrustworthy because of Demosthenes' trial. He ought to have been executed for his previous political policies. He is subject to all the curses imposed by the city. (47) He has sworn falsely on the Areopagus by the awful goddesses and the other gods, by whom it is traditional to swear solemnly there, and has become accursed at every Assembly. He has been proved to have taken bribes against the city, and has deceived both the people and the council regardless of the curse. He speaks one thing and

φρονῶν, ἰδίᾳ δὲ συμβεβουλευκὼς Ἀριστάρχῳ δεινὰς καὶ παρανόμους συμβουλάς· ἀνθ᾽ ὧν – εἴπερ ἔστι που δικαία τιμωρία κατὰ τῶν ἐπιόρκων καὶ πονηρῶν, ὥσπερ ἔστι – δώσει δίκην οὗτος ἐν τῇ τήμερον ἡμέρᾳ. ἀκούσατ᾽, ἄνδρες δικασταί, τῆς ἀρᾶς.

ΑΡΑ

48 Ἀλλ᾽ ὅμως, ἄνδρες δικασταί, οὕτω Δημοσθένης τῷ ψεύδεσθαι καὶ μηδὲν ὑγιὲς λέγειν ἑτοίμως χρῆται, καὶ οὔτ᾽ αἰσχύνης οὔτ᾽ ἐλέγχου οὔτ᾽ ἀρᾶς οὐδὲν αὐτῷ μέλει, ὥστε καὶ περὶ ἐμοῦ τολμήσει λέγειν, ὡς ἀκούω, ὡς ἄρα κἀμοῦ κατέγνω πρότερον ἡ βουλή, καὶ ποιῶ πάντων ἀτοπώτατον, ὡς οὗτός φησι, πρότερον μὲν ἐναντίον τῇ τῆς βουλῆς ἀποφάσει ἀγών· ἀπολογούμενος ὑπὲρ ἐμαυτοῦ, νυνὶ δὲ συνηγορῶν αὐτῇ, κατηγορῶν τούτου, περὶ τῆς γεγενημένης ἀποφάσεως· πρᾶγμα κατασκευάζων οὐ γεγενημένον, ἀλλὰ ψεύδεσθαι πρὸς ὑμᾶς
49 τολμῶν. ἵν᾽ οὖν, ἐὰν ἐπὶ τοῦτον ἴῃ τὸν λόγον, μὴ ἐπιτρέπητ᾽ αὐτῷ, ἀλλ᾽ εἰδῆτ᾽ ἀκριβῶς ὅτι οὔτε μ᾽ ἀπέφηνεν ἡ βουλὴ οὔτ᾽ ἐμέλλησεν, ἠδικήθην δ᾽ ὑφ᾽ ἑνὸς ἀνθρώπου πονηροῦ καὶ δίκην δεδωκότος παρ᾽ ὑμῖν, ἀκούσατέ μου βραχέα· ἔπειτ᾽ ἐπὶ τοῦτον πάλιν βαδιοῦμαι.
50 Ἀνάγκη τὴν βουλήν, ὦ ἄνδρες, τὴν ἐξ Ἀρείου πάγου κατὰ δύο τρόπους ποιεῖσθαι τὰς ἀποφάσεις πάσας. τίνας τούτους; ἤτοι αὐτὴν προελομένην, ἢ ζητήσασαν τοῦ δήμου προστάξαντος αὐτῇ. χωρὶς τούτων οὐκ ἔστιν ὅντιν᾽ ἂν τρόπον ποιήσειεν. εἰ μὲν τοίνυν φῄς, ὦ μιαρὸν σὺ θηρίον, τοῦ δήμου προστάξαντος ζητήσασαν τὴν βουλὴν περὶ ἐμοῦ ποιήσασθαι
51 τὴν ἀπόφασιν, δεῖξον τὸ ψήφισμα καὶ τίνες ἐγένοντό μου κατήγοροι γενομένης τῆς ἀποφάσεως, ὥσπερ νῦν ἀμφότερα γέγονε, καὶ ψήφισμα καθ᾽ ὃ ἐζήτησεν ἡ βουλή, καὶ κατήγοροι χειροτονήσαντος τοῦ δήμου, παρ᾽ ὧν νῦν οἱ δικασταὶ τἀδικήματα πυνθάνονται. κἂν ᾖ ταῦτ᾽ ἀληθῆ, ἀποθνῄσκειν ἕτοιμός εἰμι. εἰ δ᾽ αὐτὴν προελομένην ἀποφῆναί με φῄς, παράσχου μάρτυρας τοὺς Ἀρεοπαγίτας, ὥσπερ ἐγὼ παρέξομαι
52 ὅτι οὐκ ἀπεφάνθην. καταψευσάμενον μέντοι κἀμοῦ καὶ τῆς βουλῆς ὥσπερ σὺ καὶ πονηρὸν καὶ προδότην ὄντ᾽

thinks another, and he recommended a cruel and illegal course in private to Aristarchus. For these crimes – if there is any power to exact a just penalty from perjurers and criminals, as there surely is – this man will today meet with justice. Gentlemen of the jury, listen to the curse.

CURSE

(48) Nevertheless, gentlemen of the jury, Demosthenes is so willing with his lies and dishonest speeches, not at all worried by shame or refutation or curse, that he will dare to say about me, so I hear, that the council previously found against me. I am now being utterly inconsistent, so this man says, because previously I opposed the report of the Areopagus and pleaded my own case, and now I am appearing on its behalf, and accusing this man over the present report. This story is contrived, not factual, but he dares to lie to you. (49) Therefore, so that you pay no attention to him if he tells this story, but know well that the council did not report against me nor intended to do so – that I was wronged by one miserable man who has suffered punishment among you – let me briefly tell you. Then I will get back to this man.

(50) Gentlemen, the Council of the Areopagus has to produce all its reports following two procedures. What are these? It can investigate either on its own initiative or when the people in Assembly order it. Apart from these, there is no other procedure it could follow. If then you, you scummy creature, say that the council investigated me on the orders of the people and published its report, (51) show the decree and who my prosecutors were when the report was made, just as now the two exist: both a decree by which the council was to investigate and prosecutors elected by the people, from whom now the jurors are learning about the crimes. If indeed what you say is true, then I am ready to die. But if you say the council reported me on its own initiative, then summon the Areopagites as witnesses, just as I shall produce them to say that I was not reported. (52) Moreover, having impeached this criminal and traitor who had slandered myself and the

εἰσαγγείλας καὶ ἐξελέγξας ἐν πεντακοσίοις καὶ δισχιλίοις
τῶν πολιτῶν ὅτι μισθώσας αὑτὸν Πυθοκλεῖ κατ' ἐμοῦ ταῦτ'
ἔπραξεν, ἐτιμωρησάμην μετὰ τῶν τότε δικασάντων. λαβέ μοι
σὺ τὴν μαρτυρίαν, ἣν καὶ πρότερον παρεσχόμην
μαρτυρουμένην τοῖς δικασταῖς καὶ οὐδεὶς ἐπεσκήψαθ' ὡς
ψευδεῖ οὔσῃ, ἣν καὶ νῦν παρέξομαι. λέγε τὴν μαρτυρίαν.

ΜΑΡΤΥΡΙΑ

53 Εἶτ' οὐ δεινόν, ὦ 'Αθηναῖοι, εἰ ὅτι μὲν εἷς ἀνὴρ ἔφησε
Πιστίας 'Αρεοπαγίτης ὢν ἀδικεῖν με, καταψευδόμενος κἀμοῦ
καὶ τῆς βουλῆς, ἴσχυσεν ἂν τὸ ψεῦδος τῆς ἀληθείας μᾶλλον,
εἰ διὰ τὴν ἀσθένειαν τὴν τότε καὶ τὴν ἐρημίαν τὴν ἐμὴν
ἐπιστεύθησαν αἱ κατ' ἐμοῦ ψευδεῖς γενόμεναι κατασκευαί·
ἐπειδὴ δὲ τἀληθὲς παρὰ πάσης τῆς ἐξ 'Αρείου πάγου βουλῆς
ὁμολογεῖται, Δημοσθένην εἰληφέναι εἴκοσι τάλαντα χρυσίου
καθ' ὑμῶν καὶ ταῦτα πεποιηκότ' ἀδικεῖν, καὶ ὁ δημαγωγὸς
ὑμῖν, ἐν ᾧ τὰς ἐλπίδας ἔχουσί τινες, ἐπ' αὐτοφώρῳ χρήματα
54 λαμβάνων εἴληπται, νῦν τὰ νόμιμα τἀκεῖθεν καὶ τὰ δίκαια
καὶ τἀληθῆ ἀσθενέστερα γενήσεται τῶν Δημοσθένους λόγων,
καὶ ἰσχύσει μᾶλλον τῆς ἀληθείας ἡ παρὰ τούτου ῥηθησομένη
κατὰ τοῦ συνεδρίου διαβολή, ὡς ἄρα πολλοὺς ἡ βουλὴ
ἀποπέφαγκεν ἀδικεῖν τὸν δῆμον, οἳ ἀποπεφεύγασιν
εἰσελθόντες εἰς τὸ δικαστήριον, καὶ ἐπ' ἐνίων τὸ πέμπτον
μέρος οὐ μετείληφε τῶν ψήφων; τοῦτο δ' ὃν τρόπον γίγνεται,
55 ῥᾳδίως ἅπαντες μαθήσεσθε. ἡ βουλή, ὦ ἄνδρες, ζητεῖ τὰ
προσταχθένθ' ὑφ' ὑμῶν καὶ τὰ γεγενημένα παρ' αὐτοῖς
ἀδικήματα οὐχ ὡς ὑμεῖς – καί μοι μὴ ὀργισθῆτε – δικάζειν
ἐνίοτ' εἴθισθε, τῇ συγγνώμῃ πλέον ἢ τῷ δικαίῳ ἀπονέμοντες,
ἀλλ' ἁπλῶς τὸν ἔνοχον ὄντα τοῖς ζητουμένοις ἀποφαίνει καὶ
τὸν ὁποιονοῦν ἠδικηκότα παρὰ τὰ πάτρια, νομίζουσα τὸν ἐν
τοῖς μικροῖς συνεθιζόμενον ἀδικεῖν, τοῦτον τὰ μεγάλα τῶν
56 ἀδικημάτων εὐχερέστερον προσδέξεσθαι. διόπερ τὸν παρ'
αὑτῶν ἀποστερήσαντα τὸ ναῦλον τὸν πορθμέα ζημιώσασα
πρὸς ὑμᾶς ἀπέφηνε· πάλιν τὸν τὴν πεντεδραχμίαν ἐπὶ τῷ
τοῦ μὴ παρόντος ὀνόματι λαβεῖν ἀξιώσαντα, καὶ τοῦτον ὑμῖν
ἀπέφηνε, καὶ τὸν τὴν μερίδα τὴν ἐξ 'Αρείου πάγου

council, like you, and proving before 2,500 citizens that he had taken this action against me by hiring himself to Pythocles, I avenged myself with those who were jurors then. Will you take up the deposition that previously I placed before the jurors as evidence, – and no one denounced it as false – and which I shall now again produce? Read the deposition.

DEPOSITION

(53) Athenians, is it not a shocking thing that because one man, Pistias an Areopagite, said I was a criminal and lied against me and the council, that fabrication would have been stronger than the truth, if the trumped-up lies against me had been accepted because of my weakness and isolation then? But when the truth has been admitted by the entire Council of the Areopagus, that Demosthenes took twenty talents of gold against you and having done so is a criminal, and your popular leader, on whom some fix their hopes, has been caught in the act of taking bribes, (54) will the customs of that body and justice and truth now be weaker than the word of Demosthenes? Will the coming slander of this man against the council – how the council has reported many men as wronging the people who, having come into court, have been acquitted, the council in some cases not obtaining one-fifth of the votes – be stronger than the truth? There is an explanation for this, which all of you will easily understand. (55) Gentlemen, the council considers cases that have been assigned to it by you and crimes committed within itself, not like you – and don't get angry at me – who are at times prone to make judgment being swayed more by mercy than justice; but it simply reports the one subject to the enquiry or who has broken any traditional rules of conduct, considering that the man who is used to committing crimes of a small nature will more easily welcome large-scale crimes. (56) Consequently, it reported to you and fined one of its members who robbed the ferryman of his fare. Again, the man who claimed the five drachmas allowance in the name of someone not present – this man also was reported to you. And in the same way it fined and expelled the man who

τολμήσαντ᾽ ἀποδόσθαι παρὰ τὰ νόμιμα, τὸν αὐτὸν τρόπον
57 ζημιώσασ᾽ ἐξέβαλε. τούτους ὑμεῖς κρίναντες ἀφήκατε, οὐ τῆς
ἐξ Ἀρείου πάγου βουλῆς καταγιγνώσκοντες ψεύδεσθαι, ἀλλὰ
τῇ συγγνώμῃ μᾶλλον ἢ τῷ δικαίῳ προσθέμενοι, καὶ τὴν
τιμωρίαν μείζω νομίζοντες εἶναι τῆς ὑπὸ τῶν κρινομένων
γεγενημένης ἁμαρτίας. ἦ που ἄρα ἡ βουλή, Δημόσθενες, τὰ
ψευδῆ ἀπέφηνεν; οὐ δήπου. τούτους μέντοι ὦ ἄνδρες καὶ
τοιούτους ἑτέρους ἀδικεῖν παρ᾽ ἑαυτοῖς ἀποφηνάσης τῆς
58 βουλῆς ὑμεῖς ἀφήκατε. Πολύευκτον δὲ τὸν Κυδαντίδην τοῦ
δήμου προστάξαντος ζητῆσαι τὴν βουλήν, εἰ συνέρχεται τοῖς
φυγάσιν εἰς Μέγαρα, καὶ ζητήσασαν ἀποφῆναι πρὸς ὑμᾶς,
ἀπέφηνεν ἡ βουλὴ συνιέναι. κατηγόρους εἵλεσθε κατὰ τὸν
νόμον, εἰσῆλθεν εἰς τὸ δικαστήριον, ἀπελύσαθ᾽ ὑμεῖς,
ὁμολογοῦντος τοῦ Πολυεύκτου βαδίζειν εἰς Μέγαρ᾽ ὡς τὸν
Νικοφάνην· ἔχειν γὰρ τὴν αὐτοῦ μητέρα τοῦτον. οὐδὲν οὖν
ἄτοπον οὐδὲ δεινὸν ἐφαίνεθ᾽ ὑμῖν ποιεῖν, τῷ τῆς μητρὸς
ἀνδρὶ διαλεγόμενος ἠτυχηκότι καὶ συνευπορῶν, καθ᾽ ὅσον
59 δυνατὸς ἦν, ἀπεστερημένῳ τῆς πατρίδος. αὕτη, Δημόσθενες,
τῆς βουλῆς ἡ ἀπόφασις οὐκ ἐξηλέγχθη ψευδὴς οὖσα, ἀληθινῆς
δ᾽ αὐτῆς οὔσης ἔδοξε τοῖς δικασταῖς ἀφεῖναι τὸν
Πολύευκτον· τὸ μὲν γὰρ ἀληθὲς τῇ βουλῇ προσετάχθη ζητεῖν,
τὸ δὲ συγγνώμης ἄξιόν φημι τὸ δικαστήριον ἔκρινε. διὰ
τοῦτ᾽ οὐ πιστευτέον τῇ βουλῇ περὶ τῶν γενομένων
ἀποφάσεων, ἐπειδὴ σὲ καὶ τοὺς μετὰ σοῦ τὸ χρυσίον
60 ἔχοντας ἀποπέφαγκε; δεινὸν μέντ᾽ ἂν εἴη. δεῖξον γὰρ δὴ
τοῖς δικασταῖς σύ, Δημόσθενες, νυνί, ὡς τούτων τι τῶν
ἁμαρτημάτων ὅμοιόν ἐστι τοῖς σοῖς ἀδικήμασι, καὶ ὡς τὸ
δῶρα λαμβάνειν κατὰ τῆς πατρίδος συγγνώμης ἐστὶν ἄξιον,
ὥστ᾽ ἀποφύγοις ἂν παρὰ τούτοις εἰκότως. ἀλλ᾽ οἱ νόμοι περὶ
μὲν τῶν ἄλλων ἀδικημάτων τῶν εἰς ἀργυρίου λόγον
ἀνηκόντων διπλῆν τὴν βλάβην ὀφείλειν κελεύουσι, περὶ δὲ
τῶν δωροδοκούντων δύο μόνον τιμήματα πεποιήκασιν, ἢ
θάνατον, ἵνα ταύτης τυχὼν τῆς ζημίας ὁ λαβὼν παράδειγμα
γένηται τοῖς ἄλλοις, ἢ δεκαπλοῦν τοῦ ἐξ ἀρχῆς λήμματος τὸ
τίμημα τῶν δώρων, ἵνα μὴ λυσιτελήσῃ τοῖς τοῦτο τολμῶσι
ποιεῖν.
61   Ἢ τοῦτο μὲν οὐκ ἐπιχειρήσεις λέγειν, ὅτι δὲ τῶν
πρότερον ἀποφανθέντων ὑπὸ τῆς βουλῆς τοῖς μὲν ἄλλοις
ὡμολογηκέναι συμβέβηκεν ἀξίαν εἶναι τὴν τῆς βουλῆς ζημίαν,

dared to sell the Areopagite meat portion contrary to the laws. (57) Having tried these men, you acquitted them. You were not accusing the Council of the Areopagus of lying, but gave more feeling to mercy than to justice, and considered the penalty greater than the crime committed by the accused. Demosthenes, do you think that the council made a false report? Not at all. Nevertheless, gentlemen, you yourselves acquitted these men and others like them, even though the council reported them guilty. (58) When the people in the Assembly ordered the Areopagus to investigate Polyeuctus of Cydantidae, whether he was accompanying the exiles to Megara, and having conducted the investigation to report back to you, the council reported he had gone there. You selected prosecutors in accordance with the law, he came into court, and you acquitted him, since Polyeuctus admitted that he went to Megara to Nicophanes, who was the husband of his mother. You did not think that he was doing anything odd or terrible, in keeping in contact with his mother's husband, who had fallen on hard times, and helping him, as much as he could, when he was banished from his country. (59) This report of the council was not proved false, Demosthenes, it was quite true, but it was considered fit by the jurors to acquit Polyeuctus. I say again, the discovery of the truth was entrusted to the council, but the court judged what was worthy of pardon. Because of this, should one not trust the council over the present reports, when it has stated that you and your cronies have the gold? That would indeed be terrible!

(60) Now, Demosthenes, convince the jurors that any one of these crimes is the same as those of yours, and that to accept bribes against the country is worthy of pardon, so that you would justly be acquitted by these men. The laws lay down double the damages owed for other crimes involving money, but concerning the taking of bribes they have laid down only the two penalties: either death, so that by meeting this penalty the guilty party is made an example to others, or tenfold the original amount received as the penalty for bribes, so that those who dare to do this shall not gain by it.

(61) Or will you not try to say that, but insist that the penalty imposed by the council on those previously reported by it has been agreed to be fitting

σοὶ δὲ μόνῳ τὰ περὶ αὐτῆς ἠναντιῶσθαι; ἀλλὰ μόνος σὺ τῶν πώποτ' ἀποπεφασμένων ἠξίωσας ἑκὼν σεαυτῷ τούτους κριτὰς καὶ ζητητὰς γενέσθαι, καὶ ἔγραψας κατὰ σεαυτοῦ τὸ ψήφισμα, καὶ τὸν δῆμον ἐποιήσω μάρτυρα τῶν ὡμολογημένων, ὁρισάμενος σεαυτῷ ζημίαν εἶναι θάνατον, ἐὰν ἀποφήνῃ σ' ἡ βουλὴ τῶν χρημάτων εἰληφότα τι τῶν εἰς τὴν χώραν ὑφ'

62 Ἁρπάλου κομισθέντων. ἀλλὰ μὴν πρότερον ἔγραψας σύ, Δημόσθενες, κατὰ πάντων τούτων καὶ τῶν ἄλλων Ἀθηναίων κυρίαν εἶναι τὴν ἐξ Ἀρείου πάγου βουλὴν κολάσαι τὸν παρὰ τοὺς νόμους πλημμελοῦντα, χρωμένην τοῖς πατρίοις νόμοις· καὶ παρέδωκας σὺ καὶ ἐνεχείρισας τὴν πόλιν ἅπασαν ταύτῃ, ἣν αὐτίκα φήσεις ὀλιγαρχικὴν εἶναι· καὶ τεθνᾶσι κατὰ τὸ σὸν ψήφισμα δύο τῶν πολιτῶν, πατὴρ καὶ υἱός, παραδοθέντες

63 τῷ ἐπὶ τῷ ὀρύγματι· ἐδέθη τῶν ἀφ' Ἁρμοδίου γεγονότων εἷς κατὰ τὸ σὸν πρόσταγμα· ἐστρέβλωσαν Ἀντιφῶντα καὶ ἀπέκτειναν οὗτοι τῇ τῆς βουλῆς ἀποφάσει πεισθέντες· ἐξέβαλες σὺ Χαρῖνον ἐκ τῆς πόλεως ἐπὶ προδοσίᾳ κατὰ τὴν τῆς βουλῆς ἀπόφασιν καὶ τιμωρίαν. κατὰ δὲ σαυτοῦ καὶ ταῦτα γράψας αὐτὸς τὸ ψήφισμ' ἀκυροῖς; καὶ ποῦ ταῦτα δίκαι' ἢ νόμιμ' ἐστί;

64 Μαρτύρομαι τὰς σεμνὰς θεάς, ἄνδρες Ἀθηναῖοι, καὶ τὸν τόπον ὃν ἐκεῖναι κατέχουσι, καὶ τοὺς ἥρωας τοὺς ἐγχωρίους, καὶ τὴν Ἀθηνᾶν τὴν Πολιάδα, καὶ τοὺς ἄλλους θεοὺς οἳ τὴν πόλιν καὶ τὴν χώραν ἡμῶν εἰλήχασιν, ὅτι τοῦ δήμου παραδεδωκότος ὑμῖν τιμωρήσασθαι τὸν εἰληφότα τι τῶν ‹κομισθέντων χρηματών› κατὰ τῆς πατρίδος, τὸν λελυμασμένον καὶ ἐφθαρκότα τὴν τῆς πόλεως εὐδαιμονίαν, τὸν περικεχαρακωμένην προδεδωκότα τὴν πατρίδα ταῖς αὑτοῦ

65 συμβουλίαις, ὃν οἱ μὲν ἐχθροὶ καὶ κακόνοι τῇ πόλει ζῆν ἂν βούλοιντο, συμφορὰν ἡγούμενοι τῆς πόλεως εἶναι, ὅσοι δ' εὖνοι τοῖς ὑμετέροις πράγμασι, καὶ μεταπεσούσης τῆς τύχης ἐλπίζουσιν ἐπὶ τὸ βέλτιον ἂν τὰ τῆς πόλεως πράγματ' ἐλθεῖν, τὴν ἀξίαν δίκην δόντα τῶν πεπραγμένων ἀπολωλέναι βούλονται, καὶ ταῦτ' εὔχονται τοῖς θεοῖς. οὓς κἀγὼ συμπαρακαλῶ σῶσαι τὴν πατρίδα, κινδυνεύουσαν ὁρῶν ὑπὲρ σωτηρίας, ὑπὲρ παίδων, ὑπὲρ γυναικῶν, ὑπὲρ δόξης, ὑπὲρ τῶν

66 ἄλλων ἀγαθῶν ἁπάντων. τί γὰρ ἐροῦμεν, ὦ Ἀθηναῖοι,

by others, while you alone have protested against it? But of all those ever reported, you alone of your own volition requested that these men be your judges and examiners, and you proposed the decree against yourself, and made the people witnesses of what was agreed, laying down the death penalty on yourself if the council should report that you had taken any of the money brought into the country by Harpalus. **(62)** Now, Demosthenes, you yourself proposed previously that the Council of the Areopagus should have power over all these men and the other Athenians to punish anyone violating the law and to enforce the laws of the land. You yourself surrendered and entrusted the entire city to this body, which soon you will tell us is oligarchic. Two of the citizens, a father and son, were handed over to the executioner and put to death in accordance with your decree. **(63)** One of the descendants of Harmodius was imprisoned in keeping with your command. These men, induced by the report of the Areopagus, tortured and executed Antiphon. You yourselves banished Charinus from the city for treason, in accordance with the report and punishment of the council. Will you, who have proposed this measure against yourself, now invalidate the decree? How can that be just and lawful?

(64) Gentlemen of Athens, I call to witness the awful goddesses and the place in which they live, and the heroes of the land, and Athena Polias, and the other gods who have taken our city and land as home, that when the people handed over to you for punishment the one who took a part of the imported money against the country, corrupted and destroyed the well-being of the city, and betrayed the country he once claimed to have fortified by his diplomacy, **(65)** enemies and those ill-disposed to the city would wish that man alive, considering this a misfortune for the city. But those who are sympathetically minded to your current circumstances and hope that the affairs of the city would improve with a change of fortune, wish the penalty worthy of his deeds to be exacted and he die, and this is what they pray to the gods. And I myself join in beseeching them to save the country, seeing it in danger on behalf of its freedom, its children, its women, its dignity – on behalf of every decent thing. **(66)** Athenians, when we come out of the court

πρὸς τοὺς περιεστηκότας ἐξελθόντες ἐκ τοῦ δικαστηρίου, ἐάν,
ὃ μὴ γένοιτο, παρακρουσθῆθ' ὑπὸ τῆς τούτου γοητείας· τίσιν
ὀφθαλμοῖς ἕκαστος ὑμῶν τὴν πατρῴαν ἑστίαν οἴκαδ' ἀπελθὼν
ἰδεῖν τολμήσει, ἀπολελυκότες μὲν τὸν προδότην τὸν πρῶτον
εἰς τὸν ἴδιον οἶκον εἰσενεγκάμενον τὸ δεδωροδοκημένον
χρυσίον, κατεγνωκότες δὲ μηδὲν ἀληθὲς μήτε ζητεῖν μήθ'
εὑρίσκειν τὸ παρὰ πᾶσιν ἀνθρώποις εἶναι σεμνότατον
67 νομιζόμενον συνέδριον; τίνας δ', ὦ Ἀθηναῖοι, – σκοπεῖτε γὰρ
πρὸς ὑμᾶς αὐτούς – τίνας τὰς ἐλπίδας ἕξομεν, ἐὰν κίνδυνός
τις καταλάβῃ τὴν πόλιν, τὸ μὲν δῶρα λαμβάνειν κατὰ τῆς
πατρίδος ἀσφαλὲς εἶναι πεποιηκότες, τὸ δὲ τὴν φυλακὴν
ἔχον συνέδριον τῆς πόλεως ἐν τοῖς τοιούτοις κινδύνοις
68 ἀδόκιμον καταστήσαντες; τί δ' ἐάν – τιθῶμεν γὰρ ταῦτα –
ἐὰν κατὰ τὸ ψήφισμα τὸ Δημοσθένους ἀπαιτῇ πέμψας ἡμᾶς
Ἀλέξανδρος τὸ χρυσίον τὸ κομισθὲν εἰς τὴν χώραν ὑφ'
Ἁρπάλου, καὶ πρὸς τῷ γεγενῆσθαι τὴν τῆς βουλῆς ἀπόφασιν
τοὺς παῖδας καταπέμψῃ πρὸς ἡμᾶς τοὺς νῦν ὡς ἑαυτὸν
ἀνακεκομισμένους, καὶ τούτων ἀξιοῖ πυνθάνεσθαι τὴν ἀλήθειαν
69 ἡμᾶς, πρὸς θεῶν, ὦ ἄνδρες, τί ἐροῦμεν; γράψεις σύ,
Δημόσθενες, πολεμεῖν ἡμᾶς, ἐπειδὴ καὶ τοὺς πρότερον
πολέμους καλῶς διῴκησας; καὶ πότερόν ἐστι δικαιότερον, ἂν
ταῦτα δόξῃ καὶ τοῖς ἄλλοις Ἀθηναίοις, εἰς τὸν πόλεμον
ὑπάρχειν μετὰ τῶν ἄλλων καὶ τὸ παρὰ σοῦ χρυσίον, ἢ τοὺς
μὲν ἄλλους ἀπὸ τῶν ἰδίων κτημάτων ἕκαστον εἰσφέρειν καὶ
καταχωνεύειν τὸν ἴδιον κόσμον τῶν γυναικῶν καὶ τὰ
ἐκπώματα καὶ πάντα τὰ ἐν τῇ χώρᾳ ἀναθήματα τῶν θεῶν,
ὥσπερ ἔφησθα σὺ γράψειν, αὐτὸς εἰσενεγκὼν πεντήκοντα
δραχμὰς ἀπὸ τῆς οἰκίας τῆς ἐν Πειραιεῖ καὶ τῆς ἐν ἄστει·
τοσοῦτον γὰρ κατὰ τὴν προτέραν εἰσφορὰν εἰσενηνοχὼς
70 εἴκοσι τάλαντ' ἔχεις. ἢ πολεμεῖν μὲν οὐ γράψεις, ἀποδιδόναι
δὲ κατὰ τὸ γεγραμμένον ὑπὸ σοῦ ψήφισμα κελεύσεις
Ἀλεξάνδρῳ τὸ κεκομισμένον χρυσίον; οὐκοῦν ὑπὲρ σοῦ τὸν
δῆμον ἀποδιδόναι δεήσει. καὶ ποῦ τοῦτ' ἐστὶ δίκαιον ἢ κοινὸν
ἢ δημοτικόν, τοὺς μὲν ἐργαζομένους εἰσφέρειν, σὲ δ'
ἁρπάζειν καὶ κλέπτειν; καὶ τοὺς μὲν φανερὰν κεκτῆσθαι τὴν
οὐσίαν καὶ ἀπὸ ταύτης εἰσφέρειν, σὲ δὲ πλείω ἢ πεντήκοντα
καὶ ἑκατὸν τάλαντα τὰ μὲν ἐκ τῶν βασιλικῶν τὰ δ' ἐκ τῶν

what shall we say to the bystanders if – let this not be the case – you are deceived by the sorcery of this man? How will each of you, when you return home, dare to look at his ancestral hearth, if you have acquitted the traitor who first brought into his own home the gold he had received as a bribe, and have thus voted that the council, which is considered to be the most revered by all men, is not at all true in both its investigation and findings? (67) Athenians, what hopes – consider amongst yourselves – what hopes shall we have if any danger befalls the city, when we have made it safe to take bribes against the country and have rendered disreputable the council that has the power to protect the city in these times of crisis? (68) And what if – for let us imagine this scenario – Alexander sends an envoy and, in accordance with Demosthenes' decree, demands from us the gold brought into the country by Harpalus, and, relying on the fact of the report of the Areopagus, sends us the slaves, recently returned to him, expecting us to find out the truth from them? By the gods, gentlemen, what shall we say?

(69) Demosthenes, will you propose that we go to war, when you have managed previous wars so well? Suppose this course is decided on by the other Athenians, which is the more fair: for yours and other people's gold to be used for war, or for all the others to contribute from their own possessions and to melt down the private ornaments of their wives, the drinking cups and all the votive offerings of the country to the gods, as you said you would propose, you yourself contributing fifty drachmas from your house in the Piraeus and that in the city? This was what you had contributed at the previous levy; now you have twenty talents. (70) Or perhaps you will not propose war, but will order us to give the gold brought here back to Alexander, according to the decree that you proposed? Then surely it will be for you that the people have to return it! Is it then just or right or democratic for those who work to contribute, but you to snatch and steal? And for others to make clear the property that they own and pay proportionate contributions, while you, who have taken more than 150 talents from the

Ἀλεξάνδρου χρημάτων εἰληφέναι, μηδὲν δὲ φανερὸν ἐν τῇ πόλει κεκτῆσθαι, ἀλλὰ διεσκευάσθαι πρὸς τὸν δῆμον, ὡς οὐ

71 πιστεύοντα τοῖς ἑαυτῷ πεπολιτευμένοις· καὶ τοὺς μὲν νόμους προλέγειν τῷ ῥήτορι καὶ τῷ στρατηγῷ, τῷ τὴν παρὰ τοῦ δήμου πίστιν ἀξιοῦντι λαμβάνειν, παιδοποιεῖσθαι κατὰ τοὺς νόμους, γῆν ἐντὸς ὅρων κεκτῆσθαι, πάσας τὰς δικαίας πίστεις παρακαταθέμενον, οὕτως ἀξιοῦν προεστάναι τοῦ δήμου· σὲ δὲ τὴν μὲν πατρῴαν γῆν πεπρακέναι, τοὺς δ' οὐ γεγενημένους υἱεῖς σαυτῷ προσποιεῖσθαι παρὰ τοὺς νόμους τῶν ἐν ταῖς κρίσεσιν ἕνεκα γιγνομένων ὅρκων, ἐπιτάττειν δὲ τοῖς ἄλλοις στρατεύεσθαι λιπόντ' αὐτὸν τὴν κοινὴν τάξιν;

72 Ὦ Ἀθηναῖοι, παρὰ τί οἴεσθε τὰς πόλεις τοτὲ μὲν εὖ τοτὲ δὲ φαύλως πράττειν; οὐδὲν εὑρήσετ' ἄλλο πλὴν παρὰ τοὺς συμβούλους καὶ τοὺς ἡγεμόνας. ἐπιβλέψατε δ' ἐπὶ τὴν Θηβαίων πόλιν. ἐγένετο πόλις, ἐγένετο μεγίστη· πότε καὶ τίνων τυχοῦσ' ἡγεμόνων καὶ στρατηγῶν; ἅπαντες ἂν ὁμολογήσαιεν οἱ πρεσβύτεροι, παρ' ὧνπερ κἀγὼ τοὺς λόγους

73 ἀκούων ἐρῶ, ὅτε Πελοπίδας, ὥς φασιν, ἡγεῖτο τοῦ ἱεροῦ λόχου καὶ Ἐπαμεινώνδας ἐστρατήγει καὶ οἱ μετὰ τούτων· τότε τὴν ἐν Λεύκτροις μάχην ἐνίκησεν ἡ τῶν Θηβαίων πόλις, τότ' εἰς τὴν ἀπόρθητον νομιζομένην εἶναι Λακεδαιμονίων χώραν εἰσέβαλον, κατ' ἐκείνους τοὺς χρόνους πολλὰ καὶ καλὰ διεπράξαντ' ἔργα, Μεσσήνην τετρακοσιοστῷ ἔτει κατῴκισαν, Ἀρκάδας αὐτονόμους ἐποίησαν, ἔνδοξοι παρὰ πᾶσιν ἦσαν.

74 πότε δ' αὖ τοὐναντίον ταπεινὰ καὶ τοῦ φρονήματος ἀνάξια διεπράξαντο; ὅτ' ἐδωροδόκει μὲν λαμβάνων χρήματα παρὰ Φιλίππου Τιμόλαος ὁ τούτου φίλος, ἐπὶ δὲ τοῖς ξένοις τοῖς εἰς Ἄμφισσαν συλλεγεῖσι Πρόξενος ὁ προδότης ἐγένετο, ἡγεμὼν δὲ τῆς φάλαγγος κατέστη Θεαγένης, ἄνθρωπος ἀτυχὴς καὶ δωροδόκος ὥσπερ οὗτος. τότε διὰ τρεῖς γ' ἀνθρώπους οὓς εἶπον ἅπασ' ἡ πόλις ἐκ τῶν Ἑλλήνων ἀπώλετο καὶ διεφθάρη. οὐ γὰρ ψεῦδός ἐστιν ἀλλὰ καὶ λίαν ἀληθὲς τὸ τοὺς ἡγεμόνας αἰτίους ἁπάντων γίγνεσθαι καὶ τῶν

75 ἀγαθῶν καὶ τῶν ἐναντίων τοῖς πολίταις. θεωρήσατε δὴ πάλιν καὶ ἐπὶ τῆς ἡμετέρας πόλεως, τὸν αὐτὸν τρόπον ἐξ-ετάσαντες. ἡ πόλις ἡμῶν ἦν μεγάλη καὶ ἔνδοξος παρὰ τοῖς Ἕλλησι καὶ τῶν προγόνων ἀξία, μετά γε τὰς ἀρχαίας ἐκείνας πράξεις, ὅτε Κόνων, ὡς οἱ πρεσβύτεροι λέγουσιν,

Persian king and from the money of Alexander, have not made it clear what you own in the city, but have prepared yourself against the people as not trusting in your own administration of the state? **(71)** Is it fitting that while the laws order the orator and the general, who want to obtain the confidence of the people, to have children in accordance with the laws, own land within the boundaries, pledge all the lawful oaths, and thus claim to be worthy to be leader of the people, you sold the land belonging to your father, and are passing off children not your own as yours, against the laws that control oaths at trials, and are ordering others to take the field when you yourself deserted the battle-line?

(72) Athenians, what do you think is the reason why at times cities enjoy prosperity and at times bad luck? You will not find anything other than the advisers and leaders. Look upon the city of Thebes. It was a city and it was among the greatest. When was this? And under what leaders and generals? All the older men, from whom I myself have heard the story and will speak it, would agree: **(73)** when Pelopidas, they say, led the Sacred Band and Epaminondas was general and those with them. Then the city of the Thebans won victory at the battle of Leuctra, then they invaded the land of the Spartans which, it was thought, was inviolable, and they performed many and great deeds during that time: they established Messene in the four hundredth year, made the Arcadians autonomous, and they were highly regarded by all men. **(74)** But when, though, did the opposite apply and their achievements were lowly and unworthy of their spirit? When Timolaus the friend of this man was bribed and took money from Philip, and Proxenus the traitor was in charge of the mercenaries levied for Amphissa, and Theagenes was leader of the phalanx, a man of misfortune and open to bribery, just like this man. Then the entire city was destroyed and obliterated from the whole of Greece because of the three men about whom I spoke. For it is not false but indeed only too true that the leaders are responsible for all the good and the contrary fortunes affecting the citizens. **(75)** Think again, in the same way, about our own city. Our city was great, held in high esteem by the Greeks and worthy of our ancestors, after those famous deeds from the past, when Conon, so the elders say, won victory at

ἐνίκησε τὴν ἐν Κνίδῳ ναυμαχίαν, ὅτ᾽ Ἰφικράτης ἀνεῖλε τὴν Λακεδαιμονίων μόραν, ὅτε Χαβρίας ἐν Νάξῳ κατεναυμάχησε τὰς Λακεδαιμονίων τριήρεις, ὅτε Τιμόθεος τὴν ἐν Κερκύρᾳ

76 ναυμαχίαν ἐνίκησε. τότ᾽, ὦ Ἀθηναῖοι, τότε οἱ μὲν πρότερον ὄντες λαμπροὶ διὰ τοὺς ἡγεμόνας Λακεδαιμόνιοι καὶ ὑπὸ τοῖς ἐκείνων ἤθεσι τραφέντες ταπεινοὶ πρὸς τὴν πόλιν ἡμῶν ἧκον, δεόμενοι τῆς παρὰ τῶν ἡμετέρων προγόνων σωτηρίας, ὁ δὲ καταλυθεὶς ὑπ᾽ ἐκείνων δῆμος διὰ τοὺς τότε γενομένους παρ᾽ ἡμῖν συμβούλους πάλιν ἡγεμὼν ἦν τῶν Ἑλλήνων, δικαίως οἶμαι, στρατηγῶν μὲν τοιούτων τετυχηκὼς οἵων εἶπον ἀρτίως, συμβούλους δ᾽ ἔχων Ἀρχῖνον καὶ Κέφαλον τὸν Κολλυτέα. μία γὰρ αὕτη σωτηρία καὶ πόλεως καὶ ἔθνους ἐστί, τὸ προστατῶν

77 ἀνδρῶν ἀγαθῶν καὶ συμβούλων σπουδαίων τυχεῖν. διόπερ, ὦ Ἀθηναῖοι, δεῖ ταῦθ᾽ ὑμᾶς ὁρῶντας καὶ λογιζομένους, μὴ μὰ Δία τὸν πλείω χρόνον τῆς Δημοσθένους δωροδοκίας καὶ ἀτυχίας κοινωνεῖν, μηδ᾽ ἐν τούτῳ τὰς ἐλπίδας τῆς σωτηρίας ἔχειν, μηδ᾽ οἴεσθαι ἀπορήσειν ἀνδρῶν ἀγαθῶν καὶ συμβούλων σπουδαίων, ἀλλὰ τὴν τῶν προγόνων λαβόντας ὀργὴν τὸν ἐπ᾽ αὐτοφώρῳ κλέπτην εἰλημμένον καὶ προδότην, τὸν οὐκ ἀπεχόμενον τῶν εἰς τὴν πόλιν ἀφικνουμένων χρημάτων, τὸν εἰς τὰς δεινοτάτας ἀτυχίας ἐμβεβληκότα τὴν πόλιν, τὸν τῆς Ἑλλάδος ἀλιτήριον ἀποκτείναντας ἐξόριστον ἐκ τῆς πόλεως ποιῆσαι, καὶ μεταβαλέσθαι τὴν τῆς πόλεως τύχην ἐᾶσαι, καὶ προσδοκῆσαι τούτων γενομένων βέλτιον πράξειν.

78 Ἀκούσατ᾽, ὦ Ἀθηναῖοι, κἀκείνου τοῦ ψηφίσματος τοῦ γραφέντος ὑπὸ Δημοσθένους, ὃ τεταραγμένης τῆς πόλεως μετὰ τὴν ἐν Χαιρωνείᾳ μάχην ἔγραψεν ὁ δημοτικὸς οὗτος, καὶ τῆς μαντείας τῆς ἐλθούσης ἐκ Δωδώνης παρὰ τοῦ Διὸς τοῦ Δωδωναίου· σαφῶς γὰρ ὑμῖν πάλαι προείρηκε φυλάττεσθαι τοὺς ἡγεμόνας καὶ τοὺς συμβούλους. λέγε τὴν μαντείαν πρῶτον.

MANTEIA

79 λέγε δὴ τὸ καλὸν ψήφισμα τὸ τούτου.

the naval battle at Cnidus, when Iphicrates destroyed the Spartan company, when Chabrias at Naxos defeated at sea the Spartan triremes, when Timotheus won the naval battle at Corcyra. (76) At that time, Athenians, at that time the Spartans, who before were famous because of their leaders and had been reared in the principles of those men, came humbly to our city, beseeching our ancestors for safety. The democracy which was overthrown by them was made the leading power of Greece again thanks to the advisers we then had, and I think rightly so, for they had got such generals as I have just been talking about and had Archinus and Cephalus of Collytus as advisers. For there is one only means of safety for both a city and a nation: to obtain brave men and wise advisers as leaders. (77) Athenians, if you yourselves recognise and give thought to these things, then, by Zeus, you should not share in Demosthenes' venality and ill fortune any longer, nor place your hopes of safety on this man, nor think you will be without brave men and wise advisers. Take up the spirit of your ancestors. Have this robber and traitor, who has been caught in the act, executed, and his body cast beyond the borders; this traitor, who does not keep his hands off the gold brought into the city, who has cast the city into the most calamitous misfortunes, this human plague of Greece, and allow the fortune of the city to change. And having done this, look forward to a better lot.

(78) Athenians, listen also to that decree proposed by Demosthenes, which this democrat proposed after the battle of Chaeronea when the city was in dire straits, and the oracle which came from Zeus of Dodona. It has been clearly telling you for a long time to be on your guard against your leaders and advisers. First read the oracle.

ORACLE

(79) Now read his fine decree.

ΨΗΦΙΣΜΑ

Δημοτικός γ' ὁ διατάττων ἑαυτὸν μέν, ἐπειδὴ ἀνδρεῖος καὶ εὔψυχός ἐστιν, ἐν τοῖς ὅπλοις μένειν, οὓς δ' ἂν οὗτος ἀποδοκιμάσῃ τῶν πολιτῶν, ἐπὶ τὰ ἔργ' ἀπιέναι, καὶ ἐάν τι ἄλλο τούτῳ δόξῃ ἐπιτήδειον εἶναι, τοῦτο ποιεῖν. λέγε τὰ λοιπά.

ΨΗΦΙΣΜΑ

80 Ἀκούετ', ἄνδρες δικασταί. ἀπιέναι φησὶ τὰς ἡρημένας πρεσβείας. ἐπειδὴ γὰρ ἤκουσε μετὰ τὴν μάχην τὴν ἐν Χαιρωνείᾳ Φίλιππον εἰς τὴν χώραν ἡμῶν μέλλειν εἰσβάλλειν, αὐτὸς ἑαυτὸν πρεσβευτὴν κατασκευάσας, ἵν' ἐκ τῆς πόλεως ἀποδραίη, ᾤχετο συσκευασάμενος ἐκ τῆς διοικήσεως ὀκτὼ τάλαντα, οὐδὲν φροντίσας τῆς τότε παρούσης ἀπορίας, ἡνίχ' οἱ ἄλλοι πάντες ἐκ τῶν ἰδίων ἐπεδίδοσαν εἰς τὴν ὑμετέραν 81 σωτηρίαν. τοιοῦτος ὑμῖν ὁ σύμβουλος, καὶ δύο ταύτας μόνας ἐν τῷ βίῳ Δημοσθένης πεποίηται ἀποδημίας, μετὰ τὴν μάχην ὅτ' ἀπεδίδρασκεν ἐκ τῆς πόλεως, καὶ νῦν εἰς Ὀλυμπίαν, ἐπεὶ Νικάνορι διὰ τῆς ἀρχεθεωρίας ἐντυχεῖν ἐβούλετο. ἄξιόν γε τούτῳ παρακαταθέσθαι τὴν πόλιν καὶ ἐπιτρέψαι κινδυνεύειν μέλλοντας, ὃς ὅτε μὲν ἔδει μάχεσθαι μετὰ τῶν ἄλλων τοῖς πολεμίοις, λιπὼν τὴν τάξιν ᾤχετ' ἀπιὼν οἴκαδε, ἐπειδὴ δὲ προσῆκεν οἴκοι κινδυνεύειν μετὰ τῶν ἄλλων, πρεσβευτὴν αὐτὸς αὑτὸν προβαλόμενος ᾤχετ' ἐκ τῆς πόλεως ἀποδράς; 82 ἐπειδὴ δὲ πρεσβεύειν ἔδει περὶ τῆς εἰρήνης, οὐκ ἂν ἔφασκεν ἐκ τῆς πόλεως ἐξελθεῖν οὐδὲ τὸν ἕτερον πόδα, ἐπειδὴ δὲ τοὺς φυγάδας Ἀλέξανδρον ἔφασαν κατάγειν καὶ Νικάνωρ εἰς Ὀλυμπίαν ἧκεν, ἀρχεθέωρον αὐτὸν ἐπέδωκε τῇ βουλῇ. τοιοῦτος οὗτος, ἐν μὲν ταῖς παρατάξεσιν οἰκουρός, ἐν δὲ τοῖς οἴκοι μένουσι πρεσβευτής, ἐν δὲ τοῖς πρεσβευταῖς δραπέτης ἐστίν.

Λέγε δὴ ⟨τὸ σὸν ψήφισμα περὶ δυοῖν τῶν πολιτῶν⟩ καὶ τὸ περὶ τῆς ζητήσεως τῶν χρημάτων ψήφισμα, ἃ ἔγραψε Δημοσθένης τῇ ἐξ Ἀρείου πάγου βουλῇ περὶ αὑτοῦ τε καὶ ὑμῶν, ἵνα παρ' ἄλληλα θεωρήσαντες εἰδῆτε τὴν Δημοσθένους ἀπόνοιαν.

DECREE

A democrat indeed is this one! He arranges for himself, since he is a brave and fearless man, to remain in arms, but those of the citizens whom this man rejects as unfit he orders to go off to their work, and to do anything else he thinks of as appropriate. Read the remainder.

DECREE

(80) Gentlemen of the jury, hear this. He says that the chosen embassies shall set out. For when he heard that Philip was intending to invade our land after the battle of Chaeronea he appointed himself envoy in order that he might escape from the city. He went off, having snatched up eight talents from the treasury, thinking nothing of the current dearth of funds, and at a time when everyone else was contributing from his own resources towards your safety. (81) Such is your political adviser; and Demosthenes in his life has made only these two journeys abroad: after the battle when he fled from the city, and now to Olympia, since through his presidency of the sacred embassy he wanted to meet up with Nicanor. Is it right to entrust and turn over the city to this man as danger threatens, who, when it was necessary to fight the enemy with his fellows, deserted the rank and went off home, and, when he needed to be at home to face danger with the others, he put himself forward as an envoy and went away and fled from the city? (82) But when it was necessary to have envoys concerning the peace he said he would not leave the city by even a foot, but when it was said that Alexander was restoring the exiles and Nicanor had come to Olympia, he volunteered himself as President of the Sacred Embassy to the council. In a nutshell he is this sort of man: in the battle-line he is a stay-at-home, among those who remain at home he is an envoy, and among envoys he is a runaway.

Now read your decree over the two citizens and the decree for the investigation into the money, which Demosthenes proposed for the Council of the Areopagus concerning both himself and you, so that by considering both together you will see Demosthenes' madness.

ΨΗΦΙΣΜΑ

83 Ἔγραψας σὺ τοῦτο, Δημόσθενες; ἔγραψας· οὐκ ἔστιν ἀντειπεῖν. ἐγένεθ᾽ ἡ βουλὴ κυρία σοῦ προστάξαντος; ἐγένετο. τεθνᾶσι τῶν πολιτῶν ἄνδρες; τεθνᾶσι. κύριον ἦν τὸ σὸν ψήφισμα κατ᾽ ἐκείνων; ἀδύνατον ἀντειπεῖν. λέγε δὴ πάλιν ὃ Δημοσθένης κατὰ Δημοσθένους ἔγραψε. προσέχετ᾽, ὦ ἄνδρες.

ΨΗΦΙΣΜΑ

84 Ἡ βουλὴ εὕρηκε Δημοσθένην. τί δεῖ πολλῶν λόγων; ἀποπέφαγκεν, ὦ Ἀθηναῖοι. τὸ μὲν τοίνυν δίκαιον ἦν ὑφ᾽ ἑαυτοῦ κεκριμένον εὐθὺς ἀποθνήσκειν· ἐπειδὴ δ᾽ εἰς τὰς ὑμετέρας ἥκει χεῖρας, τῶν ὑπὲρ τοῦ δήμου συνειλεγμένων καὶ τῶν ὀμωμοκότων πείσεσθαι τοῖς νόμοις καὶ τοῖς τοῦ δήμου ψηφίσμασι, τί ποιήσετε; προήσεσθε τὴν πρὸς τοὺς θεοὺς εὐσέβειαν καὶ τὰ παρὰ πᾶσιν ἀνθρώποις δίκαια νομιζόμενα;
85 μή, ὦ Ἀθηναῖοι, μή· αἰσχρὸν γὰρ καὶ δεινὸν ἑτέρους μὲν ὑπὸ τῶν Δημοσθένους ψηφισμάτων, οὐδὲν ὄντας τούτου χείρους οὐδὲ τοσαῦτ᾽ ἠδικηκότας ὅσα περ οὗτος, ἀπολωλέναι, τουτονὶ δὲ καταφρονοῦνθ᾽ ὑμῶν καὶ τῶν νόμων ἀτιμώρητον ἐν τῇ πόλει περιιέναι, αὐτὸν ὑφ᾽ ἑαυτοῦ καὶ τῶν ψηφισμάτων ὧν ἔγραψεν ἑαλωκότα. ταὐτὸ συνέδριον ὦ Ἀθηναῖοι, καὶ ὁ αὐτὸς
86 τόπος, καὶ ταὐτὰ δίκαια. ὁ αὐτὸς ῥήτωρ ἐκείνοις τ᾽ αἴτιος ἐγένετο τῶν συμβάντων κακῶν καὶ αὐτῷ τῶν νῦν συμβησομένων. ἐπέτρεψεν αὐτὸς οὗτος ἐν τῷ δήμῳ τῷ συνεδρίῳ τούτῳ κρῖναι περὶ αὐτοῦ, μάρτυρας ὑμᾶς πεποιημένος. ἔθετο συνθήκας μετὰ τοῦ δήμου, γράψας τὸ ψήφισμα καθ᾽ ἑαυτοῦ, παρὰ τὴν Μητέρα τῶν θεῶν, ἣ πάντων τῶν ἐν τοῖς γράμμασι δικαίων φύλαξ τῇ πόλει καθέστηκε. διὸ καὶ οὐχ ὅσιον ὑμῖν ἐστι ταύτας ἀκύρους ποιεῖν, οὐδὲ τοὺς θεοὺς ὀμωμοκόσι περὶ ταύτης τῆς κρίσεως ταῖς αὐτῶν τῶν
87 θεῶν πράξεσιν ἐναντίαν τὴν ψῆφον ἐνεγκεῖν. κρίσεως Ποσειδῶν ἀποτυχὼν τῆς ὑπὲρ Ἀλιρροθίου πρὸς Ἄρη γενομένης ἐνέμεινεν· ἐνέμειναν αὐταὶ αἱ σεμναὶ θεαὶ τῇ πρὸς Ὀρέστην ἐν τούτῳ τῷ συνεδρίῳ κρίσει γενομένῃ, καὶ τῇ τούτου ἀληθείᾳ συνοίκους ἑαυτὰς εἰς τὸν λοιπὸν χρόνον κατέστησαν. ὑμεῖς δὲ τί ποιήσεθ᾽ οἱ πάντων εἶναι

DECREE

(83) Did you propose this, Demosthenes? You did propose it – it cannot be denied. Was the council given power according to your motion? It was. Have these men from the citizenry been put to death? They have been executed. Was your decree valid against them? It is impossible to contradict this. Now read again what Demosthenes proposed against Demosthenes. Gentlemen, pay attention.

DECREE

(84) The council has declared against Demosthenes. Is it necessary to say anything else? Athenians: it has reported him! Justice thus dictates that, having been condemned by himself, he be executed straightaway. But since he has come into your hands, you who have been gathered together by the people and have sworn that you will obey the laws and the decrees of the people, what will you do? Will you abandon the reverence towards the gods and the justice recognised by all mankind? (85) No, Athenians, you must not. It would be an utter disgrace if when others have been executed by the decrees of Demosthenes, who were no worse than this man nor have committed crimes of the same magnitude as he, he with his disdain for you and the laws should go around in the city unpunished, when he has been convicted by his own motion and the decrees that he proposed. Athenians, the same council, the same place, and the same rights are in question. (86) The same orator was responsible for the adversities that afflicted them and that he himself will encounter now. This man himself in the Assembly asked this council to judge his case and made you his witnesses. He made a compact with the people and proposed the decree against himself to be kept by the mother of the gods, who is the guardian of all the written agreements in the city. It is not right for you to make these invalid, nor, having sworn by the gods in the present case, to deliver a vote in contradiction of the actions of the gods themselves. (87) When Poseidon failed to obtain the vote against Ares over Halirrothius he accepted the decision. The awful goddesses themselves accepted the verdict of this council in the case against Orestes, and associated themselves with the truthfulness of this body for the future. What will you do, you who claim to be most pious in everything?

φάσκοντες εὐσεβέστατοι; τὴν τοῦ συνεδρίου γνώμην ἄκυρον

88 καταστήσετε τῇ Δημοσθένους ἐπακολουθήσαντες πονηρίᾳ; οὔκ, ἐὰν σωφρονῆτ', ὦ 'Αθηναῖοι· οὐ γὰρ περὶ μικρῶν οὐδὲ τῶν τυχόντων ἐν τῇ τήμερον ἡμέρᾳ δικάζετε, ἀλλὰ περὶ σωτηρίας τῆς πόλεως ἁπάσης καὶ πρὸς τούτοις περὶ δωροδοκίας, ἔθους πονηροῦ καὶ πράγματος ἀλυσιτελοῦς ὑμῖν καὶ πάντας ἀνθρώπους ἀπολωλεκότος. ὃ εἰ μὲν καθ' ὅσον ἐστὶ δυνατὸν ἐκβαλεῖτ' ἐκ τῆς πόλεως καὶ παύσετε τοὺς ῥᾳδίως καθ' ὑμῶν χρήματα λαμβάνοντας, σωθησόμεθα θεῶν βουλομένων· εἰ δ' ἐπιτρέψετε τοῖς ῥήτορσι πωλεῖν σφᾶς αὐτούς, περιόψεσθε τὴν πόλιν ἀνατραπεῖσαν ὑπὸ τούτων.

89 Ἔγραψεν αὐτὸς ἐν τῷ δήμῳ Δημοσθένης, ὡς δηλονότι δικαίου τοῦ πράγματος ὄντος, φυλάττειν 'Αλεξάνδρῳ τὰ εἰς τὴν 'Αττικὴν ἀφικόμενα μεθ' 'Αρπάλου χρήματα. οὕτως οὖν, ὦ ἄριστ', εἰπέ μοι, φυλάξομεν, ἐὰν σὺ μὲν εἴκοσι τάλαντα λαβὼν ἔχῃς ἰδίᾳ, ἕτερος δὲ πεντεκαίδεκα, Δημάδης δ' ἑξακισχιλίους χρυσοῦ στατῆρας, ἕτεροι δ' ὅσα δή ποτ' ἀποπεφασμένοι εἰσί; τέτταρα γὰρ τάλαντ' ἐστὶ καὶ ἑξήκοντα ἤδη εὑρημένα, ὧν οἴεσθε τὴν αἰτίαν τούτοις δεῖν ἀναθεῖναι.

90 καὶ πότερα κάλλιόν ἐστι, πρὸς δὲ δικαιότερον, ἅπαντ' ἐν τῷ κοινῷ φυλάττεσθαι, ἕως ἄν τι δίκαιον ὁ δῆμος βουλεύσηται, ἢ τοὺς ῥήτορας καὶ τῶν στρατηγῶν ἐνίους διηρπακότας ἔχειν; ἐγὼ μὲν γὰρ οἶμαι τὸ μὲν ἐν τῷ κοινῷ φυλάττειν παρὰ πάντων ὁμολογούμενον εἶναι δίκαιον, τὸ δὲ τούτους ἔχειν μηδέν' ἂν εἰπεῖν ὡς ἔστι καλῶς ἔχον.

91 Πολλοὺς οὗτος εἴρηκε καὶ παντοδαποὺς λόγους, ὦ ἄνδρες, καὶ οὐδεπώποτε τοὺς αὐτούς. ὁρᾷ γὰρ ὑμᾶς τὸν ἅπαντα χρόνον ἐλπίσι κεναῖς καὶ ψευδέσι λόγοις ἐξηπατημένους ὑφ' ἑαυτοῦ, καὶ μέχρι τούτου μνημονεύοντας τὰς ὑποσχέσεις, μέχρι ἂν ῥηθῶσιν. εἰ μὲν οὖν ἔτι δεῖ τὴν πόλιν τῆς Δημοσθένους πονηρίας καὶ ἀτυχίας ἀπολαύειν, ἵνα πλείω κακοδαιμονῶμεν – οὐ γὰρ ἔχω τί ἄλλο εἴπω –, στερκτέον ἂν

92 εἴη τοῖς συμβαίνουσιν· εἰ δέ τι κηδόμεθα τῆς πατρίδος καὶ τοὺς πονηροὺς καὶ δωροδόκους μισοῦμεν καὶ μετοιωνίσασθαι τὴν τύχην καὶ μεταλλάξασθαι βουλόμεθα, οὐ προετέον ἐστὶν ὑμᾶς αὐτούς, ὦ 'Αθηναῖοι, ταῖς τοῦ μιαροῦ καὶ γόητος

Will you render invalid the decision of the council and follow the baseness of Demosthenes? **(88)** No, Athenians, if you are wise. For you are judging no small or occasional matter on this day, but the safety of the entire city, and, in addition to this, bribery, a shameful custom and an unprofitable practice to you and the ruin of all men. If you suppress as best you can those who gladly take bribes against you and expel them from the city, then we shall be saved by the grace of the gods. But if you leave it to the orators to sell themselves, then you will watch the city ruined by them.

(89) Demosthenes himself proposed in the Assembly to guard for Alexander the money brought into Attica with Harpalus, clearly showing how this was a just measure. Well, my good friend, tell me how we are to guard it, when you have taken twenty talents for your own pocket, someone else fifteen, Demades six thousand gold staters and others the amounts attributed to them? Sixty-four talents have been discovered, for which you must see that the guilt must be placed on these men. **(90)** Which is the better and in addition the more just alternative: to guard all of the money in the treasury until the people shall have reached a right decision, or for some of the orators and the generals to seize it as plunder? I myself think that to guard it in the treasury is accepted as right by everyone, and that no one would say it was right for these men to have it.

(91) Gentlemen, this man has made a multitude of differing statements, but never the same one. He sees that he all along has deceived you with empty hopes and false claims, and you remember his promises only while they are being made. If the city must reap the rewards of Demosthenes' dishonesty and misfortune so that we are even more possessed by an evil spirit – I'm at a loss to describe it any other way – we should acquiesce in our current circumstances. **(92)** But if we have any feeling for our country and hate criminals and those who take bribes, and we want our fortune to change and to improve, you must not, Athenians, be swayed by the entreaties

τούτου δεήσεσιν, οὐδὲ προσδεκτέον τοὺς οἴκτους καὶ τοὺς
φενακισμοὺς τοὺς τούτου· ἱκανὴν γὰρ εἰλήφατε πεῖραν αὐτοῦ
93 καὶ τῶν λόγων καὶ τῶν ἔργων καὶ τῆς τύχης. τίς οὕτως
εὔελπις ὑμῶν ἐστιν, ὦ Ἀθηναῖοι, τίς οὕτως ἀλόγιστος, τίς
τῶν προγεγενημένων καὶ νῦν ἐνεστηκότων πραγμάτων
ἄπειρος, ὅστις ἐλπίζει τὸν ἐκ τοσαύτης εὐδαιμονίας εἰς
τοσαύτην ἀδοξίαν καταστήσαντα τὴν πόλιν δι᾽ ἡντιναδήποτ᾽
αἰτίαν ἢ τύχην – ἐῶ γὰρ τοῦτο – νῦν, ἐπειδὴ πρὸς ταῖς
ἄλλαις ἀπορίαις καὶ τοῖς περιεστηκόσιν ἡμᾶς κινδύνοις καὶ ἡ
τῶν ἐξ αὐτῆς τῆς πόλεως δωροδοκία προσγέγονε, καὶ περὶ
αἰσχρᾶς αἰτίας κοινῇ πάντες ἀγωνιζόμεθα καὶ περὶ τοῦ μὴ
δοκεῖν τὰ ἰδίᾳ παρά τισιν ὄντα χρήματα κοινῇ τὸν δῆμον
ἔχειν, τηνικαῦτα συμβουλεύοντα καὶ διοικοῦντα τοῦτον σώσειν
94 ἡμᾶς; ἐῶ γὰρ τἆλλ᾽ ὅσα μεταβαλλόμενος ἐν τοῖς πράγμασι
καὶ δημηγορῶν οὐδὲν ὑγιὲς διατετέλεκε, καὶ τοτὲ μὲν γράφων
καὶ ἀπαγορεύων μηδένα νομίζειν ἄλλον θεὸν ἢ τοὺς
παραδεδομένους, τοτὲ δὲ λέγων ὡς οὐ δεῖ τὸν δῆμον
ἀμφισβητεῖν τῶν ἐν οὐρανῷ τιμῶν Ἀλεξάνδρῳ, ὅταν δὲ μέλλῃ
κριθήσεσθαι παρ᾽ ὑμῖν, Καλλιμέδοντ᾽ εἰσαγγέλλων συνιέναι ἐν
Μεγάροις τοῖς φυγάσιν ἐπὶ καταλύσει τοῦ δήμου, καὶ ταύτην
95 τὴν εἰσαγγελίαν εὐθὺς παραχρῆμ᾽ ἀναιρούμενος, ἐν δὲ τῇ
ἐκκλησίᾳ ταύτῃ τῇ πρώην γεγενημένῃ προσάγων καὶ
κατασκευάζων ψευδῆ μηνυτὴν ὡς ἐπιβουλευομένων τῶν
νεωρίων, καὶ περὶ τούτων γράφων μὲν οὐδέν, αἰτίας δ᾽ ἕνεκα
τοῦ παρόντος ἀγῶνος παρασκευάζων· τούτων γὰρ ἁπάντων
ὑμεῖς τούτῳ μάρτυρές ἐστε. γόης οὗτος, ἄνδρες Ἀθηναῖοι,
καὶ μιαρὸς ἄνθρωπός ἐστι, καὶ οὔτε τῷ γένει τῆς πόλεως
πολίτης οὔτε τοῖς πεπολιτευμένοις αὐτῷ καὶ πεπραγμένοις.
96 ποῖαι γὰρ τριήρεις εἰσὶ κατεσκευασμέναι διὰ τοῦτον, ὥσπερ
ἐπ᾽ Εὐβούλου, τῇ πόλει; ἢ ποῖοι νεώσοικοι τούτου
πολιτευομένου γεγόνασι; πόθ᾽ οὗτος ἢ διὰ ψηφίσματος ἢ
νόμου ἐπηνώρθωσε τὸ ἱππικόν; τίνα κατεσκεύασε δύναμιν,
τοιούτων καιρῶν παραγενομένων μετὰ τὴν ἐν Χαιρωνείᾳ
μάχην, ἢ πεζὴν ἢ ναυτικήν; τίς ἀνενήνεκται τῇ θεῷ κόσμος
εἰς ἀκρόπολιν ὑπὸ τούτου; τί κατεσκεύακεν οἰκοδόμημα
Δημοσθένης ἐν τῷ ἐμπορίῳ τῷ ὑμετέρῳ, ἢ ἐν τῷ ἄστει, ἢ
97 ἄλλοθί που τῆς χώρας; οὐδεὶς ἂν οὐδαμοῦ δείξειεν. ἔπειτα
τὸν μὲν ἐν ταῖς πολεμικαῖς πράξεσιν ἄπιστον γεγενημένον,

of this scummy juggler, nor must you listen to his lamentations and deceptions. You have had sufficient experience of him, his speeches, his deeds, and his luck. (93) Athenians, which one of you is so hopeful, which so reckless, which so ignorant of affairs past and present, that he expects that the man who has reduced the city from such prosperity to such disrepute, through whatever cause or fortune – and I disregard that – will now save us by serving as adviser and administrator? As well as the other difficulties and dangers that face us, there is the added venality of those in the city itself, and all of us together are disputing a shocking charge, so that all the people should not be thought to have the money that a certain few keep for themselves. (94) I disregard the other fluctuations in his policies and continuous ill-judged speeches, how at one time he introduced a proposal banning anyone from believing in any god other than the traditional ones, and then said that it was necessary for the people not to dispute deifying Alexander. Or, when he was about to be tried before you, how he impeached Callimedon for scheming with the exiles at Megara to subvert the democracy, and then suddenly rescinded this impeachment. (95) How he brought forward and primed a false informer at the recent meeting of the Assembly to say there was a plot against the dockyards. He made no proposals about these matters, but was preparing allegations to use in the present trial. You yourselves are witnesses of all these things against him. Gentlemen of Athens, this man is a cheat and an abomination, unworthy by either his birth or his administration and actions of being a citizen of the city. (96) What triremes are there which have been built by this man for the city, as in the time of Eubulus? What dockyards have been constructed under his administration? When has this man either by decree or law increased the cavalry? When such opportunities presented themselves after the battle of Chaeronea, what force did he levy, either by land or by sea? What ornament to the goddess has this man carried up to the Acropolis? What building did Demosthenes construct in your Exchange, or in the city, or anywhere else in the country? No one could show one anywhere! (97) If someone has been untrustworthy in matters of war, and worthless in the administration of the

ἐν δὲ ταῖς κατὰ τὴν πόλιν οἰκονομίαις ἄχρηστον, περιεορακότα δὲ τοὺς ἀντιπολιτευομένους ἅπαντα διαπεπραγμένους ὅσ' ἐβουλήθησαν, μεταβεβλημένον δ' αὐτὸν καὶ τὰς ὑπὲρ τοῦ δήμου πράξεις ἐγκαταλελοιπότα, τοῦτον 98 περιποιῆσαι βουλήσεσθε; οὔκ, ἐὰν σωφρονῆτε καὶ καλῶς καὶ ὑπὲρ ὑμῶν αὐτῶν καὶ τῆς πόλεως βουλεύησθε· ἀλλὰ δέξεσθε τὴν ἀγαθὴν τύχην, ἣ τιμωρήσασθαι παρέδωκε τῶν ῥητόρων τοὺς τὴν πόλιν διὰ τὴν αὐτῶν δωροδοκίαν ταπεινὴν πεποιηκότας, καὶ φυλάξεσθε, καθάπερ οἱ θεοὶ προειρήκασιν ὑμῖν ἐν ταῖς μαντείαις πολλάκις, τοὺς τοιούτους ἡγεμόνας καὶ συμβούλους. ἀκούσατε δ' αὐτῆς τῆς μαντείας. λέγε τὴν μαντείαν.

ΜΑΝΤΕΙΑ

99 Πῶς οὖν μίαν γνώμην ἕξομεν ὦ Ἀθηναῖοι, πῶς ὁμονοήσομεν ἅπαντες ὑπὲρ τῶν κοινῇ συμφερόντων, ὅταν οἱ ἡγεμόνες καὶ οἱ δημαγωγοὶ χρήματα λαμβάνοντες προίωνται τὰ τῆς πατρίδος συμφέροντα, καὶ ὑμεῖς μὲν καὶ ὁ δῆμος ἅπας κινδυνεύῃ περὶ τοῦ ἐδάφους τοῦ τῆς πόλεως καὶ τῶν ἱερῶν τῶν πατρῴων καὶ παίδων καὶ γυναικῶν, οἱ δὲ διηλλαγμένοι πρὸς αὐτοὺς ἐν μὲν ταῖς ἐκκλησίαις λοιδορῶνται καὶ προσκρούωσιν ἀλλήλοις ἐξεπίτηδες, ἰδίᾳ δὲ ταὐτὰ πράττωσιν ἐξαπατῶντες ὑμᾶς τοὺς ῥᾷστα πειθομένους 100 τοῖς τούτων λόγοις; τί γάρ ἐστι ῥήτορος δημοτικοῦ καὶ μισοῦντος τοὺς κατὰ τῆς πόλεως λέγοντας καὶ γράφοντας; ἢ τί φασι τοὺς πρὸ ὑμῶν γεγενημένους, ὦ Δημόσθενες καὶ Πολύευκτε, διατελεῖν ποιοῦντας, καὶ ταῦτ' οὐδενὸς δεινοῦ τότε τὴν πόλιν περιεστηκότος; οὐ κρίνειν ἀλλήλους; οὐκ εἰσαγγέλλειν; οὐ γράφεσθαι παρανόμων; ἔστιν οὖν ὅ τι πεποιήκατε τούτων ὑμεῖς οἱ φάσκοντες τοῦ δήμου κήδεσθαι 101 καὶ τὴν σωτηρίαν ὑμῖν ἐν τῇ τούτων εἶναι ψήφῳ; γέγραψαι ψήφισμα, Δημόσθενες, πολλῶν ὄντων καὶ δεινῶν καὶ παρανόμων ὧν Δημάδης γέγραφε; κεκώλυκάς τινα πρᾶξιν ὧν ἐκεῖνος προελόμενος κατὰ τοῦ δήμου πεπολίτευται; οὐδ' ἡντινοῦν. εἰσήγγελκας τὸν παρὰ τὰ τοῦ δήμου ψηφίσματα

city, and has disregarded those of the opposing party accomplishing everything they wished, changing his own position and neglecting actions in support of the people, will you want to preserve this man? **(98)** Not if you are wise and want what is best for you and the city. You will welcome the good fortune that handed over for punishment those orators whose corruption made the city degraded. And you will be on your guard against such leaders and advisers, as the gods have many times warned you in the oracles. Listen to the oracle itself. Read the oracle.

ORACLE

(99) Athenians, how then shall we have the one opinion? How shall we all agree on the interests of the state when the leaders and the demagogues take money and betray the well-being of the country, and you and all the people are in danger concerning the very soil of the city, the temples of your fathers, and your children and wives, while these men having been reconciled to each other deliberately vilify and attack each other in the Assembly, but in private they are united to deceive you, you who are too easily persuaded by their speeches? **(100)** What is the duty of a democratic orator who hates those speaking and making proposals against the people? What, Demosthenes and Polyeuctus, are we told about your predecessors, and what they continued to do, even when nothing fearful then surrounded the city? Did they not try each other? Not impeach each other? Not bring suit for illegal proposals? Have you done any of these things, you who allege that you have the people at heart and that your safety rests upon the vote of these men? **(101)** Have you censured a decree, Demosthenes, given the many scandalous and illegal ones that Demades proposed? Have you checked any move that that man undertook against the well-being of the people? Not a single one. Have you impeached the man who worked

καὶ τοὺς νόμους πολλὰ διαπεπραγμένον; οὐδεπώποτε, ἀλλὰ
περιεῖδες αὐτὸν ἐν τῇ ἀγορᾷ χαλκοῦν σταθέντα καὶ τῆς ἐν
πρυτανείῳ σιτήσεως κεκοινωνηκότα τοῖς Ἁρμοδίου καὶ
102 Ἀριστογείτονος ἀπογόνοις. ἔπειτα ποῦ τῆς εὐνοίας τῆς σῆς
ὁ δῆμος ἔλαβε πεῖραν, ἢ ποῦ τὴν τοῦ ῥήτορος βοήθειαν καὶ
δύναμιν ἐξεταζομένην εἴδομεν; ἢ ἐνταῦθα φήσετ' εἶναι δεινοί,
εἰ παρακρούεσθε τούτους ἀεὶ λέγοντες ὡς "οὐκ ἔστιν ἔξω τῆς
πατρίδος ἡμῖν ἐξελθεῖν", "οὐκ ἔστιν ἄλλη καταφυγὴ χωρὶς τῆς
ὑμετέρας εὐνοίας"; φανεροὺς ἐχρῆν γεγενημένους ἀντι-
πράττοντας καὶ λόγῳ καὶ ἔργῳ τοῖς κατὰ τοῦ δήμου
γραφομένοις ψηφίσμασιν, οὕτω πείθειν τούτους λέγοντας ὡς
οὐκ ἔστιν ὑμῖν οὐδεμία σωτηρία χωρὶς τῆς παρὰ τοῦ δήμου
103 βοηθείας. ὑμεῖς δ' ἐν τοῖς ἔξω τὰς ἐλπίδας ἔχετε,
ἁμιλλώμενοι ταῖς κολακείαις πρὸς τοὺς ὁμολογοῦντας ὑπὲρ
Ἀλεξάνδρου πράττειν καὶ δῶρ' εἰληφέναι παρὰ τῶν αὐτῶν
ὧνπερ νῦν ἀποπέφαγκεν ὑμᾶς ἡ βουλή. καὶ σὺ πάντων
ἐναντίον τῶν Ἑλλήνων διειλεγμένος Νικάνορι καὶ
κεχρηματικὼς ἐν Ὀλυμπίᾳ περὶ ὧν ἐβουλήθης, ἐλεεινὸν νῦν
σεαυτὸν κατασκευάζεις προδότης ὢν καὶ δωροδόκος, ὡς
ἐπιλησομένους τούτους τῆς σῆς πονηρίας, καὶ οὐ δώσων
104 δίκην ὑπὲρ ὧν εἴληψαι πεποιηκώς, τοσούτῳ τολμηρότερον
Δημάδου, ὥσθ' ὁ μὲν προειρηκὼς ἐν τῷ δήμῳ τὸν ἑαυτοῦ
τρόπον καὶ τὴν ἀπόνοιαν, καὶ ὁμολογῶν λαμβάνειν καὶ
λήψεσθαι, ὅμως οὐ τετόλμηκε τούτοις δεῖξαι τὸ πρόσωπον,
οὐδ' ἐναντία τῇ τῆς βουλῆς ἀποφάσει λέγειν ἠξίωσε – καίτοι
οὐκ ἔγραψεν ἐκεῖνος περὶ αὑτοῦ κυρίαν εἶναι τὴν βουλήν,
οὐδὲ θάνατον ὡρίσατο, ἐὰν ἀποφανθῇ χρήματ' εἰληφώς –· σὺ
δ' οὕτω σφόδρα πεπίστευκας τοῖς σεαυτοῦ λόγοις καὶ
καταπεφρόνηκας τῆς τούτων εὐηθείας, ὥστε πείσειν οἴει τοὺς
δικαστὰς ὡς μόνου σοῦ κατέψευσται τὸ συνέδριον καὶ μόνον
οὐκ εἰληφότα σὲ τὸ χρυσίον ἀποπέφαγκεν. καὶ τίς ἂν ταῦτα
πεισθείη;
105 Ὁρᾶτ', ὦ Ἀθηναῖοι, τί μέλλετε ποιεῖν. παρειλήφατε παρὰ
τοῦ δήμου τὸ πρᾶγμα τὸ γεγενημένον εἰδότος, τιμωρίας δ'
ἕνεκα τῆς κατὰ τῶν ἐνόχων ὄντων ταῖς ἀποφάσεσι.
Δημοσθένης εἰσάγεται πρῶτος. κατηγορήκαμεν ἡμεῖς οὐδὲν
106 οὐδενὶ καταχαρισάμενοι τῶν κοινῶν δικαίων. πότερ'
ἀμελήσαντες τῶν γεγενημένων ἁπάντων ἀφήσετε τὸν

against the decrees and the laws of the people? Never. But you permitted him to set up his bronze statue in the Agora and to share public maintenance in the Prytaneum with the descendants of Harmodius and Aristogeiton. (102) In what way, then, did the people have experience of your benevolence, or where did we see the protecting power of the orator in action? Or will you say that your skills lie in how you deceive these men by always saying that 'It is not possible for us to leave the country' and 'There is no other place of refuge apart from your goodwill'? You should have made it clear that in word and deed you sought to counteract decrees proposed against the people's interests, and thus persuade these men that you have no avenue of safety apart from the support of the people. (103) But you fix your hopes on those from abroad and compete in flattery with those who confess to work for Alexander, to taking bribes from the same sources as those from which the council has now reported you were bribed. And you, having consulted with Nicanor at Olympia in the presence of all the Greeks, and arranging everything as you wanted, you, a traitor and receiver of bribes, now set yourself up as piteous, as though these men will overlook your venality and you will not be punished for the crimes you have been caught committing. (104) In this you are more daring than Demades. Although he declared his deranged streak in the Assembly and confessed that he takes bribes and will continue to do so, nevertheless he did not dare to show his face before these men nor did he think it right to contest the Council's report. And yet he did not move that the council should have power over him or agree to death if it should be proved that he took money. But you have such enormous faith in your own arguments and derision for the simplicity of these men that you anticipate you will convince the jurors that in your case alone the council has been deceived, and that, of those it reported, you alone did not take the gold. Who on earth would be persuaded by that?

(105) Athenians, consider what you are going to do. You have taken over the case from the people who know the facts and to punish those subject to the reports. Demosthenes is brought in first. We have made our accusation and made no concession to anyone in the interests of common justice. (106) Overlooking all that has taken place, will you acquit the first man brought

πρῶτον εἰσεληλυθότα πρὸς ὑμᾶς, καὶ τὰ δίκαια παρὰ τῷ δήμῳ κα' ῆ βουλῇ τῇ ἐξ Ἀρείου πάγου δόξαντ' εἶναι καὶ τοῖς ἄλλοις ἅπασιν ἀνθρώποις; ταῦθ' ὑμεῖς οἱ κύριοι πάντων

107 λύσετε, καὶ τὴν πονηρίαν αὐτοὶ τὴν τούτων ἀναδέξεσθε; ἢ πᾶσιν ἀνθρώποις παράδειγμ' ἐξοίσετε κοινὸν ὑπὲρ τῆς πόλεως, ὅτι μισεῖτε τοὺς προδότας καὶ τοὺς χρημάτων ἕνεκα προϊεμένους τὰ τοῦ δήμου συμφέροντα; ταῦτα γὰρ ἅπαντ' ἐστὶν ἐφ' ὑμῖν νῦν, καὶ πεντακόσιοι καὶ χίλιοι ὄντες τὴν ἁπάσης τῆς πόλεως σωτηρίαν ἐν ταῖς χερσὶν ἔχετε, καὶ ἡ τήμερον ἡμέρα καὶ ἡ ὑμετέρα ψῆφος πολλὴν ἀσφάλειαν τῇ πόλει καταστήσει τὰ δίκαι' ὑμῶν ἐθελόντων κρίνειν, ἢ μοχθηρὰς ἐλπίδας ἔχειν ποιήσετε πάντας τοιαῦθ' ὑμῶν ἔθη καθιστάντων.

108 Οὐ καταπληκτέον ἐστίν, ἄνδρες Ἀθηναῖοι, οὐδὲ προετέον, ἐὰν σωφρονῆτε, τοῖς Δημοσθένους ἐλέοις τὴν κοινὴν καὶ δικαίαν ὑπὲρ τῆς πόλεως ἀπολογίαν. οὐδεὶς γὰρ ὑμῶν ἠνάγκαζε τοῦτον τὰ μὴ προσήκοντα χρήματα λαμβάνειν καθ' ὑμῶν, πολλῷ πλείω τῶν ἱκανῶν δι' ὑμᾶς ἕτερα κεκτημένον, οὐδ' ἀπολογεῖσθαι νῦν ὑπὲρ τῶν ὡμολογημένων ἀδικημάτων, γράψαντα καθ' ἑαυτοῦ θάνατον τὴν ζημίαν· ἀλλ' ἡ ἐκ τοῦ ἄλλου βίου ἔμφυτος αἰσχροκέρδεια καὶ πονηρία ταῦτ' εἰς τὴν

109 κεφαλὴν αὐτῷ τέτραφε. μὴ οὖν ἄχθεσθ' αὐτοῦ κλαίοντος καὶ ὀδυρομένου· πολὺ γὰρ ἂν δικαιότερον ἐλεήσαιτε τὴν χώραν, ἣν οὗτος καθίστησιν εἰς τοὺς κινδύνους τοιαῦτα πράττων, ἢ τοὺς ἐξ ἑαυτῆς γεγενημένους ὑμᾶς ἱκετεύει, παραστησαμένη τὰ ὑμέτερα τέκνα καὶ γυναῖκας, τιμωρήσασθαι τὸν προδότην καὶ σώζειν ἑαυτήν, ὑπὲρ ἧς οἱ πρόγονοι πολλοὺς καὶ καλοὺς κινδύνους ὑπομείναντες ἐλευθέραν ὑμῖν αὐτὴν παραδεδώκασιν, ἐν ᾗ πολλὰ καὶ καλὰ παραδείγματα λέλειπται τῆς τῶν

110 τελευτησάντων ἀρετῆς. εἰς ταύτην ἀποβλέψαντας, ὦ Ἀθηναῖοι, καὶ τὰς ἐν αὐτῇ γιγνομένας πατρίους θυσίας καὶ τὰς τῶν προγόνων θήκας, φέρειν δεῖ τοὺς εὖ φρονοῦντας τὴν ψῆφον. καὶ ὅταν Δημοσθένης ἐξαπατῆσαι βουλόμενος καὶ παρακρουόμενος ὑμᾶς οἰκτίζηται καὶ δακρύῃ, ὑμεῖς εἰς τὸ τῆς πόλεως σῶμ' ἀποβλέψαντες καὶ τὴν πρότερον δόξαν ὑπάρχουσαν αὐτῇ, ἀντίθετε, πότερον ἡ πόλις ἐλεεινοτέρα διὰ

111 τοῦτον γέγονεν ἢ διὰ τὴν πόλιν Δημοσθένης. εὑρήσετε γὰρ τοῦτον μὲν λαμπρὸν ἐξ οὗ προσελήλυθε πρὸς τὸ πολιτεύεσθαι

before you, and discard the decisions considered right by the people and by the Council of the Areopagus and by all mankind? Will you, who are sovereign in all things, overturn those judgements and take upon yourselves the corruption of these men? **(107)** Or will you make a demonstration to all mankind on behalf of the city that you detest traitors and those who betray the well-being of the people for the sake of money? All of this is now up to you: the fifteen hundred of you have the safety of the entire city in your hands. Today your vote will bring great security for the city if you are willing to make the right decision; otherwise if you condone this type of practice you will bring wretched hopes for everyone.

(108) Gentlemen of Athens, if you are wise you must not be cowed or throw away the just defence of the city because of Demosthenes' entreaties. None of you forced this man to take the money, which did not belong to him, to your detriment, when he has acquired far more than is sufficient thanks to you, nor to defend himself now for the confessed crimes when he proposed the death penalty against himself. But the shamelessness and venality innate from his whole life style have brought this upon his own head. **(109)** Do not be troubled by his weeping and wailing; you would far more justly feel pity for the land, which this man lays open to danger by doing such things, which beseeches you who are born of it, by your children and wives, to punish the traitor and save it. Your ancestors faced many and glorious dangers on behalf of it and handed it over to you free. In it many distinguished examples have been left of the virtue of those who died. **(110)** Athenians, right-thinking men must look to this land, to the traditional sacrifices celebrated in it, and to the tombs of our ancestors when delivering the vote. And when Demosthenes wants to deceive you and distracts you by lamenting and weeping, think of the city's reputation and the former glory that belonged to it, and judge whether the city deserves more pity because of him, or Demosthenes because of the city. **(111)** You will find that this man has become affluent from the time he entered political life. In place of being

γεγενημένον, καὶ ἀντὶ μὲν λογογράφου καὶ μισθοῦ τὰς δίκας
λέγοντος ὑπὲρ Κτησίππου καὶ Φορμίωνος καὶ ἑτέρων πολλῶν
πλουσιώτατον ὄντα τῶν ἐν τῇ πόλει, ἀντὶ δ' ἀγνῶτος καὶ
οὐδεμίαν πατρικὴν δόξαν παρὰ τῶν προγόνων παρειληφότος
ἔνδοξον γεγενημένον, τὴν δὲ πόλιν οὐκ ἀξίως ἑαυτῆς οὐδὲ
τῆς τῶν προγόνων δόξης διακειμένην. ἀφέντες οὖν τοὺς
ἐλέους καὶ τοὺς φενακισμοὺς τοὺς τούτου τὴν ὁσίαν καὶ τὴν
δικαίαν φέρετε ψῆφον, καὶ σκοπεῖτε τὸ τῇ πατρίδι συμφέρον,
μὴ τὸ Δημοσθένει· τοῦτο γάρ ἐστι καλῶν κἀγαθῶν δικαστῶν
112 ἔργον. καὶ ὅταν ἀναβαίνῃ τις συνηγορήσων Δημοσθένει,
λογίζεσθ' ὅτι οὗτος ὁ ἄνθρωπος, εἰ μὲν μὴ ἔνοχος ὢν ταῖς
μελλούσαις ἀποφάσεσιν ἀναβαίνει, κακόνους ἐστὶ τῇ πολιτείᾳ,
καὶ τοὺς ἐπὶ τῷ δήμῳ δῶρα λαμβάνοντας οὐ βουλόμενος
δίκην δοῦναι, καὶ τὴν κοινὴν τῶν ὑμετέρων σωμάτων φυλακήν,
ἐφ' ᾗ τέτακται τὸ ἐν Ἀρείῳ πάγῳ συνέδριον, καταλυθῆναι
βούλεται καὶ συγκεχύσθαι πάντα τὰ ἐν τῇ πόλει δίκαια· εἰ
δὲ ῥήτωρ ἢ στρατηγός, οἳ τὴν προσδοκωμένην καθ' αὑτῶν
ἀπόφασιν ἄπιστον βουλόμενοι γενέσθαι συνηγορήσουσιν, οὐ
προσεκτέον ὑμῖν ἐστι τοῖς τούτων λόγοις, εἰδότας ὅτι ἐκ
πάντων τούτων γεγένηται συνεργία περὶ τὸν Ἁρπάλου
113 κατάπλουν καὶ τὴν ἄφεσιν. νομίσαντες οὖν, ὦ Ἀθηναῖοι, καθ'
ὑμῶν πάντας τούτους ἀναβαίνειν καὶ κοινοὺς ἐχθροὺς εἶναι
τῶν νόμων καὶ τῆς πόλεως ἁπάσης, μὴ ἀποδέχεσθ' αὐτῶν,
ἀλλὰ κελεύετ' ἀπολογεῖσθαι περὶ τῶν κατηγορημένων· μηδὲ
τὴν αὐτοῦ τούτου μανίαν, ὃς μέγα φρονεῖ ἐπὶ τῷ δύνασθαι
λέγειν, καὶ ἐπειδὰν φανερὸς ὑμῖν γένηται δωροδοκῶν, ἔτι
μᾶλλον ἐξελήλεγκται φενακίζων ὑμᾶς, ἀλλὰ τιμωρήσασθ' ὑμῶν
αὐτῶν καὶ τῆς πόλεως ἀξίως. εἰ δὲ μή, μιᾷ ψήφῳ καὶ ἑνὶ
ἀγῶνι πάντας τοὺς ἀποπεφασμένους καὶ τοὺς μέλλοντας
ἀφέντες, εἰς ὑμᾶς αὐτοὺς καὶ τὸν δῆμον τὴν τούτων
δωροδοκίαν τρέψετε, κἂν ὕστερον ἐγκαλῆτε τοῖς ἀφεῖσιν, ὅτ'
οὐδὲν ἔσται πλέον ὑμῖν.
114 Ἐγὼ μὲν οὖν, ὅσον εἰς τὸ μέρος τοὐμὸν τῆς κατηγορίας
ἥκει, βεβοήθηκα, τἆλλα πάντα παριδὼν πλὴν τοῦ δικαίου καὶ
τοῦ συμφέροντος ὑμῖν. οὐκ ἐγκαταλέλοιπα τὴν πόλιν, οὐ
χάριν προὐργιαιτέραν τῆς τοῦ δήμου χειροτονίας ἐποιησάμην.
ἀξιῶν δὲ καὶ ὑμᾶς τὴν αὐτὴν γνώμην ἔχειν, παραδίδωμι τὸ
ὕδωρ τοῖς ἄλλοις κατηγόροις.

a speechwriter and a paid advocate for Ctesippus and Phormion and many others he is the richest man in the city. From obscurity and inheriting no family esteem from his forebears he has become renowned. But the city has fallen into a plight unworthy of itself or of the glory of our ancestors. Therefore disregard his appeals and trickery, and deliver a vote both proper and just, and give heed to the interests of the country and not those of Demosthenes. For this is the duty of good and noble jurors. (112) And when anyone comes forward to speak in support of Demosthenes, remember that this man, if he is not a subject of the forthcoming reports, is ill-disposed to the constitution, unwilling that punishment be exacted from those taking bribes against the people, and wants destroyed the common protection of your persons, for which the Council of the Areopagus has been set up, and all the rights in the city to be abolished. But if an orator or a general speaks in the defence from the desire to weaken the effect of the report expected in relation to themselves, you must not listen to their arguments, knowing that a conspiracy arose between all of these men over the arrival and escape of Harpalus. (113) Athenians, consider that all these men come forward against your interests and are common enemies of the laws and of the entire city. Do not listen to them but order them to make their defence speeches in relation to the charges. Nor listen to his own ravings for he has a high opinion of his ability to speak. When you see clearly that he takes bribes, the fact that he cheats you has been proved even more strongly. Punish him, as you yourselves and the city deserve. Otherwise, by one vote and at one trial you will release all those who have been reported and who will be in the future, and you will bring the corruption of these men onto your own heads and the people. Even if you later indict those who acquitted them, by then this will be absolutely no use to you.

(114) I have done my best with what falls within my share of the prosecution, disregarding everything else apart from justice and your interests. I have not deserted the city, nor have I attached greater weight to personal regard than the vote of the people. Appealing to you now to have the same disposition, I hand over the water to the other prosecutors.

ΥΠΕΡΕΙΔΟΥ

5. ΚΑΤΑ ΔΗΜΟΣΘΕΝΟΥΣ ΥΠΕΡ ΤΩΝ ΑΡΠΑΛΕΙΩΝ

Frag. I

col. 1 Ἀλλ' ἐγώ, ὦ ἄνδρες δικασταί, [ὅπερ καὶ] πρὸς τοὺ[ς
παρακαθημέ]νους [ἀρτίως ἔ]λ[εγον,] θαυ[μάζω] τουτὶ τὸ πρᾶ[γμα,
εἰ δ]ὴ νὴ Δία κατὰ Δημοσθένους μόνου τῶν ἐν τῇ πόλει
μήτε οἱ νόμοι ἰσχύουσιν οἱ κελεύοντες κύρια εἶναι ὅσα ἂν
τις αὐτὸς καθ' αὑτοῦ διάθηται, μήτε τὰ ψηφίσματα τοῦ
δήμου, καθ' ἃ ὑμεῖς μὲν ὀμωμόκατε τὴν ψῆφον οἴσειν,
ἔγραψεν δὲ αὐτὰ οὐδεὶς τῶν ἐχθρῶν τῶν Δημοσθένους, ἀλλ'
αὐτὸς οὗτος, ἐψηφίσατο δὲ ὁ δῆμος τούτου κελεύοντος [καὶ
μόνον] οὐχ ἑκου[σίως αὐτὸν ἀπο]λλύ[οντος]

col. 2 [καίτοι τὸ] δίκαιον, ὦ ἄνδρες δικασταί, ἁπλοῦν ὑπολαμβάνω
ἡμῖν εἶναι πρὸς Δημοσθένη. ὥσπερ γὰρ ἐπὶ τῶν ἰδίων
ἐγκλημάτων πολλὰ διὰ προκλήσεων κρίνεται, οὕτως καὶ τουτὶ
τὸ πρᾶγμα κέκριται. σκέψασθε γὰρ, ὦ ἄνδρες δικασταί,
οὑτωσί. ᾐτιάσατό σε, ὦ Δημόσθενες, ὁ δῆμος εἰληφέναι
εἴκοσι τάλαντα [ἐπὶ] τῇ πολιτείᾳ καὶ τοῖς νόμοις. ταῦτα σὺ
ἔξαρνος ἐγένου μὴ λαβεῖν, καὶ πρόκλησιν γράψας ἐν
ψηφίσματι προσήνεγκας τῷ δήμῳ, ἐπιτρέπων ὑπὲρ ὧν τὴν
αἰτίαν ἔσχες τῇ βουλῇ τῇ ἐξ Ἀρείου πάγου

Frag. II

col. 3 καὶ συκοφαντεῖς τὴν βουλὴν, προκλήσεις ἐκτιθεὶς καὶ ἐρωτῶν
ἐν ταῖς προκλήσεσιν, πόθεν ἔλαβες τὸ χρυσίον, καὶ τίς ἦν
σοι ὁ δούς, καὶ ποῦ. τελευτῶν δ' ἴσως ἐρωτήσεις καὶ ὅτι
ἐχρήσω λαβὼν τῷ χρυσίῳ, ὥσπερ τραπεζιτικὸν λόγον παρὰ
col. 4 τῆς βουλῆς ἀπαιτῶν. ἐγω δὲ τοὐναντίον Ι [ἡδέως ἂ]ν παρὰ
σοῦ [πυθοίμ]ην τίνος [ἂν ἕν]εκα ἡ ἐξ Ἀρείου Ι [πάγου βουλ]ὴ
ἔφη

Hyperides 5, *Against Demosthenes*

(The papyrus is badly fragmented and a large part of the speech is lost. Whereas Dinarchus 1 and Hyperides 6 are divided numerically into sections (small paragraphs), the much more fragmentary Hyperides 5 is presented according to the numbering of the fragments and the columns of the papyrus. The lacunae are so great in some sections that the sense cannot be understood, making a full translation impossible. I have not followed Colin's practice in the Budé text of proposed translations to make sense of the missing sections, for at times almost anything could fit.)

Fragment 1

(1) Gentlemen of the jury, as I was just saying to those sitting next to me, I am taken aback by this situation: that, by Zeus, everyone in the city is subject to the laws which enforce an arrangement proposed by someone against his own best interests apart from Demosthenes, and he is not subject to the decrees of the people, which you swore to uphold in your vote. No enemy of Demosthenes proposed this but the man himself, and the people voted on his instructions, just as if he had a death wish.

–   –   –   –   –

(2) And yet, gentlemen of the jury, I see that justice in this case is straightforward enough – it is in our favour and against Demosthenes. For just as in private cases many things are decided by challenges, so has this case been decided. Gentlemen of the jury, consider in this way. The people accused you, Demosthenes, of having taken twenty talents against the state and against the laws. You denied having taken this amount, and you drew up a challenge in the form of a decree which you brought before the people, handing over investigation of the accusations against you to the Council of the Areopagus

–   –   –   –   –

Fragment 2

(3) You malign the Areopagus, you issue challenges, asking in them what was the source of the gold that you took, who was the one who gave it to you, and where. Perhaps eventually you will also ask what you used the gold for when you had taken it, just as if you were asking for a bank statement from the Areopagus. I, on the contrary, (4) would be keen to hear from you why the Areopagus reported

–   –   –   –   –

Frag. III

col. 5 —   —   —   —   —

τὰς ἀποφάσεις. οὐκ ἔστι ταῦτα, ἀλλὰ πάντων φανήσονται
μάλιστα δημο[τικώ]τατα τῷ πράγματι κεχρημένοι· τοὺς μὲν
γὰρ ἀδικοῦντας ἀπέφηναν, καὶ ταῦτ' οὐχ ἑκοντες, ἀλλ' ὑπὸ
τοῦ δήμου πολλάκις ἀναγκαζόμενοι· τὸ [δὲ κο]λάσαι τοὺς
ἀδι[κοῦντα]ς οὐκ ἐφ' αὑτοῖς [ἐποί]ησαν, ἀλλ' ὑμῖν ἀπέδ[οσαν
col. 6 τοῖς κυρίοις. Δ[ημοσθένης] δ' οὐ μόνον ἐπὶ τοῦ | αὐτοῦ
ἀγῶνος οἴεται δεῖν ὑμᾶς παρακρούσασθαι διαβαλὼν τὴν
ἀπόφασιν, ἀλλὰ καὶ τοὺς ἄλλους ἀγῶνας ἅπαντας ἀφελέσθαι
ζητεῖ τοὺς τῆς πόλεως· ὑπὲρ οὗ δεῖ ὑμᾶς νυνὶ βουλεύσασθαι
προσέχοντας τὸν νοῦν, καὶ μὴ τῷ λόγῳ ὑπὸ τούτου
ἐξαπατηθῆναι. τὰς γὰρ ἀποφάσεις ταύτας τὰς ὑπὲρ τῶν
χρημάτων Ἁρπάλου πάσας ὁμοίως ἡ βουλὴ πεποίηται καὶ τὰς
αὐτὰς κατὰ πάντων, καὶ οὐδεμιᾷ προσγέγραφεν διὰ τί
ἕκαστον ἀποφαίνει, ἀλλὰ ἐπὶ κεφαλαίου γράψασα ὁπόσον
ἕκαστος εἴληφεν χρυσίον, τοῦτ' οὖν [ὀφ]ειλέτω. ἢ ἰσχύ[σει
col. 7 Δημοσθ]ένης παρ' ὑμῖ[ν τῆς κατ' αὐτοῦ] ἀπο[φάσεως μᾶλλον;]
οὐκ ἀ[ ]ες[. . .] ἀπογ[. . . .] ἀποφα[. . . .] ἔλαβεν [. .
. .]σι καὶ οἱ ἄ[λλοι πάντες.] οὐ γὰρ δή[που Δημο]σθένει
[μόνῳ τοῦ]το ἰσχυρό[ν ἔσται, τοῖς] δ' ἄλλοις ο[ὔχ. ὥστε νῦν]
οὐχ ὑπὲρ [εἴκοσι τα]λάντων δ[ικάζετε,] ἀλλ' ὑπὲρ τ[ετρακο]σίων,
οὐδ' ὑ[πὲρ ἑνὸς] ἀδικήματο[ς, ἀλλ' ὑ]πὲρ ἁπάντ[ων· ἡ γάρ] σὴ
ἀπόνο[ια, ὦ Δημό]σθενες, ὑπ[ὲρ πάντων] τῶν ἀδικούντων νῦν
προκινδυνεύει καὶ προαναισχυν[υν]τεῖ. ἐγὼ δ' ὅτι μὲν ἔλαβες
τὸ χρυσίον ἱκανὸν οἶμαι εἶναι σημεῖον τοῖς δικασταῖς τὸ τὴν
col. 8 βουλήν σου καταγνῶναι, | [ᾗ σαυτὸν ἐ]πέτρεψας· [τίνων δὲ
ἕ]νεκα ἔλαβες [καὶ ἐπὶ τ]ίσιν αἰτίαις [πᾶσαν τὴ]ν πόλιν καὶ[.
. . .]ενος [. . . .] χρυσί[. . . .]ος τοὺς [. . . ὥσ]περ εἰ[
. . . φανε]ρὸν ποιήσω. ἐπ]ειδὴ γὰρ ἦλ[θεν, ὦ ἄν]δρες
δικα[σταί, Ἅ]ρπαλος εἰς τὴν ['Αττικὴ]ν καὶ οἱ πα[ρὰ
Φιλοξέ]νου ἐξαι[τοῦντες α]ὐτὸν ἅμα [προσήχθησ]αν πρὸς [τὸν
δῆμον, τότε παρελθὼν Δημοσθένης [διεξῆλθεν] μακρὸν [λόγον,
φά]σκων οὔτε [τοῖς παρ]ὰ Φιλοξένου ἐλθο]ῦσι καλῶς [ἔχειν
τὸν] Ἅρπαλον [ἐκδοῦναι τ]ὴν πόλιν [οὔτε δεῖν] αἰτίαν
οὐ[δεμίαν τ]ῷ δήμῳ [δι' ἐκεῖνο]ν παρ' 'Α[λεξάνδρο]υ
col. 9 καταλεί[πε]σθαι, ἀσφαλέστατον δ' εἶναι τ[ῇ πόλει]

Fragment 3

(5) the reports. Quite the reverse; as you will see, they have shown a staggeringly democratic attitude in the way they have handled the matter. They reported the criminals, not willingly but because they were being compelled to do so many times by the people. They did not take on themselves to impose punishment on the guilty but handed this over to you, as is your right. But Demosthenes not only thinks that he must mislead you in connection with his own **(6)** trial when he slanders the report, but also he seeks to put an end to all the other prosecutions being heard in the city. You must keep this point in your mind now in your deliberations and not be deceived by this man's argument. The Council has produced all these reports on the matter of Harpalus' money in a uniform manner; they are the same for all of those accused. It did not add why it found against someone in any case, but in a nutshell said how much gold each man had taken and that he therefore should owe this amount. Shall Demosthenes have more credit with you **(7)** than the report against him? . . . For if this argument applies in Demosthenes' case, it also applies to the others. And so now you are passing judgement not on twenty talents but on four hundred, and not on one crime but all of them. Of all the criminals, Demosthenes, your mad conduct makes you foremost in danger and shamelessness today. I think that sufficient proof to the jurors that you took the gold is that the Council, to which you entrusted yourself, found against you. **(8)** But why you took it and for what reasons . . . the whole city . . ., I will make clear. Gentlemen of the jury, when Harpalus came to Attica, and at the same time the envoys from Philoxenus demanding him were brought into the Assembly, Demosthenes then stepped forward and delivered a long speech. He said that the city could not rightly hand over Harpalus to the envoys who had come from Philoxenus, but that it was essential that no blame be attached to the people by Alexander on account of him. **(9)** The safest course for the

τά τε χρήματα [καὶ τὸν] ἄνδρα φυλάτ[τειν] καὶ ἀναφερει[ν τὰ
χρή]ματα ἄπαντα εἰς τὴν ἀκρόπολιν, ἃ ἦλθεν ἔχων "Αρπαλος
εἰς τὴν 'Αττικήν, ἐν τῇ αὔριον ἡμέρᾳ, "Αρπαλο[ν δ' ἤ]δη
ἀποδεῖξαι τὰ χρήματα ὁπόσα ἐστίν· οὐχ ὅπως πύθοιτο τὸν
ἀριθμὸν αὐτῶν, ὡς ἔοικεν, ὁπόσα ἦν, ἀλλ' ἵνα εἰδῇ ἀφ' ὅσων
αὐτὸν δεῖ τὸν μισθὸν πράττεσθαι. καὶ καθήμενος κάτω ὑπὸ
τῇ κατατομῇ, οὗπερ εἴωθε καθῆσθαι, ἐκέλευε Μ[νησ]ίθεον τὸν
χορευτὴν ἐρωτῆσαι τὸν "Αρπαλον ὁπόσα εἴη τὰ χρήματα τὰ
ἀνοισθησόμενα εἰς τὴν ἀκρόπολιν. ὁ δ' ἀπεκρίνατο ὅτι
col. 10 ἑπτα‖κόσια τάλαντα]

– – – – –

[τα χρήματα εἶναι τη]λικ[αῦτα] αὐτὸς ἐν τῷ δ[ήμῳ] πρὸς ὑμᾶς
ε[ἰπών], ἀναφερομέν[ων τρια]κοσίων ταλα[ντων καὶ πεντ]ήκοντα
ἀνθ' ἑπτακοσίων, λ[αβὼν] τὰ εἴκοσι τάλα[ντα οὐ]δένα λόγον
ἐπ[οιήσα]το

– – – – –

ἐν τῷ δήμῳ ἑ[πτα]κόσια φήσας εἶναι τάλαντα νῦν τὰ ἡ[μί]ση
col. 11 ἀναφέρεις κα[ὶ. | . .]ω ὅτι τοῦ [. . . ἀν]ενεχθῆναι [. . .]
εἰς ἀκρόπολιν [. . τα]ῦτα τὰ πρά[γματα]

– – – – –

[. . .] ον λι [. . . .]ἔκρινον τ[.]ν [. . . οὔτ'] ἂν ἐπρί[ατο
"Αρπαλος τὰς [ ]φε[. . . ο]ὔτ' ἂν ἡ πόλις [ἐν αἰτίαις] καὶ
διαβο[λαῖς ἦν.] ἀλλὰ πάν[τω]ν τούτων, ὦ Δημό[σθενες,]

– – – – –

col. 12 [. . . σ]τατῆ[ρας ἔλαβε· σὺ δ' ὁ τῷ ψηφίσματι τοῦ σώματος
αὐτοῦ τὴν φυλακὴν καταστήσας καὶ οὔτ' ἐκλειπομένην
ἐπανορθῶν οὔτε καταλυθείσης τοὺς αἰτίους κρίνας, προῖκα
δηλονότι τὸν καιρὸν τοῦτον τεταμίευσαι; καὶ τοῖς μὲν
ἐλάττοσι ῥήτορσιν ἀπέτινεν ὁ "Αρπαλος χρυσίον, τοῖς θορύβου
μόνον καὶ κραυγῆς κυρίοις, σὲ δὲ τὸν τῶν ὅλων πραγμάτων

city, he said, was to guard both the money and Harpalus, and to carry up all of the money, which Harpalus had brought with him to Attica, to the Acropolis the next day, and that Harpalus should now make it known how much money there was. He did not do this, as it seems, so as to discover how big the sum was, but to determine from how large a sum he should claim his payment from him. Sitting down below in the niche, where he is accustomed to sit, he ordered Mnesitheus the dancer to ask Harpalus how much was the money that would be carried up to the Acropolis. And Harpalus replied seven hundred (10) talents.

—   —   —   —   —

He himself said in front of you, in the Assembly, that the sum of money was this, but he said nothing when 350 and not 700 talents were carried up to the Acropolis, having by then taken his twenty

—   —   —   —   —

You said in the Assembly that there were 700 talents, but now you can bring up only half

(11)   —   —   —   —   —

Harpalus would not have bought . . ., nor would the city have been subject to accusations and slanders. But of all these things, Demosthenes,

—   —   —   —   —

(12) he took staters. You were the one who decreed that a guard should be set up over Harpalus, but when it was found wanting you did not set it up again, nor when it was dismissed did you bring suit against those responsible, and you clearly did not take pay for the way you dealt with these circumstances. When Harpalus handed out gold to the lesser orators who can only raise a din and shout, did he overlook you who were in charge

ἐπιστάτην παρεῖδεν; καὶ τῷ τοῦτο πιστόν; τοσοῦτον δ᾽, ὦ
ἄνδρες δικασταί, τοῦ πράγματος καταπεφρόνηκεν Δημοσθένης,
μᾶλλον δέ, εἰ δεῖ μετὰ παρρησίας εἰπεῖν, ὑμῶν καὶ τῶν
col. 13 νόμων, ὥστε τὸ μὲν πρῶτον, ὡς [ἔοι]κεν, | ὁμο[λογεῖν μὲν
εἰληφέ]ναι τὰ χρήματ[α ἀλλὰ] κατακεχρῆσθαι αὐτὰ ὑμῖν
προδεδανεισμένος εἰς τὸ θεωρικόν· καὶ περιὼν Κνωσίων καὶ
οἱ ἄλλοι φίλοι αὐτοῦ ἔλεγον ὅτι ἀναγκάσουσι τὸν ἄνθρωπον
οἱ αἰτιώμενοι εἰς τὸ φανερὸν ἐνεγκεῖν ἃ οὐ βούλεται, καὶ
εἰπεῖν ὅτι τῷ δήμῳ προδεδάνεισται τὰ χρήματα εἰς τὴν
διοίκησιν. ἐπειδὴ δ᾽ ὑμῶν οἱ ἀκούσαντες πολλῷ μᾶλλον
ἠγανάκτουν ἐπὶ τοῖς κατὰ τοῦ πλήθους τοῦ ὑμετέρου λόγοις,
εἰ μὴ μόνον ἱκανὸν εἴη αὐτῷ ἰδίᾳ δεδωροδοκηκέναι, [ἀλλὰ καὶ
τὸν δῆμ]ον [. . . . .]πιμ[

col. 14   − | −   −   −   −

λέγων καὶ αἰτιώμενος, ὅτι ᾽Αλεξάνδρῳ χαριζομένη ἡ βουλὴ
ἀνελεῖν αὐτὸν βούλεται· ὥσπερ οὐ πάντας ὑμᾶς εἰδότας ὅτι
οὐδεὶς τὸν τοιοῦτον ἀναιρεῖ ὃν ἔστιν πρίασθαι, ἀλλ᾽ ὅντινα
μήτε πεῖσαι ἔστιν μήτε χρήμασιν διαφθεῖραι, τοῦτον δ[ὴ]
σκοποῦσιν ὅπως ἐκ παντὸς τρόπου ἐκποδὼν ποιήσουσιν.
κίνδυνος δ᾽ ὡς ἔοικεν ἐστὶν μὴ σύ, ὦ Δημόσθενες,
ἀπαραίτητος καὶ ἄπειστος εἶ πρὸς δωροδ[οκίαν.]
col. 15 | Μὴ νομίζ[ετε δὲ διὰ] τῆς τούτω[ν δωρο]δοκίας τὰ
τυ[χόντα τῶν] πραγμάτων [ἁλίσ]κεσθαι. ο[ὐ γὰρ ἄδηλόν] ἐστιν
ὅτι [πάντες] οἱ ἐπιβουλεύοντες τοῖς ῾Ελληνικοῖς πράγμασιν
τὰς μὲν μικρὰς πόλεις τοῖς ὅπλοις συσκευάζονται, τὰς δὲ
μεγάλας τοὺς δυναμένους ἐν αὐταῖς ὠνούμενοι, οὐδ᾽ ὅτι
Φίλιππος [τηλικ]οῦτος ἐγένετο [ἐξ ἀρχ]ῆς χρήματα δια[πέμψα]ς
εἰς Πελο[πόννη]σον καὶ Θετ[ταλίαν] καὶ τὴν ἄλλην [῾Ελλάδα],
καὶ τοὺς ἐν [δυνάμει] ὄντας ἐν [ταῖς πόλε]σιν καὶ
προ[εστῶτας]

        −   −   −   −   −

of our entire policy? Who can believe that? Gentlemen of the jury, Demosthenes has had such a contemptuous attitude to the affair, or rather, speaking frankly, to you and the laws, that at first, as it seems, **(13)** he admitted that he did take the money but said that he had used it on your behalf by borrowing it for the Theoric Fund. Cnosion and his other friends were going around saying that his accusers would force Demosthenes to reveal facts which he did not wish to, and to say that he had borrowed money for the state to meet expenditure. When those of you who heard them were even more incensed by the aspersions on your democracy, as if it was not enough for him to have taken bribes himself but he [thought it necessary also to involve] the people

(14) –   –   –   –   –

speaking and making accusations that the Council was seeking Alexander's favour and so wanted to destroy him – as if you all did not know that no one destroys the type of man who can be bought, but men plot to get out of the way by any and all means the man who cannot be persuaded or corrupted with bribes. There is a danger, as it seems, Demosthenes, that you are not moved by prayers and are resistant to taking bribes!

(15) Do not consider that only matters of less importance are adversely affected by the venality of these men. It is obvious that all who plot to win power in Greece seize control of the smaller cities by arms and the larger ones by buying the powerful citizens in them. Philip became so powerful because from the very beginning he sent money to the Peloponnese, Thessaly, and the rest of Greece, and [he bought] those in power and with authority in the cities

–   –   –   –   –

Frag. IV

col. 16   –   –   –   –   –

col. 17 [τερα]τεύῃ, καὶ οὐχ ἅπασιν οἴει φανερὸν εἶναι ὅτι, φάσκων
ὑπὲρ τοῦ δήμου λέγειν, ὑπὲρ ['Αλεξά]νδρου φανερῶς
[ἐδημηγ]όρεις; ἐγὼ γὰρ [οἶμαι καὶ] ἔμπροσθεν [γνῶναι]
ἅπαντας ὅτι [τοῦτ' ἐ]ποίησας καὶ περὶ Θηβαίων καὶ περὶ τῶν
ἄλλων ἁπάντων, καὶ ὅτι χρήματα εἰς [ταῦτα] δοθέντα ἐκ τῆς
['Ασίας αὐ]τὸς σαυτῷ [ἰδίᾳ περιπ]οιησάμε[νος κατηνάλω]σας τὰ
[πολλὰ· καὶ νῦν δὲ ναυ]τικοῖς ἐργάζῃ χ[ρημα]σιν καὶ ἐκδόσεις
δί[δως] καί, πριάμενος ο[ἰκί]αν [ ]μο[ ]ιυ[ ] πα[ ]ν τω[ ]ρῳ,
οὐκ οἰκεῖς ἐ[ν Π]ειραιεῖ, ἀλλ' ἐξορμεῖς ἐκ τῆς πόλεως. δεῖ
δὲ τὸν δίκαιον δημαγωγὸν [σω]τῆρα τῆς [ἑαυτοῦ πατρίδος
εἶναι, μὴ δραπέτην.]

col. 18 ['Επειδὴ δὲ νῦν "Αρπαλος οὕτως ἐξαίφνης] πρὸς τὴν
Ἑλλάδα προσέ[πε]σεν ὥστε μηδένα προαισθέσθαι, τὰ δ' ἐν
Πελοποννήσῳ καὶ τῇ ἄλλῃ Ἑλλάδι οὕτως ἔχοντα κατέλαβεν
ὑπὸ τῆς ἀφίξεως τῆς Νικάνορος καὶ τῶν ἐπιταγμάτων ὧν
ἧκεν φέρων παρ' 'Αλεξάνδρου περί τε τῶν φυγάδων καὶ περὶ
τοῦ τοὺς κοινοὺς συλλόγους 'Αχαιῶν τε καὶ 'Αρκάδων [καὶ
Β]οι[ω]τῶ[ν καὶ τῶν ἄλλων μὴ γίγνεσθαι]

    –   –   –   –   –

col. 19 ταῦτα σὺ πα[ρεσκεύ]ακας τῷ ψηφ[ίσματι], συλλαβὼν τὸ[ν
"Αρπα]λον, καὶ τοὺς μὲν Ἕλληνας ἅπαντας πρεσβεύεσθαι
πεπ[οίη]κας ὡς 'Αλέξανδρον, οὐκ ἔχοντας ἄλλην οὐδεμίαν
ἀποσ[τρο]φήν, τοὺς δὲ σ[ατράπας], οἳ αὐτοὶ ἂν ἧκο[ν ἑκόν]τες
πρὸς ταύτη[ν τὴν] δύναμιν, ἔχοντες τὰ χρήματα καὶ τοὺς
στρατιώτας ὅσους ἕκαστος αὐτῶν εἶχεν, τούτους σύμπαντας
οὐ μόνον κεκώλυκας ἀποστῆναι ἐκείνου τῇ συλλήψει τῇ
'Αρπάλου, ἀλλὰ καὶ[. . ἕ]καστον

    –   –   –   –   –

Fragment 4

(16)   –   –   –   –   –

(17) you make monstrous claims, and do not realise that what you were doing is clear to everyone, how you alleged that you were speaking in the best interests of the people but clearly were speaking on behalf of Alexander? I think also that in the past everyone knew that you acted in this way over the Thebans, and over all of the rest, and that you diverted to yourself money sent from Asia for these affairs and spent the majority of it, and now you are involved in maritime commerce and make bottomry loans, and have bought a house . . . you don't live in the Piraeus but anchor yourself outside the city! A just leader of the people should be the saviour of his own country, not a deserter.

(18) And just now, when Harpalus so suddenly descended on Greece that he took everyone by surprise, and he found the Peloponnese and the rest of Greece in this state of affairs owing to the arrival of Nicanor and the orders which he brought with him from Alexander concerning both the exiles and the prohibition of the joint military levies of the Achaeans, Arcadians, Boeotians and the rest

–   –   –   –   –

(19) You brought about this situation thanks to your decree and the arrest of Harpalus. You made the whole of Greece send envoys to Alexander, for they had no other avenue to pursue, and as for the satraps, who would willingly have joined this force themselves, each with their own money and army, not only did you prevent them from revolting *en masse* from Alexander by the arrest of Harpalus but also . . . each one of them

–   –   –   –   –

Frag. V

col. 20   –   –   –   –   –

[ὑπὸ Δη]μοσθένο[υς ἀπο]σταλείς, παρὰ [δ᾽ Ὀλυμ]πιάδι Καλλίας
ὁ [Χαλ]κιδεύς, ὁ Ταυροσθένους ἀδελφός· τούτους γὰρ ἔγραψε
Δημοσθένης ᾽Αθηναίους εἶναι καὶ χρῆται τούτοις πάντων
μάλιστα. καὶ οὐδὲν θαυμαστόν· οὐδέποτε γὰρ οἶμαι ἐπὶ τῶν
αὐτῶν μένων εἰκότως φί[λους] τοὺς ἀπ᾽ Εὐρίπου κέκτηται.
    Εἶτα σὺ περὶ [φιλ]ί̣ας πρὸς ἐμὲ τολ[μήσεις αὐτίκα μά]λα
col. 21 [λέγειν]; . . | . . . [ταύτην τὴν φιλίαν διέ]λυσας αὐ[τὸ]ς
ὅ[τε χρ]υσ̣ίον κατὰ τῆς [πατρί]δος ἔλαβες καὶ [μετ]εβάλο[υ]·
καὶ κατα[γέλα]στον μὲν σαυτὸν ἐποίησας, κατῃ[σχυν]ας δὲ
τοὺς ἐκ τῶν [ἔμπρ]οσθεν χρόνων [τῶν α]ὐτῶν τί σοι
προ[ελομέ]νους· καὶ ἔξον [ἡμῖν] λαμπροτάτοις [εἶναι] παρὰ τῷ
δήμῳ [καὶ τὸ]ν ὑπόλοιπον [βίον ὑ]πὸ δόξης χρησ[τῆς
πα]ραπεμφθῆν[αι, ἄπα]ντα ταῦτα ἀνέτρ[εψας, κα]ὶ οὐκ αἰσχύνει
νυνὶ τηλικοῦτος ὢν ὑπὸ μειρακίων κρινόμενος περὶ
δωροδοκίας. καίτοι ἔδει τοὐναντίον ὑφ᾽ ὑμῶν παιδεύεσθαι
τοὺς νεωτέρους τῶν ῥητόρων, καὶ εἴ τι προπετέστερον |
col. 22 ἔπραττον ἐπιτιμᾶσθαι καὶ κολάζεσθαι. νῦν δὲ τοὐναντίον οἱ
νέοι τοὺς ὑπὲρ ἑξήκοντα ἔτη σωφρονίζουσιν. διόπερ, ὦ
ἄνδρες δικασταί, δικαίως ἂν ὀργίζοισθε Δημοσθένει εἰ, καὶ
δόξης ἱκανῆς καὶ πλούτου πολλοῦ δ[ι ὑ]μᾶς μετεσχηκώ[ς], μηδ᾽
ἐπὶ γήρως [ὁ]δῷ κήδεται τῆς πατρίδος. ἀλλ᾽ ὑμεῖς μὲν
ᾐσχύνεσθε ἐπὶ τῆ[ς . . . . υ] τοὺς περιεστηκότας τῶν
Ἑλλήνων ὅτε [τινῶν] κατεχειροτονεῖτε, εἰ τοιούτο[υς καὶ]
δημαγωγοὺς κα[ὶ στρ]ατηγοὺς καὶ φύλακας τῶν πραγμ[άτων]

col. 23   – | –   –   –   –

Frag. VI

col. 24 οὐ γάρ ἐστιν ὁμοίως [δεινὸ]ν εἴ τις ἔλα[βεν], ἀλλ᾽ εἰ ὅθεν μὴ
[δεῖ, ο]ὐδέ γ᾽ ὁμοίως [ἀδι]κοῦσιν οἱ ἰδιῶται [οἱ λαβ]όντες τὸ
χρυσίον καὶ οἱ ῥήτορες καὶ οἱ στρατηγοί. διὰ τί; ὅτι τοῖς
μὲν ἰδιώταις ῞Αρπαλος ἔδωκεν φυλάττειν τὸ χρυσίον. οἱ δὲ
στρατηγοὶ καὶ οἱ ῥήτο[ρες πρ]άξεων ἕνεκα [εἰλή]φασιν. οἱ δὲ
νό[μοι τ]οῖς μὲν ἀδικοῦσιν ἁπλᾶ, τοῖς δὲ δω[ροδοκοῦσι]ν
δεκαπλᾶ [τὰ ὀφλήματα προστάτ[τουσιν] ἀποδιδόναι· [ὥσπερ
οὖ]ν τὸ τίμη[μα . .]σαι ἔστιν ἐκ [τῶν νόμ]ων τούτοις [. . .
]ς, οὕτω καὶ [. . .]ι παρ᾽ ὑμῶν [. . .]σι κατ᾽ αὐτῶν [. . .
]αι. ὅπερ γὰρ [καὶ ἐν τ]ῷ δήμῳ εἶ[πον, π]ολλὰ ὑμεῖς, ὦ

Fragment 5

(20)   –   –   –   –   –

sent by Demosthenes, and, with Olympias, Callias the Chalcidean, the brother of Taurosthenes. Demosthenes proposed these men for Athenian citizenship, and he consorts with them in particular more than anyone else. No need to be amazed at this! I think that since he is never able to hold to the same policy himself he has logically made friends with those from the Euripus!

Will you dare, then, to speak to me about friendship . . . **(21)** You yourself destroyed that friendship when you took gold against your country and changed your loyalties. You made yourself a laughing stock and you shamed those who in previous years shared in some aspects of your policy. When it was possible for us to become the most distinguished in the eyes of the people and to have enjoyed the best of reputations for the rest of our lives you upset all of this, and you are not ashamed now at your advanced age to be tried by young men for accepting bribes. And yet, the opposite should apply: the younger orators should be educated by people like you, and if they did something foolhardy **(22)** they should be reprimanded and punished by you. But the reverse now applies: the young men are correcting those over sixty! Therefore, gentlemen of the jury, rightly might you feel anger towards Demosthenes, who because of you acquired a good reputation and much wealth but now even in his twilight years he has no loyalty to his country. However, you used to feel shame . . . before those of the Greeks who were present, when you convicted certain men, if you [gave the impression of having] such men as leaders of the people and generals and overseers of state affairs

–   **(23)**   –   –   –   –

Fragment 6

(24) For if someone takes money this is not as terrible as taking it from an improper source, and the private individuals who took the gold are not guilty in the same way as the orators and the generals. Why? Because Harpalus gave the gold to the private individuals for safe-keeping; the generals and the orators took it for particular services. The laws stipulate that ordinary criminals should pay back the simple sum they took, but in the case of those taking bribes ten times the amount they have taken; as then the punishment . . . can be inflicted by law against these men . . . As I said in the Assembly,

col. 25 ἄνδρες δικασταί, δί[δοτε ἑ]κόντες τοῖς Ι στρατηγοῖς καὶ τοῖς
ῥήτορσιν ὠφελεῖσθαι, οὐ τῶν νόμων αὐτοῖς δεδωκότων τοῦτο
ποιεῖν, ἀλλὰ τῆς ὑμετέρας πραότητος καὶ φιλανθρωπίας, ἐν
μόνον παραφυλάττοντες, ὅπως δι᾽ ὑμᾶς καὶ μὴ καθ᾽ ὑμῶν
ἔσται τὸ λαμβανόμενον· καὶ Δημοσθένη καὶ Δημάδην ἀπ᾽
αὐτῶν τῶν ἐν τῇ πόλει ψηφισμάτων καὶ προξενιῶν οἶμαι
πλείω ἢ ἑξήκοντα τάλαντα ἑκάτερον εἰληφέναι, ἔξω τῶν
βασιλικῶν καὶ τῶν παρ᾽ Ἀλεξάνδρου. οἷς δὲ μήτε ταῦτα
ἱκανά ἐστιν μήτ᾽ ἐκεῖνα, ἀλλ᾽ ἤδη ἐπ᾽ αὐτῷ τῷ σώματι τῆς
πόλεως δῶρα εἰλήφασι, πῶς οὐκ ἄξιον τούτους κολάζειν

col. 26 ἐστίν; ἀλλὰ τῶν μὲν ἰδιωτῶν ὑμῶν ἐάν Ι τις ἀρχήν τιν[α
ἄρχων] δι᾽ ἄγνοιαν ἢ [δι᾽ ἀπει]ρίαν ἁμάρτῃ τ[ι, οὗτος] ὑπὸ
τούτων κ[αταρρη]τορευθεὶς ἐν τῷ δικαστηρίῳ ἢ ἀποθανεῖται ἢ
ἐκ τῆς πατρίδος ἐκπεσεῖται· αὐτ[οὶ δὲ] τηλικαῦτα
ἀδικήσαντες τὴν πόλιν οὐδεμιᾶς τιμωρία[ς τεύ]ξονται; καὶ
Κον[ων] μὲν ὁ Παιανιεύς, [ὅτι] ὑπὲρ τοῦ υἱοῦ ἔλαβεν τὸ
θεωρικὸν ἀπ[οδη]μοῦντος, πέντε δραχμῶν ἕνεκεν [ἱκε]τεύων
ὑμᾶς τάλαντον ὦφλεν ἐν τῷ δικαστηρίῳ τούτων
κατηγορούντων· καὶ Ἀριστόμαχος ἐπιστάτης γενόμενος τῆς
Ἀκαδημείας, ὅτι σκαφεῖον ἐκ τῆς παλαίστρας μετενεγκὼν
εἰς τὸν κῆπον τὸν αὐτοῦ πλησίον ὄντα ἐχρῆτο καὶ ἔφη

col. 27   —   —   —   —

Frag. VII

col. 28   —   —   —   —

[οὐ μέντοι] ἡμᾶς ὁ δῆμ[ος ἐν τῷ] μετὰ ταῦτα χρ[όνῳ] οὐκ εἴα
προσ[ιέναι] αὐτῷ οὐδὲ δια[λέγε]σθαι, ἀλλὰ καὶ συ[μβούλοις
ἐχ]ρῆτο καὶ σ[υνηγόροις] . . . . . [τοῦ δ]ὲ ἐπιόν[τος . . .
ἐ]πὶ τὴν δι[οίκησιν τῶ]ν αὐτοῦ ἅπασαν [ταμ]ί[αν
ἐχειροτόνησ[εν, ὑπ]ολαμβάνων [χ]άριν αὐτῷ παρ᾽ ἡμῶν
ὀφείλεσθαι, ὅπερ δίκαιον ἦν. καὶ πρὸς τούτοις ἀγώνων ἡμῖν
ὕστερον πολλῶν γεγενημένων [ἐξ ἐ]κείνων τῶν [πραγ]μάτων

col. 29 [και αὐ]τοῦ τοῦ π]ολέμου, οὐδε[πώποτε ἡ]μῶν ο[ὗ]τοι
[κατε]ψηφίσαντο, ἀλλ᾽ ἐκ πάντων ἔσωσαν, [ὅπερ μ]έγιστον καὶ
[ἀξιοπι]στότατον τῆς [τοῦ δήμ]ου [εὐ]νοίας [σημεῖον. καὶ
γρά]ψαι, ὦ [Δημόσθενες,]

gentlemen of the jury, you allow the **(25)** generals and the orators to enrich themselves substantially, when it is not the laws giving them the chance to do this but your toleration and philanthropy. You are careful about just one point, that the money which is taken should be by your approval and not against your interests. Demosthenes and Demades have each received, I think, more than sixty talents from actual decrees passed in the city and from proxenies, apart from money from the Great King and from Alexander. If neither of these sources is sufficient for them, and they have now taken bribes against the very life of the city, how then is it not right to punish them? If one of you private citizens **(26)** serves in some office and makes an error owing to ignorance or inexperience, he will be overcome in a court of law by the rhetoric of these men, and will either be executed or banished from his country. Shall they themselves when they have done so much damage to the city, escape without punishment? Conon of Paeania took the theoric allowance for his son who was away from home, and, when he was prosecuted by these men for it, despite appealing to you in court, he was fined a talent for the sake of five drachmas. And also Aristomachus, who was in charge of the Academy, because he brought a spade from the wrestling-school across to his own garden, which was close by, and used it, and said

(27)   –   –   –   –   –

Fragment 7

(28)   –   –   –   –   –

The people did not prevent us approaching or conversing with them in the period after this, but used us as advisers and counsellors . . . but in the following . . . they elected him treasurer-in-chief of all their financial affairs, considering that we owed him a debt of gratitude – as was only right. And in addition to this, even though we were put on trial many times on account of our actions in this period and **(29)** from the war itself, these men never voted against us but saved us from everything, thereby showing the greatest and most positive sign of the people's goodwill. And to propose, Demosthenes,

−   −   −   −   −

[ὑ]πὸ το[ῦ ψη]φίσματος [ἡλωκέ]ναι σε αὐτόμ[ατον, οὐ]κ
ἐποίησαν [. . .] γενομεν[

−   −   −   −   −

col. 30 [ὁ δῆ]μος ἐποίησεν, ὥστ', αὐτὸς ὑπὸ τῆς τύχης ἀφαιρεθεὶς
τὸν στέφανον, ἡμῶν ὃν ἔδωκεν οὐκ ἀφείλετο. οὕτως οὖν
ἡμῖν τοῦ δήμου προσενηνεγμένου, οὐ παντ' ἂν δι[καίως] αὐτῷ
[ὑπη]ρετοῖμεν, καὶ, εἰ δ[έοι, ἀ]ποθνήσκοιμεν [ὑπὲρ] αὐτοῦ; ἐγὼ
[μὲν οἶμαι· ἀλλὰ σ]ὺ κατα

−   −   −   −   −

σ]θαι εὐεργετήματα· οὐ γὰρ τὴν ἑτέρων πατρίδα εὖ ποιεῖν
[αὐ]τοὺς, ἀλλὰ τὴν ἑαυ[τῶν, ο]ὐδὲ

−   −   −   −   −

col. 31 αν] καὶ λόγου δύναμιν ἀποδεικνύμενος διατετέλεκας. καὶ ὅτε
μὲν ἡγοῦ τὴν βουλὴν ἀποφανεῖν τοὺς ἔχοντας τὸ χρυσίον,
πολεμικὸς ὢν καὶ ταράττων τὴν πόλιν, ἵνα τὴν ζήτησιν
ἐκκρούοις· ἐπειδὴ δὲ ἀναβάλοιτο τὸ ἀποφῆναι ἡ βουλή, οὔπω
φάσκουσα εὑρηκέναι, τότ' ἐν, τῷ δήμῳ συγχωρῶν 'Αλεξάνδρῳ
καὶ τοῦ Διὸς καὶ τοῦ Ποσειδῶνος εἶ[ναι εἰ βούλ]οιτο

col. 32   −   −   −   − | −

ἐβούλετ[ο ἐν τῇ ἀγορᾷ] στῆσαι εἰκό[να 'Αλεξάν]δρου βασιλέως,
τοῦ ἀνι]κήτου θε[οῦ]

—   —   —   —   —

that you were inevitably caught by the decree, they did not

—   —   —   —   —

(**30**) the people so acted that, although owing to chance they were deprived of their crown of victory, they did not deprive us of the crown they had granted. Since the people acted in this manner towards us, should we not serve them justly in everything, and if necessary die for them? I think so; you, however,

—   —   —   —   · —

public-spirited actions; for it was not that they were benefitting the lands of other people, but their own

—   —   —   —   —

(**31**) and you have persisted in showing off the power of your eloquence. When you expected that the Council would report those who had the gold you grew antagonistic and ready to throw the city into confusion in order that you might frustrate the enquiry; when the Areopagus delayed its report, saying that it had not yet discovered the facts, you then in the Assembly conceded that Alexander could be the son of Zeus and of Poseidon if he wanted

(**32**)   —   —   —   —   —

he wanted to erect in the Agora a statue of King Alexander, the invincible god

—   —   —   —   —

Frag, VIII

col. 33   –   –   –   –   –

col. 34 [τῶν ἐγ]κλημάτων, καὶ κήρυγμα περὶ [τού]των ἐποιήσατο· οἱ
δὲ [ἀντὶ] τοῦ ἀποδόντες ἃ ἔλαβον ἀπηλλάχθαι, τιμωρίας καθ᾽
αὑτῶν καὶ ζητήσεις ἔγραφον. τοὺς δὴ τὸ μὲν ἐξ ἀρχῆς
ἀδικήσαντας καὶ δωροδοκήσαντας, ἀδείας δ᾽ αὐτοῖς δοθείσης
μὴ ἀποδόντας τὸ χρυσίον, τί χρὴ ποιεῖν; ἐᾶν ἀτιμωρήτους;
ἀλλ᾽ αἰσχρόν, ὦ ἄνδρες δικασταί, ἰδίων ἔνεκα ἐγκ[λη]μάτων
πόλεως σωτηρίαν κινδυνεύειν. οὐ γὰρ ἔ[στι]ν ὑμᾶς τούτων
ἀποψηφίσασθαι, μὴ [οἰομένους] ἀναδέξα[σθαι δεῖν ἀδική]μα[τα]

col. 35   – | –   –   –   –

Μ[ὴ τοίνυν, ὦ ἄνδρες] δικασ[ταί, προτιμᾶτε] τὴν τούτω[ν
πλεο]νεξίαν τ[ῆς ὑμετέ]ρας αὐτῶν [σωτηρί]ας· μηδὲ
λη[μμάτων] αἰσχρῶν ἕν[εκα τὸν] πόλεμον, ἀλ[λὰ πρα]γμάτων
col. 36 ἀξιω[τέρων | καὶ] μεταλ[λ]α[γῆς ἀμείνονος] ποιή[σησθε.]

   –   –   –   –   –

Frag. IX

col. 37   –   –   –   –   –

ὑ]πὲρ αὐτῶν ἐ[. .]οις τὴν εἰρή[νην ἐπ]οιησάμεθα. [. . .]
βουλευω

   –   –   –   –   –

col. 38 αὐτῷ παρ᾽ ἑκάστου ἡμῶν γίγνεσθαι· καὶ τὸ μὲν κατηγορεῖν
ἐν τῷ δικαστηρίῳ καὶ ἐξελέγχειν τοὺς εἰληφότας τὰ χρήματα
καὶ δεδωροδοκηκότας κατὰ τῆς πατρίδος ἡ[μῖν] προσέταξεν
[τοῖς ἡρημένοις] κατη[γόροις], τὸ δ᾽ ἀπ[οφῆναι τοὺς ε]ἰληφότας
[ἀπέδωκεν τ]ῇ βουλῇ [τῇ ἐξ Ἀρείου] πάγου, ἣ [τούτους εἰς
τ]ὸν δῆ[μον ἀπέδει]ξεν, τὸ [δὲ κολάσαι τ]οὺς [ἀδικοῦντας ὑμῖν]

   –   –   –   –   –

col. 39 [ἐξ Ἀρείου] πάγου. ἐὰν δὲ ἡ ψῆφος μὴ ἀκόλουθος γένηται
τοῖς νόμοις καὶ τοῖς δικαίοις, τοῦτο δή, ὦ ἄνδρες δικασταί,
παρ᾽ ὑμῖν ἔσται καταλελειμμένον. διόπερ δεῖ πάντας ὑμᾶ[ς]

Fragment 8

(33)   –   –   –   –   –

(34) of the accusations, and made a proclamation about them. But these men proposed penalties and investigations against themselves instead of handing back what they took and ending the affair. What must we do to those who from the outset committed crimes and took bribes, but when immunity was granted to them did not return the gold? Shall we allow them to go unpunished? Gentlemen of the jury, it would be shocking to endanger the safety of the city as a result of the indictments brought against individuals. You cannot acquit these men unless you think that you must share the responsibility for their crimes

–   **(35)** –   –   –   –

Gentlemen of the jury, do not prefer their greed to your own safety. Do not wage war for their shamelessly taking money for themselves, but for more worthy matters **(36)** and a change to better fortunes

–   –   –   .   –   –

Fragment 9

(37)   –   –   –   –   –

on their behalf . . . we made the peace

–   –   –   –   –

(38) to be given to it by each of us. The people instructed us as the selected prosecutors to undertake the prosecuting in court and the convicting of those who had taken the money and accepted bribes against their country; the reporting of those who took the money it gave to the Council of the Areopagus, which made the identity of these men known to the people; and the punishment of the wrongdoers it allotted to you.

–   –   –   –   –

(39) from the Areopagus. If the vote is not in accordance with the laws and with justice, then, gentlemen of the jury, this decision will live with you forever. Therefore you must all

— — — — —

[εἰς τὴ]ν σωτη[ρίαν τῆς π]όλεως και τὴν ἄλ[λη]ν εὐδαιμονίαν
τὴν ὑπάρχουσαν ὑμῖν ἐν τῇ χώρᾳ, καὶ κοινῇ πᾶσι καὶ ἰδίᾳ
ἑνὶ ἑκάστῳ, καὶ εἰς τοὺς τάφους τοὺς τῶν προγόνων,
τιμωρήσασθαι τοὺς ἀδικοῦντας ὑπὲρ ἁπάσης τῆς πόλεως, καὶ
μήτε λόγου παράκλησιν [μήτε]

— — — — —

col. 40 [τοὺς εἰληφό]τας δῶ[ρα κατὰ τῆς] πατρίδος καὶ τ[ῶν] νόμων·
μηδ[ὲ τοῖς] δακρύοις τοῖς Ἀγ[νω]νίδου προσέχετε [τὸν] νοῦν,
ἐκεῖνο λο[γιζό]μενοι, ὅτι ἀτυχ[ήσαν]τι μὲν

— — — — —

οὗτος δ’ ἂν [κλαίων] οὐ δίκαια ποιήσ[ειεν], ὥσπερ καὶ οἱ
λ[ῃσταὶ] οἱ ἐπὶ τοῦ τροχ[οῦ κλαί]οντες, ἐξὸν αὐ[τοῖς] μὴ
ἐμβαίνε[ιν εἰς] τὸ πλοῖον. οὕτω καὶ Δη[μο]σθένης τί
προσ[ῆκον] κλαιήσει, ἐ[ξὸν αὐτῷ] μὴ λαμ[βάνειν τὰ χρήματα¡]

— — — — —

–   –   –   –   –

to the safety of the city and its prosperity in general, which each and every one of you together and as individuals enjoy in this country, and to the tombs of your forefathers, and punish the guilty ones on behalf of the whole city, and not be swayed either by their verbal appeals

–   –   –   ·–   –

(40) those who have taken bribes against their country and its laws. Do not pay attention to the tears of Hagnonides, considering that to a person who has been unlucky

–   –   –   –   –

this man would have no right to cry, as is the case with pirates who weep upon the wheel when they need not have embarked in the boat. The same thing applies to Demosthenes – what will he make as a fitting excuse for tears when he need not have taken the money?

–   –   –   –   –

ΥΠΕΡΕΙΔΟΥ

6. ΕΠΙΤΑΦΙΟΣ

1 Τῶν μὲν λόγων τῶν μελλόντων ῥηθήσεσ[θαι ἐπὶ] τῷδε τῷ τάφῳ
[περί τε] Λεωσθένους τοῦ στρατηγοῦ καὶ περὶ τῶν ἄλλων τῶν
μετ' ἐκείνου τετελευτηκότων ἐν τῷ πολέμῳ, ὡς ἦσαν ἄνδρες
ἀγαθοί, μάρτ[υς αὐτὸς ὁ χ]ρόνος ὁ σ[. . . . .]ῳ τας πρ[. . .
. .]ς ἀνθρω[π . . . . .]ιν πω κα[. . . . .]ἑ[ώ]ρακε ω[. . . . .]ἐν
τῷ π]άντι αἰῶ[νι . . . . . γ]εγενη[μέν . . . οὔτε] ἄνδρας
[ἀμείνους τῶν] τετελευτηκότων οὔτε πρ[άξεις μεγαλο-
2 πρεπεστ[έρας. διὸ] καὶ μάλιστα [φοβοῦ]μαι, μή μοι συμβῇ τὸν
λόγον ἐλάττ[ω φαίν]εσθαι τῶν ἔργων τῶν γεγενημένων. πλὴν
κατ' [ἐκεῖ]νό γε πάλιν θα[ρρῶ, ὅ]τι τὰ ὑπ' ἐμοῦ ἐκλειπόμενα
ὑμεῖς οἱ ἀκούοντες προσθήσετε· οὐ γὰρ ἐν τοῖς τυχοῦσιν οἱ
λόγοι ῥηθήσονται ἀλλ' ἐν αὐτοῖς τοῖς μάρτυσι τῶν ἐκείνοις
3 πεπραγμένων. ἄξιον δέ ἐστιν ἐπαινεῖν τὴν μὲν πόλιν ἡμῶν τῆς
προαιρέσεως ἕνεκεν, τὸ προελέσθαι ὅμοια καὶ ἔτι σεμνότερα καὶ
καλλίω τῶν πρότερον αὐτῇ πεπραγμένων, τοὺς δὲ τετελευτηκότας τῆς ἀνδρείας τῆς ἐν τῷ πολέμῳ, τὸ μὴ καταισχῦναι
τὰς τῶν προγόνων ἀρετάς, τὸν δὲ στρατηγὸν Λεωσθένη διὰ
ἀμφότερα· τῆς τε γὰρ προαιρέσεως εἰσηγητὴς τῇ πόλει
ἐγένετο, καὶ τῆς στρατείας ἡγεμὼν τοῖς πολίταις κατέστη.
4   Περὶ μὲν οὖν τῆς πόλεως διεξιέναι τὸ καθ' ἕκαστον ὧν
πρότερον πᾶσαν τὴν Ἑλλάδα εὐεργέτηκεν οὔτε ὁ χρόνος ὁ
παρὼν ἱκανός, οὔτε ὁ καιρὸς ἁρμόττων τῷ μακρολογεῖν, οὔτε
ῥᾴδιον ἕνα ὄντα τοσαύτας καὶ τηλικαύτας πράξεις ἐπελθεῖν καὶ
μνημονεῦσαι. ἐπὶ κεφαλαίου δὲ οὐκ ὀκνήσω εἰπεῖν περὶ αὐτῆς·
5 ὥσπερ [γὰρ] ὁ ἥλιος πᾶσαν τὴν οἰκουμένην ἐπέρχεται, τὰ[ς μὲν]
ὥρας διακρίνων κατὰ τὸ πρέπον καὶ καλῶ[ς πάντα καθ]ιστάς,
τοῖς δὲ σ[ώφροσι καὶ ἐπι]εικέσι τ[ῶν ἀνθρώπ]ων ἐπιμ[ελούμενος
κ]αὶ γεν[έσεως καὶ τροφῆ]ς κὰι [καρπῶν κ]αὶ τῶν ἄ[λλων
ἁ[πά]ντων τῶν εἰς τὸν βίον χρησίμων, οὕτως καὶ ἡ πόλις ἡμῶν
διατελεῖ τοὺς μὲν κακοὺς κολάζουσα, τοῖς δὲ δικαίοις
β[οηθοῦσα], τὸ δὲ ἴσον ἀν[τὶ] τῆς ἀδι[κίας ἄπασιν [ἀπονέμουσα,
τ]οῖς δὲ ἰδί[οις κινδύνοις κα]ὶ δαπάναι[ς κοινὴν ἄδει]αν τοῖς
6 Ἕλλη[σιν παρασκευάζουσα. [ἀλλὰ περὶ μὲ]ν τῶν κοινῶ[ν ἔργων
τῆς πόλ[εως ὥσπερ [προεῖπον φρά]σαι [παρ]αλείψω, περὶ δὲ
Λεωσθέν]ους καὶ τῶν ἄλ[λων τοὺς λόγ]ους ποιήσομ[αι. νῦ]ν δὲ

Hyperides 6, *Funeral Oration*

(1) Time itself will be the witness of the words to be spoken over this grave about Leosthenes the general and the others who died with him in the war, that they were good and brave men.

—   —   —   —   —

neither braver men than those who died nor more magnificent deeds. **(2)** For this reason I am very much afraid that my speech may seem inadequate compared with the deeds they performed. However, I take heart by this thought: that you who hear me will add what is left unsaid by me. For my words will not be spoken before an uninformed audience but before actual witnesses of what they did. **(3)** It is right to praise both our city for its policies, for its course of action not just equalling but even more notable and grand than its achievements in the past, and those who died for their bravery in the war, for not shaming the virtue of their ancestors; and on both accounts the general Leosthenes: for he was both the proposer of the city's policy and the citizens' general on campaign.

(4) In the case of Athens, there is neither sufficient time to recount each of the benefits conferred by it in times past on the whole of Greece, nor is the occasion suitable for speaking at length, nor is it easy for one man to deal with and recall so many deeds such as these. However, I will not hesitate to say something about the city in summary fashion. **(5)** Just as the sun traverses the whole world, dividing up the seasons as is fitting and establishing everything for the best, and, for men who are wise and good, controlling their birth and nourishment and crops and all the other necessities of life, so our city continues to punish wrongdoers, helps the just, deals out fairness instead of injustice to all men, and at its own danger and cost provides a common freedom from fear for the Greeks. **(6)** However, as I said before, I will pass over discussion of the public achievements of the city, and I will make Leosthenes and the others the subject of my speech.

πόθεν ἄρξωμα[ι λέγων] ἢ τίνος πρῶτον μνησθῶ; πότερα περὶ
τοῦ γένους αὐτῶν ἑκάστου διεξέλθω; ἀλλ' εὔηθες εἶναι
7 ὑπολαμβάνω· τὸν μὲν γὰρ ἄλλους τινὰς ἀνθρώπους
ἐγκωμιάζοντα, οἳ πολλαχόθεν εἰς μίαν πόλιν συνεληλυθότες
οἰκοῦσι γένος ἴδιον ἕκαστος συνεισενεγκάμενος, τοῦτον μὲν
δεῖ κατ' ἄνδρα γενεαλογεῖν ἕκαστον· περὶ δὲ Ἀθηναίων ἀνδρῶν
τοὺς λόγους ποιούμενον, οἷς ἡ κοινὴ γένεσις α[ὐτόχ]θοσιν
οὖσιν ἀνυπέρβλητον τὴν εὐγένειαν ἔχει, περίεργον ἡγοῦμαι
8 εἶναι ἰδίᾳ τὰ γένη ἐγκωμιάζειν. ἀλλὰ περὶ τῆς παιδείας αὐτῶν
ἐπιμνησθῶ, καὶ ὡς ἐν πολλῇ σωφροσύνῃ παῖδες ὄντ[ες
ἐτράφησαν καὶ ἐπαιδε[ύθησαν], ὅπερ εἰώθασίν [τινες ποι]ε[ῖν; ἀλλ'
οἶμαι π[άντας] εἰδέναι ὅτι τούτο[υ ἕνεκα] τοὺς παῖδας
παιδεύομεν, ἵνα ἄνδρες ἀγαθοὶ γ[ίγνων]ται· τοὺς δὲ
γεγενημένους ἐν τῷ πολεμῳ ἄνδρας ὑπερβάλλοντας τῇ ἀρετῇ
πρόδηλόν ἐστιν ὅτι παῖδες ὄντες καλῶς ἐπαιδεύθησαν.
9 ἁπλούστατον οὖν ἡγοῦμαι εἶναι τὴν ἐν τῷ πολέμῳ διεξελθεῖν
ἀρετήν, καὶ ὡς πολλῶν ἀγαθῶν αἴτιοι γεγένηνται τῇ πατρίδι
καὶ τοῖς ἄλλοις Ἕλλησιν. ἄρξομαι δὲ πρῶτον ἀπὸ τοῦ
στρατηγοῦ· καὶ γὰρ δίκαιον.
10 Λεωσθένης γὰρ ὁρῶν τὴν Ἑλλάδα πᾶσαν τεταπεινωμένην καὶ
[. . .] ἐπτη[χυῖ]αν, κατεφθαρμένην ὑπὸ τῶν δωροδοκούντων
παρὰ Φιλίππου καὶ Ἀλεξάνδρου κατὰ τῶν πατρίδων τῶν αὐτῶν,
καὶ τὴν μὲν πόλιν ἡμῶν [δεομέ]νην ἀνδρός, τὴν δ' Ἑλλάδα
πᾶσαν πόλεως, ἥτις προστῆναι δυν]ήσεται τῆς ἡγεμονίας,
[ἐπέδ]ωκεν ἑαυτὸν μὲν τῇ πατρίδι, τὴν δὲ πόλιν τοῖς Ἕλλησιν
11 εἰς τὴν ἐλευθερίαν· καὶ ξενικὴν μὲν δύναμιν συστησάμενος, τῆς
δὲ πολιτικῆς ἡγεμὼν καταστὰς τοὺς πρώτους ἀντιταξαμένους
τῇ τῶν Ἑλλήνων ἐλευθερίᾳ Βοιωτοὺς καὶ Μακεδόνας καὶ
Εὐβοέας καὶ τοὺς ἄλλους συμμάχους αὐτῶν ἐνίκησε μαχόμενος
12 ἐν τῇ Βοιωτίᾳ. ἐντεῦθεν δ' ἐλθὼν εἰς Πύλας καὶ καταλαβὼν
τὰς [παρ]όδους δι' ὧν καὶ πρότερον ἐπὶ τοὺς Ἕλληνας οἱ
βάρβαροι ἐπορεύθησαν, τῆς μὲν ἐπὶ τὴν Ἑλλάδα πορείας
Ἀντίπατρον ἐκώλυσεν. αὐτὸν δὲ καταλαβὼν ἐν τοῖς τόποις
τούτοις καὶ μάχῃ νικήσας ἐπολιόρκει κατακλείσας εἰς Λαμίαν·
13 Θετταλοὺς δὲ καὶ Φωκέας καὶ Αἰτωλοὺς καὶ τοὺς ἄλλους
ἅπαντας τοὺς ἐν τῷ τόπῳ συμμάχους ἐποιήσατο, καὶ ὧν
Φίλιππος καὶ Ἀλέξανδρος ἀκόντων ἡγούμενοι ἐσεμνύνοντο,
τούτων Λεωσθένης ἑκόντων τὴν ἡγεμονίαν ἔλαβεν. συνέβη δ'
αὐτῷ τῶν μὲν πραγμάτων ὧν προείλετο κρατῆσαι, τῆς δὲ

But from what point shall I begin to speak and what shall I recall first? Should I outline the ancestry of each of those men? I accept that this would be silly. **(7)** The man who speaks in praise of others who have banded together from many areas and live in the one city, each one contributing his own private ancestry, must trace each one's ancestry individually; but, when speaking about Athenians, who are born from their own soil and whose common lineage gives them an unsurpassable racial purity, I think that a eulogy on each man's ancestry becomes redundant. **(8)** Shall I recall their education, and how as children they were brought up and trained in good behaviour, as other speakers are accustomed to do? I think that everyone knows that we educate children for one reason: that they may become good men; and men who proved in the war that they surpass others in courage were clearly brought up well as children. **(9)** Therefore I think the simplest thing is to speak about their courage in the war, and how they were responsible for many benefits to their country and to the rest of Greece. I will start first with the general, for that is only right.

(10) Leosthenes saw that the whole of Greece was humiliated and cowed, corrupted by those accepting bribes from Philip and Alexander to the detriment of their own countries. Realising that our city needed a man, and the whole of Greece a city, able to undertake the role of leader, he gave himself to his country and the city to the Greeks for the sake of freedom. **(11)** When he had raised a force of mercenaries, and been appointed to command the citizen force, he defeated in battle in Boeotia the first opponents of Greek freedom, the Boeotians, Macedonians, Euboeans and their other allies. **(12)** From there he came to Thermopylae and seized the pass through which in a previous time the barbarians had marched against the Greeks, and he prevented Antipater from entering Greece. He caught up with him in those parts, and having defeated him in battle shut him up in Lamia and besieged him. **(13)** He made the Thessalians, and the Phocians, Aetolians, and all the other peoples in that area his allies. Over those whom Philip and Alexander gloried in controlling against their wishes, Leosthenes assumed leadership with their consent. He was able to succeed

14 εἱμαρμένης οὐκ ἦν περιγενέσθαι. δίκαιον δ᾽ ἐστὶν μὴ μόνον ὧν ἔπραξεν Λεωσθέν[ης ἀε]ὶ χάριν ἔχειν αὐτῷ πρ[ώτῳ, ἀ]λλὰ καὶ τῆς ὕστερον [γενομέν]ης μάχης μετὰ τ[ὸν ἐκείνο]υ θάνατον καὶ τῶν [ἄλλων ἀγ]αθῶν τῶν ἐν τῇ σ[τρατείᾳ τ]αύτῃ συμβάντων τοῖς Ἕλλησιν· ἐπὶ γὰρ τοῖς ὑπὸ Λεωσθένους τεθεῖσιν θεμελίοις οἰκοδομοῦσιν οἱ νῦν τὰς ὕστερον πράξεις.

15 Καὶ μηδεὶς ὑπολάβῃ με τῶν ἄλλων πολιτῶν μηδένα λόγον ποιεῖσθαι, [ἀλλὰ] Λεωσθένη μόνον ἐγκωμιάζειν. συμβαίνει γὰρ τὸν Λεωσθένους ἔπαινον ἐπὶ ταῖς μάχαις ἐγκώμιον τῶν ἄλλων πολιτῶν εἶναι· τοῦ μὲν γὰρ βουλεύεσθαι καλῶς ὁ στρατηγὸς αἴτιος, τοῦ δὲ νικᾶν μαχομένους οἱ κινδυνεύειν ἐθέλοντες τοῖς σώμασ[ιν· ὥστ]ε ὅταν ἐπαινῶ τὴν γεγονυῖαν νίκην, ἅμα τῇ Λεωσθένους ἡγεμονίᾳ καὶ τὴν τῶν ἄλλων ἀρετὴν ἐγκωμ[ιάζ]ω.

16 τίς γὰρ οὐκ ἂν δικαίως ἐπαινοίη τῶν πολιτῶν τοὺς ἐν τῷδε τῷ πολέμῳ τελευτήσαντας, οἳ τὰς ἑαυτῶν ψυχὰς ἔδωκαν ὑπὲρ τῆς τῶν Ἑλλήνων ἐλευθερίας, φανερωτάτην ἀπόδειξιν τ[αύτ]ην ἡγούμενοι εἶναι τοῦ [βούλ]εσθαι τῇ Ἑλλάδι τὴν ἐλε[υθερ]ίαν

17 περιθεῖναι τὸ μαχομ[ένους] τελευτῆσαι ὑπὲρ αὐτ[ῆς]. μ[έγα δ᾽ αὐτοῖς συνεβάλετο εἰς τὸ προθύμως ὑπὲρ τῆς [Ἑλλάδος ἀγωνίσασθαι τὸ ἐν τῇ Βοιωτίᾳ τὴν μάχην τὴν π[ροτέραν] γενέσθαι. ἑώρων γὰ[ρ τὴν μὲν π]όλιν τῶν Θηβαίων οἰκτ[ρῶς ἠφα]νισμένην ἐξ ἀνθρώπων, [τὴν δὲ ἀ]κρόπολιν αὐτῆς φρουρου[μένην] ὑπὸ τῶν Μακεδόνων, τὰ δὲ σώματα τῶν ἐνοικούντων ἐξηνδραποδισμένα, τὴν δὲ χώραν ἄλλους διανεμομένους, ὥστε πρὸ ὀφθαλμῶν ὁρώμενα αὐτοῖς τὰ δεινὰ ἄοκνον παρεῖχε τόλμαν εἰς τὸ κινδυνεύειν προχείρως.

18 Ἀλλὰ μὴν τήν γε περὶ Πύλας καὶ Λαμίαν μάχην γενομένην οὐχ ἧττον αὐτοῖς ἔνδοξον γενέσθαι συμβέβηκεν ἧς ἐν Βοιωτοῖς ἠγωνίσαντο, οὐ μόνον τῷ μαχομένους νικᾶν Ἀντίπατρον καὶ τοὺς συμμάχους, ἀλλὰ καὶ τῷ τόπῳ, τῷ ἐνταυθοῖ γεγενῆσθαι τὴν μάχην. ἀφικνούμενοι γὰρ οἱ Ἕλληνες ἅπαντες δὶς τοῦ ἐνιαυτοῦ εἰς [τὴν Πυλ]αίαν θεωροὶ γενήσονται τῶν ἔργων τῶν πεπραγμένων αὐτοῖς· ἅμα γὰρ εἰς τὸν τόπον ἀθροισθήσονται

19 καὶ τῆς τούτων ἀρετῆς μνήσθοντ[αι]. ο]ὐδένες γὰρ πώποτε τῶν γεγονότων οὔτε περὶ καλλιόνων οὔτε πρὸς ἰσχυροτέρους οὔτε μετ᾽ ἐλαττόνων ἠγωνίσαντο, τὴν ἀρετὴν ἰσχὺν καὶ τὴν ἀνδρείαν πλῆθος, ἀλλ᾽ οὐ τὸν πολὺν ἀριθμὸν τῶν σωμάτων εἶναι κρίνοντες. καὶ τὴν μὲν ἐλευθερίαν εἰς τὸ κοινὸν πᾶσιν

in his strategical decisions, but not able to survive what was decreed by fate. **(14)** It is right that for all time Leosthenes has our gratitude first and foremost, not only for what he did but also for the later battle fought after his death and for the other benefits which came to the Greeks by this campaign. For the actions of his successors today are built upon the foundations laid by Leosthenes.

(15) Let no one think that in making my speech I am ignoring the other citizens and eulogising Leosthenes alone.   For the praise heaped on Leosthenes for these battles is also a eulogy for the other citizens. A general is responsible for the right battle strategy, but those willing to put their lives at risk ensure victory in the actual fighting. Consequently, when I praise the victory which was gained, I am paying tribute at the same time to the leadership of Leosthenes and the courage of his men. **(16)** For who would not rightly praise those citizens who died in this war, who gave their lives for the freedom of the Greeks, thinking this the clearest proof of their wish to confer freedom on Greece: to die fighting in battle on its behalf? **(17)** One factor particularly contributed to their readiness to fight hard for Greece, and that was to have fought the first battle in Boeotia. They saw that the city of the Thebans had been piteously eradicated from mankind, that the Macedonians garrisoned its Acropolis, and that the bodies of its inhabitants had been enslaved, while strangers divided up the land. Consequently, such terrible deeds revealed before their eyes gave them a resolute courage to face danger readily.

(18) Moreover, the battle fought in the area of Thermopylae and Lamia was no less glorious for them than the one fought in Boeotia, not only for the victory over Antipater and his allies in the fighting but also for the location, the fact that the battle took place at that spot. For all the Greeks come twice a year to Thermopylae as envoys and will see their deeds, and as they collect together in the place they will remember the courage of these men. **(19)** Never did men fight either for a more noble cause, or against stronger foes, or with fewer allies, judging courage to be strength and manliness to give a multitude rather than the actual numbers of men.   They established

κατέθεσαν, τὴν δ' εὐδοξίαν ἀπὸ τῶν πράξεων ἴδιον στέφανον τῇ πατρίδ[ι περι]έθηκαν.

20 Ἄξιον τοίνυν συλλογίσασθαι καὶ τί ἂν συμβῆναι νομίζοιμεν μὴ κατὰ τρόπον τούτων ἀγωνισαμένων. ἆρ' οὐκ ἂν ἑνὸς μὲν δεσπότου τὴν οἰκουμένην ὑπήκοον ἅπασαν εἶναι, νόμῳ δὲ τῷ τούτου τρόπῳ ἐξ ἀνάγκης χρῆσθαι τὴν Ἑλλάδα; συνελόντα δ' εἰπεῖν, τὴν Μακεδόνων ὑπερηφανίαν καὶ μὴ τὴν τοῦ δικαίου δύναμιν ἰσχύειν παρ' ἑκάστοις, ὥστε μήτε γυναικῶν μήτε παρθένων μήτε παίδων ὕβρεις ἂν ἐκλείπους ἑκάστοις

21 καθεστάναι; φανερὸν δ' ἐξ ὧν ἀναγκαζόμεθα καὶ νῦν ἔτι· θυσίας μὲν ἀνθρώποις γ[ιγνο]μένας ἐφορᾶν, ἀγάλματα δὲ καὶ βωμοὺς καὶ ναοὺς τοῖς μὲν θεοῖς ἀμελῶς, τοῖς δὲ ἀνθρώποις ἐπιμελῶς συντελούμενα, καὶ τοὺς τούτων οἰκέτας ὥσπερ ἥρωας

22 τιμᾶν ἡμᾶς ἀναγκαζομένους. ὅπου δὲ τὰ πρὸς τοὺς θεοὺς ὅσια διὰ τὴν Μακεδόνων τόλμαν ἀνῄρηται, τί τὰ πρὸς τοὺς ἀνθρώπους χρὴ νομίζειν; ἆρ' οὐκ ἂν παντελῶς καταλελύσθαι; ὥστε ὅσῳ δεινότερα τὰ προσδοκώμεν' ἂν γενέσθαι κρίνοιμεν, τοσούτῳ μειζόνων ἐπαίνων τοὺς τετελευτηκότας ἀξίους χρὴ

23 νομίζειν. οὐδεμία γὰρ στρατεία τὴν τῶν στρατευομένων ἀρετὴν ἐνεφάνισεν μᾶλλον τῆς νῦν γεγενημένης, ἐν ᾗ γε παρατάττεσθαι μὲν ὁσημέραι ἀναγκαῖον ἦν, πλείους δὲ μάχας ἠγωνίσθαι διὰ μιᾶς στρατείας ἢ τοὺς ἄλλους πάντας πληγὰς λαμβάνειν ἐν τῷ παρεληλυθότι χρόνῳ, χειμώνων δ' ὑπερβολὰς καὶ τῶν καθ' ἡμέραν ἀναγκαίων ἐνδείας τοσαύτας καὶ τηλικαύτας οὕτως ἐγκρατῶς ὑπομεμενηκένα[ι ὥσ]τε καὶ τῷ λόγῳ χαλεπὸν εἶναι φράσαι.

24 Τὸν δὴ τοιαύτας καρτερίας ἀόκνως ὑπομεῖναι τοὺς πολίτας προτρεψάμενον Λεωσθένη, καὶ τοὺς τῷ τοιούτῳ στρατηγῷ προθύμως συναγωνιστὰς σφᾶς αὐτοὺς παρασχόντας, ἆρ' οὐ διὰ τὴν τῆς ἀρετῆς ἀπόδειξιν εὐτυχεῖς μᾶλλον ἢ διὰ τὴν τοῦ ζῆν ἀπόλειψιν ἀτυχεῖς νομιστέον; οἵτινες θνητοῦ σώματος ἀθάνατον δόξαν ἐκτήσαντο καὶ διὰ τὴν ἰδίαν ἀρετὴν τὴν κοινὴν

25 ἐλευθερίαν τοῖς Ἕλλησιν ἐβεβαίωσαν. φέρει γὰρ οὐδὲν εὐδαιμονίαν ἄνευ τῆς αὐτονομίας. οὐ γὰρ ἀνδρὸς ἀπειλὴν ἀλλὰ νόμου φωνὴν κυριεύειν δεῖ τῶν εὐδαιμόνων, οὐδ' αἰτίαν φοβερὰν εἶναι τοῖς ἐλευθέροις ἀλλ' ἔλεγχον, οὐδ' ἐπὶ τοῖς κολακεύουσιν τοὺς δυνάστας καὶ διαβάλλουσιν τοὺς πολίτας τὸ τῶν πολιτῶν ἀσφαλές, ἀλλ' ἐπὶ τῇ τῶν νόμων πίστει γενέσθαι.

26 ὑπὲρ ὧν ἁπάντων οὗτοι πόνους πόνων διαδόχους ποιούμενοι

freedom for all Greece in common, but conferred the glory from their deeds as a particular crown on their country.

(20) Therefore it is worth considering what would have happened in our opinion if those men in their campaign had not done what was right. Would not the whole world be under the control of one master, and Greece forced to treat his will as law? To put it simply: the contempt of the Macedonians and not the power of right would hold sway over every city, so that no outrages against grown women, young girls and boys would be left uncommitted in any place. (21) This is clear from what we are forced even now to see: sacrifices being performed to men, statues and altars and temples to the gods uncared for, but being carefully established for men, and we ourselves forced to honour the servants of those men as heroes. (22) If the practices accorded to the gods have been abolished because of Macedonian audacity, what must we think would have happened to the practices towards men? Would they not have been completely subverted? The more terrible we judge what the consequences would have been, the greater the praise must we consider deserved by those who died. (23) For no campaign has illustrated the courage of those who fought better than this most recent one, in which every day it was necessary for them to be deployed for battle, and to fight more battles in one campaign than the defeats suffered by all other armies in the past, and so steadfastly to face extreme weather conditions and so many severe deprivations of daily necessities that they are hard to describe in words.

(24) Leosthenes exhorted the citizens to endure these hardships without hesitation, and they eagerly gave their support in the war to such a general. Must they not be deemed fortunate because of their show of courage rather than unfortunate because of their sacrifice of life? In place of an ephemeral body they acquired eternal glory, and they assured the universal freedom of the Greeks by their individual courage. (25) For there cannot be happiness without autonomy. The voice of law must be sovereign over happy people, not threats from a man, nor should an accusation be frightening to free men, but only proof that they are guilty; nor must the safety of the citizens depend on those who fawn on tyrants and slander their fellows, but on trust in the laws. (26) These men undertook hardships on top of hardships for the sake

καὶ τοῖς καθ' ἡμέραν κινδύνοις τοὺς εἰς τὸν ἅπαντα χρόνον φόβους τῶν πολιτῶν καὶ τῶν Ἑλλήνων παραιρούμενοι τὸ ζῆν

27 ἀνήλωσαν εἰς τὸ τοὺς ἄλλους καλῶς ζῆν. διὰ τούτους πατέρες ἔνδοξοι, μητέρες περίβλεπτοι τοῖς πολίταις γεγόνασι, ἀδελφαὶ γάμων τῶν προσηκόντων ἐννόμως τετυχήκασι καὶ τεύξονται, παῖδες ἐφόδιον εἰς τὴν πρὸς τὸν δῆμον ε[ὔνοι]αν τὴν τῶν οὐκ ἀπολωλότων ἀρετήν – οὐ γὰρ θεμιτὸν τούτου τοῦ ὀνόματος τυχεῖν τοὺς οὕτως ὑπὲρ καλῶν τὸν βίον ἐκλιπόντας – ἀλλὰ

28 τῶν τὸ ζῆν εἰς αἰώνιον τάξιν μεταλλαχότων ἕξουσιν. εἰ γὰρ [ὁ τοῖ]ς ἄλλοις ὢν ἀνιαρότατος θάνατος τούτοις ἀρχηγὸς μεγάλων ἀγαθῶν γέγονε, πῶς τούτους οὐκ εὐτυχεῖς κρίνειν δίκαιον; ἢ πῶς ἐκλελοιπέναι τὸν βίον, ἀλλ' οὐκ ἐξ ἀρχῆς γεγονέναι καλλίω γένεσιν τῆς πρώτης ὑπαρξάσης; τότε μὲν γὰρ παῖδες ὄντες ἄφρονες ἦσαν, νῦν δ' ἄνδρες ἀγαθοὶ

29 γεγόνασι· καὶ τότε μὲν ἐν πολλῷ χρόνῳ καὶ διὰ πολλῶν κινδύνων τὴν ἀρετὴν ἀπέδειξαν· νῦν δ' ἀπὸ ταύτης ἔξεστ' εὐθὺς γνωρίμους πᾶσι καὶ μνημονευτοὺς διὰ ἀνδραγαθίαν γεγονέναι.

30 Τίς γὰρ καιρὸς ἐν ᾧ τῆς τούτων ἀρετῆς οὐ μνημονεύσομεν; τίς τόπος ἐν ᾧ ζήλου καὶ τῶν ἐντιμοτάτων ἐπαίνων τυγχάνοντας οὐκ ὀψόμεθα; πότερον οὐκ ἐν τοῖς τῆς πόλεως ἀγαθοῖς; ἀλλὰ τὰ διὰ τούτους γεγονότα τίνας ἄλλους ἢ τούτους ἐπαινεῖσθαι καὶ μνήμης τυγχάνειν ποιήσει; ἀλλ' οὐκ ἐν ταῖς ἰδίαις εὐπραξίαις; ἀλλ' ἐν τῇ τούτων ἀρετῇ βεβαίως

31 αὐτῶν ἀπολαύσομεν. παρὰ ποίᾳ δὲ τῶν ἡλικιῶν οὐ μακαριστοὶ γενήσο[νται; πότερον οὐ πα]ρὰ τοῖς π[ρεσβυτέροις; ἀλλ' ἄ]φοβον ἄ[ξειν τὸν λοιπὸν] βίον κα[ὶ ἐν ἀσφαλεῖ] γεγενῆσ[θαι ἡγήσονται] διὰ τού[τους. ἀλλ' οὐ παρὰ τοῖς] ἡλικιώτ[αις; . . . . .] τελευτὴ φ[. . . . .] καλῶς ω[. . . . .] παρὰ πο[. . . . .]αι

32 γέγον[εν. ἀλλ' οὐ παρὰ τοῖς] νεωτέρο[ις;. . . . .]τα οὐ τὸν [. . . . .]σιν αὐτ[ῶν . . . . . σπου]δάσουσιν [. . . . . πα]ράδειγμ[α . . . . .]ου τὴν ἀ[ρετὴν . . . .]πασι. οὐκ [. . . . .]ζειν

33 αὐ[τοὺς . . . .]μη; ἢ τίνε[ς . . . .]φοι λει[. . . .] Ἑλλην[. . . .] τῶν πε[. . . .] παρὰ πο[. . . .] Φρυγῶν κ[. . . στρα]τείας ἐγ[. . . .] δὲ τῆς ελ[. . . .]τατοις ε[.

34 . . . .] ἅπασιν κ[αὶ λόγοις καὶ ᾠδαῖς ἐπαι[ν . . . ἀμφό]τερα γὰρ ε[. . . .] περὶ Λεωσ[θένους . . .] καὶ τῶν

of all these things, and with the dangers of each passing day they ended the fears for all time of their fellow citizens and the other Greeks, laying down their lives so that others might live well. **(27)** Fathers have become famous because of these men, mothers highly regarded by the citizens, sisters have made and will make marriages as befit them lawfully, children will receive an introduction to the goodwill of the people in the courage of those who have not died – for this is not a word that should be used of those who gave their lives in this way for a righteous cause – but have passed on from this life to an everlasting battle array. **(28)** For if death, which is most distressing to others, has been the prime cause of great benefits for these men, how should we not judge them fortunate, or how can we say that they have departed this life, rather than that they are born again, in a nobler birth than the first time? For then they were children and foolish, but now they have become noble men. **(29)** Then, over a long period of time and through many dangers, they demonstrated their courage; now, from this rebirth, they may straightaway be well-known to all and remembered for their bravery.

(30) For on what occasion shall we forget the courage of these men? In what place shall we not see them receiving admiration and the highest of praise? Will it be in the good times of the city? No! Whom else, other than these men, will the results of their actions cause to be praised and remembered? Will it be in our private prosperity? No again; for in the courage of these men we will enjoy those times with confidence. **(31)** Will there be anyone of any age who does not deem them happy? What about those of the older generation? No! They will think that the rest of their lives will be devoid of fear and that they have been placed in safety because of these men. What about their own generation?

–   –   –   –   –

(32) What about younger men?

–   –   **(33)**   –   –   –

(34) There are two reasons to glorify the actions of both Leosthenes and

τ[ελευτησάντων] ἐν τῷ πολέμῳ. εἰ μὲν γὰρ] ἡδονῆς ἕν[εκεν
μνημονεύ]ουσιν τὰς τ[οιαύτας καρ]τερίας, τί γέ[νοιτ᾽ ἂν τοῖς
Ἕλλησιν ἥδι[ον ἢ ἔπαινος τῶν] τὴν ἐλευθερί[αν . . . .]σάντων
ἀ[πὸ τῶν Μακεδό]νων; εἰ δὲ [ὠφελίας ἕνεκεν ἡ τοια[ύτη μνήμη]
γίγνεται, τίς ἂν λόγος ὠφελήσειεν μᾶλλον τὰς τῶν
ἀκουσόντων ψυχὰς τοῦ τὴν ἀρετὴν ἐγκωμιάσοντος καὶ τοὺς
ἀγαθοὺς ἄνδρας;

35 Ἀλλὰ μὴν ὅτι παρ᾽ ἡμῖν καὶ τοῖς λοιποῖς πᾶσιν εὐδοκιμεῖν
αὐτοὺς ἀναγκαῖον, ἐκ τούτων φανερόν ἐστιν· ἐν Ἅιδου δὲ
λογίσασθαι ἄξιον, τίνες οἱ τὸν ἡγεμόνα δεξιωσόμενοι τὸν
τούτων. ἆρ᾽ οὐκ ἂν οἰόμεθα ὁρᾶν Λεωσθένη δεξιουμένους καὶ
θαυμάζοντας τῶν ἡμιθέων καλουμένων τοὺς ἐπὶ Τροίαν
στρατεύσαντας, ὧν οὗτος ἀδελφὰς πράξεις ἐνστησάμενος
τοσοῦτον διήνεγκε, ὥστε οἱ μὲν μετὰ πάσης τῆς Ἑλλάδος μίαν
πόλιν εἷλον, ὁ δὲ μετὰ τῆς ἑαυτοῦ πατρίδος μόνης πᾶσαν τὴν
τῆς Εὐρώπης καὶ τῆς Ἀσίας ἄρχουσαν δύναμιν ἐταπείνωσεν.

36 κἀκεῖνοι μὲν ἕνεκα μιᾶς γυναικὸς ὑβρισθείσης ἤμυναν, ὁ δὲ
πασῶν τῶν Ἑλληνίδων τὰς ἐπιφερομένας ὕβρεις ἐκώλυσεν μετὰ

37 τῶν συνθαπτομένων νῦν αὐτῷ ἀνδρῶν. τῶν δὲ μετ᾽ ἐκείνους
μὲν γεγενημένων, ἄξια δὲ τῆς ἐκείνων ἀρετῆς διαπεπραγμένων,
λέγω δὴ τοὺς περὶ Μιλτιάδην καὶ Θεμιστοκλέα καὶ τοὺς
ἄλλους, οἳ τὴν Ἑλλάδα ἐλευθερώσαντες ἔντιμον μὲν τὴν

38 πατρίδα κατέστησαν, ἔνδοξον δὲ τὸν αὐτῶν βίον ἐποίησαν, ὧν
οὗτος τοσοῦτον ὑπερέσχεν ἀνδρείᾳ καὶ φρονήσει, ὅσον οἱ μὲν
ἐπελθοῦσαν τὴν τῶν βαρβάρων δύναμιν ἠμύναντο, ὁ δὲ μηδ᾽
ἐπελθεῖν ἐποίησεν. κἀκεῖνοι μὲν ἐν τῇ οἰκείᾳ τοὺς ἐχθροὺς
ἐπεῖδον ἀγωνιζομένους, οὗτος δὲ ἐν τῇ τῶν ἐχθρῶν

39 περιεγένετο τῶν ἀντιπάλων. οἶμαι δὲ καὶ τοὺς τὴν πρὸς
ἀλλήλους φιλίαν τῷ δήμῳ βεβαιότατα ἐνδειξαμένους, λέγω δὲ
Ἀρμόδιον καὶ Ἀριστογείτονα, οὐδαμῶς αὐτοὺς οἰκειοτέρους
ὑμῖν εἶναι νομίζειν ἢ Λεωσθένη καὶ τοὺς ἐκείνῳ
συναγωνισαμένους, οὐδ᾽ ἔστιν οἷς ἂν μᾶλλον ἢ τούτοις
πλησιάσειαν ἐν Ἅιδου. εἰκότως· οὐκ ἐλάττω γὰρ ἐκείνων
ἔργα διεπράξαντο, ἀλλ᾽ εἰ δέον εἰπεῖν καὶ μείζω. οἱ μὲν γὰρ
τοὺς τῆς πατρίδος τυράννους κατέλυσαν, οὗτοι δὲ τοὺς τῆς
Ἑλλάδος ἁπάσης.

40 Ὦ καλῆς μὲν καὶ παραδόξου τόλμης τῆς πραχθείσης ὑπὸ
τῶνδε τῶν ἀνδρῶν, ἐνδόξου δὲ καὶ μεγαλοπρεποῦς προαιρέσεως

those who died in the war. If it is for pleasure that men recount such steadfast deeds, what could be more pleasing to the Greeks than praise of those who brought about freedom from the Macedonians? But if this sort of recollection is motivated by the benefit that it brings, what speech could bring greater benefit to the souls of those who will hear it than the one which eulogises courage and brave men?

(35) It is clear from these arguments that with us and with everyone else they must be held in high esteem; but it is worth considering who will be greeting the leader of these men in Hades. Would we not expect to see greeting and marvelling at Leosthenes those alleged demi-gods who took part in the campaign against Troy? This man performed parallel actions, but surpassed them in so far as they, with the whole of Greece, took one city, but he, with only his own city, brought down completely the power which controlled Europe and Asia. (36) They came to the defence of one woman who had been shamefully treated, while he, with the men now being buried with him, prevented the outrages which were threatened against all Greek women. (37) And those who were born after them, but performed deeds that were worthy of their courage – I speak of Miltiades and Themistocles and those with them, and the others who by setting Greece free brought honour to their country and made their own lives glorious – (38) Leosthenes excelled them in bravery and forethought in that while those men held back the invading force of the barbarians, he prevented it from invading at all; those men saw the enemy fighting in their own country, but he defeated his enemies in their land.

. (39) I think also that those who demonstrated to the people their friendship towards each other in the most assured fashion – I speak of Harmodius and Aristogeiton – in no way consider themselves closer to you than Leosthenes and those who served with him, nor are there any with whom they would rather associate in Hades than these men. Quite right too. For they performed deeds not less worthy than theirs, but, if one must give an opinion, more so. For Harmodius and Aristogeiton brought down the tyrants of their country; these men those of the whole of Greece.

(40) How fine and incredible was the daring practised by these men, how admirable and magnificent the choice they made, how awe-inspiring the

ἧς προείλοντο, ὑπερβαλλούσης δὲ ἀρετῆς καὶ ἀνδραγαθίας τῆς
ἐν τοῖς κινδύνοις, ἣν οὗτοι παρασχόμενοι εἰς τὴν κοινὴν
ἐλευθερίαν τῶν Ἑλλήνων

—   —   —   —   —

41   Χαλεπὸν μὲν ἴσως ἐστὶ τοὺς ἐν τοῖς τοιούτοις ὄντας
πάθεσι παραμυθεῖσθαι· τὰ γὰρ πένθη οὔτε λόγῳ οὔτε νόμῳ
κοιμίζεται, ἀλλ' ἡ φύσις ἑκάστου καὶ φιλία πρὸς τὸν
τελευτήσαντα ὁρισμὸν ἔχει τοῦ λυπεῖσθαι. ὅμως δὲ χρὴ
θαρρεῖν καὶ τῆς λύπης παραιρεῖν εἰς τὸ ἐνδεχόμενον, καὶ
μεμνῆσθαι μὴ μόνον τοῦ θανάτου τῶν τετελευτηκότων, ἀλλὰ
42   καὶ τῆς ἀρετῆς ἧς καταλελοίπασιν. οὐ γὰρ θρήνων ἄξια
πεπόνθασιν, ἀλλ' ἐπαίνων μεγάλων πεποιήκασιν. εἰ δὲ γήρως
θνητοῦ μὴ μετέσχον, ἀλλ' εὐδοξίαν ἀγήρατον εἰλήφασιν,
εὐδαίμονές τε γεγόνασι κατὰ πάντα. ὅσοι μὲν γὰρ αὐτῶν
ἄπαιδες τετελευτήκασιν, οἱ παρὰ τῶν Ἑλλήνων ἔπαινοι παῖδες
αὐτῶν ἀθάνατοι ἔσονται. ὅσοι δὲ παῖδας καταλελοίπασιν, ἡ
τῆς πατρίδος εὔνοια ἐπίτροπος αὐτοῖς τῶν παίδων
43   καταστήσεται. πρὸς δὲ τούτοις, εἰ μέν ἐστι τὸ ἀποθανεῖν
ὅμοιον τῷ μὴ γενέσθαι, ἀπηλλαγμένοι εἰσὶ νόσων καὶ λύπης
καὶ τῶν ἄλλων τῶν προσπιπτόντων εἰς τὸν ἀνθρώπινον βίον·
εἰ δ' ἔστιν αἴσθησις ἐν Ἅιδου καὶ ἐπιμέλεια παρὰ τοῦ
δαιμονίου, ὥσπερ ὑπολαμβάνομεν, εἰκὸς τοὺς ταῖς τιμαῖς τῶν
θεῶν καταλυομέναις βοηθήσαντας πλείστης ἐπιμελείας καὶ
κηδεμονίας ὑπὸ τοῦ δαιμονίου τυγχάνειν.

—   —   —   —   —

courage and bravery which they showed in times of danger for the common freedom of the Greeks

—   —   —   —   —

(41) Perhaps it is hard to console those who are suffering such grief. For sorrows are not put to rest by words or by law; the character of each man and the warmth of his feelings towards the dead determines the level of grief. Nevertheless, we must be brave and lighten our distress to the best of our ability, and remember not only the deaths of those who fell but also the courage which they have left behind. (42) For they have not suffered what merits our tears, but done what deserves the highest praise. While they did not reach old age in this mortal life, they have acquired eternal glory and become fortunate in every way. For those of them who were without children when they died, the praises of the Greeks will be their immortal children; for those who have left children behind, the goodwill of the country will become guardian of their children. (43) In addition to all this, if death is the same as not having been born, then they have been released from sickness, from pain and from the other things which inflict themselves on human life. But if, as we assume, there is consciousness in Hades, and the power of a god looks after us there, then it is reasonable to expect that those who gave help when the honours of the gods were being subverted will win most care and favour from the immortal judge.

—   —   —   —   —

Dinarchus 1. *Against Demosthenes*
The following are the differences from Conomis' Teubner text:

This edition			Conomis
1	6	καὶ περὶ	περὶ
8	2	κατὰ σοῦ	σ'
9	7	διαθήκας	θήκας
11	6	τῶν ἀποφάσεων τῶν	τῆς ἀποφάσεως τῆς
		. . . γεγενημένων	. . . γεγενημένης
20	2	ἐν οἷς	ἐν οἵοις
25	7	περιορᾶν ἐάν τις ᾿Αθηναίων	† μὴ περιορᾶν ἐάν τις ὅπλα
		ὅπλα διὰ τῆς χώρας	διὰ τῆς χώρας τῆς ᾿Αθηναίων †
30	5	ἀνατέτραφεν	ἀνατέτροφεν
33	9	καταλύουσιν; δεῖ ὑμᾶς	< . . . ; . . . >
34	1	κατασκευὴν	παρασκευὴν
	7	κακῶν;	κακῶν.
35	7	ἐπιστολὴν	ἐπιστολὰς
39	7	τῶν Λακεδαιμονίων	Λακεδαιμονίων
43	3	σταθησομένην	ἀνατεθησομένην
45	7	Δημοσθένην	διὰ Δημοσθένην
55	2	τὰ γεγενημένα . . . τοῖς	ἀποφαίνει τὰ γεγενημένα. . .
		ζητουμένοις ἀποφαίνει	τοῖς ζητουμένοις
63	4	τὴν . . . ἀπόφασιν και	τὰς . . . ἀποφάσεις καὶ
		τιμωρίαν	τιμωρίας
64	6	κομισθέντων χρημάτων	om. (lacuna after
			πατρίδος)
65	5	δίκην δόντα	δόντα δίκην
66	8	παρὰ πᾶσιν ἀνθρώποις	σεμνότατον παρὰ πᾶσιν
		εἶναι σεμνότατον	ἀνθρώποις εἶναι
74	7	ἐκ τῶν Ἑλλήνων	μετὰ τῶν ἄλλων ἑλλήνων
81	9	ἀποδράς;	ἀποδράς,
82	8	τὸ σὸν ψήφισμα περὶ δυοῖν	< . . . . >
		τῶν πολιτῶν	
93	11	διοικοῦντα	πολέμους διοικοῦντα
103	6	ἐν Ὀλυμπίᾳ	om.
106	5	ἀνθρώποις;	ἀνθρώποις,
108	9	τέτραφε	τέτροφε
109	3	καθίστησιν εἰς τοὺς κινδύνους	εἰς τοὺς κινδύνους καθίστησιν
	7	κινδύνους	ἀγῶνας
110	6	σῶμ'	ὄνομα
111	9	τὴν ὁσίαν καὶ τὴν δικαίαν	τὴν δικαίαν καὶ τὴν ὁσίαν

Hyperides

The following are the significant differences from Jensen's Teubner text:

5. Against Demosthenes

		This edition	Jensen
col. 1	8	καὶ μόνον	om.
7	1	μᾶλλον	μεῖζον
	4	οὐχ. ὥστε νῦν	οὔ. καὶ γὰρ
	5	τετρακοσίων	τριακοσίων
	7	πάντων	ἀπάντων
15	1	Μὴ νομίζετε δὲ	ἢ μὴ νομίζῃ τις
17	7	καὶ νῦν δὲ	om.
		ναυτικοῖς ... πατρίδος	
		εἶναι	placed in col. 16
	11	μὴ δραπέτην	om.
18	1	Ἐπείδη δὲ νῦν	om.
	7	καὶ τῶν ἄλλων μὴ	
		γίγνεσθαι	om.
24	8	]σαι	τιμῆ]σαι
26	11	ἔφη	ἐφη
28	1	οὐ μέντοι	om.
30	3	πάντ' ἂν δικαίως	πάντα τὰ δίκαι' ἂν
	5	κατα	κατὰ τοῦ δήμου
32	1	ἐν τῇ ἀγορᾷ	om.
34	8	οἰομένους ἀναδέξασθαι	ἐθέλοντας ἀναδέξασθαι
		δεῖν ἀδικήματα	καὶ τὰ ἀδικήματα αὐτῶν
39	4	εἰς	om.
40	7	τὰ χρήματα	om.

Hyperides

6. *Funeral Oration*

		This edition	Jensen
2	1	φοβοῦμαι	πεφόβημαι
4	4	ἐπελθεῖν	διεξελθεῖν
5	2	κατὰ	εἰς
6	1	ἀλλὰ περὶ μὲν	περὶ μὲν οὖν
	2	παραλείψω	om.
	4	πρῶτον	πρώτου
7	5	ποιούμενον	ποιούμενος
15	7	ἐγκωμιάζω	ἐγκωμιάσω
19	6	ἀπὸ	τὴν ἀπὸ
20	2	νομίζοιμεν	νομίζομεν
	7	ἂν ἐκλείπτους	ἀνεκλείπτους
21	1	ἔτι	ἔστι
2λ	4	κρίνοιμεν	κρίνομεν
25	1	οὐδὲν	πᾶσαν
	2	ἄνευ τῆς αὐτονομίας	† ἡ αὐτονομία
29	2	ἔξεστ' εὐθὺς	om.
31	2	ἀλλ'	οἳ
	3	ἡγήσονται	νομίζουσι
32-3		Many supplements removed	
34	5	]σάντων	παρασκευα]σάντων
	8	ἀκουσόντων	ἀκουόντων
		ἐγκωμιάσοντος	ἐκωμιάζοντος
39	3	οὐδαμῶς αὐτοὺς οἰκειοτέρους	† οὐθένας οὕτως οἰκείους
41	4	ὁρισμὸν	τὸν ὁρισμὸν
42	1	οὐ	εἰ

Commentary

Dinarchus 1, *Against Demosthenes*

(In the secondary-level structures given in the introduction to each part of Dinarchus 1, the abbreviation A stands for the Areopagus/Areopagites and D for Demosthenes. For discussion of the use of ring composition in the speech see Introduction, Section 3.)

A (1-4) Introduction

- (1) D imposed his own death sentence if found guilty of bribery.
  - (2) The A expressed just and true opinions in its report against D.
    - (2) Appeal is made to the jurors not to surrender the city's rights.
    - (3) D is on trial before his peers; so are the jurors before their fellows.
    - (3) They await the jurors' conclusion about the country's interests.
  - (3) The A's report was intended to punish those guilty of this crime.
- (4) D proposed the decree that the A should investigate the affair.

(1-4) The speaker briefly refers to Demosthenes' actions when he was accused of accepting a bribe from Harpalus, and to the findings of the Areopagus when ordered to investigate the matter (1, 3-4). The main theme of the introduction is to gain the support of the jurors in spite of the repetition of subject matter from the preceeding speech of Stratocles (1; cf. 20 and 21). The speaker apologises and exhorts the jurors not to betray the city by acquitting Demosthenes, a theme that permeates the speech. They are urged to think of the trial in terms not just of the present law court but of Attica as a whole by the analogy that while Demosthenes is on trial before his peers so are they before their fellow citizens (2-3).

(1) **Athenians, your popular leader . . . he opposed:** That is, Demosthenes. For rhetorical effect Dinarchus places *demagogos* ('leader of the people') at the opening of the speech in order to contrast this trustworthy position with Demosthenes' treacherous betrayal of the people.

When Harpalus fled from Athens only 350 of his alleged seven hundred talents were found, and most of the leading statesmen were accused of accepting bribes, presumably from him, to allow his escape: see Introduction, p. 9. At a meeting of the Assembly called to discuss the affair Demosthenes proposed a formal investigation into the scandal by means of an *apophasis* (4, 6, 68, 82-83, 86, Hyp. 5.1, 2, 8, 34), a judicial procedure under which the Areopagus, on the orders of the Assembly, enquired (*zetein*) into those suspected of subversive or treasonable actions and delivered a preliminary verdict or 'report' (*apophasis*). If this report indicated guilt, then the accused was tried in a normal lawcourt. Demosthenes further agreed to submit to the death penalty if found guilty by this 'decree against himself' to which Dinarchus refers (8, 40, 61, 63, 83-84, 86, 104, 108, Hyp. 5.1), and others also under suspicion followed suit, such as Philocles (Din. 3.2, 5, 16, 21; cf. Hyp. 5.34 for unnamed others). At the end of a six months' enquiry or *zetesis* (45) the Areopagus published its report and accused several people of *dorodokia* (treason by taking bribes against the state), including Demosthenes for receiving twenty talents from Harpalus: 6, 45, 53, 69, 89, Hyp. 5.2, 7, 10, Plut. *Demosthenes* 25.4-5. Although the penalty for *dorodokia* was a tenfold fine or death (60, Din. 2.17, Hyp. 5.24, *AP* 54.2), he was fined fifty talents.

It is impossible to give a modern monetary equivalent to Demosthenes' alleged bribe of twenty talents; suffice it to say that it was an enormous sum since one talent equalled 36,000 obols (the smallest unit of currency), and three obols was the daily pay for an Athenian juror in the late fifth and fourth centuries BC.

What is also at issue in the allegation is the fine line between acceptance of gifts *per se* and as bribes. The receipt of gifts was an inherent part of Greek diplomacy; however, taking gifts as bribes to the detriment of Athens was a crime that the Athenians regarded as particularly heinous. See, for example, S. Perlman, 'On Bribing Athenian Ambassadors', *GRBS* 17 (1976), 223-233, J. Cargill, 'Demosthenes, Aischines and the Crop of Traitors', *Ancient World* 11 (1985), 75-85, F.D. Harvey, '*Dona Ferentes*: Some Aspects of Bribery in Greek Politics', *Crux. Essays in Greek History Presented to G.E.M. de Ste. Croix on his 75th Birthday*, edd. P.A. Cartledge and F.D. Harvey (London: 1985), 76-113 and B.S. Strauss, 'The Cultural Significance of Bribery and Embezzlement in Athenian Politics', *Ancient World* 11 (1985), 67-74.

The use of φανερῶς ('unequivocally') is rhetorical since the Areopagus cited no evidence to substantiate its accusation that Demosthenes accepted a bribe from Harpalus (Hyp. 5.6-7, Dem. *Epistle* 2.1, 15 and 3.42; cf. Din. 2.21). The prestige and reputation of the Areopagus form one of the major themes of the speech and are constantly emphasised in order to secure acceptance of its report and thus disguise the fact that no proof against those accused in the affair existed: see Introduction, pp. 10-11 and 26.

Since Stratocles has said a great deal . . . the pertinent decrees: Stratocles was a wealthy orator from the deme of Diomeia. In the Harpalus trials of 323 ten orators were chosen as state prosecutors (Din. 2.6; cf. 1.51 and Hyp. 5.38), and Stratocles spoke first in the trial of Demosthenes. In view of his youth (he was about 25 years old at the time) he may have delivered what was only an introductory speech, setting out the charges and evidence, preceding a lengthier and more important one by the unknown client of Dinarchus, for whom the latter wrote his speech. On Stratocles see *PA* 12938, Berve, *Alexander* 2, no. 724, Davies, *APF*, 494-495; cf. F. Blass, *Die attische Beredsamkeit*[2], 3.2 (Leipzig: 1898), 333-336.

(2)   **it remains for us . . . pleadings of the defendant:** The start of a general exhortation, which is rhetorically exaggerated: could a case such as the present one have never before been experienced in Athens? Demosthenes had been accused of accepting bribes many times in the past: for example, from Persia (Aes. 3.156, 173, 209, 238-240, 259; cf. Din. 1.10, 15, 70, Hyp. 5.25), from Philip II and Alexander (Din. 1.28, Hyp. 5.25) and from other men (Aes. 3.85, 103, 146).

The exhortation, which takes up one of Dinarchus' characteristically long sentences, is meant to offset impatience on the part of the jurors since we should expect much repetition in ten prosecution speeches against Demosthenes, irrespective of their length.

(3)   **You should consider . . . findings were declared:** Here, ὁρᾶτε is an imperative, not an indicative. The challenge to the jurors, who now find themselves on trial before their fellows, forms the core of this part of the speech: if Demosthenes is acquitted then they too will be seen as corrupt.

The passage ends with an example of Dinarchus' oratorical style in the 'stacking' of verbs: ἀφῆτε ζητεῖν προσετάξατε ('You did not order [the Areopagus'] investigation so that you could acquit [them]').

(4)   **This decision is now up to you . . . began its enquiry:** The decree is that of the Assembly, which officially instigated the Areopagus' investigation under the *apophasis* procedure into the affair. Dinarchus is guilty of exaggeration in his implication that the council had held the power for centuries since *apophasis* developed only in the mid-fourth century. However, since the case against Demosthenes and the others was treasonable (*prodosia*), which would involve the traditional role of the Areopagus, Dinarchus is probably referring generally to the Areopagus' former right of guardianship of the laws, on which see R.W. Wallace, *The Areopagos Council* (Baltimore & London: 1989), 55-64 with E.M. Carawan, '*Apophasis* and *Eisangelia*: The Rôle of the Areopagus in Athenian Political Trials', *GRBS* 26 (1985), 115-140.

Dinarchus concludes the introduction of the speech with the Areopagus investigating the alleged missing money and the corruption of the leading statesmen.

B (5-11)   Justification of Report

  (5) The A's investigation had been on behalf of its country.
  (6) The sovereign powers of the A.
  (7) Although D says the A lied, he ordered similar investigations before.
  (8) D proposed his own death penalty if the A condemned him.
  (8-9) D adhered to the A's report before, but now he maligns it.
  (9) The sovereign powers of the A.
  (10-11) In the present case the A had investigated for the good of the city.

(5-11) In the second part of the speech Dinarchus' aim is to persuade the jurors that the Areopagus' decision should be accepted without question – a necessary objective as no evidence existed against Demosthenes (see Introduction, pp. 10-11). Dinarchus describes the Areopagus' sovereign powers in the state, its integrity, and how its previous investigations met with unanimous approval (7, 8-9). This is linked to the present case, in which the accused now hypocritically rejects the Areopagus' findings, a *volte face* from his previous stance (8-9, 10-11). Guilt, then, is shown to be the motive for Demosthenes' inconsistency. His character is contrasted with the noble Areopagus, which ignored any challenges in order to reach a just decision for the well-being of the city (5-6, 10-11).

(5)   **Regardless of your challenges . . . directed against it:** During the course of the Areopagus' six-month investigation (*zetesis*) Demosthenes issued a *proklesis* ('challenge') to the people to present that body with evidence of his guilt: 5 with Hyperides 5.2. When he was named in the report (*apophasis*), he issued a second *proklesis* to compel the Areopagites to produce proof: 6 (cf. 61) and Hyperides 5.3. This form of defence was in vain, and he was brought to trial.

(6)   **Although it seemed . . . twenty talents of gold:** See commentary on 5. In addition to his official challenges Demosthenes toured the Agora and elsewhere denouncing the Areopagus and the people.
  Shall the Council . . . Demosthenes?: Dinarchus refers here to the Areopagus' traditional right of investigating, and judging, cases of intentional murder (Aes. 1.92, Dem. 23.66, [Dem.] 59.80, Lycurgus 1.12).

Before the legislation of Ephialtes in 462/1 the Areopagus had wide-ranging political and judicial powers (*AP* 4.4 and 8.4 with P.J. Rhodes, *A Commentary on the Aristotelian Athenaion Politeia* [Oxford: 1981], *ad loc.*, though see now Wallace, *Areopagos*, 32-46), and it may also have been able to impose *atimia* (loss of civic rights) on those found guilty (*AP* 8.4 and 16.10 [with Rhodes, *Commentary*, 155-156 and 220-222], Plut. *Solon* 19.4). Ephialtes' legislation of 462 deprived it of all of its political functions, which were transferred to the Boule, Assembly, and law courts (*AP* 25.2, Aristotle, *Politics* 1274a 7, Plut. *Pericles* 9.5 and *Cimon* 15.2, [Plut.] *Moralia* 812d, Diod. 11.77.6). The Areopagus still maintained some of its judicial powers, and in the fourth century it played a more integral role in Athenian political affairs. In the mid-fourth century it was empowered to investigate crimes other than murder under the procedure known as *apophasis* (Wallace, *Areopagos*, 115-119). See further Rhodes, *Commentary*, 313-319, Wallace, *Areopagos*, 77-93.

(7) **Yes! Because the council . . . as it seems:** Dinarchus anticipates what will be the core of Demosthenes' defence speech, and this is a perfectly logical assumption to make on account of Demosthenes' *prokleseis* (challenges). Much of section 7 and the opening of 8 has been found recently on a papyrus fragment of the late second/early third century A.D. (*P. Oxy.* 49, 3436).

ὡς ἔοικεν ('as it seems') is a common rhetorical trick, since it allowed the orators virtually unlimited freedom in expressing themselves and abusing their adversaries as they wished by avoiding specific statements, but it would nevertheless influence the opinions of the audience (cf. 6, 7, 48, Hyp. 5.13).

Demades was an active politician and diplomat. For example, he persuaded Alexander not to insist on the surrender to him of several leading statesmen after the fall of Thebes in 335 (see commentary on 82). As a result, Alexander insisted only on the expulsion of Charidemus (32). He also played a role in keeping Athens neutral in the war of Agis III of Sparta ([Plut.] *Moralia* 818e-f), on which see commentary on 34. However, he proposed divine honours for Alexander in 324, but later he was indicted under a *graphe paranomon* (making an illegal proposal) and fined ten talents (Athenaeus 6.251b, Polybius 12.12b3, Aelian, *VH* 5.12, Valerius Maximus 7.2.13), one of the three *graphai paranomon* brought against him by which he was convicted. The last trial may be dated during the Lamian War of 323-322 (on which see Introduction, pp. 12-16), when he was especially vulnerable. Since he was convicted a third time he lost his civic rights but these were restored and the fine waived in the crisis of 322 when his diplomatic powers were again needed (Diod. 18.18.1-2, Plut. *Phocion* 26.2). For a summary of Demades' decrees and offices see M.H. Hansen, *The Athenian Ecclesia* 2 (Copenhagen: 1989), 40, and C. Schwenk, *Athens in the Age of Alexander* (Chicago: 1985), nos. 4, 5, 7, 8, 23, 24, 37, 51 and 87; and on Demades' active political career see J.M. Williams, 'Demades' Last Years, 323/2-319/8 B.C.: A 'Revisionist' Interpretation', *Ancient World* 19 (1989), 19-30.

This is the first pairing of Demosthenes and Demades in the speech (cf. 11, 45, 89, 101, 104, and also Din. 2.14 and Hyp. 5.25-26), perhaps because he was the next to be tried (it seems clear from 2.15 that Demosthenes and Demades had already stood trial), although it is likely that Demades did not remain in Athens but was condemned *in absentia* (see commentary on 29 and 104). Dinarchus tends to pair those with similar political sympathies (for example, Aristides and Themistocles at 37), and comparing Demosthenes with the 'disreputable' Demades (presumably over his proposal to deify Alexander) allowed him the convenience of creating further prejudice against Demosthenes.

Did you not order . . . Dear Heracles!: In order to persuade the jurors to accept the Areopagus' verdict, Dinarchus refers to previous occasions when Demosthenes initiated its enquiries and approved its results. The oath by Heracles is repeated only at Dinarchus 2.3. An oath was a common rhetorical device to lend weight to an argument on pious grounds (R.J. Bonner and G. Smith, *The Administration of Justice from Homer to Aristotle* 1 [Chicago: 1930], 145-146), and Dinarchus, like Hyperides, exploits the device often, especially to Zeus (40, 43, 77, and 3.15; cf. 36: Athena and Zeus) and the gods (64, 68, and 3.1), rather than deified heroes (there are the only two instances of an appeal to Heracles). Less common are appeals to Athena, as at 45 and 64 (cf. 36), the 'awful goddesses' at 64 (cf. their use at 47 and 87), the Mother of the Gods at 86, and Good Luck at 29 and 98. Compare also the use of Poseidon and Ares at 87.

(8) **Why then . . . reports of the Council:** On Demosthenes' decree against himself, see commentary on 1. These two questions are rhetorical; Dinarchus' client would theatrically point an accusing finger at Demosthenes when asking them. They also form the core component of this part of the speech and highlight the fate that should befall Demosthenes because of his own decree, the Areopagus' findings, and his declared faith in that body.

Blass emended the text σοῦ to σε (followed by Conomis and by Nouhaud and Dors-Méary), but I prefer κατὰ σοῦ of Hieronymus Wolf (followed also by Burtt); cf. 61.

What body shall the people . . . the truth: A rhetorical question addressed to the jurors *en masse*; cf. similar appeals at 46, 67 and 88.

(9) **Despite claiming to be . . . the Council:** That is, the Areopagus; τὸ συνέδριον is one of the rarer names by which Dinarchus refers to the body.

previously held in high repute . . . slander it: Dinarchus' description of Demosthenes as a *demotikos*, followed by the terms *politeia* and *demokrateia*, is calculated to portray him in an unappealing light: someone who claims (φάσκων) to be a leader of the people would not be expected to attack one of the bastions of the Athenian democracy, the Areopagus. Note a similar attack at section 44 when Demosthenes the *demotikos* 'pollutes' Athenian citizenship by proposing Taurosthenes for citizenship.

has protected your life . . . the city depends: On the Areopagus, see also commentary on 6 and 62. It is unknown what the 'sacred deposits' are (reading διαθήκας of manuscript A), but the general view is that they were oracles (so Burtt, 178 note a, Nouhaud and Dors-Méary, 57 n. 9). ἀπορρητούς suggest something not so much 'sacred' as 'mystical' in the sense of something that is not to be divulged to outsides or even non-initiates. Certainly though the reference is rhetorical exaggeration in that the city's safety rested solely on these mystic deposits.

(10) **The Council . . . what I think:** The emphatic repetitious opening to a sentence is one of Dinarchus' stylistic characteristics – compare 15: 'I'm almost speechless with rage'. Both of these comments appear extemporaneous, and are added for rhetorical effect: the outrage of the speaker breaking through as he loses his self-control at the thought of Demosthenes' actions!

It had two alternatives . . . due punishment: The first of two alternatives that faced the Areopagus.

In 336 the Persian king Darius III contributed money towards a Greek revolt against the Macedonian hegemony in order to divert Alexander's attention from his projected invasion of Asia. The revolt was quickly terminated by Alexander, but in 335 Thebes again revolted, receiving support from several states including, it seems, the Athenians (Aes. 3.240-241, Din. 1.18-21, Arr. 1.7.4 and 1.10.1-3, Diod. 17.8.5-6). The Theban rebellion was short-lived: as punishment the city was razed to the ground and those of the population who survived the carnage were enslaved (Diod. 17.14.1, Arr. 1.7.1 ff. with A.B. Bosworth, *A Historical Commentary on Arrian's History of Alexander*, 1 [Oxford: 1980], 73-91, Plut. *Alexander* 11.7 ff.; cf. *Demosthenes* 23.1 ff., Diod. 17.8.3 ff., Justin 11.3.6 ff.). T.T.B. Ryder, *Koine Eirene* (Oxford: 1965), 103-107, argues that Alexander acted constitutionally against Thebes, but the severity of the punishment must have been deliberate, to serve as a warning to rebellious states.

The amount given by Darius and Demosthenes' involvement in the Persian conspiracy are controversial. Dinarchus' allegation here must be taken with that made in sections 18-21, that Demosthenes accepted money from the Persian king to help support a Greek revolt in 336 and that he himself betrayed Thebes to its destruction. See in detail Worthington, *Dinarchus*, 139-143 and 160-168; the arguments are briefly summarised here.

Only Aeschines 3.239 and Dinarchus 1.10 and 18 specify the actual sum of money (three hundred talents), and it is only the orators who link the receipt of Persian gold with Demosthenes' betrayal of Thebes in 335 (Aes. 3.156-157; cf. 173, 209, 259, Din. 1.15, 20, 26, Hyp. 5.17 and 25). Moreover, there is contradiction within them, which shows their unreliability. Aeschines 3.239-240 says that Darius offered three hundred talents but accuses Demosthenes of taking seventy. Dinarchus accuses Demosthenes with others of keeping some of the money (1.10), of taking all of it (1.18), and that he acquired over 150 talents in his dealings with Persia and Alexander (1.70). Thus, we have four differing sums of money allegedly taken by Demosthenes: in Aeschines, seventy talents, and in Dinarchus, part of three hundred talents, three hundred talents, and less than 150 talents.

Dinarchus tends to follow Aeschines' account of the Persian gold and the fall of Thebes, and it is plausible that he used Aeschines' accusation at 3.239-240 and opted to charge Demosthenes with refusing to part with ten talents (at 1.10 and 18). Rounding-up and exaggerating of figures was a common practice in oratory.

All of this does not preclude a kernel of truth: Darius III may well have offered a large sum of money to the Athenians, which they refused to accept, but then Demosthenes (and others) took some of this as a bribe, perhaps to influence Athenian opinion towards a possible alliance with Persia against Alexander since Demosthenes' general policy had been the hope that the Persians would defeat Alexander (cf. G.L. Cawkwell, 'The Crowning of Demosthenes', *CQ²* 19 [1969], 176-180). Any such dealings then were to backfire on him later.

The Persian money and the betrayal of Thebes (on which see commentary on 18-21, especially 21) together formed a common topos to the discredit of Demosthenes (on topoi see the Introduction, p. 37). It was first used by Aeschines in 330 and reused by Dinarchus in 323 (and also by Stratocles if a fragment of a speech is correctly attributed to him: see commentary on 24). Moreover, the complexity of this part of the speech in its structure leads one to believe that compositional sophistication to cover a weak argument – and for rhetorical effect – has taken precedence over historical accuracy.

(11) **Or, if you wanted . . . the previous case:** The second alternative facing the Areopagus was to refuse the investigation under the *apophasis* procedure into those who had received bribes from Harpalus, but only if the people desired the acquittal of Demosthenes and the others, and thereby to bring danger and harm to the city. Such rhetorical influencing of the jury is far from subtle, but it was effective since Demosthenes was condemned.

C (11-28)   Past History I

(11-13) Three of D's past actions are used to help illustrate his corruptibility.

(14) Timotheus' noble deeds, but nevertheless he was punished.

(15-16) D's actions ultimately led to the betrayal of his city.

(16-17) Timotheus did not argue the court's verdict and was prepared to die.

(18-21) Destruction of Thebes, attributed to D, is indicative of his ignoble past.

(22-23) Appeal is made to condemn D, as jury condemned others previously.

(24-26) D has betrayed Athens' allies despite his policies.

(26-27) Call made to punish men of note like D.

(28) Three of D's past exploits are used to help cast aspersions on his character.

(11-28) Dinarchus returns to the other major theme of his speech, selected events from Athens' past history to show that Demosthenes' policies were detrimental to the interests of both Athens and its allies. He is also contrasted to Timotheus, who, when accused of taking a bribe, accepted the penalty without question despite his heroic deeds (14-17). Much use is made of the destruction of Thebes (18-21 and 24), as Dinarchus lays responsibility for its fate squarely on Demosthenes' shoulders; the latter's apparent inactivity in procuring Arcadian help appears the more reprehensible when related to the Theban aid given to Athens in the restoration of democracy in 404/3 (25). By these arguments, especially when coupled with effectively integrated exhortations against him, the impression is conveyed that Demosthenes' actions warrant his execution and that it is the duty of the jurors to declare against him.

The framework for this lengthy part of the speech follows the progression (a) specific action, (b) exhortation/abuse against Demosthenes, and (c) specific action, dividing thus:

(11/12) Demosthenes' past exploits (3)

(13) Abuse of Demosthenes

(14) Timotheus' noble deeds

(15) Abuse/call to condemn Demosthenes

(16) Demosthenes' deeds contrasted to Timotheus and Conon

(17) Timotheus' deeds used as contrast for those of Demosthenes

(18-21) Call to execute Demosthenes from allusion to Theban history

(22-23) Execute Demosthenes

(24-25) Thebes

(26-27) Execute Demosthenes
(28) Demosthenes' past actions (3)

This division does not correspond exactly with the secondary-level ring structure, and this double framework gives us an insight into how the speech was composed. In the lengthier parts of the speech Dinarchus would need a rough outline of the topics he had selected and of their sequence for maximum effect, hence the above linear progression. Once he had this, he could then compose the whole part in ring composition (see Introduction, pp. 24-26).

(11) **Yet in spite of the excellence . . . consequence:** On the reports see commentary on 1. Because of the plurality of people involved in this passage I have emended τῆς ἀποφάσεως τῆς . . . γεγενημένης to τῶν ἀποφάσεων τῶν . . . γεγενημένων (cf. 63): see 'On the Use of ἀπόφασις and ἀποφάσεις in Deinarchus I and III', *Philologus* 130 (1986), 184-186, in which I argue that singular instances of *apophasis* refer to individuals and not to all of those charged collectively.

(12) **Demosthenes . . . to deceive you:** It appears that as well as his two *prokleseis* (see commentary on 5) Demosthenes toured the Agora and elsewhere the people might collect denouncing the Areopagus and pleading his own defence in public. This he has done before, as Aeschines, in a speech of 345, says: 'He therefore goes up and down the market-place expressing his wonder and amazement' (1.94). Dinarchus will have heard Demosthenes' public denunciations and so gained insight into what he would include in his defence speech. Ditto Hyperides, who expects Demosthenes to protest that he is being used as a political scapegoat, and has Demosthenes' supporters speaking on his behalf (5.13-14). Dinarchus now moves to selected exploits from Demosthenes' past to show his corruptibility.

'I made the Thebans your allies' . . . states: The reference is to the alliance Demosthenes' procured between Athens and Thebes in 339. The news that Philip II had seized Elatea in that year and that, to all intents and purposes, Athens would be the next target threw the Athenians into no small panic (Aes. 3.84, 140-151, 237-240, 256, Dem. 18.168-188. and 211 ff., Diod. 16.84-85.2, Plut. *Demosthenes* 17.5 ff.). Demosthenes' description of this panic and how he responded to the crisis in his Crown oration of 330 (18.169 ff.) is one of the greatest pieces of oratory to survive, although we must allow for exaggeration. Demosthenes' role in the treaty is generally lauded: see (with background and discussion) A. Schäfer, *Demosthenes und seine Zeit*[2] 2 (Leipzig: 1885), 545-553, A.W. Pickard-Cambridge, *Demosthenes* (London: 1914), 370-376, P. Cloché, *Démosthène et la fin de la démocratie Athénienne* (Paris: 1937), 191-195, Hammond & Griffith, *HM* 2, 589-596, N.G.L. Hammond, *Philip of Macedon* (London: 1994), 143-147; more critically, see J.R. Ellis, *Philip II and Macedonian Imperialism* (London: 1976), 191-193.

'I brought everyone into line at Chaeronea' . . . the line there: Demosthenes is taunted with desertion of his post at the battle of Chaeronea in 338 (see further commentary on 78) by Aeschines in 330 (3.7, 148, 151-152, 159, 175-176, 181, 187, 244 and 253), and by Dinarchus now (71 and 81); cf. Hyperides 5.17 with commentary. The anecdote that Demosthenes' cloak caught on a bramble bush and, thinking that he had been captured, he appealed to be taken alive, is quoted by later sources (Plut. *Demosthenes* 20.2 and [Plut.] *Moralia* 845f). This is invention as under Athenian law deserters lost their personal rights (Andocides 1.74: 'According to a second [form of disfranchisement] delinquents lost all personal rights . . . this class included . . . all who deserted on the field of battle, who were found guilty of evasion of military service, of cowardice . . . all who threw away their shields . . .'). It is likely that Plutarch refers to this penalty (at *Demosthenes* 21.1-2) when he states that Demosthenes' enemies were preparing indictments against him. Demosthenes was certainly not under any cloud, for he was selected to deliver the *epitaphios* over the fallen Athenians in the battle.

'I was an ambassador . . . your behalf': In 13 Dinarchus says that Demosthenes toured all of the Greek world (cf. 16 and 24 on plural embassies to Thebes), but both this and the statement here contradict, and are contradicted by, 81, which states that Demosthenes made only two journeys abroad in his life.

(13)   **I do not know . . . against the people:** Note how Dinarchus distorts facts and uses rhetoric to exploit the tensions between rich and poor by arguing that the receipt of bribes, calculated to harm the city and people, was despicable; cf. J. Ober, *Mass and Elite in Democratic Athens* (Princeton: 1989), 200-216.

(14)   **Athenians . . . twenty other cities as well:** It is ironic that Demosthenes, who had praised the exploits of Timotheus and his father Conon (8.74-75, 20.68 ff.; cf. 84-86 and 22.72), now found himself ignominiously contrasted with them.

Timotheus defeated a Spartan fleet off Corcyra in 375 (Isocrates, *Antidosis* 107 ff., [Dem.] 13.22, Xenophon, *Hellenica* 5.4.64 ff., Diod. 15.47), which severely crippled Spartan naval power. In 367/6 he captured Samos after a ten month siege (*IG* ii² 108, Isocrates, *Antidosis* 111-112, Dem. 15.9, Nepos, *Timotheus* 1.2), and Athenian cleruchs were sent there in 365/4 (Aristotle, *Rhetoric* 2.1384b32-35, Diod. 18.8.9, Strabo 14.4.18), in 361/0 (Scholiast on Aes. 1.53), and then some two thousand more in 352/1 (Philochorus, *FGrH* 328 F 154, Diod. 18.8.9, Strabo 14.639.18). Subsequently Timotheus was appointed to retake Amphipolis (cf. Dem. 23.149). While campaigning in Macedonia he was occupied with various sieges – as Dinarchus mentions – at Methone, Pydna, Potidaea, and apparently twenty other cities (cf. Din. 3.17).

Conon's reputation as expounded by Dinarchus here and earlier by Demosthenes (20.69) stems from his victory at the battle of Cnidus in 394 when, with Persian help, he annihilated the Peloponnesian fleet in the so-called Corinthian War of 395-386 (Dem. 20.68, 70, Isocrates, *Philip* 64, *Areopagiticus* 12 and 65, *Evagoras* 56 and 68, Xenophon, *Hellenica* 4.3.10-14, 8.1, Diod. 14.83.4-7). This victory was followed by the liberation of many cities on the coast of Asia Minor from the oppressive rule of Sparta, including Erythrae, which bestowed a statue and citizenship on Conon (M.N. Tod, *Greek Historical Inscriptions* 2 [Oxford: 1948], no. 106).

Demosthenes tells us (20.70) that Conon was the first to receive (in 394) a publicly erected statue in Athens since that of the 'tyrannicides' Harmodius and Aristogeiton, who murdered Hipparchus, son of the tyrant Pisistratus, then joint ruler of Athens with his brother Hippias (see commentary on 101). This set a trend of public dedications for those who performed public services. Pausanias talks of monuments to Conon and Timotheus in the Agora (1.3.2), and on the Acropolis (1.24.3; cf. Tod, *Greek Historical Inscriptions* 2, no. 128), as well as bronze statues of them in the Sanctuary of Hera on Samos and at Ephesus (Pausanias 6.3.16). See further on this genre A. Stewart, *Attika. Studies in Athenian Sculpture of the Hellenistic Age*

(London: 1979), 115-132, M.K. Walsh, 'Honorary Statues in Ancient Greece', *BSA* 11 (1904/5), 32-49. On Timotheus and Conon see further *PA* 13700 and 8707 and Davies, *APF*, 506-511.

Dinarchus has probably inserted Samos into his speech for emotional effect, given that under Alexander's Exiles Decree the Athenians were ordered to return the island to its native owners, a move they resisted (see Introduction, p. 7). At the same time, the exploits of Timotheus and of Conon formed a patriotic topos (on which see Introduction, p. 37), which appealed to the glorious deeds of the Athenians' ancestors, and it is repeated at 75 and Dinarchus 3.17. This offers something of an interesting twist, since in sources such as Isocrates Timotheus is not a democratic hero, and Conon's liberationist tactics were undertaken for the Persians and not the Athenians, but the Athenians nevertheless were to exploit his deeds to their own advantage.

You did not treat ... one hundred talents: The orators frequently mention the oath of the jurors. Each year 6,000 citizens were selected to serve as jurors, and they swore an oath to vote in accordance with the laws. The oath (Dem. 24.149-151) is quoted in the commentary on Hyperides 5.1.

In 356/5 the Athenians sent a fleet of sixty triremes under Iphicrates, Menestheus and Timotheus to aid Chares, then occupied with the allied revolt against the Second Athenian Confederacy known as the Social War (Diod. 16.21.1, Nepos, *Timotheus* 3.1-4). Quarrels between the commanders resulting in lack of support for Chares at the battle of Embata led to Chares bringing the three to trial for accepting a bribe (Isocrates, *Antidosis* 129, Din. 1.16-17, Diod. 16.21.4, Nepos, *Timotheus* 3.4-5), probably in the winter of 356/5. Iphicrates and Menestheus were acquitted but Timotheus was fined the huge sum of one hundred talents. He was unable to pay, and so was forced into exile in Chalcis where he died two or three years later (Isocrates, *Antidosis* 129-130, Nepos, *Timotheus* 3.5; cf. [Dem.] 49.9 ff.). Timotheus' trial and career are interwoven with the politics and leading politicians of Athens at that time, on which see R. Sealey 'Athens after the Social War', *JHS* 75 (1955), 74-81 (= *Essays in Greek Politics* [New York: 1967], 164-182) and 'Callistratus of Aphidna and His Contemporaries', *Historia* 5 (1956), 178-203 (= *Essays in Greek Politics*, 133-163), R.A. Moysey, 'Chares and Athenian Foreign Policy', *CJ* 80 (1985), 223-227 and 'Isokrates and Chares: A Study in the Political Spectrum of Mid-Fourth Century Athens', *Ancient World* 15 (1987), 83-86.

because Aristophon ... Chians and the Rhodians: Aristophon from the deme Azenia was an orator who lived a remarkably long life, almost 100 years. He first came to prominence in political life against the Thirty in 404/3, and he was the leading prosecutor of Timotheus at his trial ([Plut.] *Moralia* 187a). Demosthenes (18.249) says that Aristophon's opponents indicted him every day for a while, and Aristophon himself boasts of being acquitted of indictment under the *graphe paranomon* procedure (for illegal proposals) seventy-five times. See further *PA* 2108, Davies, *APF*, 65 and D. Whitehead, 'The Political Career of Aristophon', *CPh* 81 (1986), 313-319.

(15)   Will you not punish this despicable creature and Scythian: Demosthenes' illegitimacy is stated elsewhere (Aes. 3.171-172, [Plut.] *Moralia* 847f, Rutilius Lupus 3.9), but this can hardly be true given Pericles' citizenship law of 451/0 (*AP* 26.4, Plut. *Pericles* 37.3), which stated that both parents must be Athenian citizens for children to be legitimate (quoted at 71 below).

Demosthenes, born either in 385/4 or 384/3 (Davies, *APF*, 121-122), would have been debarred from political and judicial life if he were illegitimate. An opponent's parentage was often an area to attack given the invective in oratory (see P. Harding, 'Rhetoric and Politics in Fourth-century Athens', *Phoenix* 41 [1987], 29-32), and the mother's profession, for example, is included in the topoi of invective of the Attic orators: thus Demosthenes (18.129-130; cf. 261) makes Aeschines' father an uneducated slave and mother a whore. See also commentary on 71, where the legitimacy of Demosthenes' children is questioned.

I'm almost speechless with rage: Cf. 10. This is probably a 'simulated' or pretend extemporaneous comment effectively emphasising the speaker's outrage.

whom not one man . . . own expense: Reference to the Areopagus' enquiry (*zetesis*) and to its report against Demosthenes, which found him guilty of taking a bribe: see commentary on 1. On his apparent possession of Persian gold, see commentary on 10.

Several measures reported to have earned Demosthenes much wealth are described at 42-45; cf. 111, with commentary. The reference here is to Demosthenes' income from domestic and not foreign sources, the subject of the previous clause, as revealed by the οὐ μόνον . . . ἀλλὰ καί construction.

and just recently . . . by Harpalus: This clause is separate from the one immediately preceding it, making Dinarchus refer here to Demosthenes' most recent (νῦν) income as opposed to his *earlier* income (the subject of the two previous clauses).

(16) **And yet, what fraction . . . Read it:** Dinarchus may be referring to Demosthenes' embassies to Thebes here, presumably in connection with the alliance of 339 (although this seems to have been the product of a *single* mission).

For the exploits of Timotheus and Conon see 14 with commentary. The decree on Timotheus will be that recording his punishment and its circumstances, meted out for apparently taking money from the Chians and the Rhodians.

(17) **Such was the nature . . . their vowed duty:** That is, Timotheus. Direct address to Demosthenes for stylish rhetorical effect.

Demosthenes' inactivity and failure to serve his city are often stated in order to sharpen the contrast between him and those who have actively benefited the city like Timotheus and who respect the law and the findings of judicial bodies (cf. 37-40 and 100). Demosthenes, however, acts in the opposite way by publicly denouncing and challenging the Areopagus and its findings. There is a similarity with 87, where Poseidon and the 'awful goddesses' also bowed to the judgment of the Areopagus.

But he was ready . . . did not hold: Since Timotheus had no desire to compromise the jurors, he stood ready for condemnation, if they so decided, refusing to plead for clemency.

(18) **Gentlemen of Athens . . . its defence:** See commentary on 10 on Demosthenes' alleged receipt of Persian gold to help support the Theban revolt. Dinarchus holds Demosthenes himself directly responsible for the destruction of Thebes, and he even accuses him of refusing to pay a bribe of ten talents, demanded by the Arcadian leader Astylus, to procure Arcadian help for Thebes, even though he had allegedly received three hundred from the Persian king. Without the Arcadian support Thebes thus fell. Whether

Demosthenes was guilty or was the victim of a trumped-up charge is unknown: in the commentary on 21, the argument is put forward that Demosthenes was innocent.

The Arcadians . . . hard-pressed Thebans: Aeschines (3.240), Arrian (1.10.1) and Diodorus (17.8.5-6) attest Arcadian support for the Thebans. Dinarchus' implication that the Arcadians did not decide to commit themselves until they arrived at the isthmus is additional information.

which had reached them . . . young shoots: A picturesque detail, perhaps illustrating supplication as a ploy in diplomacy, but the qualifying ὡς ἔφασαν ('as they said') impacts on the veracity of the anecdote since it is tantamount to hearsay. Hammond (Hammond & Walbank, *HM* 3, 59) points out that the Thebans would have made their way to the Gulf of Corinth with great difficulty since a Macedonian army was encamped at Onchestus and the envoys would have had to avoid Thespiae and Plataea on their route.

(19)   **The Thebans came . . . free people:** The Thebans' decision to rebel against their enforced slavery is part of the greater Greek ideal of *eleutheria* or freedom (see also 37), which Dinarchus exploits for emotional effect in this passage. On this ideal see also commentary on Hyperides 6.10.

After the battle of Chaeronea in 338 Philip II imposed a Macedonian garrison in Thebes and appointed a council of three hundred former exiles as governing body. The Thebans' hegemony of the Boeotian League was also taken away, and a purge of anti-Macedonians followed (Diod. 16.87.3, Pausanias 9.1.8, 6.5, Justin 9.4.6-9): C. Roebuck, 'The Settlement of Philip II with the Greek States in 338 B.C.', *CPh* 43 (1948), 79-80, and Hammond & Griffith, *HM* 2, 610-612. Dinarchus implies that the conduct of the pro-Macedonian oligarchy proved too much for the Thebans, and Arrian attributes the outbreak of the rebellion to some of the returning exiles (1.7.1-3). Cf. 38, of Thebes in 382-379/8, when a Spartan garrison illegally occupied the Cadmea.

(20)   **The Arcadians . . . the Greeks:** The theme of *eleutheria* (freedom) is continued, though the ideal is devalued since Astylus demands a price for it. Dinarchus says it was then that the Arcadians decided to support Thebes (Diodorus 17.8.6 has 'the Peloponnesians' waiting at the isthmus to see what transpired), whereas Arrian 1.10.1 *implies* that they had made this decision before leaving home; cf. commentary on 18 and especially 21.

Since their general Astylus was open to bribery: This is the only source that actually names the Arcadian *strategos* (general) of 335, and although Aeschines 3.240 refers to this incident he does not name Astylus. We know nothing else about him. An assessment of the extent of bribery in Greece is limited because the sources for states other than Athens are scarce. This passage is valuable since it refers to its existence in Arcadia: see further F.D. Harvey, '*Dona Ferentes*: Some Aspects of Bribery in Greek Politics', *Crux. Essays in Greek History Presented to G.E.M. de Ste. Croix on his 75th Birthday*, edd. P.A. Cartledge and F.D. Harvey (London: 1985), 90, with 89-102 on the extent of bribery.

as Stratocles also said: On Stratocles, see commentary on 1.

and demanded ten talents . . . their city: Here and in 21 Dinarchus says that Astylus wanted a ten talent bribe, but Aeschines 3.240 has nine talents of silver. On the orators' veracity see commentary on 10. The ambassadors are the Theban ones who begged Demosthenes for ten talents from the three hundred he was supposed to have received from Persia in order to pay Astylus.

(21) **But this miserable, impious, and mercenary man . . . the Thebans:** Dinarchus uses the word αἰσχροκερδής ('mercenary') in his characterisation of Demosthenes (cf. 108, Din. 3.6) as it reinforces the impression of his venality.

Dinarchus' allegations are doubtful, for the accusation that Demosthenes was responsible for the betrayal of Thebes occurs only in Dinarchus and in Aeschines (3.239-240; cf. 133 and 155-156), and both only bring insinuations against Demosthenes. See in detail Worthington, *Dinarchus*, 160-168; the arguments are briefly summarised here.

First, we have the confusion in our sources over the receipt and amount of the Persian money (see commentary on 10). Next, Demosthenes' so-called 'betrayal' of Thebes. Diodorus (17.8.5-6) and Plutarch (*Demosthenes* 23.1; cf. [Plut.] *Moralia* 847c) say that Demosthenes initially urged the Athenians to support Thebes; they gave arms to the Thebans, but then retracted their support (Diod. 17.8.6; cf. Plut. *Demosthenes* 23.2), and Thebes was razed to the ground. However, Diodorus 17.8.6 informs us that it was the Athenians in Assembly, not Demosthenes or his advice, who ultimately decided against active support (cf. Plut. *Demosthenes* 23.2). Of course, Alexander still blamed them (Arr. 1.10.6), but this is very different from the allegations of two orators out to convict Demosthenes by fair means or foul.

We know from various sources that the Arcadians marched out (Arr. 1.10.1, Diod. 17.8.5-6), so Dinarchus refers to a historical fact. Yet, according to him and Aeschines (3.240) the Arcadians decided to support Thebes when they arrived at the isthmus and only in return for a bribe, but Arrian (1.10.1) certainly has it (cf. Diod. 17.8.6) that they had decided to help *if necessary* before leaving home. Astylus' decision not to intervene actively may have been calculated: he did not wish to do so until necessary, but by then it was too late (A.B. Bosworth, *A Historical Commentary on Arrian's History of Alexander*, 1 [Oxford: 1980], 76; cf. A. Schäfer, *Demosthenes und seine Zeit*[2] 3 [Leipzig: 1887], 133-134). The story was then fabricated that he remained passive unless paid a bribe, something that Demosthenes refused to do despite his alleged huge sum of money. Indeed it is odd that Thebes and its large resources could not have paid out nine or ten talents from its own funds.

This does not of course preclude a kernel of truth in the account; however, if some of the jurors were aware of the events, this presupposes that the transactions at the isthmus must have been common knowledge. Perhaps if speeches were given in the Assembly denouncing or explaining what happened, there would be reference to them in Aeschines and Dinarchus, for such would support their own cases admirably. More likely is that we have a distortion of historical facts and accuracy for rhetorical reasons. Moreover, Dinarchus' composition must also be borne in mind: these sections display such complex ring structures that go beyond the secondary level (see Worthington, *Dinarchus*, 344 and 351-352) that it is hard to reconcile historical accuracy with the level of composition.

(22) **Do you think . . . such iniquities:** Rhetorical approach to convict Demosthenes and have him executed, as the penalty for *dorodokia* allowed, in the light of what has preceded. Dinarchus involves the jury directly in the proceedings with the analogy that they are on trial before their peers, as we have already seen him do in the introduction to the speech (3). These

questions are meant to provoke dicastic *thorubos*, that is, inciting a crowd (here the jury) to raise an uproar which would fuel their indignation of the defendant and in an emotionally-charged atmosphere lead to them declaring against him; see V. Bers, 'Dikastic *Thorubos*', *Crux. Essays in Greek History Presented to G.E.M. de Ste. Croix on his 75th Birthday*, edd. P.A. Cartledge and F.D. Harvey (London: 1985), 1-15.

(23)   **You are those . . . his mill:** References now to three men executed for less noteworthy crimes than that of Demosthenes to influence the jury against him; cf. 60. The details of the case against Menon the miller are unknown. Presumably they were sufficiently well-known that Dinarchus could cite the case so tersely. It was against the law to confine an Athenian citizen; hence, the death penalty was imposed on Menon for incarcerating this young boy from the Attic deme Pellene in his mill.

You inflicted death on Themistius . . . Eleusinia: This is all we know about Themistius. Under Athenian law, any person assaulting another while attending a religious festival (specifically the festivals of the Great Dionysia, Dionysia at Piraeus, Lenaea, Thargelia, and the Eleusinian Mysteries) was liable to the death sentence under the procedure called *graphe hubreos* (Dem. 21.8-11, 147, 175 ff.). The case was first heard by the Assembly, and if it decided against the defendant then the case proceeded to court (R.J. Bonner and G. Smith, *The Administration of Justice from Homer to Aristotle* 2 [Chicago: 1938], 24-25, A.R.W. Harrison, *The Law of Athens* 2 [Oxford: 1971], 59-64, D.M. MacDowell, *The Law in Classical Athens* [London: 1978], 194-197).

The most famous of cases under this procedure was that of Demosthenes against Meidias in 347/6, which may be mentioned here since the murder of Meidias' supporter Nicodemus, in which Demosthenes was implicated, is the subject of section 30 (see commentary). At the Dionysia of 348, Meidias punched Demosthenes, who was a *choregos* (a provider of a chorus at a dramatic performance), in the face, and he indicted Meidias under a *graphe hubreos*. After a year (Dem. 21.13), Meidias paid thirty minas in an out-of-court settlement (Aes. 3.52, Plut. *Demosthenes* 12.3-6). Demosthenes' speech survives as Oration 21 in the Demosthenic corpus.

and on Euthymachus . . . his brothel: This is all we know of Euthymachus, though the case must have been well known (as with that against Themistius above) for Dinarchus to refer to it so sketchily. A. Schäfer, *Demosthenes und seine Zeit*2 2 (Leipzig: 1885), 155-156 with n. 2, connects this episode with the betrayal of Olynthus, the chief city of the Chalcidian League, to Philip II in 348 (see commentary on 26 and 28).

(24)   **But thanks to this traitor . . . barbarians:** When Thebes was razed to the ground in 335, the survivors were sold as slaves. Dinarchus implies that the women and children became property, distributed at will among the 'barbarian' Macedonians.

a neighbouring and allied city has been ripped up from the middle of Greece: Cf. 74 (where Thebes' destruction is attributed to three Theban commanders), and note the imagery carried over from Aeschines 3.133: 'But Thebes! Thebes, our neighbour, has in one day been swept from the midst of Hellas.'

the city of the Thebans . . . ploughed and sown: The vivid imagery from the metaphor seems also to have been used by Stratocles in his speech against Demosthenes, if the attribution of a fragment of a speech to him in

Agatharchides is correct (F. Blass, *Die attische Beredsamkeit²*, 3.2 [Leipzig: 1898], 319-320): ἀροῦται καὶ σπείρεται τὸ Θηβαίων ἄστυ τῶν συναγωνισαμένων ὑμῖν τὸν πρὸς Φίλιππον πόλεμον ('the city of the Thebans, which fought on the same side in the war against Philip with you, is being ploughed and sown'). The Athenian-Theban alliance against Philip II would be that of 339 (see commentary on 12), which was shattered by him after the battle of Chaeronea in 338 (on which see commentary on 78). The repetition for effect is typical of Dinarchus' rhetorical style.

I tell you this contemptible man . . . your ally: Further repetition of the first person singular for emphasis. Demosthenes was the Theban *proxenos* (an individual appointed by another state – in Demosthenes' case, Thebes – to look after its ambassadors and important visitors when in Athens); for his mission to that city see commentary on 12. On *proxenoi* see F.E. Adcock and D.J. Mosley, *Diplomacy in Ancient Greece* (London: 1975), 160-163.

But those to whom . . . by misfortune: An effective way of concluding Demosthenes' 'betrayal' of the Thebans, and introducing, by way of contrast, their earlier support of the Athenians.

(25) **When the democracy . . . as our elders say:** See also 72 ('All the older men . . . would agree') and 75 ('so the elders say'), also within the context of earlier Theban history.

despite the strength . . . their territory: The corruption of the text at the end of this section has led to several proposed restorations; the word order of my proposal (περιορᾶν ἐάν τις Ἀθηναίων ὅπλα διὰ τῆς χώρας) is a plausible compromise.

In 404/3 Athens was controlled by the oppressive oligarchic regime of the Thirty Tyrants, which suppressed many of the political and judicial rights and privileges of the people: see for example C. Hignett, *A History of the Athenian Constitution* (Oxford: 1952), 285-298 and 378-389 and P.J. Rhodes, *A Commentary on the Aristotelian Athenaion Politeia* (Oxford: 1981), 415-482. Lysias, whose brother Polemarchus was murdered under the regime, presents us with a vivid contemporary picture of it in his speech *Against Eratosthenes* (12). The Spartans, in an effort to prohibit any resurgence of Athenian power, ordered that anyone discovering an exile was to return him to Athens or be fined five talents (Diod. 14.6.1; cf. Plut. *Lysander* 27.2). This was resisted by the Thebans (and Argives: Diod. 14.6.2; cf. Justin 5.9.4), who decreed that Boeotia would offer refuge to any Athenian exile and imposed a fine of one talent on any Boeotian who refused (Plut. *Lysander* 27.3, *Pelopidas* 6.4, Diod. 14.6.3 and 32.1; cf. commentary on 27). Furthermore, they secretly helped the exiled Thrasybulus of Stiria (*PA* 7310, Davies, *APF*, 240-241) to seize Phyle (Xenophon, *Hellenica* 2.4.2, *AP* 37.1, Diod. 14.32.1, Plut. *Lysander* 27.4), which was used as a base of operations against the Thirty, and in the decree to which Dinarchus refers they agreed to turn a blind eye towards any Athenian marching through their territory bearing arms (Plut. *Lysander* 27.3, *Pelopidas* 6.4).

The restoration of democracy in 403 was a favourite topos among the orators: cf. Lycurgus 1.61 and Aeschines 3.190-192, 195 and 208 with P. Harding, 'Rhetoric and Politics in Fourth-century Athens', *Phoenix* 41 (1987), 34-36. See also 38-40 with commentary.

(26) **But this man . . . their safety:** On the alleged receipt of money see commentary on 10. ὡς αὐτίκα φήσει ('as he will presently tell you') suggests that the phrase was either a later insertion after Demosthenes'

defence speech or an indication that Demosthenes had given advance warning that as part of his defence he would emphasise his relations with Thebes (cf. commentary on 7 on advance arguments).

Gentlemen . . . Thebes: In 24 Demosthenes was the betrayer of Thebes, and so too here. Olynthus was the chief city in the Chalcidice and the final one to resist Philip II's expansionist policies in that region. It fell to the king after a short siege in August or September 348 (J.R. Ellis, *Philip II and Macedonian Imperialism* [London: 1976], 99), and its citizens were either enslaved or fled into exile (Diod. 16.53.3). Philip was said to have bribed two of the city's hipparchs, Euthycrates and Lasthenes, hence Dinarchus' allusion to treachery (Diod. 16.53.2; cf. Dem. 8.40, 9.56-57, 66 ff., 19.265, 342 and 18.48 – although Demosthenes tends to attribute Philip's successes to treachery). The Olynthians had thrice appealed for help to the Athenians, but despite Demosthenes' measures in support ([Plut.] *Moralia* 845d-e), especially in the three *Olynthiac* orations, an Athenian relief fleet arrived too late. On the background see Hammond & Griffith, *HM* 2, 321-328, and N.G.L. Hammond, *Philip of Macedon* (London: 1994), 50-52 and 61-63.

The fates of Olynthus at the hands of Philip II and of Thebes by Alexander the Great were common historical topoi.

Decide wisely now . . . gods: On the inclusion of the gods as a rhetorical device see commentary on 7.

(27) **For only by one way . . . Read the letters:** Another emphatic opening of a sentence, which is typical of Dinarchus. Cf. 3 and 22 (the verdict of the jurors is awaited by the remainder of the citizens) and 5 and 11 (the Areopagus was not swayed by the powerful opposition in its quest for truth and justice).

The second decree in the speech is that of the Thebans who agreed to support the restoration of Athenian democracy in 403 (cited in 25). It is now called to be read along with additional evidence. The letters probably reflect correspondence between Demosthenes and the Thebans, as Nouhaud and Dors-Méary (58, note 26) suggest.

(28) **Athenians, this man is a hireling . . . history:** An emphatic opening statement, which is characteristic of Dinarchus; cf. 76 and 90.

This was the man . . . the first war: In 357 the Athenians declared war (the 'first war') on Philip II when he apparently reneged on a secret agreement to hand over Amphipolis to them (*IG* ii^2 127, Isocrates, *Philip* 2, Aes. 2.21, 70, 72, 3.54; cf. Diod. 16.8.2). That such an agreement was made is highly doubtful: see G.E.M. de Ste. Croix, 'The Alleged Secret Pact between Athens and Philip II Concerning Amphipolis and Pydna', *CQ*^{2} 13 (1963), 110-119. Although the war did not end until 346 proposals for peace had been put forward by Philip although the Athenians were not persuaded to consider them until after the fall of Olynthus in 348 (see commentary on 26), and the formal annexation of the Chalcidice into Macedon. Eventually, with the support of Philocrates (see next note) and Demosthenes, the war was concluded (Peace of Philocrates). For the history see J.R. Ellis, *Philip II and Macedonian Imperialism* (London: 1976), 63-67 and 93-124, Hammond & Griffith, *HM* 2, 236-243 and 315-347.

This man helped to defend Philocrates . . . exiled him: In late 348 Philocrates of Hagnus proposed that Athens send envoys to discuss Philip II's peace terms, which was technically illegal, perhaps because of a clause in the treaty between Athens and the Olynthian League, against which Philip was then campaigning (Ellis, *Philip II*, 100). Philocrates was indicted under the procedure known as *graphe paranomon* (illegal proposals – see too Aes. 2.13-14, 3.62). Demosthenes defended him, winning such a victory that his opponent Lycinus failed to obtain one-fifth of the votes cast (Aes. 2.14, 3.62), and so under Athenian law lost his political rights. Then in 343 Philocrates was impeached by Hyperides for having made proposals (in 346: see above note) contrary to the common good (cf. Hyp. 4.29-30). Although the charge was flimsy Philocrates fled into exile before the trial (not actually exiled as Dinarchus states) and was condemned to death *in absentia* (Dem. 19.114 ff., Aes. 2.6, 3.79 ff.; cf. Hyp. fr. A.16 Burtt). See further *PA* 14599 = 14576 and Ellis, *Philip II*, 100 and 148-150.

and he hired a carriage . . . the Macedonians: In 346 peace between Athens and Philip II was formally concluded when Antipater, Eurylochus, and Parmenion travelled to Athens as Philip's envoys for the actual signing (Theopompus *FGrH* 115 F 164; cf. Dem. 19.69, Aes. 3.72). Dinarchus' accusations of flattery echo those which Aeschines also levels against him in his speech of 330 (for example, 3.76: ' . . . and at daybreak he came escorting the ambassadors into the theatre, so that he was actually hissed for his unseemly flattery. And when they set out on their return journey, he hired for them three span of mules'). This need not imply plagiarism by Dinarchus, for we should expect that two enemies of Demosthenes would have common charges to use against him, and perhaps again we have here evidence of an anti-Demosthenic topos in use. Moreover, both can only insinuate rather than prove that Demosthenes was guilty of this act of flattery. It does appear that Demosthenes treated the visiting Macedonians with some degree of hospitality, but this was probably as part of a strategy to procure the acceptance of the Peace of Philocrates (cf. Ellis, *Philip II*, 125-127).

D (29-47) Past History II

    (29-30) Appeal is made to punish D.
        (30) D conspired with Aristarchus to murder Nicodemus.
            (31-33) D has infected everyone with his bad luck (he is jinxed).
                (34-36) D's past inactivity to the detriment of Greece (time of Agis' war).
                (37-40) Contrast to Athens' great ancestors, who helped the Theban exiles.
            (41-44) D in the past introduced bad legislation to the detriment of Athens.
        (45-47) D has cheated the Athenian people and is accursed.
    (47) D advanced a cruel and unlawful course to Aristarchus.
    (47) The speaker urges that D must pay the penalty for his crimes.

(29-47) In this part of the speech Dinarchus uses Athens' past history to show the determining role played by leaders in the good and bad fortunes of a city, using the prudential argument that Demosthenes will be of no use to Athens given his inactivity and ignobility in the past (30, 36). Differences are drawn between Demosthenes' sloth and the diligence of patriots and former leaders (31-36), which enhanced Athens' reputation, while he is motivated only by venal desires (37-45). Thebes is again at the core, but in this part the emphasis falls not on Demosthenes' apparent role in its downfall (as in 18-21), but on the Athenian help to Thebes in 379/8 when the Cadmea was illegally garrisoned Sparta. The heroism of Demosthenes' predecessors is thus contrasted with his reluctance to send help in 335. The sequence of events in this part of the speech follows the progression (a) abuse/exhortation against Demosthenes, (b) selected action/event, and (c) abuse/exhortation against Demosthenes, which is the reverse of the general framework of the previous part.

(29)   **Gentlemen . . . against the city:** Note the emphatic opening, which is typical of Dinarchus' style. Being caught 'red-handed' (cf. 54 and Din. 2.6) is both a dramatic phrase and has a legal foundation since in some judicial procedures (such as *apagoge*, in which any citizen could hand over a transgressor to the authorities: *AP* 12.1) the criminal had to be caught specifically 'in the act'. By the fourth century anything infamous was included under it (A.R.W. Harrison, *The Law of Athens* 2 [Oxford: 1971], 224).

Since good fortune . . . these leaders: The inclusion of the reference to good fortune (ἀγαθὴ τύχη), which is also found at 98, adds religious weight to Dinarchus' appeal for Demosthenes' execution; cf. Hyp. 5.35-36.

E. Badian, 'Harpalus', *JHS* 81 (1961), 35 with n. 144, argued that the person expelled for defiling the country is Demades, and that when he was accused he immediately went into exile without standing trial. This is plausible; cf. commentary on 104.

(30)   **For what occasion . . . ruined them:** Cf. Aeschines 3.158 ('For there is no city, there is no private man – not one – that has ever come off safe after following Demosthenes' counsel'). The dramatic tone here helps to mask to an extent the argument from probability (*eikota*) that the accused, given his career and activities to date, will not serve his city to any use in the future.

Did he not go . . . his misfortunes: Cf. 47. The story is also told by Aeschines (1.171-172, 2.148 and 166; cf. Athenaeus 13.592f), and is perhaps one of several stock topoi in the oratorical repertoire of invective against Demosthenes, and not an instance of Dinarchus' plagiarising from Aeschines.

Demosthenes is accused of becoming the lover and mentor of one Aristarchus, said to be mentally deficient (Aes. 1.171) and of persuading him to murder Nicodemus of Aphidna, who in 348 had charged Demosthenes with desertion during the Euboean campaign (Aes. 2.148). Demosthenes had gone with the Athenian force to Euboea, but returned to Athens in order to perform his liturgy (personal duties for the state paid from one's own funds) of *choregia* (providing a chorus) at the festival of the Great Dionysia. However, even though Nicodemus failed to prosecute, Demosthenes still wanted vengeance, hence the plot with Aristarchus. The latter then fled, and Demosthenes allegedly kept three talents which Aristarchus gave him and which had been intended to help him while in exile (Aes. 1.172, 2.166). Demosthenes' opponents, especially Meidias, tried to connect him with Aristarchus but failed. Although Demosthenes denied complicity (21.104-105, 116 ff.), it is plausible that the conspiracy did exist: the Euboean affair (March 348) occurred contemporaneously with the Great Dionysia, at which Meidias punched Demosthenes (cf. Aes. 3.52, 212, Plut. *Demosthenes* 12.3-6), and as a result he was subsequently indicted under a *graphe hubreos*: see commentary on 23. Meidias may have seized the opportunity for revenge by having his supporter Nicodemus charge Demosthenes with desertion, although it is odd that Demosthenes did not simply attack against Meidias but resorted to a more brutal course, which was out of character.

(31) **When he began to advise . . . and disgrace:** A.P. Dorjahn and W.D.
Fairchild ('Extemporaneous Elements in Some Minor Attic Orators', *CB* 48
[1972], 62) considered 'I will pass over his private affairs, for time does not
allow me to speak at length' extemporaneous: 'If these words were
accompanied by a glance towards the water-clock, it would create an
impression that at least in part the accuser was speaking impromptu.' This is
certainly true. See commentary on 114 on the water-clock. For similar
descriptions of the results of Demosthenes' policies, where Demosthenes
appears a jinx, see 64 ff., 88 and 109.

Has he not let slip . . . on your behalf: See also 36. Demosthenes' missed
opportunities are also used against him by Aeschines at 3.164-166
(Alexander's apparently hard-pressed position before the battle of Issus in
Persia in 333). Here Dinarchus anticipates what will be part of Demosthenes'
defence strategy, perhaps based on what he heard him say before the trial (see
commentary on 12), and in the following sections sets out to discredit it.

(32) **Charidemus sailed . . . anticipated:** The following names are also found in
Demosthenes' later *Epistle* 3.31 as patriots with whom he associated –
perhaps in order to reply to Dinarchus' charge that he was responsible for
their misfortune.

Charidemus received Athenian citizenship, probably in 357/6 (Davies,
APF, 571), for his military services for the state (Dem. 23.145, 151, 185,
187). Since he was involved in military activities in Thrace in 336 (A.
Schäfer, *Demosthenes und seine Zeit*[2] 2 [Leipzig: 1885], 87, Berve,
Alexander 2, 406-407), he was the first person to send news of Philip II's
death to Athens – specifically to Demosthenes (Aes. 3.77). He was amongst
those Athenians, including Demosthenes, whom Alexander III demanded to
be surrendered to him in 335 after the Theban revolt: Arr. 1.10.4, Plut.
Demosthenes 23.4 and *Phocion* 17.2; cf. Dem. *Epistle* 3.31, and see
commentary on 82. Although Alexander relented in his demand, he insisted
on Charidemus' exile, who fled to Darius (Arr. 1.10.6), and was eventually
killed on Darius' orders in 333 (Diod. 17.30.2-6, Curt. 3.2.10-19). On
Charidemus see Demosthenes 23.144-195 with *PA* 15380, Berve, *Alexander*
2, no. 823 and Davies, *APF*, 570-572.

Since Charidemus was exiled soon after the fall of Thebes (335), what
could have been the service which Dinarchus mentions? Perhaps to gain
Persian support in a rebellion against Alexander since Demosthenes had been
leaning towards the Persians in his policy (G.L. Cawkwell, 'The Crowning of
Demosthenes', *CQ*[2] 19 [1969], 174-180), and Darius had made overtures for
an alliance soon after Alexander became king (see commentary on 10). Yet,
faced by the terrible example of the razing of Thebes the Greeks would not
have rallied to a further call against Macedonian hegemony so soon after, nor
would one expect Demosthenes, who had so recently narrowly escaped being
surrendered to Alexander, to be making speeches so openly in public.
Dinarchus probably seized upon a historical event and reworked it to
disparage Demosthenes as one active only in words and not deeds, and note
how Dinarchus presents Charidemus' motive, who, in going to the Persian
king, wanted 'to be of service to you with actions not with words', which
echoes 17, that Timotheus 'performed great deeds for the city by actions and
not by words'.

(33) **Ephialtes . . . the city:** Ephialtes served on an embassy to Persia in 341/0,
and returned with money to support a war against Philip II, some of which

was given to Demosthenes ([Plut.] *Moralia* 847f) and to Hyperides ([Plut.] *Moralia* 848e). Hyperides may well have used this money as a stepping-stone to political power: see Introduction, p. 28. In 335 Ephialtes was one of those demanded by Alexander (Arr. 1.10.4, Plut. *Demosthenes* 23.4; cf. Dem. *Epistle* 3.31). He left Athens soon after and joined forces with the Persians, and in 334/3 he was killed while helping to defend Halicarnassus against Alexander (Diod. 17.27.3). See further *PA* 6156 and Berve, *Alexander* 2, no. 329.

Euthydicus . . . also perished: We know very little about Euthydicus; presumably he was a supporter of Demosthenes, but he was not one of those demanded by Alexander in 335. Since his name occurs with that of Ephialtes in the only two ancient sources we have for him, we may presume he served on the Persian embassy with Ephialtes (see commentary on 33). See further *PA* 5556.

Do you not think . . . the city: This is the first of three lacunae in the text (33-34, 64, and 82). The sense of the lacuna here poses no problem in restoring the text. An accusative and infinitive construction most readily fits the sense, with the whole sentence being turned into a question in view of the numerous questions before and after the lacuna. See my 'Deinarchus I.34 & 82: Two textual restorations', *LCM* 10 (1985), 152 (accepting Blass' restoration at 64).

Dinarchus now returns to his general argument with speculation on Athens' future prospects in the light of past events and of Demosthenes' leadership.

(34) **Is it not necessary for us . . . mercenaries:** I prefer the reading κατασκευὴν of manuscript A (followed by Burtt) over παρασκευὴν of N (followed by Blass, Conomis and Nouhaud and Dors-Méary).

In 331, Agis III of Sparta led a short-lived war against the Macedonian hegemony of Greece, the most important threat to that hegemony between the destruction of Thebes and Alexander's death. Agis had received support from several states including Achaea, Arcadia, Elea, Elis, and Tegea, but he was defeated and killed by Antipater, who had been appointed regent of Macedon while Alexander was campaigning in the east, at the battle of Megalopolis in either late 331 or spring 330 (Aes. 3.165-166, Diod. 17.48.1, 62.6-63.4, 73.5, Curt. 6.1; cf. Arr. 2.13.4, 3.6.3, 3.16.10). The Athenians, on the urging of Demosthenes and probably also Demades and Phocion (see commentary on 35), did not support him (cf. Aes. 3.165-166, Diod. 17.62.7, [Plut.] *Moralia* 818e-f). Antipater referred the fate of the defeated states to the Council of the League of Corinth, which fined Achaea and Elis 120 talents, but then referred the decision on Sparta to Alexander himself (Aes. 3.133, Diod. 17.73.5-6, Curt. 6.1.20). Alexander surprisingly pardoned Sparta and it ceased to pose a threat to Macedon, probably as he intended (Hammond & Walbank, *HM* 3, 78). On Agis' war see Worthington, *Dinarchus*, on 1.34-35 with bibliography cited, to which add E. Badian, 'Agis III: Revisions and Reflections', *Ventures Into Greek History. Essays in Honour of N.G.L. Hammond*, ed. Ian Worthington (Oxford: 1994), 258-292.

The Spartan punishment could have been more severe in view of the retribution that befell Thebes in 335, but it is interesting that Aeschines 3.133 laments the Spartan fate: 'And the wretched Lacedaemonians . . . they who once claimed the right to lead the Greeks, are now about to be sent to Alexander to serve as hostages, and to make an exhibition of their misfortunes . . .' This lamentation is unusual in oratory where Spartan history tends to be ignored or devalued in favour, as we would expect, of Athenian.

and Alexander, so they said, . . . misfortunes: Rhetorical exaggeration is evident here. Alexander was actually in Persia during Agis' war and did not leave for India until summer 327. Dinarchus knew this, but styled the argument of this passage for rhetorical effect, as did Aeschines, when referring to the same incident, at 3.165: 'Meanwhile Alexander had withdrawn to the uttermost regions of the North, almost beyond the borders of the inhabited world.' Thus, Alexander is fixed even further away from Greece, and therefore less likely to return, in which case if Demosthenes had acted in support of Agis III, Greece might well have rid itself of its Macedonian masters. Compare a similar type of argument at Hyperides 5.18-19 (with commentary). The depiction of the geographical extent of Alexander's conquests shows that the unparalleled conquests of the king were a ready subject of conversation: L.L. Gunderson, 'Alexander and the Attic Orators', *Ancient Macedonian Studies in Honour of C.F. Edson*, ed. H.J. Dell (Thessaloniki: 1981), 189-190. On Alexander's Indian exploits see now A.B. Bosworth, *Alexander and the East* (Oxford: 1996).

(35) **What then . . . common safety:** On Agis III's war see commentary on 34. It is implausible that Demosthenes was *solely* responsible for the lack of Athenian support for Agis, as Dinarchus would have it. He was certainly instrumental in persuading the Athenians not to intervene (Aes. 3.165-166, Diod. 17.62.7, and especially G.L. Cawkwell, 'The Crowning of Demosthenes', *CQ*[2] 19 [1969], 176-180); however, given the fate which befell Thebes in 335, Athenian neutrality in 331/0 almost certainly saved the city from a harsh penalty. As with Demosthenes' role in the 'betrayal' of Thebes to destruction (18-21), Dinarchus brings only insinuations, not actual charges, against him that his handling of the Agis affair had been detrimental to Athens and the Greeks.

Not at all . . . fingertips: That is, at the time of the battle of Issus (333), Alexander's first true victory over the Persian army. The phrasing is similar to that used by Aeschines in his speech of 330: ' . . . there was not room enough in the city to contain your odious demonstrations and the letters that you carried around, dangling them from your fingers' (3.164). On the battle see, for example, Bosworth, *Conquest and Empire*, 57-62.

παρ' αὐτῷ is the equivalent of παρὰ σαυτῷ; cf. H.A. Kleyn, 'Dinarchea', *Mnemosyne* 8 (1859), 94.

ἐπιστολὴν of the manuscripts is to be preferred over ἐπιστολὰς in the light of the continuity of the passage in question; cf. Blass, Burtt and Nouhaud and Dors-Méary.

(36) **living well . . . never better ones:** In 69 Dinarchus refers to Demosthenes' houses in the Piraeus and in the city, which is a skilful strategy to denigrate Demosthenes' character in view of the Athenians' attitude to ostentation and decadence; cf. Hyp. 5.16.

The employment of the oath introduces a pious element to Dinarchus' argument, and it is a particularly appropriate one given the argument of this passage. On Dinarchus' use of oaths see commentary on 7. The conclusion of this section has a near-jocular tone to it.

Demosthenes' position as leader of the people has elsewhere been described as *demagogos* (1) and *demotikos* (9), but here *symbouloi* ('advisers') and *hegemones* ('leaders') are specified; cf. 40 and 35. *Symboulos* denotes the most politically active of the citizens, those who propose decrees and speak in assemblies; cf. M.H. Hansen, *The Athenian Assembly in the Age of Demosthenes* (Oxford: 1987), 50-63. Dinarchus deliberately chooses this term to fit his central argument that the fortunes of a city rest upon its leaders' policies.

(37) **Gentlemen . . . the Acropolis:** The following historical citations were part of a 'bank' of historical topoi linked to the rise of Athens after the Persian Wars and the formation of the Delian League: S. Perlman, 'The Historical Example, Its Use and Importance as Political Propaganda in the Attic Orators', *SH* 7 (1961), 162-164. In this section Dinarchus has telescoped events.

We have already noted that Dinarchus linked Demosthenes and Demades together because of their political ideologies or corrupt practices (7, 11, 45, 89, 101, 104), and here we find Aristides and Themistocles similarly linked. They were joint leaders of the people in 480 (*AP* 23.3; cf. 28.2). Themistocles was responsible for enlarging the Athenian navy and thus enhancing the Athenians' fifth century empire. He was responsible for the rebuilding of the city walls and the building of those at the Piraeus (Thucydides 1.89.3 ff., *AP* 23.3-4, Plut. *Themistocles* 19.1 ff.). Perhaps his greatest claim to fame lay in his tactical brilliance at the battle of Salamis in 480, which resulted in the total defeat of the Persian navy. During a Persian invasion in 481 (Herodotus 7.138), the Greek fleet assembled at the bay of Salamis in September 480. Themistocles forced battle when the Greeks were intent on scattering by sending a slave to Xerxes, the Persian king, with the news that the Greek fleet would soon sail off and that he would aid the Persian cause (Herodotus 8.70-75, Plut. *Themistocles* 12). Xerxes immediately sailed against the Greeks, and under Themistocles' direction the Persian fleet was virtually annihilated. Xerxes himself fled back to Persia (Herodotus 8.113-120). On the battle see Herodotus 6.41-95, and on the period see, for example, N.G.L. Hammond, *A History of Greece*[3] (Oxford: 1986), 237-244.

Aristides encouraged the Ionian states to leave the Spartan alliance of 478/7 after the Persian Wars and helped to organise the Delian League, headed by Athens (Thucydides 1.96-97.1, *AP* 23.4-5, Diod. 11.44 and 46.4, Plut. *Aristides* 23). He was also responsible for the assessment of the allied tribute payable to Athens (Thucydides 1.96.1, 5.18.5, Dem. 23.209, *AP* 23.5, Diod. 11.47, Plut. *Aristides* 24, Pausanias 8.52.2, Nepos, *Aristides* 3), which was moved from Delos to Athens in 455/4 (Diod. 12.38.2, 12.54.3, 13.21.3, Plut. *Pericles* 12.1), hence the reference to the carrying of the tribute up to the Acropolis. On Aristides see *PA* 1695 and Davies, *APF*, 48-50; on Themistocles, see *PA* 6669 and Davies, *APF*, especially 214-217.

(38) **but you will remember . . . Cephalus the orator:** Cephalus came from the Attic deme Collytus (cf. 76), and he was especially influential in Athenian political life after the Peace of Antalcidas or King's Peace of 386 (T.T.B. Ryder, *Koine Eirene* [Oxford: 1965], 34-36, 39-41 and 122-124). He was also an accomplished orator (cf. Dem. 18.219), but it is probably for his role in the overthrow of the regime of the Thirty in Athens (404/3) that Dinarchus cites him here (see commentary on 25 and 76). 'Shortly before the present time' is exaggeration: the Thirty were deposed in 404/3 and Dinarchus' speech was delivered in 323 – chronological accuracy was not important to the orators. On Cephalus see *PA* 8277 and R. Sealey, 'Callistratus of

Aphidna and His Contemporaries', *Historia* 5 (1956), 185-186 (= *Essays in Greek Politics* [New York: 1967], 140).

Thrason of Herchia: Thrason is said to have been a Theban *proxenos* (Aes. 3.138), and served as an ambassador to Cetriporis in Thrace in 356/5 (*IG* ii² 127, 37). See further: *PA* 7384 and Davies, *APF*, 239-240.

Eleus: Little is known of this man, but Burtt, 201 note a, tentatively identified him with the trierarch of *Hippia Archeneidou* of *IG* ii² 1632, 144-145 (dated to 322); cf. Kirchner at *PA* 6401. See further *PA* 6400 and Davies, *APF*, 210-211.

and Phormisius: Phormisius is named at *AP* 34.3 with other men who were not members of the Thirty (cf. Xenophon, *Hellenica* 2.3.2), but he, unlike the others, does not seem to have been with Thrasybulus at the democrats' base of Phyle (see commentary on 25). See also *PA* 14945.

and other fine men . . . alive: Dinarchus is deliberately vague so as to reinforce the persuasiveness of his argument since only Eleus and perhaps Thrason would have been alive at this time. Presumably Dinarchus names these men because they supported Athenian plans to liberate Thebes from Spartan control in 379/8, to which patriotic topic he proceeds in the central section of this part of the speech (37-40).

For some of these . . . enslaved: In 382 the Spartan commander Phoebidas answered the call of a pro-Spartan element in Thebes and illegally seized the Cadmea, where he installed a Spartan garrison and exiled three hundred of the leading citizens (Diod. 20.20, Xenophon, *Hellenica* 5.2.28-31, Nepos, *Pelopidas* 1.2), perhaps as part of Spartan policy to counteract the continuing growth of Theban power after the King's Peace of 386. Although Phoebidas was brought to trial, King Agesilaus intervened on his behalf and he was merely fined. The Theban exiles fled to Athens and appealed for help on the grounds that they had helped the Athenian exiles in 404/3 (Diod. 15.25.4; see commentary on 25); in midwinter 379/8, with Athenian help proposed by Cephalus, they expelled the Spartan garrison: Diod. 15.25 ff., Xenophon, *Hellenica* 5.4.1 ff., Plut. *Pelopidas* 7 ff. (cf. 14.1), [Plut.] *Moralia* 596 ff, Nepos, *Pelopidas* 2 and 3; see now J. De Voto, 'The Liberation of Thebes in 379/8 B.C.', *Daidalikon. Studies in Memory of R.V. Schoder*, ed. R.F. Sutton (Wauconda, Wis.: 1989), 101-116. The Athenians' support was a major factor in causing them to form the Second Athenian Confederacy, on which see commentary on 39.

(39) **And others . . . worthy of your ancestors:** The Athenian assistance to the exiled Thebans in 379/8, which saw the expulsion of the Spartans and the restoration of Theban democracy (see commentary on 38), echoes section 25, where Theban help to the Athenians in 404/3, against Spartan orders, led to the expulsion of the Thirty and the restoration of Athenian democracy. In section 25 the context is Demosthenes' betrayal of Thebes despite its help in 404/3; in 39 the context is Athens' support for the Thebans in 379/8, thanks to the leaders then.

The Athenians followed their help to Thebes with a diplomatic invitation to the Greek states to join Athens in opposing Spartan imperialism. This led to the establishment of the Second Athenian Confederacy, which soon grew into a fourth century Athenian empire, on which see J. Cargill, *The Second Athenian League* (Berkeley: 1981) with his *Athenian Settlements of the Fourth Century BC* (Leiden: 1995). Diplomacy soon gave way to warfare when the Spartan Sphodrias unsuccessfully attempted to seize the Piraeus one night (Diod. 15.29.5-6, Xenophon, *Hellenica* 5.4.20-23, Plut. *Pelopidas* 14, *Agesilaus* 24.3-5), probably on the orders of King Cleombrotus. Although he was tried in Sparta he was acquitted (Diod. 15.29.6-7, Xenophon, *Hellenica* 5.4.24-34, Plut. *Agesilaus* 24.6-25), thanks to the influence of Cleombrotus and the platitudes of Agesilaus' son Archidamus on his father – echoing the result of the king's earlier help to Phoebidas.

(40) **These men . . . by Zeus:** The repetition for emphasis is one of Dinarchus' stylistic idiosyncrasies. The oath to Zeus is for rhetorical and pious effect (see commentary on 7). On the terminology *symbouloi* and *hegemones*, see also commentary on 36 with 71 and 72.

rogues such as these . . . their own decree: In sections 42-45 Dinarchus expounds on Demosthenes' other sources of illegal income; cf. 111 with commentary.

(41) **Gentlemen of Athens . . . made money:** In section 30 we are told that his 'friend' Demosthenes betrayed Aristarchus (see commentary on 30). Dinarchus moves to detail some of Demosthenes' illegal incomes, having foreshadowed such an attack in 40.

(42) **Are there any of you . . . been paid:** Dinarchus refers to Demosthenes' trierarch law of 340/39. In the fourth century a trierarchy (equipping and maintaining a trireme at personal expense for one year) became a shared rather than an individual one as had been the case in the fifth century. Those liable for the trierarchy – about 1,200 – were grouped into symmories in 357/6 by the law of Periander ([Dem.] 47.21-23; cf. Dem. 14.16), but this system was still inequitable (Dem. 21.154-155, 18.102), and in 354 Demosthenes proposed a series of reforms in his speech *On The Symmories* (14), including an increase in the number of citizens liable for the trierarchy from 1,200 to 2,000 (14.16 ff.). He was largely unsuccessful, so then he introduced the trierarch law of 340/39, under which the three hundred citizens were required to contribute in proportion to their wealth: cf. Dem. 18.102 ff., Aes. 3.55, 222 (naturally condemnatory), Hyp. fr. B.43 Burtt, Dem. 36.45, and note the remarks of G.L. Cawkwell, 'Athenian Naval power in the Fourth Century', *CQ*[2] 34 (1984), 342-345.

Dinarchus implies that Demosthenes was bribed (perhaps by the three talents specified below) to propose this law, although Demosthenes states that he was offered money *not* to introduce it and that he was tried and acquitted (18.103-104). Although it is possible that the three hundred trierarchs did try to bribe him to drop his proposed law and so maintain the *status quo* (which was in their interests), it is also possible that the *existing* trierarchs wanted to modify the list, and so bribed him to propose it.

The passage allows us a glimpse of the composition of the jurors at Demosthenes' trial if some of the three hundred richest men in Athens were there, either as jurors or as spectators. On spectators see now A. Lanni, 'Spectator Sports or Serious Politics? οἱ περιεστηκότες and the Athenian Lawcourts', *JHS* 117 (1997), 183-189.

(43) **Gentlemen, tell me . . . free gift:** This section is a long rhetorical question to the jury, and the allegations are uncertain as Dinarchus is using the Athenians' reluctance to grant citizenship to his rhetorical advantage (J. Ober, *Mass and Elite in Democratic Athens* [Princeton: 1989], 266-270).

Diphilus, son of Diopeithes of Sunium, may have been the syntrierarch of *Hegemone Nausinikou* before 325/4, and who also proposed a naval law in about 323/2: *IG* ii[2] 1631, 511 and 1632, 19 (Davies, *APF*, 169). A speech for

Diphilus is believed to have been composed by Dinarchus (Conomis, fr. XLI). See *PA* 4467 = 4487 and Davies, *APF*, 167-169.

Two types of invitation existed to public entertainment in Athens, which took place in the Prytaneum oɩ 'Town Hall' (as yet undiscovered, but situated on the north slope of the Acropolis: S.G. Miller, *The Prytaneion* [Berkeley: 1978], 38-66). The first type of invitation was to dine there on a single occasion (called *deipnon* for citizens and *xenia* for non citizens such as foreign guests and ambassadors). The second type, and the one Dinarchus refers to, was *sitesis*, the right to dine at state expense for life, bestowed on an individual and his eldest male descendant. This was the highest Athenian award and was granted *ex officio* and *ex beneficio*, the latter by decree only. Diphilus' receipt of *sitesis* (presumably for his syntrierarchy) would have been sometime in the period 334-324. See further M.J. Osborne, 'Entertainment in the Prytaneion at Athens', *ZPE* 41 (1981), 153-170, A.S. Henry, *Honours and Privileges in Athenian Decrees* (Hildesheim: 1983), 262-290, P.J. Rhodes, 'δεῖπνον and ξένια in the Prytaneum', *ZPE* 57 (1984), 193-199 and Miller, *Prytaneion*, 4-10

I agree with S.A. Naber's emendation, 'Adnotationes criticae ad Antiphontis, Aeschinis, Hyperidis, Dinarchi orationes', *Mnemosyne* 33 (1905), 182, of σταθησομένην for ἀνατεθησομένην in the erection of statues; cf. those to the Pontic tyrants (below), and to Demades in 101.

Or the conferment . . . Chaerephilus: Chaerephilus was a metic salt-fish seller (Athenaeus 3.119f, 8.339d) who owed his citizenship (as did his three sons) to Demosthenes, according to Dinarchus, in return for lavish bribes. However, Chaerephilus' family was a wealthy one (Davies, *APF*, 566, M.J. Osborne, *Naturalization in Athens* 3 [Brussels: 1983], 75-76), and citizenship is more likely to have been bestowed for benefactions to the city. The exact date of the grant is unknown, but sometime during the famine of 330-326, when money for the purchase of corn was rewarded with citizenship, is plausible (A. Schäfer, *Demosthenes und seine Zeit*[2] 3 [Leipzig: 1885], 296-297 with n. 4; cf. Davies, *APF*, 566). On Chaerephilus see *PA* 15187, Davies, *APF*, 430 and 566-567 and Osborne, *Naturalization* 3, T75.

Chaerephilus and his sons were enrolled in Demosthenes' deme of Paeania since it was customary for new citizens to be enrolled in the deme of their *prostates* (sponsor). Chaerephilus does not seem to have been very active liturgically (unlike his sons: see below).

Pheidon, Pamphilus and Pheidippus: The three brothers were enrolled in the *hippeis* class, which indicates their wealth, and were active liturgically, though Pheidon was not as active here as his brothers. Little is known about him, and he may even have died soon after his father in the 320s, aged about 45 (see *PA* 14184, Davies, *APF*, 567, Osborne, *Naturalization* 3, T76). Pamphilus may have been a councillor in 327/6 (*PA* 11555, Davies, *APF*, 567-568, Osborne, *Naturalization* 3, T77). Pheidippus was trierarch prior to 322 since in that year *IG* ii[2] 1631, d622-624 records him as owing 1,200 drachmas for the sole trierarchy of *Kytheria Aristokratous* (see further *PA* 14163, Davies, *APF*, 567-568, Osborne, *Naturalization* 3, T78).

Epigenes and Conon the bankers: We know only that Epigenes was a banker. Osborne connects the grant of citizenship (as with Conon and Chaerephilus and his sons) with a *largesse* to the city, probably during the famine, and plausibly suggests that he was also enrolled in Paeania, the deme of Demosthenes; see further *PA* 4782 and Osborne, *Naturalization* 3, T80.

Little is also known about Conon, except that he too was a banker. Osborne dates his citizenship to the same period as those named above; see also *PA* 8700, Davies, *APF*, 430 and Osborne, *Naturalization* 3, T81. He is commonly believed to be the person accused in 56 and by Hyperides at 5.26 of fraudulently obtaining theoric money (used to enable the poor to attend the festivals: see commentary on Hyperides 5.13), but this is doubtful: see commentary on 56 and 57.

Salt-fish sellers and bankers are probably singled out here because of the social stigma attached to these servile professions (normally undertaken by metics); Dinarchus vilifies Demosthenes for taking bribes to the degradation of the Athenian citizenship. We are now in the realm of rhetorical topoi, and Osborne in fact questions the extent to which Chaerephilus and his sons were involved in the salt-fish occupation, believing that much of this detail is oratorical fabrication (*Naturalization* 3, 75-76 and 4, 196-197).

Or the bronze statues . . . Pontus: Bronze statues to commemorate public services by individuals were erected in the Agora: cf. the discussion in the commentary on 14.

Paerisades I was ruler of Bosporus from 344/3-309; Satyrus and Gorgippus were two of his sons, later to share the responsibility of government with their father until his death (cf. Diod. 20.22). The Spartocid dynasty had been established in about 433; by the time of Paerisades I it was in its third generation: R. Werner, 'Die Dynastie der Spartokiden', *Historia* 4 (1955), 412-444 and Osborne, *Naturalization* 3, T21.

The Bosporan area was important for its grain exportation to Athens and that city enjoyed preferential treatment over other Greek states (Dem. 20.31, 36-37). However, Athens had recently loss its privileged position in the Pontic grain trade, a blow doubled because of the famine, but thanks to Demosthenes' diplomacy there had been a renewed agreement: S.M. Burstein, '*IG* II² 653, Demosthenes and Athenian Relations with Bosporus in the Fourth Century B.C.', *Historia* 27 (1978), 428-436. Thus, here we see one of Dinarchus' tactics of persuasion, as he subtly draws on the unpleasant effects of the famine of this period to evoke prejudice against Demosthenes by giving the impression that it was Demosthenes and not the Athenian people who benefitted the most.

from whom one thousand medimni . . . anywhere: Demosthenes' receipt of the corn as an annual bribe presupposes that he will always have a place of refuge with the Pontic tyrants. We appear to have another attempt to counter a possible defence strategy of Demosthenes, although Dinarchus may have added such remarks to a revised version of the speech after Demosthenes' own defence speech.

(44)   **Or did he introduce the proposal . . . a citizen:** Demosthenes' dealings with Euboea and especially with Callias and his brother Taurosthenes of Chalcis in Philip II's reign are recounted at Aeschines 3.85 ff., but Aeschines gives a distorted view – as does Dinarchus. Taurosthenes and Callias did not enslave their countrymen nor did they betray all of Euboea to Philip II since Carystus remained loyal to Athens.

In 343 Callias unsuccessfully sought Macedonian (and Theban) support for the creation of a Euboean League, motivated less for an alliance with Philip rather than for personal power (Aes. 3.89-91). Then in spring or early summer 341, Callias despatched three ambassadors to Athens to plead for an alliance supporting Chalcidic hegemony, under which Athens was guaranteed

Euboean allegiance. Demosthenes secured its acceptance, though he was later accused by Aeschines that he had been bribed (3.91 ff.). Then in the period 336 to 330 (Worthington, *Dinarchus*, 208), he proposed Taurosthenes and Callias for Athenian citizenship, and he was accused of taking a bribe also for this by Aeschines (3.85) and by Hyperides (5.20). On Taurosthenes see *PA* 13435 and M.J. Osborne, *Naturalization in Athens* 3 (Brussels: 1983), T7 (discussion at T73), and on the historical background see A. Schäfer, *Demosthenes und seine Zeit²* 2 (Leipzig: 1885), 418-423, J.R. Ellis, *Philip II and Macedonian Imperialism* (London: 1976), 162-166 and 169-170 and Hammond & Griffith, *HM* 2, 501-503 and 545-554.

(45) **Is it necessary for me . . . By Athena:** Athena was the patron goddess of Athens so Dinarchus chooses an appropriate oath since Demosthenes had proposed unscrupulous men for citizenship in her city; cf. 64, and on Dinarchus' use of oaths see commentary on 7. The call that Demosthenes' culpability is so well known that witnesses are redundant is rhetorical technique and should be met with scepticism. In 112 Dinarchus expects character-witnesses to appear on behalf of Demosthenes.

do you think that . . . reports to you: This is the only extant source on the length of the Areopagus' actual investigation (*zetesis*), which we are told took six months.

On Demades see commentary on 7. Cephisophon's identity is disputed, but the most likely candidate is Cephisophon of Cholargeus (*PA* 8419, Davies, *APF*, 149), whom Demosthenes tells us (18.21, 75) supported the Peace of Philocrates in 346 (see commentary on 28). Why Dinarchus cites him here is unknown, unless it foreshadows his trial.

(46) **Gentlemen, there are many . . . by the city:** The emphatic opening is one of Dinarchus' stylistic characteristics. Execution was one of the penalties for *dorodokia* (cf. commentary on 60), and Dinarchus and Hyperides repeatedly urge the jurors to inflict this fate on Demosthenes, but he was eventually fined.

(47) **He has sworn falsely . . . the curse:** On the oaths in the speech see commentary on 7. The 'awful goddesses' appear again in 64 and 87.

Meetings of the Assembly and of the Boule were preceded by the herald reciting a prayer (Aes. 1.23, Din. 2.14; cf. Aristophanes, *Thesmophoriazusae* 295-310) and invoking a curse on all traitors and enemies of the state (Andocides 1.31, Dem. 19.70-71, 20.107, 23.97, Lycurgus 1.31, Aristophanes, *Thesmophoriazusae* 331-351; cf. Din. 2.16), which Dinarchus calls to be read at the end of 47. Curses in Greek society had a political as well as religious value; the actual text of the curse has not been preserved, although it is parodied in the passages of Aristophanes, *Thesmophoriazusae* cited above. See P.J. Rhodes, *The Athenian Boule* (Oxford: 1972), 36-37, for a discussion and a reconstruction of the oath and curse; on the opening and proceedings of an Assembly, see M.H. Hansen, *The Athenian Assembly in the Age of Demosthenes* (Oxford: 1987), 88-93.

He speaks one thing . . . justice: For Demosthenes' apparent conspiracy with Aristarchus, see commentary on 30. The parenthetical 'if there is any power to exact a just penalty from perjurers and criminals, as there surely is' is extemporaneous in tone. On the penalty see commentary on 60.

Gentlemen of the jury, listen to the curse: The fourth part of the speech ends with this call to read out the curse, which implies that Demosthenes has incurred it and so deserves condemnation on religious and political grounds.

E (48-53) Judicial Process of the Areopagus

(48) D will lie that the speaker was previously condemned by the A.

(49) Prelude to the explanation of what happened to the speaker.

(50) Machinery of the A: only two methods by which it begins an investigation.

(50-52) The speaker's defence: he proves his innocence.

(53) The lies uttered against the speaker before were disbelieved.

(48-53) While each of the following three parts (E: 48-53, F: 54-60, and E¹: 61-63) forms its own structural unit, each highlighting at its core the powers of the Areopagus, collectively they form the central argument to the speech, the thrust of which is that Areopagus need not cite supporting evidence for its accusation (55). Dinarchus now returns to his major subject, the Areopagus. The two ways in which investigations by the Areopagus can be initiated are described (50), and the judicial machinery of the council is treated both as an introduction to the central part of the speech (54-60), and as a means to discredit Demosthenes' possible accusation that the speaker was found guilty by the Areopagus (50-53); it is reinforced also by the deposition to prove his innocence (52). Sections 50-63 are important for the *apophasis* procedure in the Areopagus, and show Dinarchus' value as a source for Athenian law and legal procedure.

(48) **Nevertheless, gentlemen ... against me:** As in 47 we have the rare appeal to the jurors themselves. Either ὡς ἀκούω is a *post hoc* rhetorical trick for publication, or Dinarchus had at the time heard something of Demosthenes' defence in advance; cf. 'so this man says' below, and on such remarks see commentary on 7. In the following sections Dinarchus is at pains to discredit such a form of defence by Demosthenes. The speaker's present actions are the reverse of those of Demosthenes, who previously had championed the integrity of the Areopagus but now, since it reported against him, challenges it.

I am now being ... lie to you: On the incident involving the speaker (for whom Dinarchus wrote the speech) and his earlier prosecution at the hands of the largely unknown Pistias, see commentary on 53.

(49) **Therefore ... this man:** Not Demosthenes but Pistias the Areopagite, who is named at 53. The speaker's explanation of his innocence serves also as an admonishment to the jury not to be swayed by the arguments of the accused and thereby deliver an unjust verdict: K.J. Dover, *Greek Popular Morality in the Time of Plato and Aristotle* (Oxford: 1974), 23-25; cf. C. Carey and R.A. Reid, *Demosthenes: Selected Private Speeches* (Cambridge: 1985), 9-13, on the presentation of the speakers.

(50) **Gentlemen, the Council ... its report:** τίνας τούτους ('what are these?') is a rhetorical question to involve the jurors directly in the case. As the passage indicates, the Areopagus could investigate certain important matters of a political nature either on the orders of the Assembly (*apophasis kata prostaxin*) or on its own initiative (*apophasis aute proelomene*). This procedure was known as *apophasis*, and if it found those under scrutiny guilty, then the case would be tried in a law court. The central element of this part of the speech and those of the two following parts (at sections 55 and 62) highlight the powers of the Areopagus, and serve to reinforce the argument that no man should dispute them.   On the Areopagus see commentary on 6 and 9.

(51)   **show the decree . . . crimes:** Rhetorical challenge to Demosthenes in anticipation of his claim that the speaker was the subject of an *apophasis* which was initiated by the Areopagus itself (see commentary on 50), thus making the speaker an Areopagite. We cannot say with absolute certainty whether the speaker was guilty of the crime, but the deposition produced at the end of the following section indicates he was exonerated when the case came to court.

We are told in this passage that the prosecutors in the Harpalus trials of 323 were elected by the state, and at Dinarchus 2.6 we learn that they numbered ten; the present speech was the second in the prosecution line-up.

If indeed what you say . . . was not reported: Cf. 17 on Timotheus' readiness to die − the irony would not have been lost on the jurors. Demosthenes' personal decree made himself liable to the death penalty if found guilty of accepting a bribe from Harpalus (see commentary on 1), however he protested the Areopagus' findings (see 5-6 with commentary on 5). The speaker now denies that his prosecution was the result of the second method by which the Areopagus conducts investigations (*aute proelomene*), and offers proof in the deposition read out at the end of the next section.

(52)   **Moreover, having impeached . . . Read the deposition:** 2,500 seems a large number of jurors to us, yet certain types of legal procedure involved juries of several hundreds (for example, *eisangeliae, apophaseis* and *graphae paranomon*), and at 107 we are told that the jury at Demosthenes' trial numbered 1,500: on numbers see further A.R.W. Harrison, *The Law of Athens* 2 (Oxford: 1971), 47 with n. 2. The courtroom was known as the Heliaea, which was probably situated in the South-West corner of the Agora: J.M. Camp, *The Athenian Agora* (London: 1986), 46-47, 60 and 108.

The subject is Pistias, named at 53.   Pythocles, an opponent of Demosthenes and a supporter of Aeschines (Dem. 18.285, 19.225, 314), had a political career spanning nearly forty years (from 357 to 318), and he was especially active in naval and public matters (Davies, *APF*, 485).   On Pythocles see *PA* 12444 and Davies, *APF*, 485-486. On the attack by Pistias and Pythocles on the speaker see 53 with commentary.

(53)   **Athenians . . . isolation then:** The identity of the speaker's former prosecutor is now revealed as Pistias (*PA* 11823), a member of the Areopagus. We know next to nothing about him or the case. Dinarchus has a speech against Pistias for an *eisangelia* or impeachment (Dion. Hal. *Dinarchus* 10 = Conomis, fr. XV) but this may have no connection with the case here since in 50-52 the client refers to his previous charge as a result of the *apophasis* procedure. Evidently the deposition exculpates the speaker.

But when the truth . . . taking bribes: On the findings of the Areopagus see commentary on 1. On the technical nature of the phrase ἐπ᾿ αὐτοφώρῳ (being caught 'in the act'), see commentary on 29.

F (54-60) Judicial Power of the Areopagus

    (54) D will slander the A.
       (54) D's defence: some accused by the A previously were acquitted in court.
          (55) The A's way of enquiry differs from the people's, who put mercy over justice.
          (55) The A simply issues a report against someone.
          (56-57) The people have a greater regard for mercy than for justice.
       (58-59) Polyeuctus was found guilty by the A but then acquitted in court.
       (59-60) The jury is not to be swayed by D and thus distrust the A's report.

(54-60) This is the sixth, and central, part of the speech, in which Dinarchus sets out to foil another potential line of defence that Demosthenes ought to be acquitted since other men previously condemned by the Areopagus were found innocent by the people in court (54-60). Polyeuctus of Cydantidae is singled out in some detail (58-59). The Areopagus and its character are still defended, even when the people disregarded its earlier reports (57 and 59). The core element of this part of the speech consists of the statement that the council need only issue a report against someone without offering proof or explanation (55). It attempts to counter the fact that no evidence existed against Demosthenes or those others accused of taking bribes from Harpalus (see Introduction, pp. 10-11 and 26).

(54)   **will the customs . . . understand:** If a private accuser in a lawsuit failed to obtain at least one-fifth of the votes cast he was unable by law to bring a similar suit in future: Andocides 1.33 and 4.18, Dem. 21.47 (cf. 58.6), Plato, *Apology* 36a-b, with R.J. Bonner and G. Smith, *The Administration of Justice from Homer to Aristotle* 2 (Chicago: 1938), 56-57, A.R.W. Harrison, *The Law of Athens* 2 (Oxford: 1971), 83. In 56 ff. Dinarchus takes steps to offset Demosthenes' potential defence that although accused he should be acquitted, as has happened to others before.

(55)   **Gentlemen . . . large scale-crimes:** On the Areopagus' method of investigation see commentary on 50. The phrase 'being swayed more by mercy than justice' echoes 'gave more feeling to mercy than to justice' in 57, and, as can be seen from the secondary-level ring structure above, both perfectly balance each other and strikingly frame the core element of this part of the speech. The announcement that the Areopagus need only report anyone ἁπλῶς (to be interpreted as meaning without supplying any reason or evidence for its accusation – cf. Hyperides 5.6) thus forms the core of the whole speech. It is advanced to counter the lack of evidence in the Harpalus affair and to discredit Demosthenes' repeated criticisms of the report against him and his attacks on the Areopagus (see commentary on 5).

    Conomis and Nouhaud and Dors-Méary print ἀποφαίνει after καί, following Blass, but this results in hiatus; Burtt, who places it after ζητουμένοις a few lines below, should be preferred.

(56)   **Consequently, it reported . . . the laws:** The Areopagus denounced these three men under a previous *apophasis*. We know nothing about the first man, who appears to have committed a relatively trivial crime.

    In the second case, Dinarchus alludes to theoric money, which was used to enable the poor to attend the festivals and was probably introduced by Pericles in the 450s (see commentary on Hyperides 5.13). Five drachmas was a fairly substantial amount since it is the equivalent of thirty obols, and three obols was the daily rate of pay for an Athenian juror in the late fifth and fourth centuries BC. The common opinion is that the culprit is Conon of Paeania, the banker whom Dinarchus tells us was made an Athenian citizen on the motion of Demosthenes (see 43 with commentary). This view is based on the similarity between this case and that cited at Hyperides 5.26 ('Conon of Paeania took the theoric allowance for his son who was away from home'), but this is not necessarily so. In section 57 Dinarchus tells us that the court acquitted him, whereas the Conon mentioned by Hyperides was fined the sum of one talent.

As to the third case, the μέρις was a meat allowance for members of the Areopagus, the equivalent of a modern-day sustenance allowance for those on official business. This passage indicates that any Areopagite convicted of a crime was expelled from the Areopagus: D.M. MacDowell, *Athenian Homicide Law in the Age of the Orators* (Manchester: 1963), 41.

(57) **Having tried these men . . . guilty:** Cf. 55 'prone to make judgment being swayed more by mercy than justice' (with commentary). It is surprising to learn that the court acquitted these offenders even though the Areopagus had condemned them (cf. Polyeuctus in 58–59). If Dinarchus' information here is trustworthy, then it makes any connection between the identity of the man illegally obtaining theoric money in 56 with the convicted Conon at Hyperides 5.26 impossible.

Why would Dinarchus insert this material (and that concerning Polyeuctus in 58) since it appears to strengthen any similar claims Demosthenes might make in his defence speech? Perhaps he did not anticipate this line of defence and so added this material to a revised version of the speech. More plausibly is that he is drawing a distinction between the lesser crimes and that of Demosthenes, urging the jurors not to disregard the Areopagus' declaration now as has happened in the past.

(58) **When the people . . . his country:** Cf. 59. Polyeuctus underwent an *apophasis* on the charge that he was accompanying exiles to Megara, who presumably were those returning to Athens in anticipation of Alexander the Great's Exiles Decree of 324/3 (cf. 81-82, and 103), on which see Introduction, p. 7. At 94 Dinarchus says that a certain Callimedon was also charged with conspiring with the exiles, so both cases seems to have been regarded as treason (*prodosia*). However, Polyeuctus was acquitted when his case came to court.

(59) **This report . . . terrible:** The emphatic repetition after 58 is not overdone or monotonous, as a superficial reading of the speech may indicate, but is a product of the care Dinarchus took in the composition of the speech, as the ring structures indicate. Such care also supports the theory that the Polyeuctus episode was added to the speech after oral delivery (see commentary on 57).

At section 89 we are told that the Areopagus could trace only 64 of the alleged missing 350 talents of Harpalus' money. If so, then the mention of bribes in gold suggests that Harpalus fled from Asia with gold, contrary to Diodorus' statement at 17.108.6 that he took silver: see commentary on 4.

(60) **Now, Demosthenes . . . these men:** Cf. Demosthenes' slanderous statement at 54. Here, Dinarchus exploits the fact that the Athenians viewed Demosthenes' crime against the state as especially reprehensible (see commentary on 3), and he argues that the jurors would not be justified to acquit him. This form of rhetorical persuasion is the reverse of that in 23, where we hear of three men executed for less important crimes than that of Demosthenes.

The laws lay down . . . gain by it: There is some confusion over the penalties, and perhaps deliberately so as Dinarchus would have had sound knowledge of legal procedure and penalties from his career as a speechwriter. Ordinary crimes excluding bribery were punished by a simple fine whereby the amount which had gone missing had to be repaid (*AP* 54.2). If the fine was unpaid by a due date the amount was doubled or the person imprisoned (Hyp. 5.24, *AP* 48.1 with P.J. Rhodes, *A Commentary on the Aristotelian Athenaion Politeia* [Oxford: 1981], 559 and 599). Bribery against the state (treason) was punished by a fine ten times greater than the amount taken (Din. 2.17, Hyp. 5.24, *AP* 54.2; cf. Dem. 24.112). The law concerning receipt of bribes is quoted at Demosthenes 21.113 (cf. Aes. 3.232), and it involved the loss of citizenship and confiscation of property, although Andocides 1.74 states that such criminals could retain property. Here Dinarchus adds the death penalty, which could be inflicted by means of an *eisangelia*. Since the *apophasis* procedure was very similar to *eisangelia*, the penalties may have been the same.

E¹ (61-63) Judicial Authority of the Areopagus

    (61) D will argue that in his case alone the A's report is objectionable.
        (61) D proposed the A's enquiry into the affair and his death penalty if found guilty.
        (62) D previously proposed the A's sovereignty over all where laws are involved.
        (62-63) Others have been condemned before by the reports of the A.
    (63) D nevertheless will argue that in his case the A is to be overridden.

(61-63) In the seventh part of the speech, Dinarchus sets out to trap Demosthenes by his own stance in the past. Dinarchus repeats that Demosthenes initiated the Areopagus' investigation into the Harpalus affair and proposed to submit to the death penalty if it declared against him (61), and that on a number of previous occasions he sustained the Areopagus' findings and was even responsible for an increase in its judicial powers (62-63). Demosthenes is neatly trapped by the compelling argument that he is bound by law not to disregard the report against him (63), and therefore he must suffer execution. The sovereign powers of the Areopagus form the core element of this part (62). When this element is read in conjunction with the central elements of the previous two parts (50 and 55), we can see how their sequence, which deal with the authority and power of the Areopagus, is ingeniously developed to form a persuasive case against Demosthenes.

(61) **Or will you not . . . Harpalus:** On Demosthenes' challenges see commentary on 5, and on his decree against himself see commentary on 1. The passage may be interpreted as that Demosthenes *alone* proposed such a decree, but this is negated by Dinarchus 3.2, 5, 16 and 21, where Philocles also is cited; cf. Hyperides 5.24 (unnamed others).

(62) **Now, Demosthenes . . . oligarchic:** For the power and reputation of the Areopagus see commentary on 6, with R. Wallace, *The Areopagos Council* (Baltimore and London: 1989). On the increase of the Areopagus' power at the hands of Demosthenes (which would be the introduction of the *apophasis* procedure), see Wallace, *Areopagos*, 115-119 and 176 ff. *Patrioi nomoi* in this passage is the equivalent of *patrios politeia*, the constitution of the ancestors, a common political value used by the orators in order to attract popular support: Wallace, *Areopagos*, 131 ff. E. Badian, 'Harpalus', *JHS* 81 (1961), 33-34, believes that these sections indicate that Demosthenes was relying on his good relations with the Areopagus to exonerate him, and that Hyperides 5.5 shows that the Areopagus declared against him because of popular pressure.

Two of the citizens . . . decree: The two men were probably those whom Demosthenes appointed to guard Harpalus' money when it was deposited on the Acropolis, and who were later executed on his orders when only half of it was found: see Introduction, p. 9. They are more likely the subjects of the decree read out in section 82 rather than are connected with those whom Dinarchus will name in the next section as subjects of earlier enquiries.

(63)   **One of the descendants . . . command:** This was Proxenus, a descendant of the sixth-century 'tyrannicide' Harmodius. Along with Aristogeiton, Harmodius had murdered Hipparchus, son of the tyrant Pisistratus, then joint ruler of Athens with his brother Hippias. Even though Hippias ruled for a further four years, Harmodius and Aristogeiton were still recognised as 'tyrannicides', and the incident became a popular topos for the orators (see also commentary on 101). In 347/6 Proxenus was in command of an Athenian fleet off the island of Euboea (Aes. 2.133-134, Dem. 19.50, 52, 73-74, 154-155), but had then been charged with some crime before 343 (Dem. 19.280-281). This cannot be the case to which Dinarchus refers here as the *apophasis* procedure was not introduced until about 343 (R. Wallace, *The Areopagos Council* [Baltimore and London: 1989], 115-119), and Proxenus (with Antiphon below) was one of the first to be tried under it. See further *PA* 12270 and Davies, *APF*, 478.

These men . . . Antiphon: Antiphon intended to burn the Piraeus dockyards for Philip II of Macedon sometime between 346 and 343, but had been caught by Demosthenes (Dem. 18.132-134; cf. Plut. *Demosthenes* 14.5). Since he and Proxenus (above) were among the first to be prosecuted under the *apophasis* procedure (cf. Dem. 18.133), which was not introduced until 343, the incident and trial may be dated to this year. The Areopagus' *apophasis* found him guilty, but when he was tried in a law court he was acquitted. Demosthenes involved the Areopagus again, and this time Antiphon was found guilty and executed. On Antiphon see *PA* 1281; cf. Wallace, *Areopagos*, 113-119.

You yourselves banished . . . lawful: Little is known of Charinus. The manuscripts have Ἀρχῖνον for the name, but this may be emended to Χαρῖνον on the basis of Pseudo-Demosthenes 58.37-38, which refers to Charinus' exile for treason, and the tone of the passage indicates that he was an adversary of Demosthenes. See too *PA* 15437.

The *apophasis* here refers to an individual, and so should be in the singular and not the plural, as seems to be the pattern elsewhere (11; cf. Din. 2.1, 21 and 3.5, 7): see Ian Worthington, 'On the Use of ἀπόφασις and ἀποφάσεις in Deinarchus I and III', *Philologus* 130 (1986), 184-186.

D¹ (64-85) Past History II

    (64-67) Exhortation made to condemn D.

      (68) D proposed the decree to keep Harpalus' money; the A established the truth.

      (69-71) Do not take D's advice: he does less than others and is an unworthy leader.

      (72-79) Leaders are responsible for good/bad fortunes of cities (Thebes, Athens).

      (79-82) D has not done as much as others and is no good as a leader.

    (82-83) D's decrees about Harpalus' money and the A's investigation.

    (84-85) Exhortation made to condemn D.

(64-85) As with its partner, Past History II (D: 29-47), Dinarchus in this part of the speech (64-85) focuses on the influential role played by leaders in their cities. Again he draws on selected events from the history of Athens and Thebes in order to persuade the jury that Demosthenes' policies will continue to the detriment of Athens. From a lengthy exhortation against him (64-71), Dinarchus turns to Theban history, and in particular its rise to prominence as a result of the successes of the generals Pelopidas and Epaminondas (72-73). The central section of this part of the speech focuses on Thebes' decline because of the actions of three commanders, who are likened to Demosthenes (74). Dinarchus then balances this argument with a chronicle of selected Athenian military victories thanks to its military commanders, which increased Athens' power in Greece (75-76). The contrast is thereby drawn in the closing sections between Demosthenes' cowardice and inactivity and those who performed deeds of bravery, and the contention is that Demosthenes' prolonged

The sequence of events in this part of the speech follows the same progression as its partner (D: 29-47): (a) exhortation/abuse against Demosthenes, (b) action/past event, and (c) exhortation/abuse against Demosthenes, thus showing the structural symmetry of the speech.

(64) **Gentlemen of Athens . . . as home:** Here we find invocations to a range of gods and heroes in order to give Dinarchus' case against Demosthenes a pious element (cf. commentary on 7). Athena is named here in her role of guardian of the city, which is apt since Demosthenes' actions have endangered her city; cf. a similar use at 44-45.

that when the people . . . diplomacy: That is, Demosthenes, accused by the Areopagus and brought to trial before the court, functioning on behalf of the people. Note the similarity with 40-41 and 111; cf. 24-26 (Demosthenes' diplomatic relations with Thebes). On the attitude of the people to Demosthenes' crime, see commentary on 3. The lacuna in the text after πατρίδος was restored by Blass as κομισθέντων χρημάτων, and this is almost certainly correct; cf. similar phraseology in such contexts at 15, 61, 68 and 77.

(65) **enemies and those ill-disposed . . . decent thing:** The death penalty was also (unsuccessfully) demanded by Dinarchus for Aristogeiton (Din. 2.2, 3, 4, 11, 17, 20) and for Philocles (Din. 3.5, 7).

I follow manuscript A for the word order δίκην δόντα.

(66) **Athenians, when we come . . . this man:** Cf. Hyperides 5.22. Spectators were common at trials depending on the nature of the case (certain religious cases, such as those involving the Mysteries, would not have an audience),

and the bystanders alluded to here probably included some of the Greeks who we are told were keenly watching the case and the verdict that the jurors will return. On spectators see A. Lanni, 'Spectator Sports or Serious Politics? οἱ περιεστηκότες and the Athenian Lawcourts', *JHS* 117 (1997), 183-189.

Demosthenes as a sorcerer is also found at 95; such irreverent descriptions of opponents characterise oratory.

How will each of you . . . findings?: A patriotic exhortation to the jurors. Dinarchus often cites the glorious deeds performed by past individuals (25-26, 37 ff., 75 ff.), and here the appeal is made to the higher standards of a past generation. On the powers of the Areopagus see commentary on 6. I follow manuscript A for the word order in this section (cf. Burtt).

(67) **Athenians, what hopes . . . crisis:** This emphatic opening is one of Dinarchus' stylistic characteristics; cf. Introduction, p. 23. On the Areopagus see commentary on 6 and 9. σκοπεῖτε γὰρ πρὸς ὑμᾶς αὐτούς ('consider amongst yourselves') is probably a 'simulated' extemporaneous comment, a rhetorical technique whereby a deliberately planned comment is made to appear off-the cuff for dramatic effect.

(68) **And what if . . . Harpalus:** An emphatic opening, and the passage is dramatically effective as Dinarchus excites the fear of the Athenians that Alexander may seek revenge on Athens for sheltering Harpalus. The decree here is Demosthenes' proposal to have guarded the alleged seven hundred talents which Harpalus brought with him to Athens from Taenarum (70, 89; cf. Hyp. 5.9 and [Plut.] *Moralia* 846b). The remainder of the five thousand talents which Harpalus took from Babylon (see Introduction, p. 7) were left behind at Taenarum, and not 'brought into the country'; cf. 15, 61, 64 (restored), 70 and 77.

and, relying on the fact . . . say: The whole section is aimed at panicking the jurors since Harpalus had long since left Athens (and was dead) by the time of Demosthenes' trial. On the Areopagus' report against Demosthenes, see commentary on 1; on the oath for pious effect, see commentary on 7.

Harpalus was a man of considerable wealth and power, and he had returned to Athens with two vessels (Ian Worthington, '*IG* ii² 1631, 1632 and Harpalus' Ships', *ZPE* 65 [1986], 222-224), so it is likely that he would have several slaves with him.

(69) **Demosthenes . . . so well:** An allusion to Demosthenes' cowardice at the battle of Chaeronea in 338 (see commentary on 12).

Suppose this course . . . the city: Dinarchus refers to an *eisphora* (extraordinary tax) held in the late 340s when relations between Athens and Philip II reached an *impasse* that made war inevitable. That Demosthenes, from the deme Paeania, owned a house in the Piraeus is attested elsewhere (Aes. 3.209, Hyp. 5.16), and is to be expected since those who came from other demes and became actively involved in politics would need to own (or rent) a town house (M.H. Hansen, 'Political Activity and the Organization of Attica in the Fourth Century B.C.', *GRBS* 24 [1983], 227-238).

Dinarchus is guilty of rhetorical exaggeration. If Demosthenes' house yielded fifty drachmas in an *eisphora*, and the *eisphora* was fixed at about 1% of the total value (A.H.M. Jones, *Athenian Democracy* [Oxford: 1957], 23-30), then his house would have been worth about five thousand drachmas (Davies, *APF*, 38). Perhaps Demosthenes kept most of his capital in liquid form (Davies, *APF*, 135), in which case, if the house were his only declared property, he would have been excluded, given that many properties must have been below the exemption limit.

This was what ... talents: This was the sum allegedly received as a bribe by Demosthenes from Harpalus: see commentary on 1.

(70)   **Or perhaps ... money of Alexander:** On the substances of these accusations see the commentaries on 69 and 89, and on Demosthenes' receipt of Persian gold, see commentary on 10. There are similar appeals at 15, 80, 111 and Hyperides 5.34-37, 6.10. Dinarchus outlines some ignoble ways by which Demosthenes acquired wealth at 42-45 (with commentary).

have not made it clear ... state: That is physical property, such as a house (but on this see commentary on 69), against which *eisphorai* and liturgies (personal duties for the state paid from one's own funds) were assessed (J.H. Lipsius, *Das attische Recht und Rechtsverfahren* [Leipzig: 1905], 677). *Politeuomenoi* was one of the technical terms for those who actively involved themselves in politics; cf. next note. Dinarchus throws doubt on Demosthenes' personal belief in his political abilities.

(71)   **Is it fitting ... confidence of the people:** *rhetores kai strategoi* (orators and generals) is the term the Athenians commonly used for their political leaders; cf. commentary on 1, with M.H. Hansen, *The Athenian Assembly in the Age of Demosthenes* (Oxford: 1987), 50-63. The law paraphrased by Dinarchus is controversial, and *rhetores* and *strategoi* have been grouped together for political not constitutional reasons (J. Ober, *Mass and Elite in Democratic Athens* [Princeton: 1989], 119-120).

to have children ... the people: The Athenians attached great importance to the legitimacy of their children, and Pericles' citizenship law of 451 required that both parents be citizens before offspring was legitimate (*AP* 26.4; cf. Plut. *Pericles* 37.3).

In the archonship of Antiodotus, given the large number of citizens, it was decided on the proposal of Pericles that a man should not be a member of the citizen body unless both his parents were Athenian. *Strategoi* and *hipparchoi* were required to have legitimate children and land (*AP* 4.2), and the Decree of Themistocles has the same provision for trierarchs (R. Meiggs and D.M. Lewis, *A Selection of Greek Historical Inscriptions* [Oxford: 1988], no. 23, 18-22).

you sold the land ... battle-line: To swear innocence by one's children was a common oath used by defendants. Demosthenes seems to have had only one legitimate child, a daughter, who had died in 336 since Aeschines has it that Demosthenes celebrated the murder of Philip II and led the Athenian celebrations even though she had been dead for only a week (3.77; cf. 3.160, Plut. *Demosthenes* 22.3, [Plut.] *Moralia* 847b). Athenaeus (13.592e-f) says that he had illegitimate children by a courtesan (cf. Aes. 2.149), so Dinarchus may be alluding to these. On Demosthenes' desertion at the battle of Chaeronea, see commentary on 12.

(72)   **Athenians ... generals:** Dinarchus returns to his argument that leaders control the fortunes of a city, and that Demosthenes will be unlikely to serve Athens well. He takes Thebes and not Athens as a basis for his argument, focusing on the period 371-338, during which Thebes grew to some eminence in the Greek world. As part of his argument, Dinarchus uses the term *symbouloi* for political leaders, which is often selected for rhetorical effect (P. Harding, 'Rhetoric and Politics in Fourth Century Athens', *Phoenix* 41 [1987], 36-37). *Symboulos* is used exclusively for proposers and speakers

in the Assembly (M.H. Hansen, *The Athenian Assembly in the Age of Demosthenes* [Oxford: 1987], 50-63) – in other words, men who were actively responsible for the policies of a city, and who should be dealt with severely when things went wrong.

All the older men . . . agree: Cf. 25 ('as our elders say') and 75 ('so the elders say'), perhaps indicative of the use of a popular topos.

(73) **when Pelopidas . . . with them:** Pelopidas and Epaminondas were responsible for the military supremacy of Thebes from 371 – when the Thebans defeated the Spartans at the battle of Leuctra (see below) – until 362 ('the Theban hegemony'), when they were defeated by a combined Athenian and Sparta force at the battle of Mantinea. Pelopidas died in battle in 364 against the army of Pherae, and Epaminondas in 362 at the battle of Mantinea. On this period, see J. Buckler, *The Theban Hegemony, 371-362 B.C.* (Cambridge, Mass.: 1980).

The Sacred Band was the crack Theban infantry corps, which had been commanded by Pelopidas at the battle of Leuctra. It gained everlasting fame at the battle of Chaeronea in 338 (see commentary on 78) when a Macedonian wing commanded by the future Alexander III annihilated it (Plut. *Alexander* 9.2; cf. Diod. 16.86.3-4). The restored Lion of Chaeronea could well mark the spot where the Theban Sacred Band fell – the bones of 254 men were discovered together there, who may have been these Thebans (Pausanias 9.40.10); cf. P.A. Rahe, 'The Annihilation of the Sacred Band at Chaeronea', *AJA* 85 (1981), 84-87.

Then the city . . . by all men: The Spartans' hegemony of the Greeks (cf. commentary on 38) ended with their defeat at the battle of Leuctra in 371, a defeat all the more surprising as the Spartan force of one thousand cavalry and ten thousand hoplites outnumbered the Boeotian army of six hundred cavalry and six thousand hoplites (Xenophon, *Hellenica* 6.4.4 ff., Diod. 15.55 ff., Plut. *Pelopidas* 20.3 ff., Nepos, *Epaminondas* 6.4, *Pelopidas* 4.2). Epaminondas was then invited by the Arcadians to invade Sparta (Diod. 15.62.3); he liberated Messenia and rebuilt the capital at Messene, which had been destroyed by the Spartans on a much earlier occasion (see below): Diod. 15.62.3-66.1, Plut. *Pelopidas* 24, *Agesilaus* 34.1-2, Pausanias 4.27.5-8. His action was economically disastrous for the Spartans, and robbed their state of power in Greece. On the battle of Leuctra and its aftermath, see Buckler, *Theban Hegemony*, 66-227 and T.T.B. Ryder, *Koine Eirene* (Oxford: 1965), 70-84.

Dinarchus is guilty of chronological inaccuracy in his account as the earlier events took place during the course of the Second Messenian War (c. 630-610), and thus he is a century astray. However, we are not dealing with history but rhetoric, and chronological precision is not part of the brief of the orators. Moreover, other orators, when referring to the same incident, give different, and equally incorrect, dates (Isocrates, *Archidamus* 27, Lycurgus 1.62).

(74) **But when . . . spirit:** Dinarchus now turns to men whose conduct allegedly brought disaster on the city, thanks to their contact with Demosthenes, in this the central element of this part of the speech. In sections 18-21 (cf. 24) it is Demosthenes who was responsible for Thebes' destruction; here it is three Theban commanders, although Dinarchus links Timolaus to Demosthenes which by implication connects him with Thebes' downfall.

When Timolaus . . . this man: Dinarchus may be guilty of rhetorical slander against the three commanders, especially as Pseudo-Plutarch (*Moralia* 259d, 260c) lauds Theagenes' moral decency.

Timolaus was pro-Macedonian, and he may have been exiled after the fall of Thebes in 335 (Dem. 18.48, 295-296, Polybius 18.4.4, Athenaeus 10.436b); nothing else is known about him. Proxenus, *strategos* of 339/8, secured Amphissa with ten thousand mercenaries under the Athenian general Chares soon after the Theban alliance effected by Demosthenes of that year (cf. commentary on 12), as part of a strategy to prevent Philip II from threatening Boeotia and Athens. It was defeated and Amphissa fell to Parmenion (Aes.3.146-147, Polyaenus 4.2.8). Theagenes commanded the Theban phalanx at the battle of Chaeronea ([Plut.] *Moralia* 259d, Plut. *Alexander* 12.5), and was thus the last commander of the Sacred Band (see commentary on 73).

Then the entire city . . . citizens: This statement forms a neat transition between the fortunes of Thebes and those of Athens.

I follow the original reading of A (A^(pr)) for ἐκ τῶν Ἑλλήνων (cf. 24) and A also for διεφθάρη (συνδιεφθάρη N).

(75)   **Think again . . . at Corcyra:** Cf. similar statements at 37, 39-40, 76 and 109. Dinarchus turns to a selection of successful Athenians to contrast Demosthenes' lack of achievement (cf. 96-97). The exploits and awards accorded to the following may even have formed a rhetorical topos; we find them used also in Demosthenes (20.75-86), Aeschines (2.20, 3.243), and cf. Isocrates, *Areopagiticus* 12. It is the orators' practice to depict the Spartans at a disadvantage, hence Dinarchus turns to Athenian victories over Sparta (cf. 14, 25, 38-39), and in 76 it is only after they had *humbly* come begging to Athens that they received Athenian help.

On Conon and Timotheus see commentary on 14. Iphicrates defeated a Spartan company in 390 (Xenophon, *Hellenica* 4.5.7, 11-17, Diod. 14.91.2-3, Plut. *Agesilaus* 22.2, Pausanias 3.10.1), for which he was rewarded with a public portrait in Athens, as had been Timotheus and Conon before him (see commentary on 14). However, the state honours which had been awarded to the 'tyrannicides' Harmodius and Aristogeiton (see commentary on 101) were also bestowed on him now (Aes. 3.243, Dem. 23.130, Aristotle, *Rhetoric* 2.1397b30-34, Pausanias 1.24.7). In 356/5, he sailed with Menestheus and Timotheus to Chares as joint commanders of an Athenian fleet during the Social War between Athens and its rebellious allies. These men were defeated and were then tried (see commentary on 14). See further on Iphicrates *PA* 7737, Davies, *APF*, 248-252 and L. Kallet, 'Iphikrates, Timotheos and Athens, 371-360 B.C', *GRBS* 24 (1983), 239-252.

Chabrias defeated a Spartan fleet off Naxos in 376 which secured Athenian control of the Aegean (Xenophon, *Hellenica* 5.4.40-42, Dem. 20.77, Aes. 3.222). This victory also earned him a public portrait in Athens in 375 (Dem. 13.22-23, 20.84-86, Aes. 3.243, Aristotle, *Rhetoric* 3.1411b9-11, Diod.15.33.4). It is interesting that Chabrias did not pursue the Peloponnesian fleet to almost certain annihilation but proceeded to retrieve those of his men who were shipwrecked or dead. The fate that had befallen the generals following the battle of Arginousae in 406 (Diod. 15.35), when the generals were put to death for failing to rescue Athenian crews because of bad weather, would not have been lost on him. On Chabrias see *PA* 15086, Davies, *APF*,

560-561 and A.G. Woodhead, 'Chabrias, Timotheus and the Aegean Allies, 375-373 B.C.', *Phoenix* 16 (1962), 258-266.

(76)   **At that time . . . advisers as leaders:** See commentary on 75 on the Spartans. Dinarchus refers to the 404/3 oligarchic regime of the Thirty in Athens, supported by Sparta at the end of the Peloponnesian War, which was toppled with Theban aid (see commentary on 25). Cephalus is named at section 38 in the context of Athenian aid to Thebes when Sparta garrisoned it from 382 to 379/8: see 38-39 with commentary. Archinus supported Thrasybulus in the overthrow of the Thirty in 403 (Aes. 2.176, 3.187, 195; cf. Dem. 24.135); see further *PA* 2526.

(77)   **Athenians . . . a better lot:** The argument that Demosthenes should be executed so that the city can prosper is repeated and reinforced in this section, and cf. similar lines of appeal and attack at 31-36, 46-48, 53-54, 64-66, 91-93 and 113; cf. Hyperides 5.21 ff., 27 and 34 ff. On the oath to Zeus, see 40 and 43; cf. 36 (joined with Athena); for discussion, see commentary on 7. Dinarchus also uses a similar argument in his speeches against Aristogeiton (2.3, 14) and Philocles (3.11), who are also accused of complicity in the Harpalus affair.

Dinarchus infers that Demosthenes' corruption is so great that the city has become polluted and will remain so until, in accordance with custom, he is cast beyond the borders of Attica. Demosthenes' characterisation as 'this human plague of Greece' was probably a common expression in the topoi of oratorical invective for use against an opponent; Aeschines calls Demosthenes the 'curse of Hellas' at 3.131, 157 and 253.

(78)   **Athenians . . . dire straits:** Philip II's victory at the battle of Chaeronea in 338 (see below) panicked the Athenians, who feared he would march on them next. Demosthenes proposed to fortify the city, to repair the Piraeus fortifications, and to send out embassies. Hyperides proposed to enfranchise the *atimoi* (those without civic rights), metics, and slaves, and to send the women, children, and sacred objects to the Piraeus for safety (Dem. 18.248, Hyp. fr. 18 Kenyon, Lycurgus 1.16, 41, [Dem.] 26.11, [Plut.] *Moralia* 849a). Demosthenes was also appointed a commissioner to acquire corn for the city (Aes. 3.159, 259, Dem. 18.248, [Plut.] *Moralia* 845f, 851a-b), and on his return to Athens he was selected to deliver the funeral oration (*epitaphios*) over those who had died in the battle of Chaeronea (Speech 60). In 337/6 he was appointed to the board of ten overseers of the city's fortifications (Dem. 18.113, 248, 286-289, 299, Aes. 3.14, 23-24, 27, 152, 159, 236, Plut. *Demosthenes* 21.2-4, [Plut.] *Moralia* 845f-846a, 851a).

From the disclosure at section 80 Demosthenes' corn commission is the substance of the decree here. At sections 80-82, Dinarchus calls his absence from the city desertion, but this can hardly be true since he delivered the *epitaphios* on his return – a signal honour. On funeral orations, see Introduction, pp. 34-35.

The battle of Chaeronea, fought on 2 August 338, smashed Greek resistance to Philip II in one blow. From then onwards Greece fell under the hegemony of Macedon and remained relatively passive, apart from the war headed by Agis III of Sparta (see commentary on 34), until Alexander died on 10 June 323. The Athenians alone had one thousand killed and two thousand taken as prisoners (M.N. Tod, *Greek Historical Inscriptions* 2 [Oxford: 1948], no. 176), and Philip II followed this victory by establishing the League of Corinth, which effectively controlled Greece under his headship (see

Introduction, pp. 3-4). On the battle, see Diod. 16.85.5 ff., Plut. *Alexander* 9.2; cf. *Demosthenes* 19 ff., Polyaenus 4.2.2 and 7, and in detail Hammond & Griffith, *HM* 2, 596-603. On Philip's settlement with the Greeks after the battle see C. Roebuck, 'The Settlement of Philip II with the Greek States in 338 B.C.', *CPh* 43 (1948), 73-92.

and the oracle ... oracle: This oracle appears again at section 98, and it is also found at Demosthenes 19.29. H.W. Parke, *The Oracles of Zeus* (Oxford: 1967), 140, notes that the oracle quoted by Demosthenes and by Dinarchus is something of a rhetorical trend to rouse the superstitious feelings of the jurors against their leaders.

(79) **Now read . . . Read the remainder:** This is Demosthenes' decree (sneeringly referred to as 'noble') cited at 78 and 80, by which as an official envoy he was able to leave Athens after the battle of Chaeronea in 338 as a corn commissioner (see 78). This decree introduces a more violent attack in 80-82 on Demosthenes and his activities after that battle.

(80) **Gentlemen of the jury . . . your safety:** On this episode and the battle of Chaeronea, see commentary on 78. The figure of eight talents, which Demosthenes allegedly seized, does not occur elsewhere – Aeschines, who also relates the incident (3.159 and 253), says that Demosthenes only took a trireme. A.W. Pickard-Cambridge, *Demosthenes* (London: 1914), 394, thought that Demosthenes' hurried departure was justified, but it is more likely that he exploited the corn commission in order to flee Philip and returned when Philip did not attack Athens. Lycurgus also uses the same rhetorical attack and imagery on Leocrates for desertion after Chaeronea; for example, 'Leocrates ignored all these provisions. He collected what belongings he had . . . And so he disappeared, a deserter, untouched by pity for the city's harbours from which he was putting out to sea, and unashamed in face of the walls which, for his own part, he left undefended' (1.17).

(81) **Such is your political adviser . . . the city:** A quite untrue allegation since earlier Dinarchus has referred to Demosthenes' multiple embassies (12, 13) or those elsewhere, such as to Thebes (16, 24). On the battle of Chaeronea, see commentary on 78.

and now to Olympia . . . Nicanor: Dinarchus expands this statement in 82. The Olympian *theoria* (religious delegation) had religious and political significance. Nicanor had been sent by Alexander to the Olympic Festival of 324 to proclaim the Exiles Decree (Hyp. 5.18, Diod. 17.109.1, 18.8.2-7, Curt. 10.2.4-7, Justin 13.5.2-6; see Introduction, p. 7). Athens was confronted not only by the unwelcome return of its exiles but also by the loss of the island of Samos, peopled as it then was by Athenian cleruchs (see commentary on 14). Demosthenes travelled to Olympia as *architheoros* (chief religious envoy) of the Athenian delegation in an attempt to forestall the decree's implementation; he may have achieved a stay of execution, but it was Alexander's death that rendered it null and void as far as the Greeks were concerned. On Nicanor see Berve, *Alexander* 2, no. 557.

Is it right . . . the city: The tone of this passage suggests a question, and I place a question mark after ἀποδράς and translate accordingly. The allegations here are to Demosthenes' alleged cowardice at the battle of Chaeronea (see commentary on 12) and his corn commission after the battle (see commentary on 78 and 80)

(82) **But when it was necessary . . . a foot:** A reference to the Athenian delegation to Alexander after the razing of Thebes in 335 (cf. Introduction, pp. 4-5). Alexander was lenient towards the Athenians, even though they had initially supported the Thebans, and demanded only the surrender of several leading orators, including Demosthenes. Demades was able to commute even this (cf. 101), but the king insisted on the exile of Charidemus (see commentary on 32): Diod. 17.15, Arr. 1.10.4-6, Plut. *Demosthenes* 23.4, *Phocion* 17.2, [Plut.] *Moralia* 841e, 847c, 848e, Justin 11.4.10-11; cf. Aes. 3.161. Although the sources name different statesmen who were to be surrendered, the list in Plutarch, *Demosthenes* 23.4 is to be preferred: see, for example, A.B. Bosworth, *A Historical Commentary on Arrian's History of Alexander*, 1 (Oxford: 1980), 92-96. Again we see the importance of Demades as a diplomatic figure (on Demades see commentary on 7).

but when it was said . . . runaway: This concludes the argument that Demosthenes has been concerned purely with his own safety and has neglected his duty as a *symboulos* (adviser) to Athens. In section 103 Dinarchus discredits Demosthenes' mission by alleging that his primary motive was personal gain. On the mission to Olympia see commentary on 81. ἔφασαν indicates that news of the Exiles Decree had leaked out in advance of Nicanor's arrival in Greece, well before its proclamation at Olympia (cf. Hyp. 5.18).

Now read your decree . . . madness: The second decree cited here is that of Demosthenes for the Areopagus' investigation into the Harpalus affair: see commentary on 1. It is read again at 83 for further persuasive effect.

There is a lacuna in the text here, which was first identified by E. Maetzner, *Dinarchi Orationes* 3 (Berlin: 1842), *ad loc*. However, the general sense of the passage, based on what Dinarchus says in 83, indicates that this decree refers to the father and son who were among those investigated by the Areopagus and later summarily executed (see 62). I have again restored the text as I suggested in my 'Deinarchus I.34 & 82: Two textual restorations', *LCM* 10 (1985), 152 (*contra* Worthington, *Dinarchus*, 253-254); i.e., λέγε δὴ τὸ ψήφισμα περὶ δυοῖν τῶν πολιτῶν, with the addition of σὸν after τὸ from section 62. Thus, what is read out here is the proposal for these two men's punishment, followed by the reading of Demosthenes' decree that proposed the Areopagus' investigation into the Harpalus affair.

(83) **Did you propose this . . . pay attention:** These rhetorical questions bring dramatic immediacy to the speech; cf. 89-90. The citizens are the father and son of 62, whose decree Dinarchus has just had read out (see commentary on 82). Dinarchus then refers to Demosthenes' decree by which he agreed to submit to the death penalty if found guilty of accepting a bribe from Harpalus: see commentary on 1.

(84) **The council has declared . . . all mankind:** The Areopagus found Demosthenes guilty of *dorodokia*, the punishment for which was either a tenfold fine or death: see 60 with commentary. On the heliastic oath sworn annually by the jurors, see commentary on 14.

At 51 we learn that the prosecutors were appointed by the state, and Dinarchus 2.6 tells us that they numbered ten. In the following sections and in the Conclusion (105-114) Dinarchus instructs the jury what it should do.

(85) **No, Athenians . . . in question:** Other men who were executed for lesser crimes are mentioned at 23 and 56-57, although they were not victims of Demosthenes' decrees. Dinarchus refers to the decree that initiated the *apophasis* procedure and by which Demosthenes agreed to submit to the death penalty if found guilty of *dorodokia*: see commentary on 1.

C¹ (86-103)   Past History I

    (86-88) The A declared D guilty of taking bribes; the jury must act on this.
    (89-90) Venality of politicians in taking some of Harpalus' money.
    (91-93) D should be punished for reducing his city to disgrace.
    (94-96) D does not deserve to be a citizen, because of his ignoble past.
    (97-98) D should be punished for neglecting the good of the people.
    (99-101) Venality of D and other politicians, united against the good of
        the people.
    (102-103) D took bribes as the A had reported.

(86-103)   This is the most disappointing part of Dinarchus' speech for content since it is mostly rhetorical exhortation. As with its partner, Past History I (C: 11-28), the emphasis falls on selected events and deeds in order to illustrate Demosthenes' venality and to secure his conviction. Although Demosthenes initiated the *apophasis* procedure and was condemned under it by the Areopagus, his refusal to accept its verdict (86, 103; cf. 98) brings him into conflict not with Timotheus, as in 17, but with Poseidon and the Erinyes, who though deities still bowed to its judgment (86-87). Another contrast is drawn between the patriotic actions of (unnamed) predecessors (100) and Demosthenes' apathy and corruption (101), which included acquiescence in state benefactions for Demades, who was also suspected of bribery.

    Aside from content, Dinarchus' structural symmetry and control of his subject matter are still apparent, and the broad sequence of events follows the same pattern as its partner C: (a) action/deed, (b) exhortation against Demosthenes, and (c) action/deed.

(86)   **The same orator . . . the city:** For Demosthenes' decrees, see 1 with commentary. They are read out in 82-83.

    The Mother of the Gods (Cybele), who was the protector of the laws, had a cult linked to the Boule, and she had a temple and statue next to the central record office or Metröon (P.J. Rhodes, *The Athenian Boule* [Oxford: 1972], 31). Dinarchus skillfully inserts a pious element into his appeal with the reference to her. The Metröon housed the state archives, including laws and decrees, all of which were accessible by the public (Lycurgus 1.66, Aes. 3.187), and it was situated on the west side of the Agora in the old chamber of the Boule (J.M. Camp, *The Athenian Agora* [London: 1986], 91-94). See further A.E. Boegehold, 'The Establishment of a Central Archive at Athens', *AJA* 76 (1972), 23-30 and W.C. West, 'The Public Archives in Fourth-century Athens', *GRBS* 30 (1989), 529-543.

    It is not right . . . themselves: There are corresponding appeals at 46, 64-66, 87, 110. On the heliastic oath, see commentary on 14.

(87-88)   When Poseidon . . . Demosthenes: Dinarchus indicates that popular opinion viewed *dorodokia* for the betrayal of the city and its citizens as particularly heinous and tantamount to treason.

    Poseidon prosecuted Ares for murdering his son Halirrhothius, who had raped Ares' daughter Alcippe. Ares was tried before the Areopagus but acquitted (Apollodorus 3.14.2, Pausanias 1.21.4 and 28.5). The Areopagus may take its name from this trial since Ares was the first to be tried 'on the hill' (Pausanias 1.21.4, 1.28.5; cf. D.M. MacDowell, *The Law in Classical Athens* [London: 1978], 27).

    The Erinyes of Clytemnestra pursued Orestes, who had murdered his mother Clytemnestra and her lover Aegisthus in revenge for their slaying of his father Agamemnon, to Athens (Aeschylus, *Agamemnon* and *Choephoroi*). He was tried by the Areopagus, and was acquitted thanks to the intervention of Athena (Aeschylus, *Eumenides*; cf. Dem. 13.74 and Pausanias 1.28.5). The use of mythology by the Attic orators was a frequent rhetorical topos (S. Perlman, 'The Historical Example, Its Use and Importance εε Political Propaganda in the Attic Orators', *SH* 7 [1961], 158-162; cf. L. Pearson, 'Historical Allusions in the Attic Orators', *CPh* 36 [1941], 219-222).

(89) **Demosthenes himself . . . own pocket:** For Demosthenes' decree see commentary on 68; he was found guilty of taking a bribe of twenty talents from Harpalus (see commentary on 1). Note the sarcastic reference to Demosthenes as ὦ ἄριστε ('good friend').

someone else fifteen: The identity of this person is unknown. Since fifteen talents is a huge amount of money he must have been an important and influential figure, and Schäfer (*Demosthenes und seine Zeit*[2] 3 [Leipzig: 1887], 325 n. 3 [on 326]), followed by Blass (*Die attische Beredsamkeit*[2], 3.2 [Leipzig: 1898], 316 n. 3), plausibly suggests that it was Philocles, who allowed Harpalus into Athens against the specific orders of the Assembly ([Plut.] *Moralia* 846a). Why Dinarchus does not name him is unknown. He was subsequently brought to trial, and the prosecution speech by Dinarchus (3) survives.

Demades six thousand gold staters . . . to them: On Demades see commentary on 7. If gold, then the money would be the equivalent of twenty talents, the same as Demosthenes' bribe. This is implausible, and probably six thousand silver staters (two talents) are meant: E. Badian, 'Harpalus', *JHS* 81 (1961), 35 n. 146, Bosworth, *Conquest and Empire*, 219. Forensic exaggeration on the part of Dinarchus seems likely (cf. commentary on 4). At Dinarchus 2.1 we are told that Aristogeiton was prosecuted for taking a bribe of twenty minas, but the identities (and amounts) of those others involved in the affair are unknown.

Sixty-four talents . . . men: Manuscripts A and N have τετρακόσια as their original readings; however, assuming the reading τέτταρα of the corrected A manuscript is correct, the Areopagus' six-month investigation (*zetesis*) had not met with great success. On the manuscripts, cf. Introduction, pp. 38-39. It would appear from the missing 350 talents that the large sum of 286 (350 minus 64) still remained unaccountable, which is hard to imagine: more plausible is that Harpalus arrived in Athens with about 450 talents, and thus about one hundred were given in bribes.

(90) **Which is the better . . . have it:** The contradictory use of δίκαιον and δικαιότερον nicely criticises Demosthenes' decree mentioned in 89, where it is described as δίκαιον. The question is rhetorical and the speaker, in answering it, presumably echoes the mood of the jury. On the reference to *rhetores* and *strategoi*, see commentary on 71.

(91) **Gentlemen, this man . . . circumstances:** On Demosthenes' changes of statements see also 17, 46-47, 94-95 and Hyperides 5.12-13.

The parenthetical οὐ γὰρ ἔχω τί ἄλλο εἴπω was thought by A.P. Dorjahn and W.D. Fairchild ('Extemporaneous Elements in Some Minor Attic Orators', *CB* 48 [1972], 62) to be a pseudo-extemporaneous comment for rhetorical effect (cf. on the device Introduction, p. 23). The argument in this and in the following sections is based on probability (τὸ εἰκός); that is, Demosthenes will continue to be ignoble and maintain his corrupt practices in the future: see G. Kennedy, *The Art of Persuasion in Greece* (Princeton: 1963), 30-32.

(92)   **But if we have ... his luck:** Demosthenes is also called a γόης ('juggler') by Aeschines (3.137, 207), and this is probably part of the topoi of invective used by the orators, perhaps even influenced by the pejorative terms of Old and Middle Comedy (K.J. Dover, *Greek Popular Morality in the Time of Plato and Aristotle* [Oxford: 1974], 30-34). Another rhetorical technique of persuasion is also evident in the passage, as Dinarchus admonishes the jurors not to be swayed by the arguments of the defendant into giving an acquittal (Dover, *Greek Popular Morality*, 23-25).

(93)   **Athenians, which one ... administrator:** ἐῶ γὰρ τοῦτο is a 'simulated' spontaneous comment: see commentary on 91 on the technique. On the rhetorical appeal to mass wisdom when the audience knew less, see J. Ober, *Mass and Elite in Democratic Athens* (Princeton: 1989), 149-150 and 165.

        As well as ... themselves: Dinarchus refers to the money brought into the city by Harpalus when he finally gained entry (see Introduction, p. 8). Since the Areopagus could trace only 64 of the alleged missing 350 talents (89) a few corrupt individuals *en masse* impugned the reputation of the citizens.

(94)   **I disregard the other ... Alexander:** Demosthenes negotiated with Nicanor at Olympia in an effort to forestall the implementation of the Exiles Decree, which Nicanor had brought to be proclaimed at the games: see Introduction, p. 7. It would also appear at this time that the mainland Greeks were discussing the deification of Alexander, who saw himself as a son of Zeus after his visit to the oracle of Zeus Ammon in the oasis at Siwah in the winter of 332 (Plut. *Alexander* 27.8-10; cf. Diod. 17.51, Curt. 4.7.25, Justin 11.11.2-12). It is possible that it was Alexander himself who demanded the Greeks recognise his divinity, in which case Nicanor also brought this royal directive with him. The Athenians at first resisted ([Plut.] *Moralia* 804b, 842d), as did other Greeks (Polybius 12.12b3, [Plut.] *Moralia* 219e), but then Demosthenes advocated acceptance when he returned from Olympia, which Dinarchus (cf. 103) says was the result of a bribe (cf. also Hyp. 5.31-32). More likely is that Dinarchus is taking advantage of the incident to malign Demosthenes since the Athenians were sending an embassy to Alexander to appeal the Exiles Decree, and the placatory move of recognising his divinity might have improved its chances of success. On Alexander's deification, see Bosworth, *Conquest and Empire*, 278-289, E. Badian, 'The Deification of Alexander the Great', *Ancient Macedonian Studies in Honour of C.F. Edson*, ed. H.J. Dell (Thessaloniki: 1981), 27-71 and now G.L. Cawkwell, 'The Deification of Alexander the Great: A Note', *Ventures Into Greek History. Essays in Honour of N.G.L. Hammond*, ed. Ian Worthington (Oxford: 1994), 293-306, who argues that the move to recognise Alexander as a god came not from the king but from the Greeks. See also commentary on Hyperides 5.32.

        Or, when ... impeachment: The exiles are probably Athenians, gathering at Megara in anticipation of the Exiles Decree; cf. 58, where Polyeuctus was also brought up on charges in connection with them. Callimedon played a role in political life from the 320's, and also had extensive mining interests. Demosthenes' impeachment of him must have been shortly before his own trial in mid-March 323 (Ian Worthington, 'The Chronology of the Harpalus Affair', *SO* 61 [1986], 68-69), and after the proclamation of the Exiles Decree, and it may well have been an attempt to divert attention from his apparent guilt in the Harpalus scandal. The vignette of Callimedon's dealings with the exiles is a useful supplement to our knowledge of the period, and it also indicates a possible conspiracy by the Athenian exiles in order to bring about their return since the Athenians resisted their recall (Curt. 10.2.6-7). Dinarchus is insinuating that while Demosthenes' impeachment of Callimedon was patriotic, he was bribed to drop it. On Callimedon see *PA* 8032 and Davies, *APF*, 279.

95) **How he brought forward . . . against him:** The incident is unknown. It is not the same as in section 63 (Dinarchus cites Antiphon's intention to burn the Piraeus dockyards for Philip II and his subsequent execution), on chronological grounds and because Antiphon was ultimately condemned thanks to Demosthenes' intervention: see commentary on 63.

Gentlemen of Athens . . . the city: Aeschines (3.137, 207) also abusively refers to Demosthenes as a γόης; cf. commentary on 92. That Demosthenes is unworthy of being an Athenian citizen, rather than an appeal that he simply ought to be convicted, is a deliberately chosen statement that fits the structure of this part of the speech and further questions Demosthenes' political leadership of the Athenians.

96) **What triremes . . . Eubulus:** Eubulus was a prominent Athenian statesman in the 350's and early 340's; as a result of his administration, Athens' financial situation, which at that time was severe, dramatically improved. He was able to instigate a building progamme and to introduce other economic and military measures ([Plut.] *Moralia* 852c). In this section Dinarchus focuses on the military aspects of his work, beginning with his involvement in the increase in the Athenian navy. On Eubulus see *PA* 5369, R. Sealey, 'Athens after the Social War', *JHS* 75 (1955), 75-80, and especially G.L. Cawkwell, 'Eubulus', *JHS* 83 (1963), 47-67.

What dockyards . . . cavalry: Inscriptional evidence (*IG* ii² 505) indicates that Eubulus had fortified the Piraeus dockyards. Dinarchus is the only extant source who accuses Demosthenes of doing nothing for the cavalry, and so we ought to view his criticism with some scepticism (cf. Cawkwell, 'Eubulus', 66). In 330 Demosthenes had stressed his contributions to the state (18.299 ff.), which in effect rebut Dinarchus' later claims, and so we are dealing with rhetorical manipulation of the truth on the part of either, or both, orators.

When such opportunities . . . sea: For Demosthenes' actions following the battle of Chaeronea, see 78-82 with commentary. Cawkwell ('Eubulus', 66) is critical of Dinarchus here, and suggests that Eubulus could have assigned money to the military or Stratiotic Fund.

What ornament . . . Acropolis: Rhetorical exaggeration to malign Demosthenes. His payments in the form of liturgies (**personal** duties for the state paid from one's own funds) and other public contributions (Davies, *APF*, 135-137) were so enormous that they would surely have outweighed any apparent neglect of the patron-goddess.

What building . . . anywhere: This refers to Eubulus' encouragement to trade by his establishment of trading facilities and hostels (Xenophon, *Poroi* 3.12 ff.).

In Dinarchus' citing of Eubulus' administration we see a historical topos, one patriotically relating to the Good Old Days of Athens or the 'ancestor-theme'. Moreover, at least some of the jurors would be able to remember Eubulus and the fact that Demosthenes was his opponent (Dem. 21.206-207; cf. Aes. 2.184, Sealey, 'Athens after the Social War', 75-80, Cawkwell,

'Eubulus', 49-51), hence he would be an ideal foil for Dinarchus to use. An interesting point is that Athens enjoyed great prosperity not only under Eubulus but also under the more recent administration of Lycurgus (see Introduction, p. 5). Why then does Dinarchus cite Eubulus, who was active more than two decades earlier than the present trial? Perhaps Lycurgus, who had been discredited in his later years and even indicted shortly before his death ([Plut.] *Moralia* 842e), was still under a cloud at the time of the trial, and therefore would not have been a popular choice.

(97)   **If someone has been . . . this man:** A rhetorical question, focusing on the use of leaders for the well-being of the state which peppers the speech (29 ff., 40 ff., 77 ff., 99 ff; cf. Hyp. 5.12-13 and 17). On Dinarchus' attack on Demosthenes for his inconsistent policy, cf. commentary on 17.

(98)   **Not if you are wise . . . Read the oracle:** The reference to ἀγαθὴ τύχη ('good fortune') lends a pious element to Dinarchus' argument.

The oracle of Zeus of Dodona was quoted earlier in the speech at 78 (see commentary), and the similarity between the two sections is striking. The oracle that warned against leaders who took bribes to the detriment of the city shows the extreme care taken in the protection of the state and the relationship between its leaders and people.

(99)   **Athenians, how then . . . their speeches**: Note the similarities with 12-13, 40, 106 ff., 112 ff., and Hyperides 5.12-13 – perhaps this series of rhetorical questions to incite the jurors is something of a common appeal used by orators against their more powerful opponents. On the term *demagogoi* for political leaders, see commentary on 1.

(100) **What is the duty . . . these men:** For some of Demosthenes' actions against potential state enemies, see 63 and 94-95. The exploits of the Athenians' ancestors have been cited several times in the speech, and here the exhortation is to strive for the higher standards of previous generations. Polyeuctus is probably Polyeuctus of Sphettus, who was also accused of *dorodokia* in the Harpalus affair and apparently acquitted: see Introduction, p. 10. Dinarchus is our only source to connect Polyeuctus with the Harpalus affair, but the identification is generally accepted. A third century A.D. papyrus, *P. Oxy.* 15, 1804 fr. 3, 7-8 (= Conomis, fr. IVb), refers to a speech by Dinarchus against Polyeuctus (see Introduction, p. 39). On Polyeuctus see *PA* 11950, Berve, *Alexander* 2, no. 650 and Davies, *APF*, 7.

(101) **Have you censured . . . Aristogeiton:** On Demades see commentary on 7. He received a statue and *sitesis* (the right to dine at state expense for life) in 335 for his mission to Alexander to plead for the non-surrender of the Athenians whom the king demanded after the razing of Thebes (see commentary on 82).

Harmodius and Aristogeiton murdered Hipparchus, son of the tyrant Pisistratus, then joint ruler of Athens with his brother Hippias, in 514 (Herodotus 5.55 ff., Thucydides 6.54 ff., *AP* 18, [Plato] *Hipparchus* 229c1 ff., Diod. 10.17). Hippias ruled for a further four years until a Spartan force under King Cleomenes I expelled him (Herodotus 5.63.1), but Harmodius and Aristogeiton were still recognised as tyrannicides. They and the period became not only the ideal of democracy but also a popular topos employed by the orators (S. Perlman, 'The Historical Example, Its Use and Importance as Political Propaganda in the Attic Orators', *SH* 7 [1961], 164-166). They were the first recipients of a public statue and their descendants received these state awards for life (Isaeus 5.47, Dem. 19.280, 20.29). On Harmodius and Aristogeiton see *PA* 2232 and 1777, respectively; cf. Davies, *APF*, 473-474; on the murder of Hipparchus, quoting modern bibliography, see P.J. Rhodes, *A Commentary on the Aristotelian Athenaion Politeia* (Oxford: 1981), 227-233.

102) **In what way . . . support of the people:** Dinarchus anticipates a potential line of defence from Demosthenes: that he has no place to seek refuge if found guilty; cf. 43: 'this man who presently will tell you he may not take refuge anywhere', and 103: 'you fix your hopes on those from abroad'. Aeschines also has a similar line of attack in his speech at the Crown trial of 330 (3.209), but the fact that Dinarchus uses the same sorts of appeals does not imply plagiarism since he plausibly heard aspects of Demosthenes' defence in advance (cf. commentary on 12). Also, in *Epistle* 2.24-26 Demosthenes, then in exile, put forward this same defence, which was likely to be from his own trial speech. Dinarchus intends the contrast between the judicial steps taken by the predecessors of Demosthenes and Polyeuctus (100), and the apathy of Demosthenes and his acquiescence in Demades' awards (101), to counter any argument that Demosthenes acted for the people's best interests.

103) **But you fix your hopes . . . bribed:** See commentary on 102 for Demosthenes' overseas connections. On the charge that Demosthenes took bribes from Athens' enemies (in this case Harpalus), see commentary on 1.

And you . . . committing: On Demosthenes' mission to Olympia in connection with the Exiles Decree, see commentary on 81. Here, Dinarchus implies that Demosthenes went to Olympia in order to secure a bribe. His support of Alexander's proposed apotheosis upon his return could suggest this, but more likely is that he supported the move for political reasons: see commentary on 94. Dinarchus is thus seizing an opportunity to discredit Demosthenes, especially as he was unsuccessful in his missions to Nicanor, although he may have effected a delay in the return of the Athenian exiles (G. Colin, 'Démosthène et l'affaire d'Harpale', *REG* 39 [1926], 42, E. Badian, 'Harpalus', *JHS* 81 [1961], 32-33 with n. 122).

H.A. Kleyn's deletion of ἐν Ὀλυμπίᾳ ('Dinarchea', *Mnemosyne* 8 [1859], 102) is needless, and also causes problems with the sense of the passage.

31 (104)   Justification of Report

- (104) D is bolder than Demades, who admitted he took a bribe.
  - (104) Demades did not dare dispute the report of the A.
  - ⊢ (104) Demades did not volunteer to undergo the death penalty if found guilty.
  - (104) D intends to persuade the jury that the A's report is wrong.
- (104) D will say that he did not take any of Harpalus' money.

104) The penultimate part of the speech is very short, and it sees Dinarchus return to his other major subject, the Areopagus. Despite its size it is an integral unit in the structure, balancing the content of its partner (B: 5-11), to whose core element (8) its own is strikingly similar. In 104 Demades, all too often slandered for his treachery, is something of a hero for admitting his guilt and not contesting the Areopagus' declaration of his complicity in the Harpalus affair. Demosthenes, who did challenge the Areopagus, appears even more reprehensible as Dinarchus cleverly contrasts Demosthenes with the ignoble Demades.

(104) **In this you . . . he took money:** Cf. the similarity of the first half of this section with 61. At 89 Dinarchus alleges that Demades had taken a bribe of six thousand gold staters (= slightly less than twenty talents), but this figure is doubtful (see commentary *ad loc.*).

Demades is linked to Demosthenes several times in the speeches at the trials (7, 11, 45, 89, 101; cf. Din. 2.14, Hyp. 5.25-26) in order to emphasise political sympathies and a congruous criminal nature. However, in 104 Dinarchus denigrates Demosthenes with the argument that even a person such as Demades did not dispute the Areopagus' *apophasis* or propose his own death sentence should he be found guilty (which forms the central element of this part) – unlike Demosthenes. Although Demades was found guilty (Din. 2.15), this section, together with 29, has been plausibly taken to mean that he did not stand trial and was condemned *in absentia* (A. Schäfer, *Demosthenes und seine Zeit*[2] 3 [Leipzig: 1887], 344-345, Berve, *Alexander* 2, 132, E. Badian, 'Harpalus', *JHS* 81 [1961], 35). He was back in Athens at the time of Alexander's death in June 323 (Plut. *Phocion* 22.3). See further on Demades, commentary on 7.

But you have such . . . by that: The passage exemplifies the rhetorical technique of speakers admonishing juries not to be beguiled into giving an unjust verdict: see K.J. Dover, *Greek Popular Morality in the Time of Plato and Aristotle* (Oxford: 1974), 23-25 and J. Ober, *Mass and Elite in Democratic Athens* (Princeton: 1989), 156 ff. and 318 ff.

A¹ (105-114) Conclusion

> (105-106) D must be condemned as a traitor, as is just and fitting.
>> (107-108) For city's and people's safety, the jurors are not to give in to D.
>>> (108) D has acquired much money in his career.
>>> ├ (109) D brought his predicament on himself, so pity the endangered country.
>>> (110-111) D, now rich and famous, does not deserve pity, given Athens' plight.
>> (112-113) Do not acquit such traitors or the state will suffer.
> (114) Jury, like speaker, must concentrate on justice and people's interests.

(105-114) The conclusion (epilogue) of the speech is an exhortation against Demosthenes, for it is Dinarchus' last attempt to secure his conviction before the other prosecutors' speeches and then the defence speech of Demosthenes. Arguments such as the Areopagus' report against Demosthenes must not be disregarded (105-106); Demosthenes must be condemned for the sake of the city (107-114); Demosthenes took bribes to the detriment of Athens (108 and 111); and no credence should be given to witnesses speaking in his support, especially any orators and generals also facing prosecution (112-113) are reemphasised. The speech ends with a final appeal before Dinarchus 'hands over the water' to the other prosecutors (114).

(105) **Athenians . . . common justice:** Cf. 114. Dinarchus neatly involves the jurors here. From this passage, 106, Hyperides 5.6-7 and Demosthenes, *Epistle* 2.14, we know that Demosthenes was the first to be tried, and consequently the verdict of the jury was crucially important for the remaining cases.

(106-107) **Overlooking all . . . for everyone:** The first section should be split into two questions, rather than just the one, with the first question concluded at ἀνθρώποις. On the report of the Areopagus against Demosthenes, see commentary on 1. A jury of 1,500 accords with the type of case currently being tried; cf. commentary on 52. Again, we have the speaker's appeal to the jury not to be swayed by the defendant's arguments and so deliver an unjust verdict: K.J. Dover, *Greek Popular Morality in the Time of Plato and Aristotle* (Oxford: 1974), 23-25.

(108) **Gentlemen of Athens . . . against himself:** Sections 108-111 are partially preserved on *P. Oxy.* 49, 3436, a recently discovered papyrus fragment of the late second or early third century A.D.: see Introduction, p. 39. Dinarchus refers to the bribe taken by Demosthenes and to his decree to suffer death if found guilty: see commentary on 1. The appeal is set to provoke the jury's opposition to Demosthenes and to such leaders who have betrayed the state for money, a crime that the Athenians especially condemned.

We are given some details of the ways by which Demosthenes acquired money at 10, 42-45, 70, 89, 103, and cf. 111 with commentary. The oratorical argument that Demosthenes is so wealthy that he had no need to accept bribes is intended to emphasise Demosthenes' corruption; cf. Dinarchus 3.18, where it is used against Philocles the general.

But the shamelessness . . . head: Demosthenes is described as αἰσχροκερδής, a deliberate word to reinforce his venality; cf. 21 with commentary.

(109) **Do not be troubled . . . and wailing:** Aeschines also mocks Demosthenes' tears as part of a defence strategy in his speech of 330 (3.209 and 210). Hyperides (5.40) also scorns the tears of Hagnonides, indicating that Hagnonides was himself either soon to be tried or was to appear as a character witness for Demosthenes (cf. 112).

you would far more justly . . . died: The deeds of some of the Athenians' ancestors are frequently cited by the orators in order to stir the patriotic spirits of the jurors.

I follow manuscript A for the order καθίστησιν εἰς τοὺς κινδύνους, and manuscripts Acorr. N for the reading κινδύνους after καλοὺς (see too *P. Oxy.* 49, 3436 fr. B col. i line 31), and not ἀγῶνας (APr); cf. H. Wankel, 'Bemerkungen zu neuen Rednerpapyri', *ZPE* 53 (1983), 89.

(110) **Athenians, right-thinking men . . . because of the city:** An echo of 109 on Demosthenes' tears: see commentary. The same type of appeal is often made in the speech in order to ensure that the jury declares against Demosthenes.

The discovery of *P.Oxy.* 49, 3436 (late second/early third century A.D.) finally confirms the reading σῶμα of AN: τὸ τῆς πόλεως σῶμ' ἀποβλέψαντες. See *The Oxyrhynchus Papyri* 49, edited by A. Bülow-Jacobsen and J.E.G. Whitehorne (London: 1982), no. 3436 fr. B col. ii line 20 at pp. 22-24; *contra* H. Wankel, 'Bemerkungen zu neuen Rednerpapyri', *ZPE* 53 (1983), 89-90. Nouhaud and Dors-Méary, in the latest text of Dinarchus (Budé), disregard the papyrus reading and still print ὄνομα.

(111) **You will find . . . ancestors:** Dinarchus refers to Demosthenes' earlier career as a speechwriter. Demosthenes would have been paid a legitimate fee (*misthos*) for his services as a *logographos* (K.J. Dover, *Lysias and the Corpus Lysiacum* [Berkeley: 1968], 157-158), but Dinarchus alleges that he also took bribes, and implies that those who acquired great wealth from humble beginnings did so dishonestly.

Ctesippus, son of Chabrias (see commentary on 75), hired Demosthenes in a case against the law of Leptines of 356/4, which repealed all immunities

from liturgies (personal duties for the state paid from one's own funds)
bestowed on all individuals apart from the descendants of the tyrannicides
Harmodius and Aristogeiton (see commentary on 101). Chabrias' actions for
the state had earned him immunity, which Ctesippus had inherited, but under
Leptines' law he would once again be liable for the expensive liturgy service.
Demosthenes spoke against the law (Speech 20) but the outcome is unknown.
On Ctesippus see *PA* 8885 and Davies, *APF*, 561.

Phormion had been employed by Pasion as manager of his bank and shield-
factory, and was freed in his master's will. In 350/49 Apollodorus, eldest of
Pasion's sons, sued him for embezzlement. Demosthenes successfully
defended him (Speech 36), winning such a victory that his opponent failed to
receive one-fifth of the votes cast. On Phormion see *PA* 14951 and Davies,
APF, 431-437. On Demosthenes' early career, see A.W. Pickard-Cambridge,
Demosthenes (London: 1914), 111-141 and W. Jaeger, *Demosthenes. The
Origin and Growth of his Policy* (Berkeley: 1938), 24-41 and 64-67.

Therefore disregard . . . jurors: Again, the common appeal involving the
state to offset any dicastic sympathy for Demosthenes' defence; cf. 37 ff., 64
ff., 99 ff. and Hyperides 5.34-36.

In view of *P. Oxy.* 49, 3436 fr. B col. iii lines 27-28, supported by A, the
order τὴν ὁσίαν καὶ τὴν δικαίαν (cf. 2.20) is to be preferred over the
reverse order of N; so Burtt, *contra* Conomis and Nouhaud and Dors-Méary.

(112) And when anyone . . . Harpalus: Aeschines concludes his speech against
Ctesiphon/Demosthenes in 330 in much the same vein (3.257 ff.), and in his
prosecution speech against Leocrates in the same year Lycurgus says that the
supporters should qualify their services on behalf of the city (1.135-140). We
do not know who spoke in support of Demosthenes. Perhaps the references
to Cephisophon (45), Demades (7, 11, 45, 89, 101, 104) and Polyeuctus of
Sphettus (100), as well as to Hagnonides' tears by Hyperides (5.40), indicate
they would do so. However, Demades probably had left Athens by then
(commentary on 29), in which case his guilt could be linked with the others
in order to reinforce their discredit. J. Ober, *Mass and Elite in Democratic
Athens* (Princeton: 1989), 121-122, takes this passage as an indication that
rhetores and *strategoi* (on the term see commentary on 71) made good
character witnesses. More likely, though, is that Dinarchus takes pains to
discredit those also implicated in the affair whose trials will follow.
Athenaeus (13.592e-f) tells us that Demosthenes paraded his illegitimate
children before the jurors for emotional effect; if true, then this was to no
avail.

(113) Athenians, consider . . . no use to you: Evidently some of the others
charged with bribery were expected to support Demosthenes (see
commentary on 112), and Dinarchus cautions the jury to disregard their
testimony – as does Hyperides at 5.5-6 and 39-40.

The fundamental weakness of the Areopagus' charge of *dorodokia* against
those it accused is revealed by the appeal 'by one vote and at one trial all of
those who have been reported and those who will be in the future will be
released'. Since no evidence existed to substantiate the charge, all of the
accused should either have been condemned or acquitted. However, that
some of those accused were acquitted (Aristogeiton, for example) suggests a
political conspiracy against Demosthenes: see Introduction, p. 10.

(114) I have done my best . . . people: Cf. the start of the Epilogue: 'We have made our accusation and made no concession to anyone in the interests of common justice' (105).

Appealing to you . . . prosecutors: The water is the κλεψύδρα, water-clock, which timed speeches at trials and also other meetings such as tribal assemblies (*AP* 67.2-5). When one prosecutor in cases involving several prosecutors finished his speech, he would 'hand over the water' to his colleague, who then delivered his speech – as Dinarchus' client does at the end of his speech.

Trials usually lasted one day (*AP* 67.1, Aes. 2.126, 3.197), which was divided into three: speeches for the prosecution, that of the defence, and then speeches for the penalty if the accused was found guilty (on the last, see D.M. MacDowell, 'The Length of the Speeches on the Assessment of the Penalty in Athenian Courts', *CQ*² 35 [1985], 525-526). This gives the impression that Athenian court procedure was rushed (cf. Plato, *Laws* 855-856 and 766e). However, it is hard to accept a one-day period for public cases involving multiple prosecutors since this period fell on them all collectively and not individually. Moreover, it also included the quoting of laws and decrees and the testimony of character witnesses (the κλεψύδρα was stopped for these in private suits only: *AP* 67.3). Some public or show trials therefore must have lasted up to two or three days: see Ian Worthington, 'The Duration of an Athenian Political Trial', *JHS* 109 (1989), 204-207.

On the water clock see P.J. Rhodes, *A Commentary on the Aristotelian Athenaion Politeia* (Oxford: 1981), 719-728; photograph: J.M. Camp, *The Athenian Agora* (London: 1986), fig. 85 with p.112; see also S. Young, 'An Athenian Clepsydra', *Hesperia* 8 (1939), 274-284 and D.M. MacDowell, *The Law in Classical Athens* (London: 1978), 249-251.

With this final appeal to the jury, Dinarchus concludes his speech against Demosthenes.

Hyperides 5, *Against Demosthenes*

Whereas Dinarchus 1 and Hyperides 6 are divided numerically into sections (small paragraphs), Hyperides 5, being much more fragmentary, is presented according to the numbering of the fragments and the columns of the papyrus. Because it is so mutilated, any analysis of this speech for ring composition is impossible. We do not even know how long in its written form it was. However, it is possible to deduce the major parts of the speech from Hyperides' tone and changes of subject matter, hence the commentary is arranged accordingly.

(1-7)   Hyperides' prologue begins by accusing Demosthenes of thinking himself above the law (1). He denied that he took money from Harpalus, and he challenged the verdict of the Areopagus even though he initiated its enquiry into the missing money (1-3; cf. 6). The Areopagus' reputation and actions are commended (5), and the appeal is made to the jury not to believe Demosthenes' defence (6). Hyperides stresses the uniform manner in which the Areopagus delivered its findings against those suspected of taking bribes and that Demosthenes' acquittal would affect those others accused (6-7).

(1)   **Gentlemen of the jury . . . sitting next to me:** Hyperides is especially skilled at having the listener (and reader) caught up in the pace and thrust of a speech from the very start. Here, a sense of dramatic immediacy is introduced since Hyperides appears to have been conversing readily with his fellow prosecutors during the previous prosecution speech (which could have been that delivered by Dinarchus' client) against Demosthenes.

The speech begins with the connective ἀλλά, which seems odd at first sight. This usage is called the 'inceptive' (J.D. Denniston, *The Greek Particles*[2], revised K.J. Dover [Oxford: 1954], 20-21), and corresponds roughly to the English word 'well'. What is interesting, though, is that we do not find the other Attic orators starting their speeches with ἀλλά, and so Hyperides' unusual use of it is worthy of some comment.

Hyperides' earlier speech *In Defence of Euxenippus* (4) also began with this word, and the start of the present speech is almost verbatim that of the Euxenippus speech, and so both are worth quoting. *In Defence of Euxenippus* 1: ἀλλ' ἔγωγε, ὦ ἄνδρες δικασταί, ὅπερ καὶ πρὸς τοὺς παρακαθημένους ἀρτίως ἔλεγον, θαυμάζω εἰ μὴ προσίστανται ἤδη ὑμῖν αἱ τοιαῦται εἰσαγγελίαι ('Gentlemen of the jury, as I was just saying to those sitting next to me, I am taken aback that you are not tired of this type of impeachment by now'). *Against Demosthenes* 1: ἀλλ' ἐγώ, ὦ ἄνδρες δικασταί, ὅπερ καὶ πρὸς τοὺς παρακαθημένους ἀρτίως ἔλεγον, θαυμάζω τουτὶ τὸ πρᾶγμα ('Gentlemen of the jury, as I was just saying to those sitting next to me, I am taken aback by this situation'). Probably the use of ἀλλά as the first word and the appeal to the jury are to lend a sense of dramatic immediacy to both speeches and so capture the juror's attention from the outset. However, what is intriguing is that none of the other orators whose works survive uses this word to start a speech with the single exception of Demosthenes' *Erotic Essay* (61), an epideictic work whose authorship is in any case disputed. Moreover, we have 56 *exordia*, or openings of speeches, composed allegedly by Demosthenes as 'models' from which orators could choose to start their own speeches. Not one of these begins with ἀλλά. In view of this and the opening similarity of the Euxenippus speech to that against Demosthenes, it is therefore plausible that one of Hyperides' stylistic characteristics was to begin his forensic speeches with ἀλλά and the direct address to the jurors citing his astonishment at the background to the case for dramatic effect. The introductions of Hyperides' three other forensic speeches, *In Defence of Lycophron* (1), *Against Philippides* (2) and *Against Athenogenes* (3), are lost. The start of Hyperides' only other extant speech, the *Epitaphios* (see Speech 6 in this volume), is extant, but it does not begin in this way. However, epideictic oratory was a different genre from forensic, and unsuited to the racier beginning.

I am taken aback ... death wish: The reference to Zeus (νὴ Δία) here is not actually an oath by the god since Hyperides tends to use few such oaths in his speeches, preferring to add weight to his case by means of imagery and emotional appeal. More likely, it is the equivalent of the more common ἀλλὰ νὴ Δία, used to set up an argument ascribed to an opponent so that it can be refuted in the following speech (Denniston, *The Greek Particles*, 8-9).

Colin, in his note on this section (p. 244), points out Hyperides' use of the plural νόμοι ('laws') and ψηφίσματα ('decrees'). In practice, only one law had been contravened and Demosthenes proposed in only one decree that the Areopagus investigate into the Harpalus affair (on which, see commentary on Dinarchus 1.1). As Colin rightly says, Hyperides' use of the plural is meant to have more effect on his audience.

The decree to which Hyperides refers is that of Demosthenes which subjected himself to the death penalty if he were found guilty of taking a bribe from Harpalus (cf. 2). Dinarchus also makes frequent use of this decree in his speech against Demosthenes (for example, at 1.8: 'Why then, Demosthenes, did you agree in the Assembly to the death penalty on yourself if the council should report against you?', and at 1.40: 'For acts such as these they should have been put to death long ago, in accordance with their own decree'; cf. 1.61, 63, 83-84, 86, 104, 108): see further, commentary on Dinarchus 1.1. Since the Areopagus declared Demosthenes guilty of taking a bribe against the state while he was a public official (*dorodokia*), under the terms of his own decree he should be executed rather than declare his innocence at his trial. Hyperides is incorrect in asserting that Demosthenes alone proposed a decree against himself as others also under suspicion followed suit: for example, Philocles (Din. 3.2, 5, 16, 21); and cf. 34 for a reference to unnamed others. On those accused of taking a bribe from Harpalus see Introduction, p. 10.

which you swore to uphold: Hyperides refers to the dicastic oath (cf. 39), sworn by those who were selected as jurors for the year. The oath is given by Demosthenes at 24.149-151:

> I will give verdict in accordance with the statutes and decrees of the People of Athens and of the Council of Five-hundred. I will not vote for tyranny or oligarchy. If any man tries to subvert the Athenian democracy or makes any speech or any proposal in contravention thereof, I will not comply. I will not allow private debts to be cancelled, nor lands nor houses belonging to Athenian citizens to be redistributed. I will not restore exiles, or persons under sentence of death. I will not expel, nor suffer another to expel, persons here resident in contravention of the statutes and decrees of the Athenian

People or of the Council. I will not confirm the appointment to any office of any persons still subject to audit in respect of any other office, to wit the offices of the nine Archons or of the Recorder or any other office for which a ballot is taken on the same day as for the nine Archons, or the office of Marshal, or ambassador, or member of the Allied Congress. I will not suffer the same man to hold the same office twice, or two offices in the same year. I will not take bribes in respect of my judicial action, nor shall any other man or woman accept bribes for me with my knowledge by any subterfuge or trick whatsoever. I am not less than thirty years old. I will give impartial hearing to prosecutor and defendant alike, and I will give my verdict strictly on the charge named in the prosecution. (The juror shall swear by Zeus, Poseidon, and Demeter, and shall invoke destruction upon himself and his household if he in any way transgresses this oath, and shall pray that his prosperity may depend upon his loyal observance thereof.)

For discussion see R.J. Bonner and G. Smith, *The Administration of Justice from Homer to Aristotle* 2 (Chicago: 1938), 152-156 and D.M. MacDowell, *The Law in Classical Athens* (London: 1978), 44 and 60.

(2) **And yet, gentlemen of the jury ... the Areopagus:** In private cases (*dikai*) a challenge was an accepted form of defence, but not so in public cases (*graphai*), into which category the trial of Demosthenes for treason against the state fell; cf. A.R.W. Harrison, *The Law of Athens* 2 (Oxford: 1971), 135-136 and 153.

At the end of a six months' enquiry or *zetesis* (Din. 1.45) the Areopagus published its findings and accused Demosthenes of taking twenty talents from Harpalus (7, 10; see too Dinarchus 1.6, 45, 53, 69, 89). It is impossible to give a modern monetary equivalent to this sum; suffice it to say that it was an enormous amount since one talent equalled 36,000 obols (the smallest unit of currency), and three obols was the daily pay for an Athenian juror in the late fifth and fourth centuries BC.

During the course of the Areopagus' investigation, apparently as a result of popular feeling against him, Demosthenes issued a *proklesis* or challenge to the people to present that body with evidence for his guilt (cf. Din. 1.5).

On the Areopagus and its powers, see commentary on Dinarchus 1.6.

(3-4) **You malign the Areopagus ... reported:** Cf. 31. When formally accused by the Areopagus, Demosthenes issued a second *proklesis* (challenge), this time to compel it to produce proof of its allegation against him (cf. Din. 1.6 and 61). He seems to have toured the Agora and elsewhere denouncing the Areopagus and the people (cf. Din. 1.12, 26, 31, 43, 48 and 102).

The verb συκοφαντέω is loaded with implications. Sycophants were those who informed on, or blackmailed, people usually for personal gain (cf. Dem. 21.103, Aes. 2.5, 3.256), and were held in contempt by Athenian society. Thus, Demosthenes' challenging of the actual members of the Areopagus was just as reprehensible, and in the process he wrongly maligned the worthy reputation of that council. In 40, Hyperides refers to the sycophant Hagnonides, who seems to have been one of Demosthenes' character witnesses. In so doing, Demosthenes is depicted as even more contemptible since he asks sycophants to vouch for his character. On sycophancy see A.R.W. Harrison, *The Law of Athens* 2 (Oxford: 1971), 60-62.

(5-6) **the reports . . . your right:** The championing of the integrity of the Areopagus and of the validity of its decision permeates Dinarchus' speech as well. This is hardly surprising since no evidence against Demosthenes or against those others accused of *dorodokia* existed. Like Dinarchus, Hyperides has to build his case around the trustworthiness of the Areopagus (cf. Introduction, p. 26), hence its findings against those accused should be automatically accepted. The Areopagus could not recommend or inflict punishment on individuals by its own authority, which is why the case had to be referred to an ordinary law court.

From this passage it is possible that the Areopagus had delayed making the results of its enquiry into the missing money known until it was compelled to do so by the people. This may have been because it anticipated using Demosthenes' diplomatic powers if Alexander decided not to grant the Athenians' request over the return of their exiles under the Exiles Decree: see Introduction, p. 7.

But Demosthenes not only thinks . . . argument: On Demosthenes' slanders see 2-3 above. Presumably the reference to all the other prosecutions is to the trials of those others accused in the Harpalus affair: see Introduction, p. 10. Demosthenes' trial took place in probably March 323 and was the first (Din 1.105): on chronology see Ian Worthington, 'The Chronology of the Harpalus Affair', *SO* 61 (1986), 63-76.

The Council has produced . . . the report against him: The Areopagus merely declared those it investigated guilty and gave an amount allegedly taken by each man (cf. Din. 1.89). According to Dinarchus, it did not need to cite any supporting evidence in order to substantiate its accusations against anyone ('it simply reports the one subject to the enquiry or who has broken any traditional rules of conduct': 1.55). Certainly, it did not cite evidence against Demosthenes, as he continually stressed in letters which he wrote to the Athenians when in exile; for example, '. . . without any manifest proof or even a scrutiny of evidence on the part of the Council, condemning all the accused on the strength of the unrevealed information of that body' (*Epistle* 2.1); 'Or what proof did the Council allege against me? Or what proof could it now allege? There is none; for it is impossible to makes facts out of what never happened' (*Epistle* 2.15; cf. 3.42). The validity of the Areopagus' reports is open to doubt by the fact that several of the accused were found guilty in a court of law and others innocent: see Introduction, p. 10.

(7) **For if this argument . . . others:** Demosthenes was accused by the Areopagus of taking twenty talents from Harpalus; since he was the first to be tried (Din. 1.107) his condemnation would also affect those who were to be tried after him. However, we know that not all of those accused by the Areopagus were found guilty when brought to trial; for example, Aristogeiton and Demades. This fact immediately reveals the weakness of the Areopagus' findings as well as the biased verdict against Demosthenes at his trial: since no evidence was cited for the allegations of bribery, all of the accused should either have been condemned or acquitted (cf. Din. 1.113, 2.21). On what grounds did the jurors then decide who was guilty and who innocent? See further Introduction, pp. 10–11.

Fuhr proposed μεῖζον, but Blass' μᾶλλον is preferable; so Colin.

And so now you are passing . . . four hundred: Harpalus had allegedly left behind 350 talents when he fled (Introduction, p. 9); the figure in Hyperides' text at this point is incomplete because of a lacuna in the papyrus. The

papyrus has τ . . . σιων, which was originally restored by Sauppe in 1848 as
τ[ριακο]σίων (300). However, on the plausible grounds that the orators were
more likely to exaggerate a figure for rhetorical effect, Boeckh in the same
year rounded up the amount to τ[ετρακο]σίων (400). Other modern editors
have followed suit (though Jensen still prints τ[ριακο]σίων). Certainly,
rounding-up of figures occurs elsewhere in the orators and may have been
common practice; for example, Dinarchus at 1.10 and 18 rounds up the
amount of the bribe demanded by the Arcadians to help Thebes from
Aeschines' figure of nine talents (at 3.239-240) to ten. See also 9-10 on
restoration of the sums of money which Harpalus allegedly brought with him
and which were deposited on the Acropolis.

I prefer Colin's proposed ὥστε νῦν, which I think is in keeping with the
explanatory nature of Hyperides' subsequent comments.
and not on one crime . . . against you: Words such as shamelessness
(ἀναισχυντία) are deliberately chosen by Hyperides for their emotional
effect and to highlight the heinous nature of the crime. Dinarchus uses the
word αἰσχροκερδής ('mercenary') in his characterisation of Demosthenes
(1.21; cf. 1.108: 'the shamelessness and venality innate from his whole life
style have brought this upon his own head'; 3.6: 'there is nothing worse than
someone's wickedness being unknown') as it reinforces the impression of his
venality. See further F.D. Harvey, *'Dona Ferentes*: Some Aspects of Bribery
in Greek Politics', *Crux. Essays in Greek History Presented to G.E.M. de Ste.
Croix on his 75th Birthday*, edd. P.A. Cartledge and F.D. Harvey (London:
1985), 102-113.

(8-14) Hyperides now moves to detail the circumstances which led to the
accusations of bribery against certain Athenian statesmen. He begins by
outlining Harpalus' arrival in Athens and the Assembly debate at which
Demosthenes proposed his arrest and the confiscation of his money (8-10).
Even at this point Demosthenes was apparently keen to take some of it for
himself (9), saying nothing when only 350 of the alleged 700 talents brought
by Harpalus were put under guard (10). Hyperides alleges that Demosthenes
took money from Harpalus for relaxing that guard (12), and that when
accused of this he admitted he took it for the Theoric Fund, not as a bribe
(12-13). Once again, Demosthenes is made to show his contempt for his city
and its people (13-14).

(8)   **But why you took it . . . on account of him:** A quickening of pace as we
move into the narrative part of the speech: the listener and/or reader is now
effectively drawn into the drama and confusion that must have prevailed in
Athens at this time.

Harpalus' first attempt to enter Athens, when he was supported by a large
and powerful force of six thousand mercenaries, five thousand talents of
stolen money (Diod. 17.108.6) and thirty warships (Curt. 10.2.1), was in mid
June 324. He was unsuccessful that time as the Assembly forbade his entry
([Plut.] *Moralia* 846a). He made another attempt at the end of that month,
with a much smaller force (Ian Worthington, *'IG* ii² 1631, 1632 and
Harpalus' Ships', *ZPE* 65 [1986], 222-224), and this time he was allowed
into the city by the general Philocles. On the chronology see Ian
Worthington, 'The Chronology of the Harpalus Affair', *SO* 61 (1986), 63-76.
Soon after his arrival, Hyperides tells us that Macedonian envoys from
Philoxenus, Alexander's financial governor of Sardis, came to Athens to

demand his extradition. It is odd that someone like Philoxenus was involved and not Antipater, whom Alexander had left behind him as guardian (*epitropos*) of the Greeks (Arr. 1.11.3), although we are told that envoys did go from Antipater and also it seems from the king's mother, Olympias (Diod. 17.108.7, [Plut.] *Moralia* 846b). Philoxenus may have sent an embassy that later prompted Antipater to follow suit. On Philoxenus see Berve, *Alexander* 2, no. 793; cf. E. Badian, 'Alexander the Great and the Greeks of Asia', *Ancient Society and Institutions. Studies Presented to Victor Ehrenberg on his 75th Birthday*, ed. E. Badian (Oxford: 1966), 56-60.

Demosthenes was right to argue that the Athenians could not justly hand over Harpalus to Alexander since Harpalus had been made an Athenian citizen. This grant was in recompense for his gift of corn to the city during the famine of the 320s (Athenaeus 13.586d, 13.596a-b; cf. M.N. Tod, *Greek Historical Inscriptions* 2 [Oxford: 1948], no. 196, 5). To surrender him to Alexander would have meant betraying a citizen, who had sought sanctuary in his city.

(9)   **The safest course . . . payment from him:** At a meeting of the Assembly called to discuss the affair, at which the various envoys (see 8) and Harpalus presented their cases, it was resolved, thanks to the influence of Demosthenes, to imprison Harpalus, confiscate the money he had with him, and to send an envoy to the king rather than obey the directive of the envoys. **Sitting down below in the niche . . . talents:** The niche or κατατομή refers to what seems to have been a cutting in the Pnyx (where the Athenian Assembly met), presumably close to the *bema* or rostrum from where speeches were delivered. We might imagine that the more politically active of the citizens, who would thus speak the most, would sit closest to the *bema*, and it comes as no surprise that Demosthenes would sit here. However, there is a view that when the Athenians attended an Assembly they were grouped together in their ten tribes on the Pnyx (P.J. Bicknell and G.R Stanton, 'Voting in Tribal Groups in the Athenian Assembly', *GRBS* 28 [1987], 51-92), not least as a way of controlling several thousands of citizens who might attend a meeting. Demosthenes was a member of the third tribe (which was called Pandionis), and if the Athenians were grouped by tribes he would have been seated some distance from the *bema*. Clearly, the arguments of Bicknell and Stanton do not fully take into account the implication of the Hyperides passage here. On the Assembly see M.H. Hansen, *The Athenian Ecclesia* 1 & 2 (Copenhagen: 1983 & 1989); cf. R.K. Sinclair, *Democracy and Participation in Athens* (Cambridge: 1988) and J. Ober, *Mass and Elite in Democratic Athens* (Princeton: 1989).

The identity of Mnesitheus the dancer is unknown.

In the phrase ἀφ' ὅσων αὐτὸν δεῖ τὸν μισθὸν πράττεσθαι, αὐτὸν refers not to Demosthenes but to Harpalus, and so the sentence is translated as 'he should claim his payment <u>from him</u>'. There are parallels for this use of πράττομαι at Herodotus 3.58.4, Pindar, *Olympian* 10.30 and Demosthenes 20.32.

(10-12) **He himself . . . staters:** On Demosthenes' proposal, Harpalus' money was to be secured on the Acropolis the day after the Assembly meeting until word came back from Alexander about what was to be done with him. Harpalus' figure of 700 talents does not seem to have been checked until after he had fled, and only 350 talents were found there. Hyperides accuses Demosthenes here of covering up the discrepancy since he had already taken a bribe (of twenty talents) and did not wish that to become known. We should note that neither Hyperides nor Dinarchus accuse Demosthenes of embezzlement, and that Hyperides does not imply that Demosthenes knew of the deficit before Harpalus escaped. In other words, that he took Harpalus at his word as did the other Athenians. It is more likely, however, that Harpalus brought about 450 talents with him and simply lied about the amount.

The figure of 700 (ἑπτακοσίων) in this passage is virtually intact. That of 350 talents is a modern restoration (τρια]κοσίων ταλά[ντων καὶ πεντ[ήκοντα), but since the figure of 700 looks unassailable and Hyperides goes on to talk about 'half' of it, 350 is also secure.

The stater was a unit of currency which was the equivalent of two drachmas (on coinage see also commentary on 26). At 1.89 Dinarchus refers to someone who took his bribe in staters, who may well have been Demades: see commentary *ad loc.*

(12)   **You were the one who . . . circumstances:** The sarcasm in this section, which is one of Hyperides' stylistic characteristics, is very apparent and effective.

Demosthenes proposed that a guard be set up over Harpalus and over his money. At Dinarchus 1.62 and 83 we are told that Demosthenes proposed a motion to execute two men, a father and son, who could have been those ordered to guard Harpalus' treasure. Hyperides alleges that Demosthenes was bribed to relax the guard and so permit Harpalus to escape.

When Harpalus . . . as it seems: The reference to the lesser orators who can only resort to shouting and screaming is meant to contrast with more powerful orators such as Demosthenes who controlled state policy by their ability to persuade the people at Assemblies. In accusing Demosthenes of betraying not only the people but also the laws, Hyperides is playing on the Athenians' respect for the law, as seen in the annual dicastic oath (see commentary on 1 above).

The qualifying ὡς ἔοικεν ('as it seems') is a common rhetorical trick allowing an orator to qualify deliberate slander of an opponent or to cast another's actions in an ambiguous light. However, in this passage it is crucial in Hyperides' allegation: what might Demosthenes have said for Hyperides to interpret in this way? The answer, as Hyperides goes on to tell us (13), is Demosthenes' 'admission' that he took the money for the Theoric Fund (on which see next note).

(13)   **he admitted . . . Theoric Fund:** Hyperides alleges that Demosthenes had admitted from the first that he took money for the Theoric Fund but then, it seems, he changed this admission to outright denial. It is important to bear in mind that Hyperides qualifies Demosthenes' line of defence with the phrase 'as it seems' (see above note). Hyperides is likely to be distorting facts in order to point more blame at Demosthenes or to show his ability to switch from one statement to another. Again, then, the historical veracity of oratory poses a problem (cf. Introduction, pp. 36-38); earlier scholars, however, often accepted the accuracy of information in oratory at face-value. For example, on this passage, A.W. Pickard-Cambridge, *Demosthenes* (London: 1914), 466 says: 'It can scarcely be denied in the face of Demosthenes' own admission . . . that Demosthenes received the money'!

The verbs προδανείζομαι in this sentence mean either to negotiate a loan in advance or to negotiate a loan for (the people): see W. Wyse, 'On the Use of προδανείζειν', *CR* 6 (1892), 254-257. The implication is that Demosthenes had stated that he took the money for the common good of the people and not as repayment for a loan or as a bribe. Indeed, there are some grounds for believing that Demosthenes did borrow the money for the Theoric Fund; in other words, not for venal purposes but for the good of the city: see Introduction, pp. 11-12.

The Theoric Fund was a substantial financial reserve by the fourth century, and the elected officials who controlled it were politically very powerful (cf. note on 28 below). At 1.56 Dinarchus tells us that the individual theoric allowance was five drachmas (the equivalent of thirty obols with three obols being the daily rate of pay for an Athenian juror), so this amount multiplied by the number of eligible citizens (precise figures are unknown, but M.H. Hansen, *Three Studies in Athenian Demography* [Copenhagen: 1988], 7-13, posits between 200,000 and 250,000) testifies to its size and the power of its elected officials. The Theoric Fund took its name from the monetary donations (two obols, or one-third of a drachma) to the people which were said to have been introduced by Pericles in the 450s to allow them to attend the theatre. All budget surpluses were put into this fund, and in the fourth century Demosthenes introduced a measure by which these surpluses were deflected to military campaigns in times of war. A law was introduced which inflicted death on anyone proposing that the Theoric Fund be used for military purposes in peace-time. Anyone fraudulently obtaining the theoric allowance was indicted and subject to enormous fines: note the case of Conon of Paeania in section 26. On Eubulus and the Fund see further *PA* 5369, J.J. Buchanan, *Theorika* (New York: 1962) and G.L. Cawkwell, 'Eubulus', *JHS* 83 (1963), 53-58.

Cnosion and his other friends . . . involve] the people: The translation 'thought it necessary also to involve' is not in the Greek and is added in square brackets in order to make English sense.

Aeschines 2.149, in a speech delivered in 343, alleges that a sexual liaison took place between Demosthenes' wife and Cnosion, a member of his household, in the same year. Moreover, Aeschines says that this encounter was orchestrated by Demosthenes so that his wife would fall pregnant: '. . . who has got his children lawfully, not by putting his wife in Cnosion's bed as you, Demosthenes, did yours'. Hyperides may well have singled out Cnosion here for this reason (cf. Colin, 251; Scholia to Aeschines 323a, 323b), especially as Athenian statesmen were required to have legitimate children and the Athenians attached supreme importance to legitimacy (see commentary on Dinarchus 1.71). Any children from this liaison would have been illegitimate, and Hyperides no doubt hoped that his allusion to Cnosion would cause the jury to react adversely against Demosthenes.

The reference to Cnosion and his other friends in this section is an interesting example of supporters publicly canvassing on behalf of a statesman, here Demosthenes. It may also be an example of how 'politicians' marshalled their support, given that the Athenian political system was very different from that of today: see P.J. Rhodes, 'Political Activity in Classical Athens', *JHS* 106 (1986), 132-144 and R.K. Sinclair, *Democracy and Participation in Athens* (Cambridge: 1988), 106-190. For a good, succinct account of the differences between Athenian and modern democracy see J. Ober, *Mass and Elite in Democratic Athens* (Princeton: 1989), 3-17.

(14)   **speaking and making accusations . . . taking bribes:** Of linguistic interest here is Hyperides' unusual use of the accusative absolute ὥσπερ οὐ πάντας ὑμᾶς εἰδότας ('as if you all did not know'), where a genitive might be expected. See Kühner-Gerth, *Ausführliche Grammatik der griechischen Sprache*[4] (Hanover: 1955), 2.97, where however this example is not quoted.

Demosthenes believed that he was being set up as a political scapegoat and that the Areopagus was declaring against him in its report for this hidden agenda. I suggest that there could well be some truth to this. The Areopagus' report (*apophasis*) was published when the diplomatic mission to Alexander to plead against the Exiles Decree returned to report its failure. The political sacrifice of the man who opposed Harpalus' extradition was a potential means of endearing the Athenian cause to Alexander in any further appeal: see further Introduction, pp. 10-11.

(15-37) After this brief factual outline Hyperides moves to an appeal to the jury to condemn Demosthenes based on the latter's venality throughout his political career and the dangers of corrupt leaders. He outlines how corruption has wreaked havoc in Greece, and that individuals, including Philip II, have been able to exploit some individuals and thus affect the downfall of various cities (15-16). Demosthenes, Hyperides alleges, is working for Alexander (17), as can be seen from Demosthenes' treatment of Harpalus which prevented Greece uniting in revolt against Macedon (17-19). Again, Demosthenes has shown only contempt for Athens by proposing unscrupulous men as citizens and accepting bribes (20-21), so much so that he can never be a role-model for the younger generation (21-22). Ordinary criminals are not as bad as leaders who betray popular trust (24) and grow rich from exploiting the people and taking bribes from the city's enemies, like Demosthenes and Demades (25). Others have been punished in the past (26), just as those who served the state well were rewarded (28-30), but Demosthenes now wants only to malign the Areopagus in order to escape his just punishment (31-34). The jurors are urged to feel no hesitation in condemning him (34-37).

(15)   **Do not consider . . . in the cities:** The translation 'he bought' is not in the Greek and is added in square brackets in order to make English sense.

As so often in oratory, factual events are not given in their chronological order. This is true here. In many of his speeches exhorting the Athenians to oppose Philip II, king of Macedon from 359 to 336, Demosthenes says that many of his successes over the Greeks were achieved by bribery and treachery. Thus, Olynthus, the chief city in the Chalcidice, fell to Philip after a short siege in 348 (see further, commentary on Dinarchus 1.26, with bibliography cited). Demosthenes alleges that Philip achieved success at Olynthus by bribing two of the city's cavalry commanders: '. . . Euthycrates and Lasthenes, the Olynthians, who thought they were such bosom-friends of his, and then, when they had betrayed their city, met the most ignominious fate of all' (8.40; see too 9.56-57, 19.265, 342 and 18.48; cf. Din. 1.24-26). Demosthenes also has similar allusions to treachery at Amphipolis and Pydna, which fell to Philip in 357 and 356: 'They know how he treated those Amphipolitans who betrayed their city to him and those Pydnaeans who opened their gates to him' (1.5).

Three hundred years later Diodorus Siculus, perhaps unduly influenced by Demosthenes, says much the same thing (16.54.3-4):

> Hence the anecdote that when Philip wished to take a certain city with unusually strong fortifications and one of the inhabitants remarked that it was impregnable, he asked if even gold could not

scale its walls. For he had learned from experience that what could not be subdued by force of arms could easily be vanquished by gold. So, organising bands of traitors in the several cities by means of bribes and calling those who accepted his gold 'guests' and 'friends', by his evil communications he corrupted the morals of the people.

After Philip took such towns, he installed pro-Macedonian oligarchies in them in order to ensure loyalty to him. Perhaps in some cases Philip did bribe influential citizens to win over cities opposed to him – Philip was not the sort of person who wasted manpower and time. However, we must bear in mind that Demosthenes' allegations are rhetorical, intending to misrepresent the situation and to persuade the people that Philip was not invincible.

The references to the Peloponnese, Thessaly and the rest of Greece for the most part are exaggerated; cf. similar historical falsifications at Hyperides 6.13 (with commentary). In the Peloponnese Philip's influence was not great and Sparta always opposed him. Thessaly was a different matter: the state was fertile and provided Philip with the horses for his cavalry. He had become involved in it in 358 when the city of Larissa called on him for support in a dispute with another Thessalian city, Pherae (Diod. 16.35 ff.). In 352 he was elected to the constitutional office of leader or *tagos* of Thessaly. Further intervention was necessary in 344 which resulted in his dividing the state into four parts and appointing governors over each of these parts. This move did not adversely affect the Thessalians (cf. J.R. Ellis, *Philip II and Macedonian Imperialism* [London: 1976], 138-143), and the state remained loyal to Macedon from then until the Lamian War (323-322).

I follow Colin's restoration of Μὴ νομίζετε δὲ (also followed by Burtt) as opposed to Kenyon's ἢ μὴ νομίζῃ τις, which Jensen follows (cf. Blass).

(17)   you make monstrous claims ... majority of it: Jensen reversed much of the order of sections 16-18 given the gaps in the papyrus; however, I follow Blass' order which seems to fit the general sense more readily, as do Kenyon, Colin and Burtt.

The reference here is to Demosthenes' alleged venality and his deception of the people, behaviour which smacks of treason and would warrant the death penalty. Dinarchus argued in similar fashion in his speech (1.10, 18-21, 42-45). The money from Asia is that which Demosthenes allegedly received from the Persian king to support a Greek revolt on the accession of Alexander the Great in 336 and his alleged role in the betrayal of Thebes to its destruction in 335: see further, commentary on Dinarchus 1.10 and 18-21. On Demosthenes' other activities and illegal incomes see Dinarchus 1.42-45 with discussion.

Hyperides also obliquely refers to Demosthenes' apparent betrayal of others ('and over all of the rest'). This is simply rhetorical exaggeration as no hard evidence to support this allegation exists. Hyperides cannot resist the opportunity to depict Demosthenes in as unfavourable a light as possible, and thus support his own arguments, by magnifying the extent of his corruption. This is also part of the rhetorical technique whereby the orator led the jury through a critical scrutiny of an opponent's arguments so that the jurors themselves would end up totally discrediting and ridiculing those arguments. Hyperides resorts to this tactic often, not only in this speech but also in his other speeches (cf. *In Defence of Lycophron* 5-8, *In Defence of Euxenippus* 1-3).

And now you are involved in . . . the city: Bottomry loans (money lent on any ship that would not return with corn or certain other goods for Athens) were illegal, but because of the huge returns on such a loan which individuals could make (cf. Xenophon, *Poroi* 3.9) many of these loans were made. Given Athens' dependence on imported corn from the Black Sea area, Demosthenes' alleged action here is not only illegal but also harmful to the well-being of the city and its people. On bottomry loans see A.R.W. Harrison, *The Law of Athens* 2 (Oxford: 1971), 109-115.

Dinarchus 1.69 (cf. Aes. 3.209) mentions houses owned by Demosthenes in the Piraeus, the port of Athens, and in the city. Although Demosthenes came from the nearby Attic deme Paeania, considerable time to walk or ride there and back would have elapsed. Therefore, in view of his political activity he is likely to have had a house in the city. See further M.H. Hansen, 'Political Activity and the Organization of Attica in the Fourth Century B.C.', *GRBS* 24 (1983), 227-238.

The nautical metaphor of this passage is taken from Aeschines 3.209: ἐκλιπὼν μὲν τὸ ἄστυ οὐκ οἰκεῖς, ὡς δοκεῖς, ἐν Πειραιεῖ, ἀλλ' ἐξορμεῖς ἐκ τῆς πόλεως ('You have left the upper city; and the Piraeus, as it seems, is not so much your home, as an anchorage for you, off the city's coast'); Hyperides has actually taken over the phrase from Aeschines.

A just leader . . . a deserter: The phrase 'not a deserter' was suggested by Blass and fits the sense of this context perfectly.

'Demosthenes the runaway' refers to his alleged cowardice at the battle of Chaeronea in 338, when Aeschines in 330 (3.7, 148, 151-152, 159, 175-176, 181, 187, 244, 253) and Dinarchus in 323 (1.12, 71, 81) say that he deserted his post (cf. Plut. *Demosthenes* 20.2 and [Plut.] *Moralia* 845f). We are told that such cowardice in battle was an indictable offence and involved loss of personal rights (and thus by extension the ability to take part in political life): 'According to a second [form of disfranchisement] delinquents lost all personal rights . . . this class included . . . all who deserted on the field of battle, who were found guilty of evasion of military service, of cowardice . . . all who threw away their shields . . .' (Andocides 1.74). However, the allegation against Demosthenes is likely to have been fabricated by the orators and mistakenly believed by later sources such as Plutarch, for Demosthenes was selected to deliver the *epitaphios* over the fallen Athenians in the battle of Chaeronea, and he continued to enjoy a political career (see commentary on Dinarchus 1.12).

(18)   **And just now . . . by surprise:** On Harpalus' arrival see Introduction, p. 7. His unexpected arrival was in keeping with his hasty flight as Alexander returned from India punishing any venal satraps and generals (on the background to this see E. Badian, 'Harpalus', *JHS* 81 [1961], 16-25; cf. Worthington, *Dinarchus*, 41-42). Harpalus' corrupt lifestyle at his headquarters in Babylon made him a prime candidate for execution, and he fled to Athens in an effort to instigate a revolt against Alexander since Athens represented his last real chance of security in the future: see Introduction, p. 7.

and he found the Peloponnese . . . Alexander: The passage refers to the consternation on the part of the Greeks over Alexander's Exiles Decree, which was brought to Greece by the royal messenger Nicanor. Under its terms, all exiles were to return to their cities (apart from murderers and the Thebans) and Alexander empowered Antipater to coerce any unwilling city to obey the terms – 'We have written to Antipater about this, to the end that if any cities are not willing to restore you [the exiles], he may constrain them' (Diod. 18.8.4). This directive was to be read out at the end of the Olympic Games, held from 31 July to 4 August, 324. However, Hyperides indicates that its contents were known in advance since Nicanor arrived in Greece shortly before Harpalus at the end of June 324.

N.G. Ashton, 'The Lamian War – A False Start?', *Antichthon* 17 (1983), 47-63, argues that this and the following passage indicate that the Greeks were organising a revolt against Macedonian hegemony *before* Harpalus' arrival. This view is quite wrong: see Ian Worthington, 'The Harpalus Affair and the Greek Response to the Macedonian Hegemony', *Ventures Into Greek History. Essays in Honour of N.G.L. Hammond*, ed. Ian Worthington (Oxford: 1994), 307-330.

concerning both . . . the rest: I argue for the restoration καὶ τῶν ἄλλων μὴ γίγνεσθαι in my 'Hyp. 5.18 and Alexander's Second Directive to the Greeks', *Classica et Mediaevalia* 37 (1986), 115-121.

Alexander must have expected opposition to the Exiles Decree from the mainland Greeks since it so clearly flouted the autonomy of the Greek cities and thus the terms of the League of Corinth. Opposition of a military nature cannot have been ruled out (the reason why Harpalus selected Athens as a refuge was because the city could still have posed a threat to the king), especially as contacts of a military nature had been maintained by several Greek states during Alexander's reign – for example, the Athenians, Aetolians, Locrians and Phocians (Diod. 18.8.5; cf. *IG* ii^2 367 and *IG* ii^2 370). Hence a further directive from the king to prohibit a joint military levy of some of the more powerful Greek forces is to be expected, and indeed Hyperides in this section refers to plural ἐπιτάγματα ('decrees').

(19)   You brought about this situation . . . one of them: The decree is that of Demosthenes at the Assembly meeting which had Harpalus arrested, his money confiscated and an embassy sent to Alexander over the matter. Hyperides had opposed Demosthenes' policy and was in favour of using Harpalus' offer of men and money to revolt from Alexander, but he had been thwarted by Demosthenes: see Introduction, p. 8. This was probably the occasion when Hyperides parted company with Demosthenes over the stance to be taken towards Macedon. The implication of Hyperides' argument here is that if his own view had prevailed the Greeks would not be meekly sending embassies to Alexander to protest the Exiles Decree as they would have united together in opposition against Alexander. Compare a similar argument at Dinarchus 1.33-34 (with commentary).

This line of argument cannot be used, as Ashton does (see note on 18 above), as a basis for a view that the Greeks were already planning a revolt prior to Harpalus' arrival. Moreover, it must be pointed out that the restoration 'satraps' is almost total (σ[ατράπας]) and that even the first letter is unclear! It is odd that our historical sources do not refer to any satraps fleeing to Taenarum, and Hyperides must be lying (cf. Colin, 255). The fact that the Greeks were resorting to diplomatic means (embassies) as opposed to military means explains why Harpalus met with such little enthusiasm; see Introduction, pp. 17-18.

(20) **sent by Demosthenes . . . at this:** The opening context is lost. Taurosthenes and his brother Callias were supposed to have made their fellow citizens slaves by betraying the whole of the island of Euboea to Philip II in the late 340s. Demosthenes had proposed Athenian citizenship for them, probably in 336-330, for which Dinarchus accused Demosthenes of taking a bribe (Din. 1.44; cf. Aes. 3.85): for further discussion, see commentary on Dinarchus 1.44.

Olympias here is presumably Alexander the Great's mother, Philip II's third wife. She had apparently demanded Harpalus' surrender from the Athenians (see commentary on 8), but contacts between her and Demosthenes are unknown. She was certainly hated in Athens and seems to have interfered in religious matters, especially those which affected the oracle of Zeus at Dodona, in her native Epirus (cf. Hyp. 4.14-26).

I think that . . . friendship: The tides of the Euripus strait (which separates Euboea from the mainland) were legendary for their daily continual changing, hence Hyperides makes this sarcastic analogy with Demosthenes' continual changes of policy. Aeschines (3.90) uses the same imagery when talking of Callias' political inconsistency: 'Then [Callias] abandoning them also, and making more twists and turns than the Euripus, by whose shores he used to live. . .' Whether Demosthenes did change so frequently is hard to determine; certainly, Plutarch did not think so, and he criticises those who say that Demosthenes did and compares him to Cimon, Thucydides and Pericles (*Demosthenes* 13).

(21-22) **you yourself destroyed . . . punished by you:** A direct appeal to the jurors here for rhetorical effect.

Hyperides presumably refers here to the friendship which he had shared with Demosthenes as joint opponents of Macedonian imperialism in the 330's and 320's. Their anti-Macedonian stance allied the two until the arrival of Harpalus, when Demosthenes' cautious advice to the people set him at odds with the more militant Hyperides, who wanted to use Harpalus' offer of money and men in a revolt against Alexander. Thus, as well as his attack on Demosthenes' character and failures, Hyperides needs to distance himself from Demosthenes given his own political leanings, and so persuade the jurors that he himself did not share in Demosthenes' venality. On relations between the two men see G. Colin, 'Démosthène et l'affaire d'Harpale', *REG* 39 (1926), 83-86 and F.W. Mitchel, 'Lykourgan Athens: 338-332', *Semple Lectures* 2 (Cincinnati: 1970).

Note by contrast Hyperides 6.8 and 32, on the importance of good role models in educating the young.

The plural ὑμῶν is translated as 'people like you' to show that Demosthenes was one of several accused of complicity in the Harpalus affair, and thus on trial at this time.

(22) **But the reverse now applies . . . sixty:** Demosthenes was born in either 385/4 or 384/3 (Davies, *APF*, 121-122), and so he would have been in his early sixties at the time of the present trial in March 323. The reference to those on trial in their sixties supports this. Certainly some of those prosecuting him were from a younger generation; for example, Stratocles of Diomeia (*PA* 12938, Berve, *Alexander* 2, no. 724, Davies, *APF*, 494-495; cf. F. Blass, *Die attische Beredsamkeit*[2], 3.2 [Leipzig: 1898], 333-336), who was probably in his twenties: see commentary on Dinarchus 1.1.

Therefore, gentlemen . . . country: Demosthenes acquired a huge amount of wealth during his career as is evidenced by the large numbers of liturgies (personal duties for the state paid from one's own funds) which he performed: see Davies, *APF*, 135-137; for his other incomes (attributed to the receipt of bribes), see Dinarchus 1.42-45 with commentary.

even in his twilight years: The phrase ἐπὶ γήρως ὁδῷ ('even in his twilight years') is a poetic expression. It is not Attic Greek but Homeric; cf. ἐπὶ γήραος οὐδῷ at *Iliad* 22.60. Quotations from Homer occur often in oratory in order to lend weight to a particular argument or viewpoint given the importance attached to Homer in Greek education.

However, you used to feel shame . . . state affairs: The translation 'gave the impression of having' is not in the Greek and is added in square brackets in order to make English sense.

Spectators often listened to trials depending on the nature of the case; cf. the references to bystanders at Dinarchus 1.3, 22, 46, 66 and 107. Some trials after all were as much a form of entertainment as a day at the theatre, given the invective, gossip and drama found in speeches. On spectators see A. Lanni, 'Spectator Sports or Serious Politics? οἱ περιεστηκότες and the Athenian Lawcourts', *JHS* 117 (1997), 183-189. Like Dinarchus, Hyperides is putting pressure on the present jury to find against Demosthenes since the jurors' vote – and by extension themselves – will be scrutinised by the people as a whole.

The Athenians moved fast to censure incompetence and corruption on the part of their leaders and generals. The latter were especially vulnerable to prosecution with severe penalties: see W.K. Pritchett, *The Greek State at War* Part II (Berkeley: 1974), 4-33 and 126-132; cf. J. Ober, *Mass and Elite in Democratic Athens* (Princeton: 1989), 200 ff.

(24) **For if someone takes money . . . generals:** The Athenians had no word for our 'politician', and they most commonly called their political leaders *rhetores kai strategoi* (orators and generals), thus showing the intimate role of the generals in political life. In his speech against Aeschines in 330 Demosthenes (18.212) refers to himself as 'an adviser (*symboulos*) and a speaker (*rhetor*)'. On nomenclature see further M.H. Hansen, *The Athenian Assembly in the Age of Demosthenes* (Oxford: 1987), 50-63. The law binding on *rhetores kai strategoi* is quoted at Dinarchus 1.71 (see commentary).

Why . . . services: Harpalus of course did not give any of his gold to individuals for safe-keeping since the day after his arrest allegedly all of it was carried up to the Acropolis (see 9-11); he did however give out some of it in bribes to influential statesmen. Hyperides is simply drawing a distinction between private citizens and those entrusted with civic and military responsibilities, such as Demosthenes, who believe that in return for performing public services they are free to take payment. In this, Hyperides is also playing on the fine line between the receipt of gifts, an inherent part of Greek diplomacy, and the taking of bribes against the well-being of the city or its people. The issue here is not whether Demosthenes received gifts during his career – he certainly would have on his various embassies – but whether he took them as bribes to the detriment of Athens (that is, treason).

On bribery of officials see further S. Perlman, 'On Bribing Athenian Ambassadors', *GRBS* 17 (1976), 223-233, J. Cargill, 'Demosthenes, Aischines and the Crop of Traitors', *Ancient World* 11 (1985), 75-85, F.D. Harvey, '*Dona Ferentes*: Some Aspects of Bribery in Greek Politics', *Crux*.

Essays in Greek History Presented to G.E.M. de Ste. Croix on his 75th Birthday, edd. P.A. Cartledge and F.D. Harvey (London: 1985), 76-113 and B.S. Strauss, 'The Cultural Significance of Bribery and Embezzlement in Athenian Politics', *Ancient World* 11 (1985), 67-74.

The laws stipulate . . . gentlemen of the jury: ἀδικεῖν refers to milder examples of corruption punishable by the repayment of the exact sum that had been taken (cf. *AP* 54.2). Those who took bribes against the state, which was treason, were punished by a tenfold fine or even by death, and Dinarchus 1.60 calls for the latter.

Blass restored τίμη[μα τιμῆ]σαι (followed by Kenyon, Jensen, Colin and ?urtt), but the papyrus here is so badly fragmented and the discussion of the legal punishments so distorted that any such restoration is doubtful.

(25-26) you allow the generals . . . your interests: An echo of the argument used by Dinarchus against Demosthenes (1.55 ff.), where the speaker says that the peop e are easily hoodwinked by emotional arguments and put mercy over justice. We cannot dispute this observation, based on what we know of the Athenian jury system!

Demosthenes and Demades . . . punish them: Demosthenes and Demades are paired together by Dinarchus (1.7, 11, 45, 89, 101, 104; cf. 2.15), perhaps because Demades was the next to be tried – in his speech against Aristogeiton, Dinarchus implies that Demosthenes and Demades had already been tried (2.15: 'You decided to show no mercy towards Demades and Demosthenes because it was proved that they took bribes against your interests'). However, it is likely that Demades fled before his actual trial and was condemned *in absentia*. Like Demosthenes, Demades was politically active and was responsible for introducing many decrees in the Assembly and performing various magistracies. Hyperides says that Demades took bribes from interested parties when doing so. On Demades see further commentary on Dinarchus 1.7. On Demosthenes' alleged illegal incomes, see commentary on Dinarchus 1.42-45.

The proxeny system was akin to a network of diplomatic relations. *Proxenoi* were individuals in certain cities who were appointed to look after another state's ambassadors and important visitors when travelling to their city. The proxeny system soon became a lucrative one given the honours and benefits bestowed on *proxenoi*, and competition was no doubt fierce. Hyperides implies that Demosthenes and Demades had amassed considerable wealth from serving as *proxenoi*. See further F.E. Adcock and D.J. Mosley, *Diplomacy in Ancient Greece* (London: 1975), 160-164; cf. 201-202.

If one of you . . . punishment: An example here of the Athenian view that ignorance is not a defence: those serving in the various magistracies were indictable if found to be inept or corrupt. Note the harshness of the penalty: execution or banishment.

The reference to the dangerous power of rhetoric is interesting; after all, Hyperides himself was also a practitioner of the art. However, it could be abused, and clearly those who lacked rhetorical ability were at a disadvantage in the law courts and must also have been in the Assembly, where the real political power lay in the hands of the orators or *rhetores*. Note Gorgias' response to Socrates' question on what is the greatest good for men in which Gorgias claims expertise (Plato, *Gorgias* 452e4):

The ability to use words to persuade jurors in a jury court and councillors in a council house and those assembled in an Assembly, and in any other meeting which is of a civic nature.

Conon of Paeania . . . five drachmas: Little is known about Conon, a banker who was made a citizen thanks to Demosthenes and lived in the same deme (Paeania) as him (Din. 1.43). This passage is often cited to support the view that the Conon referred to here is the person whom Dinarchus at 1.56 says fraudulently obtained theoric money, but this identification is doubtful: see commentary on Dinarchus 1.56. One talent was 6,000 drachmas, and thus the fine imposed on Conon for taking five drachmas was enormous and shows the sacrilegious nature of the crime. On theoric money, see commentary on 13 above, and on Conon see also *PA* 8700 and Davies, *APF*, 430.

And also Aristomachus . . . and said: The implication here is that the most charges were applied against individuals, evidence of the Athenian love of litigation and of the actions of the sycophants, especially in the fourth century. The Academy was the school founded by Plato in the early fourth century which taught science and philosophy, and was meant to train men for participation in political life. It was located in an area sacred to the hero Academus, hence its name. We know nothing about Aristomachus.

(28) **The people . . . following:** The opening context is lost because of the fragmentary nature of the papyrus here.

they elected him treasurer-in-chief . . . right: Hyperides refers to the administration of Lycurgus, the treasurer of the Theoric Fund (on which, see commentary on 13), under whose administration (336-324) a financially exhausted Athens prospered greatly. The date of Lycurgus' financial control of Athens is controversial, but 336-324 is now commonly accepted; for example, by Davies, *APF*, 351; J.J. Buchanan, *Theorika* (New York: 1962), 75-77, believes that Lycurgus began his financial leadership in 337/6 and occupied that position until 326/5.

Lycurgus' administration was a great period in later fourth century Athenian history: see Introduction, p. 5. Amongst other things, a building programme was inaugurated, statues were cast of the three fifth-century tragedians Aeschylus, Sophocles and Euripides, together with official recensions of their plays (perhaps contributing greatly to their 'canonisation' in Alexandrian times), and the ephebic system, a form of military conscription for 18-20 year old Athenian youths, was introduced. All of this was in keeping with a new, grander, phase in Athens' history after a bleak period of financial exhaustion and revolts from the Athenians' allies. Lycurgus died in 324, and Stratocles, the first prosecutor of Demosthenes at his trial (see commentary on Dinarchus 1.1), proposed his posthumous deification ([Plut.] *Moralia* 852). We have only one extant speech by Lycurgus, that against Leocrates in 330: see Introduction, p. 6. On Lycurgus see further F.W. Mitchel, 'Lykourgan Athens, 338-322', *Semple Lectures* 2 (Cincinnati: 1970), C.J. Schwenk, *Athens in the Age of Alexander* (Chicago: 1985), Bosworth, *Conquest and Empire*, 204-215, and J.D. Mikalson, *Religion in Hellenistic Athens* (Berkeley and Los Angeles), 11-45.

And in addition to this . . . period: Lycurgus and Hyperides must have shared similar anti-Macedonian feelings, though Hyperides was the more radical of the two (see Introduction, pp. 8 and 12-13). Elected officials were legally indictable if found to be corrupt during their term of office, and the

Athenians' love of litigation and of censuring their officials meant there were many such trials. Hyperides was accused of misconduct several times (see Introduction, p. 29). Despite Lycurgus' great services to the state, he was indicted in late 324 and had to be carried into court on a bed since he was close to death ([Plut.] *Moralia* 842e). The case was unresolved when he died, and his children were then prosecuted for their father's alleged misdeeds ([Plut.] *Moralia* 842e). They were acquitted thanks to the intervention of Demosthenes, who wrote on their behalf when he was in exile (*Epistle* 3; cf. [Plut.] *Moralia* 842e).

I follow Blass' restoration οὐ μέντοι at the start of this section, as do Kenyon, Colin and Burtt.

(29)   **and from the war itself . . . Demosthenes:** The reference to a war in the Lycurgan period is puzzling unless Hyperides refers to that of Agis III in the late 330's; however, Athens took no part in this: see Introduction, p. 5. Certainly Athens was not at war with Macedon until after Alexander had died in June 323. Perhaps Hyperides refers to the aftermath of Philip II's assassination in 336 when the Greeks rose in revolt, or even back to the time of Philip II, when the Athenians were twice at war with him in 357-346 and 340-338. On these historical contexts see Introduction, pp. 2-4.
That you were inevitably . . . did not: Hyperides refers to Demosthenes' decree which subjected himself to the death penalty if he were found guilty of taking a bribe from Harpalus (cf. 1-2). See further, commentary on Dinarchus 1.1.

(30)   **the people so acted . . . their own:** We should expect much repetition of arguments and appeals given that there were ten prosecution speeches against Demosthenes at his trial; cf. Dinarchus 1.2 ('Firstly, be sympathetic to those of us still to speak should we repeat points previously made'). The papyrus is badly fragmented here, and the full sense of this section of the speech, like so many others, is impossible to restore.

The use of the crown metaphor is striking, and Hyperides also uses it at 6.19 in the context of those Athenians who fell in the first year of the Lamian War: 'They gave freedom to all of Greece in common, and they conferred the glory from their deeds as a particular crown on their country'. The crown metaphor has interesting affinities with the crown which had been proposed for Demosthenes on the motion of Ctesiphon for his services to the state in 336 and for which Ctesiphon (and by extension Demosthenes) was finally brought to trial in 330 by Aeschines: see Introduction, p. 6. The speeches of Demosthenes (18) and Aeschines (3) from this trial survive. Such an allusion would not have been lost on the audience, given that the 'Crown' trial took place only six years before the present one. On the background to this trial and politics involved see further S. Usher, *Demosthenes On The Crown* (Warminster: 1993), 13-17.

I follow Blass' supplement to the reading of the papyrus, πάντ' ἂν δικαίως, as does Kenyon; Jensen, Colin and Burtt follow Fuhr with πάντα τὰ δίκαι' ἂν.

(31)   **and you have persisted . . . the power of your eloquence:** On the power of speech see the comment by Gorgias in the note on 26 above.
When you expected . . . the enquiry: Dinarchus 1.10 refers to an investigation by the Areopagus in 335, evidently under the *apophasis* procedure, into alleged Persian gold in Athens, but it did not pursue the investigation further. E. Badian believes that some sort of patriotic

compromise between Demosthenes and the Areopagus was struck in the period under consideration, with the former acknowledging Alexander's divinity and the latter refusing to publish the results of its investigation ('Harpalus', *JHS* 81 [1961], 33-34). This is implausible. Hyperides in this passage is seeking to malign Demosthenes and the tone indicates this.

When Demosthenes was accused of treason (*dorodokia*) in 324/3 for accepting a bribe from Harpalus he initiated an *apophasis*, which was then ratified by the Assembly, and the Areopagus conducted an investigation (see commentary on Dinarchus 1.1). Hyperides here refers to how Demosthenes threw the city into confusion (ταράττων) by the two challenges (*prokleseis*) which he issued during the Areopagus' investigation. The first challenge was to the people to present the Areopagus with evidence for his guilt (cf. Din. 1.5), and the second, when he was formally accused by it, was to its members to produce proof for their charge (cf. Din. 1.6, 61). He also seems to have toured the Agora and elsewhere denouncing the Areopagus and the people (cf. Din. 1.12, 26, 31, 43, 48 and 102).

when the Areopagus . . . if he wanted: In 324/3 the Greeks had been discussing divine honours for Alexander while he was still alive (the indefinite ἐπειδὴ ἀναβάλοιτο suggests more than one occasion). In Athens, resistance had come from Demosthenes (Polybius 12.12b3), Lycurgus and Pytheas ([Plut.] *Moralia* 804b and 842d); however, both Dinarchus (1.94, 103) and Hyperides indicate that after Demosthenes met with Nicanor at Olympia over the Exiles Decree (see commentary on 18 above), he changed his mind and apparently advised the Athenians to accept Alexander's apotheosis. Hyperides here, like Dinarchus, is alleging that Demosthenes changed his mind because he was bribed to do so by the Macedonians. In other words, he is showing Demosthenes' inability to pursue a consistent policy and his treachery in wanting to appease the enemies of the city.

The contemptuous tone of Hyperides' comment is very similar to one attributed to the Spartan king Damis ([Plut.] *Moralia* 219e), which is worthwhile quoting in the Greek as well:

Δᾶμις πρὸς τὰ ἐπισταλέντα παρὰ τοῦ Ἀλεξάνδρου θεὸν εἶναι ψηφίσασθαι, 'συγχωροῦμεν,' ἔφη, ' ' Ἀλεξάνδρῳ, ἐὰν θέλῃ, θεὸς καλεῖσθαι.'

Damis, with reference to the instructions sent from Alexander that they should pass a formal vote deifying him, said, 'We concede to Alexander that, if he so wishes, he may be called a god.'

The orators may well have accused Demosthenes of saying this and used it as a basis to vilify him further. However, the fact that a similar expression occurs in this much later work impacts on the veracity of their allegation and suggests that the phrase is a stock one. For discussion of Alexander's divinity with modern bibliography, see commentary on Dinarchus 1.94.

(32)   **he wanted . . . invincible god:** Cf. Hyperides 6.21-22 with commentary. Though almost all of the Greek text here is missing, the restoration as originally proposed by Sauppe is followed by most modern editors (excluding Kenyon) and fits the sense of the passage. Colin plausibly added the location of this statue (ἐν τῇ ἀγορᾷ) which would have been positioned in the Athenian Agora.

E.A. Fredricksmeyer, 'Three Notes on Alexander's Deification', *AJAH* 4 (1979), 6-7, believes that the reference to Zeus in this passage is an indication that an official proposal and then a cult of Alexander existed in Athens to acknowledge him as the son of Zeus Ammon. This is implausible. Although in the east Alexander would appear as Ammon with purple robes and ram's horns, and Ephippus (Athenaeus 12.537e-538b = Ephippus, *FGH* 126 F 5) talks of incense being burned before him and of a reverential silence (all indicative of a cult), Hyperides significantly uses the word for a secular statue (εἰκών) as opposed to a temple statue (ἄγαλμα); cf. his practice at 6.21. Now, εἰκών is the standard word in the late fourth century and hellenistic period for a portrait of a man and no cult was connected to one until the second century BC, and then only in Asia Minor (A. Stewart, *Faces of Power. Alexander's Image and Hellenistic Politics* [Berkeley and Los Angeles: 1993], 208; cf. 100-102). That being the case, I suggest that Hyperides was being heavily sarcastic here and echoing a popular sentiment that divine honours for the living Alexander were an object of ridicule. Stewart also does not believe in a statue for Alexander: (ibid., 101-103 and 207-209). However Badian has recently suggested that whereas the Athenians refused to establish a cult to Alexander they were prepared to compromise and erect a portrait statue of him on which he would be described as divine (E. Badian, 'Alexander the Great between Two Thrones and Heaven: Variations on an Old Theme', in *Subject and Ruler: The Cult of the Ruling Power in Classical Antiquity*, ed. A. Small [Ann Arbor: 1996], 25-26). This is perhaps an over-ingenious interpretation of this passage, especially as Alexander, had he returned to the mainland and desired full divine honours, would have been quite aware of the distinction. Mainland Greece was not the exotic east, and if there was such a proposal to erect a statue of Alexander in Athens – and by extension to establish a cult of him in his lifetime – it was soon forgotten when news came of his death in June 323.

(34)   **of the accusations . . . for their crimes:** Hyperides refers to the charges of several influential Athenians (including Demosthenes and Phocion) suspected of complicity in the Harpalus affair by which they agreed to submit to the death penalty if they were accused by the Areopagus of taking bribes from Harpalus: see commentary on 1. Hyperides stresses that since the Areopagus accused Demosthenes and others of accepting bribes, they must be condemned given the decrees against themselves so that the safety of the city will not be endangered.

We have very common rhetorical appeals here and in column 35. On improving the fortunes of the city; compare, for example, Dinarchus 1.65: 'But those who are sympathetically minded to your current circumstances and hope that the affairs of the city would improve with a change of fortune . . .', and 1.92: 'But if we have any feeling for our country and hate criminals and those who take bribes, and we want our fortune to change and to improve . . .'

The involvement of the jurors in the crimes of the accused is another common rhetorical device. Dinarchus uses it often in his speeches (for example, 1.3: 'You should consider, Athenians, that just as this man Demosthenes is on trial before you, so before your peers are you. These are the ones who are waiting to see what decision you will bring concerning the country's interests: whether you will surrender yourselves to the personal corruption and venality of these men, or whether you will make clear to all mankind that you detest those taking bribes to the detriment of the country'), as does Aeschines (for example, 3.246: 'Cast your vote, then, not only as men who are rendering a verdict, but also as men who are in the public eye, to be called to account by the citizens who, though they are not now present, will nevertheless ask you what your verdict was'; cf. 3.254). The device was to influence the jurors to declare against the accused so as to escape the suspicion of condoning the action or even collusion with those charged.

(35-37) Gentleman of the jury . . . the peace: In this badly fragmented part of the papyrus the rhetorical appeal to persuade the jurors to find Demosthenes guilty of the heinous crime appears to bring this part of the speech to an end.

The Athenians were not at war against Macedon when this speech was delivered, therefore the reference to their waging a war is at first sight puzzling. However, the context is those leaders who took money from Harpalus, which he of course stole from Alexander. At 1.68-70, Dinarchus suggests that Alexander might demand the return of all the money which Harpalus brought with him to Athens. In order to comply the people as a whole would need to sacrifice their own wealth as well as that of the city, otherwise they could then find themselves fighting a war against Macedon which had its origins in the venality of a few individuals. Hyperides was very likely arguing a similar case here: that the Athenians should not risk war with Alexander because of the corruption of Demosthenes and a few others like him.

(38-40) Hyperides now moves to the epilogue or conclusion of the speech. The epilogue usually contained a final summation of the case and appeal to the jury to convict the accused. Hyperides stresses that the prosecutors have conducted their cases lawfully (38), and that the Areopagus has conducted its enquiry in accordance with the laws and decrees of the city (38-39). Therefore, for the safety of Athens and its people, the jury must ignore the pleadings of Demosthenes and find him guilty (39-40).

(38) **to be given to it . . . allotted to you:** This section represents the division of responsibility between the prosecutors, the Areopagus and the jury. After the Areopagus issued its *apophasis*, those accused were then tried in court as was the procedure in Athenian law. Ten orators were commissioned by the state and prosecuted Demosthenes at his trial (Din. 2.6; cf. 1.51) before a jury of 1,500 citizens (Din. 1.107). It is unknown whether the same number prosecuted the others accused of complicity in the affair. For Demosthenes' prosecutors see Introduction, p. 10.

(39) **If the vote . . . verbal appeals:** Again, Hyperides cautions the jurors to be wary of the dangerous power of rhetoric: cf. 26, and see too 34-37. The 6,000 male citizens over the age of thirty who were selected annually as jurors took a dicastic oath to uphold and vote in accordance with the laws: this oath is quoted in the commentary on 1 above. See also Hyperides 6.25 with commentary on the 'rule of the law' in Athens.

the tombs of your forefathers: The Athenians considered the establishment and maintenance of ancestral tombs especially important, and one of the questions asked at the preliminary enquiry (*dokimasia*) of potential magistrates was whether they had looked after their ancestral tombs (cf. Din. 1.71). Note how Dinarchus refers to ancestral tombs as the basis of an appeal to the jurors at 1.110: 'Athenians, right-thinking men must look to this land, to the traditional sacrifices celebrated in it, and to the tombs of our ancestors when delivering the vote.' Athenian law decreed that children were to support their parents in old age and then to give them a proper burial when deceased (Andocides 1.74, *AP* 56.6 with P.J. Rhodes, *A Commentary on the*

Aristotelian Athenaion Politeia [Oxford: 1981], 629-630; cf. W.K. Lacey, *The Family in Classical Greece* [London: 1968], 116-118). If they failed to do so, then they could be legally indicted and held up as an object of contempt. Thus, in his speech against Aristogeiton, Dinarchus uses Aristogeiton's desertion of his father Cydimachus and refusal to fund his burial against him (2.8, 18).

I retain the preposition εἰς, suggested by Boeckh, as do Kenyon and Colin; *contra* Burtt and Jensen.

(40) **those who have taken . . . right to cry:** Weeping also was a rhetorical device to win the sympathy of the jurors. We do not know who supported Demosthenes in his defence, but character witnesses and others, including those implicated in the Harpalus affair, were expected (cf. Din. 1.112). Hagnonides was a sycophant (Plut. *Phocion* 29.3), and thus a contemptible member of Athenian society: see commentary on 3-4. He may well have been a character witness at the present trial, or even implicated in the Harpalus scandal and so soon to be tried. If so, he was not condemned, for he was one of the Athenians exiled when Antipater imposed an oligarchy in Athens in 322 (see Introduction, p. 16). Phocion was able to persuade Antipater to allow Hagnonides (and other exiles) to live in the Peloponnese (Plut. *Phocion* 29.3), although Hagnonides evidently thought little of Phocion's diplomatic overtures on his behalf as he was one of the prosecutors at his trial in 318 (Phocion was condemned to death). Shortly after Phocion's execution, Hagnonides was himself condemned by the people (Plut. *Phocion* 38.1), a fitting end for such an odious character.

as is the case with pirates . . . the boat: Any set penalty for piracy in Greek law is largely unknown. However, from this passage it would appear that pirates were tied to a wheel and their bodies broken on it as it rotated either as a punishment before death or to obtain a confession. The wheel was also used for punishing slaves. Thus, the slave-girl who administered the poison to her master and his friend as described in Antiphon's speech *Prosecution of the Step-Mother for Poisoning* was also tortured on the wheel (1.20). For further references to the wheel see G. Thür, *Beweisführung vor den Schwurgerichtshöfen Athens: die Proklesis zur Basanos* (Vienna: 1977), 183 n. 96.

The same thing . . . the money: Given the accusation which Hyperides is levelling at Demosthenes, I venture that τὰ χρήματα ('the money') is the most likely restoration.

The ending of the speech is lost, but to judge from the tone of this section the actual speech may not have been much longer.

Hyperides 6, *Funeral Oration*

Although the *Epitaphios* is more intact than Hyperides' speech against Demosthenes (5), it is still very fragmentary in parts and its conclusion is missing. Thus, as with Hyperides 5, any analysis of it for ring composition is impossible. We do not even know how long the speech was in its written form as the ending is missing. The last three sections of the speech which we have do not come from the papyrus but are quoted in an early fifth century A.D. anthology of quotations by Stobaeus. However, it is possible to deduce the major parts of the speech from Hyperides' tone and the changes of subject matter; hence, the commentary is arranged accordingly.

Thucydides 2.34 gives us the details of the ceremony involved in honouring those who had died in battle:

> The bones of the departed lie in state for the space of three days in a tent erected for that purpose, and each one brings to his own dead any offering he desires. On the day of the funeral coffins of cypress wood are borne on wagons, one for each tribe, and the bones of each are in the coffin of his tribe. One empty bier, covered with a pall, is carried in the procession for the missing whose bodies could not be found for burial. Anyone who wishes, whether citizen or stranger, may take part in the funeral procession, and the women who are related to the deceased are present at the burial and make lamentation. The coffins are laid in the public sepulchre, which is situated in the most beautiful suburb of the city; there they always bury those fallen in war, except indeed those who fell at Marathon; for their valour the Athenians judged to be preeminent and they buried them on the spot where they fell. But when the remains have been laid away in the earth, a man chosen by the state, who is regarded as best endowed with wisdom and is foremost in public esteem, delivers over them an appropriate eulogy. After this the people depart.

On the battle of Marathon (fought in 490 against the Persian army), see commentary on 37.

(1-3) Hyperides' prologue begins with an appeal to gain the goodwill of his audience lest he omit any facts which his listeners consider worthier than he does (1-2). He also introduces the general Leosthenes as the central figure of his speech (3).

(1) **Time itself will be the witness . . . magnificent deeds:** As is to be expected from an *epitaphios*, Hyperides must show that the deeds performed by the dead will stand as an everlasting memorial to their bravery and valour on behalf of Athens and the Greeks; cf. 27-29. The invocation to Time is a common rhetorical device, which is found also in poetry (cf. Pindar, *Olympian* 10.53).

Leosthenes was without doubt the most important general of the late 320's. He single-handedly masterminded the Athenian preparations for the revolt known as the Lamian War (see Introduction, pp. 12-16), at one stage defeating Antipater and besieging him in the town of Lamia (see 12), and his death in late 323 at the siege of Lamia (see 13) was a major blow. So great was his reputation that a painting of him was commissioned by the state (Pausanias 1.13), and of course the present speech stands as a memorial to him. As well as his military abilities Leosthenes was an outstanding orator in this period, thereby showing the influence that generals could wield in political affairs: on Leosthenes' political role see L. Tritle, 'Leosthenes and Plutarch's View of the Athenian *Strategia*', *AHB* 1 (1987), 6-9. Although his earlier career is largely unknown, evidence exists to show that he had been a trierarch in Athens in 325/4, before becoming a general in 324/3: see Ian Worthington, 'The Earlier Career of Leosthenes and *IG* ii² 1631', *Historia* 36 (1987), 489-491. His activities are more fully documented from 324, when he was responsible for arranging the passage of 50,000 ex-mercenaries from Asia to the mercenary base at Taenarum (Pausanias 1.25.5; cf. 8.52.5).

On Leosthenes see further: *PA* 9142 and 9144, Berve, *Alexander* 2, no. 471, Davies, *APF*, 9142, and E. Lepore, 'Leostene e le Origini della Guerra Lamiaca', *PP* 10 (1955), 161-185.

(2)   **For this reason . . . the deeds they performed:** Hyperides delivered this speech at the end of the first year of the Lamian War, probably in the spring of 322, a few months before Antipater defeated the Greeks at the battle of Crannon (Diod. 18.17.3-5). Thus, the exploits of Leosthenes and of the Athenians up to this point would still be very fresh in the minds of his audience.

Hyperides resorts to a common rhetorical technique here, called the *captatio benevolentiae*, which was meant to secure the goodwill of the audience from the outset. An *epitaphios* was intended to be a patriotic and rousing speech delivered on a sombre occasion. As such it, and the person selected by the state to deliver it, would have been viewed critically by the audience. By admitting his concerns and inviting his audience to add anything he might omit, Hyperides neatly offsets any criticism of his speech. In this respect, the opening of the speech is similar to the other funeral speeches which we have: cf. Thucydides 2.35.2, Lysias 2.1 and Demosthenes 60.1-3. On the other speeches, see Introduction, pp. 34-35.

(3)   **It is right to praise . . . their ancestors:** The reference to the previous history of Athens and the great deeds of the Athenians' ancestors was a common rhetorical technique to appeal to the patriotic spirit of the audience. The days of the Persian Wars (the battle of Salamis is most frequently cited) and the fifth century Athenian empire (such as the leadership of Pericles: cf. Isocrates 15.111, 234, 307, 16.28, Dem. 3.21, Aes. 1.25) are regularly referred to by the orators, and this type of appeal was especially used in funeral orations which were intended to rouse the spirits of their listeners at a time of grief and crisis. The other surviving *epitaphioi* show that it was accepted to refer back even as far as mythological times, especially to the Trojan War; cf. Lysias 2.4-60, Dem. 60.7-12, practically all of Socrates' speech in Plato, *Menexenus* 236d-249c, and of course Hyperides 6 at 35-36. Hyperides, like the other speakers of funeral orations, exploits the period of the Persian wars deliberately in order to draw the analogy between the war then, against a foreign foe which aimed to crush Greek freedom, and the present war, which was also being fought over the ideal of freedom (cf. Diod. 18.10.3): on this analogy see commentary on 12. On the Greeks' attitude to freedom, see commentary on 10, and cf. 12, 34 and 39 for instances of other topoi which Hyperides uses.

However, Hyperides here insinuates that the Athenians' decision to revolt on the death of Alexander in 323 (which brought about the Lamian War) bettered any previous policy. Historically, this is hard to accept. An explanation might be that even at this stage in the war there was a feeling in

Athens that a Macedonian victory was ultimately inevitable. Finding it impossible to counter this feeling, Hyperides resorted to a tactic that the Athenians at least had made a stance against Antipater and Macedonian rule well knowing they might lose. In that case, their courage and patriotism outshines the past. A more cynical explanation exists however, and that is that Hyperides himself played a key role in the outbreak of the revolt, and so he may well have taken advantage of his current situation to magnify the results of his own policy.

On the orators' use of history see further Ian Worthington, 'History and Oratory', *Persuasion. Greek Rhetoric in Action*, ed. Ian Worthington (London: 1994), 244-263, with bibliography cited.

on both accounts . . . on campaign: Leosthenes had evidently been in contact for some years with the mercenaries returning from Asia to Greece and basing themselves at Taenarum in southern Laconia. It was these men whom Harpalus' money would have hired in addition to his own force if Demosthenes had not thwarted his mission to Athens in 324 (see Introduction, p. 8). After Demosthenes' exile, his opponent Hyperides dealt secretly with Leosthenes, sending him the remainder of Harpalus' money on the Acropolis in order to hire mercenaries and encouraging him to raise more troops (Diod. 18.9.2-5).

Hyperides now ends his prologue to the speech, and, in keeping with the general pattern of an *epitaphios*, will turn to the city itself next.

4-9) Hyperides uses this part of his speech to praise Athens and its reputation for universal fairness and as the protector of the freedom of the Greeks, as is to be expected in an *epitaphios*. However, he does so surprisingly briefly (4-5) as he is anxious to give his eulogy of Leosthenes, the subject of his speech (6). The statement that there is no need to discuss the ancestry of Leosthenes or of the Athenians and the way they were raised (6-8) allows Hyperides to explain why he is proceeding immediately to the narrative of Leosthenes' recent exploits (9).

4) **In the case of Athens . . . summary fashion:** The admission here echoes section 2 (see commentary), in which Hyperides attempts to offset any criticism of his speech while keeping to the pattern of an *epitaphios*. Since Hyperides probably could speak for only an hour or so, it would have been impossible to recount the deeds of the Athenians throughout their history, hence he has to be selective. At the same time he would have been aware that elements in his audience would not have agreed with his selections or would have been displeased with his treatment of them.

(5) **Just as the sun . . . for the Greeks:** Equating the *polis* of Athens with the sun is far-fetched to say the least, but note a similar tone to Socrates' reference to the nourishment provided by nature for men at Plato, *Menexenus* 237c-238a. During the fifth century Athens, as hegemon of the Delian League (478-404), exploited its allies and ruled anything but fairly. The same is true of the Second Athenian Confederacy (378-338), which quickly turned into a fourth century empire: cf. commentary on Dinarchus 1.39. Amongst the stipulations on the decree of Aristoteles, on which the Second Athenian Confederacy was based, were that the Athenians would not impose a tribute (tax) on their allies, or set up cleruchies, or impose garrisons or governors in allied towns, or interfere in the autonomy or constitution of their allies. Such stipulations indicate that these Athenian practices had been hated in their fifth century empire. However, within a few years the Athenians were again openly exploitive.

For the decree of Aristoteles see *IG* ii² 43 = M.N. Tod, *Greek Historical Inscriptions* 2 (Oxford: 1948), no. 123; translated in P. Harding, *From the End of the Peloponnesian War to the battle of Ipsus* (Cambridge: 1985), no. 35. See further on the fourth century empire: G.T. Griffith, 'Athens in the Fourth Century', *Imperialism in the Ancient World*, edd. P.D.A. Garnsey and C.R.Whittaker (Cambridge: 1978), 127-144 and J. Cargill, *The Second Athenian League* (Berkeley: 1981). On the fifth century empire see, for example, D.W. Bradeen, 'The Popularity of the Athenian Empire', *Historia* 9 (1960), 257-269 (arguing against the view of G.E.M. de Ste Croix, 'The Character of the Athenian Empire', *Historia* 3 [1954-5], 1-41, that Athenian rule was popular).

Although Blass restored εἰς τὸ πρέπον, I believe that Kenyon's κατὰ τὸ πρέπον ('as is fitting') is preferable; so also Colin.

(6-7)   **However . . . my speech:** Since Hyperides has already told us in section 3 that the immediate context of the speech is the resolution (*proairesis*) to go to war on Alexander's death, focusing on Leosthenes and those who fought in the first year of the Lamian War is logical. In this, Hyperides is breaking from the traditional or accepted structure of an *epitaphios*, which treated mythological subjects as part of the exhortation to the people (cf. the use of myth by Lysias at 2.4-60 and Demosthenes at 60.7-11). No doubt the seriousness of the current circumstances was not lost on the people, and so Hyperides concentrated on the more immediate historical and military background.

From what point . . . recall first?: Questions conforming to the standard 'formula' of a funeral oration, and also marking a transition in the structure of the speech to a narrative of events.

Should I outline . . . silly: The reference to racial purity reflects more than the Athenians' jealous guarding of their citizenship: it shows their belief that they were born of the land itself (autochthonous). This ideal is prevalent in *epitaphioi* (cf. Thucydides 2.36, Lysias 2.47, Plato, *Menexenus* 237b, Dem. 60.4-5).

(8)   **Shall I recall . . . brought up well as children:** Children were an integral part of the *oikos* or family unit, which in turn was an integral part of the *polis*, as Aristotle proclaimed in the *Politics* (1.2):

> We must first discuss household units since the city as a whole consists of households. The subject can be subdivided into the parts of which a household is made up: a complete household consists of slaves and free persons. Since one ought to examine everything in its smallest part first, and the primary and smallest constituents of a household are master and slave, husband and wife, and father and children . . .

In Athens only legitimate male children could inherit the *oikos* and so take part in political life, and elected officials such as *strategoi* and *hipparchoi* were required to have legitimate children (*AP* 4.2; cf. Din. 1.71). In 451 Pericles passed a law that both parents had to be Athenian citizens before children from a marriage were regarded as legitimate (*AP* 26.4, Plut. *Pericles* 37.3: quoted in the commentary on Dinarchus 1.71). In addition, the security of the state rested on the ability of the citizens to fight for it, and cowardice in battle was an indictable offence (Andocides 1.74: quoted in the commentary on Hyperides 5.17). Thus, children's upbringing was of paramount importance to the well-being and future of the state. See too 42, on the city's legal responsibility to raise children orphaned by war, and the subsequent honours awarded to them.

(9) **Therefore I think . . . only right:** Hyperides prepares to speak about Leosthenes and his men and their valour in the Lamian War, on which see Introduction, pp. 12-16. He extends the focus from merely the city of Athens to the whole of Greece, given that the Macedonians had effectively controlled Greece by means of the League of Corinth from 337 (see Introduction, pp. 3-4). Again, Hyperides directs his attention to the immediate circumstances rather than to an excursus on a mythological theme, as was common in the other funeral orations. There will be a mythological treatment, but it will come later in the speech (35-36).

(10-14) Here we have the narrative proper of Leosthenes' deeds in the first year of the Lamian War. In sections 15 to 34 Hyperides will mesh Leosthenes' exploits and reputation with those of his men, but in this part of the speech (10-14) Hyperides treats Leosthenes alone. He traces his rise to prominence and foreshadows his death for the sake of freedom (10), then details his military victories in Boeotia (11), and against Antipater at Thermopylae and Lamia (12), and the support he secured from other Greek states because of his deeds and reputation (13). This part of the speech is nicely rounded off by the reference to Leosthenes' death and the gratitude which he deserves for serving Greece as he did (14).

10) **Leosthenes saw . . . countries:** Strictly speaking, Greece was not 'humiliated and cowed' during the reign of Philip II, as Hyperides alleges here, since there was widespread resistance to the king until the final defeat at Chaeronea (338), which led to the establishment of the League of Corinth (337). Only then did Greece fall under Macedonian hegemony, and it remained so until Alexander's death (323), apart from a revolt on the death of Philip II (336) which Alexander quickly ended. On the historical background, see Introduction, pp. 1-4.

All of this does not mean that prominent Athenian leaders did not take bribes during this earlier period, and Demosthenes, in his Crown oration of 330, gives us a lengthy list of bewildering names from almost every Greek city of those he considers are traitors to Greece (18.295-296). Not that Demosthenes may be excluded from any such list, for Dinarchus alludes to his receipt of bribes from various sources at 1.10, 42-45 and 70, for example. Aeschines' sarcastic comment in his speech of 343 is rather apt here: 'It appears from Demosthenes' speech that he alone cares for the city and that all the rest are traitors' (2.8). Hyperides is going too far when he says that such bribes were responsible for the downfall of Athens and Greece; however, this is part of his strategy of effectively portraying the greatness and sacrifice of Leosthenes.

Realising that . . . the sake of freedom: On the recognised leadership ability of Athens and the need for proper leaders, cf. Pericles in his alleged *epitaphios* (Thucydides 2.41). There is also an interesting parallel with Dinarchus 1.76, who talks of Athens' traditional arch-enemies the Spartans coming to Athens to beg for help: 'At that time, Athenians, at that time the Spartans, who before were famous because of their leaders and had been reared in the principles of those men, came humbly to our city, beseeching our ancestors for safety . . . For there is one only means of safety for both city and a nation: to obtain brave men and wise advisers as leaders'.

The Greeks held their common freedom or ἐλευθερία to be of utmos importance. For example, the Thebans' decision to rebel against Alexande in 335 is treated by Dinarchus (1.19) as part of this ideal: 'The Thebans . . were no longer able to bear the conduct of the Macedonians among them i the city, nor to suffer slavery, nor to witness the abuses committed against th persons of free people'. Hyperides uses ἐλευθερία eight times in this speech and, as one scholar puts it, it is the 'primary catchword of the speech' (N.G Ashton, 'The Lamian War – stat magni nominis umbra', *JHS* 94 [1984 154). Even epigraphical evidence follows suit; for example, *IG* ii² 467 (date to 306/5) says that the Lamian War was fought ὑπὲρ τῆς ἐλευθερίας τῶ Ἑλλήνων. We may also note that in section 25 αὐτονομία, individua autonomy, which is linked to the prosperity of states, is stressed. So als freedom is an important theme of the other funeral orations we have (o which see Introduction, pp. 34-35), and those who died for it are accordingl praised (cf. Lysias 2.55, 67-69 and Dem. 60.23).

Although Hyperides makes Leosthenes the subject of his speech, there is n doubt that he anchors his speech on the ideal of ἐλευθερία, thereby showin that those who fell in battle died for the noblest of causes. As with the othe speakers of *epitaphioi*, ἐλευθερία also helps to explain his analogy of th present war against Macedon to that fought against the Persians, anothe foreign foe, who also endangered the freedom of the Greeks (see commentar on 12). Diodorus also stressed the principle of freedom in his account of th origins of the Lamian War (18.10.3):

> Envoys should be sent to visit the Greek cities and tell them that formerly the Athenian people, convinced that all Greece was the common fatherland of the Greeks, had fought by sea against those barbarians who had invaded Greece to enslave her, and that now too Athens believed it necessary to risk lives and money and ships in defence of the common safety of the Greeks.

(11)   **When he had raised . . . other allies:** When Alexander the Great died i June 323 the vast majority of the Greeks revolted (the Lamian War), and th Athenians immediately sent what was left of Harpalus' money on th Acropolis to help Leosthenes hire mercenaries at their base in Taenarun southern Laconia (Diod. 18.9.4). Leosthenes already had dealings with th ex-mercenaries at Taenarum since he had recently arranged for 50,000 to b brought over from Asia (Pausanias 1.25.5; cf. 8.52.5) when Alexander ha issued his Dissolution Decree, which ordered all satraps and generals t disband their mercenary armies. Contact between Leosthenes and Hyperide who had come to political power after Demosthenes' disgrace in the Harpal affair, had been ongoing for some time (Diod. 18.9.2-3). Now, such conta was formalised and Leosthenes was appointed general.

Not every Greek state revolted from the Macedonian rule. The Boeotia and the Euboean Leagues did not; the former was perhaps worried by th possible re-emergence of Thebes, which had dominated the other towns the state in the past, and the latter hated the Athenians' brand of imperialisn Nor did Thessaly revolt at the very start of the war. Leosthenes dealt with th Boeotians and the Euboeans first. He marched from Taenarum to Aetolia link with another Greek force and then invaded Boeotia. There, he defeated combined Boeotian and Euboean army, close to Plataea, and then moved to the essential strategic town of Thermopylae (Diod. 18.11.3-5).

(12)   **From there he came to Thermopylae . . . besieged him:** Cf. 38. Hyperides confuses the chronology in this and the following sections, but such confusion is often the case in oratory where the emphasis was on presentation of information as opposed to total accuracy.

Thermopylae (the 'Hot Gates' – even today, the hot sulphur springs there are very impressive) was referred to as the 'Gates of Greece' since it controlled a major strategic pass from northern Greece into central, and thus the south beyond. At Thermopylae Leosthenes did battle with Antipater, whom Alexander had left behind as guardian (*epitropos*) of Greece and Macedon (Arr. 1.11.3). Antipater's force was numerically inferior to that of Leosthenes, but the powerful Thessalian cavalry supported him. However, the Thessalians almost immediately deserted to the Greek side and Antipater was defeated (Diod. 18.12.3-4). With some difficulty he struggled for refuge to the nearby town of Lamia, which controlled the main route from Thessaly into central Greece, and then beyond. The choice of the town was not an accident on Antipater's part; even in defeat he realised the need to prevent Leosthenes from invading Macedon, and his control of Lamia had that result. Here, Leosthenes and his army besieged him throughout the winter of 323/2 (Diod. 18.12.4-13.5, Plut. *Demosthenes* 27.1, *Phocion* 23.4-5, Polyaenus 4.4.2). The town gave its name to the Greek revolt, or Lamian War.

The reference to the barbarians at Thermopylae is to the year 480 when a Persian army under Xerxes invaded Greece. The Greeks decided that the best strategy was to defend a narrow place where the Persian cavalry would be ineffective and as far north as possible in order to stop states in that region falling into Persian hands, hence Thermopylae. For two days a Greek force from various states resisted Persian attacks at Thermopylae, but on the third day the Persians found a way to attack the Greek force from the rear, and as a result the Greeks were cut off between two lines of Persians. Leonidas, the Spartan commander of the Greeks, then dismissed the force apart from the Spartans, Thebans and the Thespians. The latter surrendered when the Persians over-ran them, but the 300 Spartans refused to surrender and were cut down to the last man (Herodotus 7.216-222). The Spartans' bravery made a great impression on the Greeks (and the Persians), and their courage became legendary throughout history. Therefore, their action became a historical topos. On the battle of Thermopylae see Herodotus 7.198-239 and, for example, N.G.L. Hammond, *A History of Greece*[3] (Oxford: 1986), 228-236.

Hyperides refers to the exploits of Themistocles later in the Persian Wars at 37: see commentary. The selection of instances from the Persian Wars is deliberate, for Hyperides uses that period, when Greece faced a foreign enemy which threatened its freedom and autonomy, as an analogy to the present war against the Macedonians, who also endangered the freedom of the Greeks (see commentary on 10). This is also the case with some of the other funeral orations we have; for example, that of Lysias (2.21-44) and those attributed to Pericles (Thucydides 2.41.5-42) and Socrates (Plato, *Menexenus* 239d-241c). On these see Introduction, pp. 34-35.

Interestingly, Hyperides' choice is likely to have been influenced also by current opinion as well as by the 'standard' references to past history demanded by an *epitaphios*. It seems that when Leosthenes was killed at

Lamia, the Greek states banded together and formed a 'Council', each state represented by one delegate, to resist Macedon and declare the League of Corinth null and void. It gave hegemony to the Athenians and made Antiphilus sole commander of its forces. The Council modelled itself on the League, which was established in 480 when the Persians invaded Greece. Thus the era of the Persian wars was very much alive in Athens, and Hyperides includes it in his speech not only to gain popularity but also to reflect the current situation.

(13) **He made the Thessalians . . . their consent:** As a result of Leosthenes' defeat of Antipater at Thermopylae (see 12) the states of Thessaly, Phocis and Aetolia in northern and central Greece remained loyal to the Greek cause; almost certainly, they would have been subdued by Antipater. Hyperides contrasts the voluntary acceptance by these states of Leosthenes' leadership with the rule apparently forced on them by Philip and Alexander. History shows a somewhat different picture. The states which Hyperides cites here did not fare badly when Philip II was king (359-336), and during the peace imposed by the Macedonians later (after 337) the Greek states generally fared well and many prospered.

To begin with Thessaly. In 358 Philip II had been invited by the city of Larissa in Thessaly to intervene in that city's dispute with another Thessalian town, Pherae (Diodorus 16.35 ff.). This invitation led to a diplomatic alliance with Larissa which included the marriage of Philip to Philinna. Then in 352, following further moves in Thessaly, the Thessalians elected Philip to the constitutional office of *tagos* (leader). Moreover, the Thessalian cavalry were always an important part of Philip's fighting force. In 344, further trouble between Larissa and Pherae again led to Philip's intervention (Diodorus 16.69.7-8, Dem. 9.12). At this time, he divided the state into four parts and appointed governors over each of these parts, and Demosthenes (19.260) talks of Philip's garrisons. This last action perhaps gives us a context for Hyperides' allegation. However, it is important to note that Demosthenes talks in general terms of plural garrisons in Thessaly but does not name any specific cities. Moreover, it seems very likely that Philip's action was an attempt to create a united Thessaly but not to reduce corporate cites such as Larissa and Pherae, which gave the country its economy (cf. J.R. Ellis, *Philip II and Macedonian Imperialism* [London: 1976], 138-143). In other words, while Philip's action gave him a much tighter control of Thessaly it did not disadvantage the Thessalians; and indeed, for a period after Alexander's death the Thessalians remained loyal to the Macedonian hegemony.

The people of Phocis also benefitted because of Philip. From 356 to 346 many Greek states waged war on the small state of Phocis in what is known as the Sacred War (Diod. 16.23 ff.). The Phocians had seized Delphi, site of the oracle of Apollo, and to maintain their war effort and hire mercenaries they had stolen the money from the sacred treasuries of the various Greek states there. The war took a decisive turn with Philip II's formal intervention in 347/6 at the request of the Boeotians, who were hard-pressed by the Phocians (Diod. 16.58.2). According to Diodorus 16.58.3, Philip was 'pleased to see their discomfiture and disposed to humble the Boeotians', so his alliance with them was for his own ends: he was eager to be involved in central Greece and to be known as the saviour of Delphi. He reached an agreement with the Phocian commander, Phalaecus, allowing his army to depart unharmed, and the state of Phocis to surrender to Philip (Diod. 16.59.2-4, Dem. 6.13, 19.126 and Aes. 2.137 ff.). By that action, he ended the Sacred War.

The sacrilegious nature of the Phocians' act in seizing the oracle of Apollo is obvious. The normal punishment was execution by being thrown from the top of Mount Parnassus, and some states such as Thessaly and Thebes wanted this. However, when the Greeks met to decide the Phocians' fate the extreme penalty was not imposed: amongst other things, the Phocians were to be disarmed and deprived of their horses until they had repaid the money taken from the temple treasuries, all of their cities were to be razed, and the people were to be moved into villages a short distance apart; however, they were left with their lands (Diod. 16.60). Although Demosthenes (19.64 ff.) thinks that the Phocian punishment was severe, it could have been far worse. The Phocians were not executed or sold into slavery, nor was their land confiscated. Moreover, the annual indemnity, which was originally fixed at sixty talents, was not enforced until 343, and in 341 it was reduced to thirty talents, and later to only ten talents per annum.

The relative lightness of the punishment was owing to the moderation of Philip and the Athenian ambassador Aeschines, who were able to persuade the other Greeks to commute the normal penalty. Thus, Hyperides is deliberately misleading in this section: Phocis may well have willingly consented to Leosthenes' leadership, but had it not been for Philip's support the people of that state would have been eradicated. During Alexander's rule, they had prospered. Hyperides cannot say this of course since he is eulogising Leosthenes and painting as disparaging a picture as he can of Macedonian rule. It is interesting to note that Demosthenes does much the same in a speech delivered in 343: he says that those Phocians who fled from Phocis before the penalty was imposed were killed (19.64 ff.). This was not so: these Phocians were placed under a curse and could be arrested, but not executed.

The Aetolians were not treated oppressively by Philip. In 342, because of a local dispute with their neighbours the Achaeans over Naupactus, they made an alliance with him. We are told that in the summer of 338 Parmenion handed them Naupactus in fulfillment of Philip's earlier promise (Dem. 9.34). In 324 they, like the other Greeks, were adversely affected by Alexander's Exiles Decree since it required them to return Oeniadae to the Acarnanian League, from which they had seized it (Diod. 18.8.6, Plut. *Alexander* 49.8). This is probably why in 323 they made a military treaty with Athens (see Ian Worthington, 'IG ii² 370 and the Date of the Athenian Alliance with Aetolia', ZPE 57 [1984], 139-144). The Aetolians supported the Theban revolt in 335 along with the Arcadians, Argives, Eleans and at first the Athenians (Aes. 3.240-241, Din. 1.21, Arr. 1.7.4), but when Thebes was captured they appealed to Alexander for mercy. He did not act against them and indeed treated the states with moderation since he needed their support for his forthcoming invasion of Persia. The Aetolian League was a powerful entity as is shown when Antipater defeated the Greeks in the Lamian War in 322: he and Craterus (who had brought Alexander's discharged veterans and wounded soldiers from Asia) then made a separate alliance with each state, apart from Athens and Aetolia (Diod. 1 ʾ.17.8). The Aetolian League fought on throughout the winter of 322/1, and it was saved from annihilation only because of the clash of Antipater and Craterus against Perdiccas (Diod. 18.24-25).

He was able . . . decreed by fate: The reference to Fate emphasises man's mortality and thus his inability to escape it. Despite Leosthenes' superior skills as a general, Greek attempts to take Lamia during the winter of 323/2 failed because of its fortifications, and during one of them in late 323 he was injured by a slinger's stone and died three days later (Diod. 18.13.5, Justin 13.5.12). Antiphilus (Diod. 18.13.6) succeeded him. Antipater then offered to surrender his force on terms, but the Athenians demanded unconditional surrender, a demand which Antipater naturally refused. About now, we may fit Demosthenes' triumphant return to Athens from his self-imposed exile, the result of his disgrace in the Harpalus affair ([Lucian] *Enc. Dem.* 31).

(14) **It is right that . . . Leosthenes:** Antiphilus, Leosthenes' successor (Diod. 18.13.6), continued the siege of Lamia. He was soon faced by a force of 20,000 infantry and 1,500 cavalry under the command of the Macedonian general Leonnatus, who had come to liberate Antipater, but in the ensuing battle Leonnatus was defeated and killed. However, Antipater was able to escape from Lamia and to make his way back to Macedon (Diod. 18.15.1-7, Plut. *Phocion* 25; cf. Justin 13.5.14-16). This proved to be a significant turning-point in the war, for Antipater was able to regroup his forces, and perhaps many in Athens realised this. In hindsight, it would have been better had the Athenians accepted Antipater's offer of surrender: see Introduction, p. 14. Certainly, no 'other benefits' came to the Greeks after this battle, for within several months Antipater and Craterus had crushed them completely.

In the spring of 322, shortly after Antiphilus' victory, the Athenians selected Hyperides ('foremost of the orators in eloquence and in hostility towards the Macedonians': Diod. 18.13.5) to deliver the present speech over those Athenians, especially Leosthenes, who had died in the first year of the Lamian War.

(15-34) In this long section Hyperides turns to praise Leosthenes' men who died for Greek freedom against Macedon. Although the soldiers seem to be the focus of this part of this speech, Leosthenes is constantly referred to and hence remains a central figure. The soldiers deserve praise because they fought and died for freedom (15-16), spurred on by the fact that their first battle was fought in Boeotia where Thebes had been razed to the ground by Alexander (17). Hyperides refers again to their battles at Thermopylae and Lamia which will bring them a universal reputation not only for their victories but because they fought for Greek freedom (18-19). But what if they had not fought for this cause: what if they had not done what was right (20)? This chilling note allows Hyperides to paint a picture of how the Macedonians would abuse the Greeks (20) – bad enough that the Greeks now have to worship certain Macedonians (21), but if Leosthenes' men had not fought as they did it would not only be the gods who were subverted (22). Once again, Hyperides says, the Greeks are in debt to those who died for freedom (23). The glory they have earned will be eternal, and this is only right given the hardships they endured and the benefits they conferred on the Greeks (24-26). Hyperides now moves to console family members who will be famous and honoured because of those men's exploits, and who may take comfort from the reputation which those men will now enjoy forever (27-29). The eulogistic tone continues as Hyperides concludes this part of the speech, again praising the courage of those men and that they are an example to the older and younger generations (30-34).

(15)   **Let no one think . . . courage of his men:** Hyperides' funeral speech is built around the great eulogy to Leosthenes. However, given that many of his audience would have lost family members and friends, he takes care not to downplay the roles of the others who lost their lives in the war so far. It is interesting that Antiphilus is not mentioned by name, despite his victory over Leonnatus (see commentary on 14).

(16)   **For who would not . . . on its behalf:** Cf. 19, 24 and 37-38. A funeral speech was meant to praise those who had died and, in an effort to exhort the listeners, to show their deaths were worthy. Here, Hyperides justifies the deaths of those who died in the war by saying their actions helped to preserve the common freedom of the Greeks. The Greeks viewed *eleutheria* or freedom as of the utmost importance: see further, commentary on 10.

(17)   **One factor . . . Boeotia:** A reference to Leosthenes' defeat of a combined Boeotian and Euboean army at the start of the war: see commentary on 11.
They saw that the city of the Thebans . . . danger readily: In 335 Thebes had defied Alexander, and he had besieged it (Diod. 17.8.3-13). After forcing the city to surrender, he razed it to the ground. Some 6,000 Thebans were killed and 30,000 were taken prisoner and sold as slaves (Diod. 17.14.1): see further, commentary on Dinarchus 1.10. Aeschines and Dinarchus also refer to the destruction of Thebes in similar vivid terminology: 'But Thebes! Thebes, our neighbour, has in one day been swept from the midst of Hellas' (Aes. 3.133); 'But thanks to this traitor the children and wives of the Thebans were divided among the tents of the barbarians, a neighbouring and allied city has been ripped up from the middle of Greece – the city of the Thebans, which shared the war against Philip with you, is being ploughed and sown' (Din. 1.24).

(18)   **Moreover, the battle . . . at that spot:** On these battles, which were fought in the first few months of the Lamian War, see commentary on 11-12.
For all the Greeks . . . courage of those men: Thermopylae was the original meeting place of the Amphictyonic League, a combination of northern and central Greek states which administered the oracle of Apollo at Delphi and convened the Pythian games there. Its Council met twice a year, and ambassadors from the various Greek states sent their representatives (θεωροί) to it. Given its control of so important an oracle in the Greek world, the League had great political power as well. For example, it was responsible for declaring the Sacred War against Phocis when that state seized Delphi in 356 (see commentary on 13), and Philip II was anxious to become a member of it (the Phocian vote on the Council was transferred to him in 346, at the end of the Sacred War).
Colin, 297, makes the intriguing suggestion that Hyperides' use of θεωροί here could indicate that Thermopylae was being established as a place of pilgrimage where those who died in the Lamian War would be honoured (Colin uses as a modern analogy 'le pèlerinage de Verdun').

(19)   **Never did men fight . . . on their country:** Cf. 16. Again, Hyperides praises those who gave their lives for the common freedom of Greece: on this ideal, see commentary on 10.
The use of the crown metaphor is striking, and Hyperides also uses it at 5.30: 'the people did this and so owing to chance they were deprived of their crown of victory but they did not deprive us of the crown they had granted'.

So too does Lycurgus, referring to those who died at the battle of Chaeronea against Philip II in 338: 'I therefore say without misgiving that their lives have been a crown for Athens' (1.50).

Numerically, the Greek forces from the start of the Lamian War in 323 to the time this speech was delivered about a year later were superior to the Macedonian, probably double in number, and most of Greece supported Athens in the Lamian War (Diod. 18.11.1-2). At the start of the war, the Greeks also had a huge fleet of 240 vessels, which included 170 Athenian ships. This combined fleet must also have been at least twice as large as that of the Macedonians (Diod. 18.9.2): see Introduction, p. 13. On the number of Athenian ships in the later fourth century, see especially N.G. Ashton, 'The Naumachia near Amorgos in 322 B.C.', *BSA* 72 (1977), 1-11 and J.S. Morrison, 'Athenian sea-power in 323/2 B.C.: Dream and reality', *JHS* 107 (1987), 88-97.

The Greeks also had a large fighting force: at the battle in Boeotia Leosthenes had about 15,000 men and 500 cavalry. This number increased dramatically, and by the time the Greeks reached Thermopylae it had risen to 30,000. The Macedonian army numbered 13,000 soldiers and 2,600 cavalry (of which 2,000 were Thessalian and deserted to the Greek side), and Diodorus (18.12.2) says that Antipater lacked 'citizen soldiers', that is Macedonians proper, at least until reinforcements arrived led by Leonnatus and later by Craterus. Leonnatus brought over 20,000 troops with him when he marched to relieve Antipater at Lamia, but Antiphilus still defeated him (see commentary on 14).

Thus, at the time of this present speech the Athenians were well supported by their allies and had more infantry and cavalry than Antipater did. Within a few months it was a different story. In the summer of 322, the Macedonian admiral Cleitus destroyed the Greek fleet at the battle of Abydus (Diod. 18.15.8-9), thereby allowing Craterus the means to ferry about 10,000 infantry, 1,500 Persian archers and 1,500 cavalry from Cilicia to Macedon (Diod. 18.16.4-5). By the time of the battle of Crannon in August 322 (at which Antipater defeated the Greeks and ended the war) the Macedonian army numbered 48,000 soldiers including 5,000 cavalry, and the Greek only 25,000 soldiers and 3,500 cavalry (Diod. 18.17.1-2).

Hyperides' factual accuracy is again questionable – at least for the first year of the war with which his speech is supposed to deal. We can understand why, given the nature of the *epitaphios* and the immediate political and military background, hence the need to exaggerate any victories and belittle the achievements of opponents.

(20) **Therefore it is worth considering . . . as law:** Cf. 22. In reality, Greece had been under Macedonian control since Philip II's victory at the battle of Chaeronea, and the rule of Alexander, especially his Exiles Decree which flouted the autonomy of the Greek states, had also proved that: see Introduction, p. 7.

νομίζοιμεν: This is the reading of the papyrus. If it is correct, ἄν must be taken with both verbs – 'What *would* we think *would have* happened?' Because this is a little difficult to parallel, most editors emend with Blass to νομίζομεν, leaving the ἄν to qualify the infinitive only. But, as P. Graindor (*Révue d'instr. publ.* 1898, p. 341) pointed out, the repetition of the same phenomenon in 22 (ἄν γένεσθαι κρίνοιμεν) suggests that we should retain the papyrus reading in both places. It seems that we may have a Hyperidean idiom.

To put it simply . . . in any place: Cf. 35-36 (with commentary), likening the Greeks' famous war against Troy over Helen to Leosthenes fighting on behalf of all Greek women. Dinarchus at 1.24 has talked of the outrages committed by the Macedonians against the Thebans, and at 1.99 and 109 he alludes to what would happen to the Athenians' wives and children if corrupt leaders are left unpunished in the city. This is a typical form of appeal in Greek oratory, and is akin to a scare tactic. Hyperides goes on to outline some of the 'outrages' which the Greek were forced to endure in the next sections. In fact, Greek women in the other states were not abused by the Macedonians, even after the end of the Lamian War, nor were they ever in danger of this.

ἂν ἐκλείπτους γένεσθαι: The difficulty faced by editors is that the word ἔκλειπτος is not found elsewhere in extant Greek; ἀνέκλειπτος is found occasionally, with the meaning 'unending', 'incessant'. However, the incidence of verbal adjectives in classical Greek is a little haphazard; had the text here read ἂν ἐκλειφθῆναι, we should not have suspected it.

(21-22) This is clear . . . completely subverted: Cf. 43, on how those who championed the gods at this time would be rewarded in Hades. These sections are often linked to Hyperides 5.31-32 in connection with the debate in Greece over Alexander's divinity in 324/3 and as evidence for a statue and cult of Alexander in Athens; cf. Dinarchus 1.94. On the deification issue and the doubtful validity of Hyperides 5.31-32 see commentary *ad loc.*

The veracity of Hyperides here also is suspect, and at the very least he is guilty of massive exaggeration. Certainly, the Athenians were not coerced to abandon worshipping their traditional gods, and there is no evidence to suggest they neglected existing temples and sanctuaries during the Macedonian hegemony. In fact, during this period as part of a building programme the Panathenaic Stadium and the Theatre of Dionysus were constructed (see Introduction, p. 5).

Moreover, in 21, Hyperides uses the word ἄγαλμα (cult image) as distinct from εἰκών (which had no cult attached at this time); contrast 5.32. An *eikon* was simply a portrait and had no cult attached to it until the second century – and then only in Asia Minor. Badian suggests that whereas the Athenians refused to establish a cult to Alexander they compromised and erected a portrait statue of him on which he would be described as divine (E. Badian, 'Alexander the Great between Two Thrones and Heaven: Variations on an Old Theme', in *Subject and Ruler: The Cult of the Ruling Power in Classical Antiquity*, ed. A. Small [Ann Arbor: 1996], 25-26). However, the distinction between being recognised as a god and simply being described as one would not be lost on Alexander, and the diplomatic embassies to the king in connection with the Exiles Decree shows how careful the Greeks were not to upset him. More importantly, no statue of Alexander is known in Athens (cf. A. Stewart, *Faces of Power. Alexander's Image and Hellenistic Politics* [Berkeley and Los Angeles: 1993], 101-103 and 207-209), and when Alexander died the Greeks immediately disregarded his Exiles Decree – the odious issue of his divine honours must have suffered the same fate. The same Athenians who, at some point in the Lamian War, prosecuted Demades for his earlier proposal of divine honours for Alexander (Athenaeus 6.251b,

Aelian, *VH* 5.12), would not have allowed any statues or temples to remain standing or performed sacrifices to him.

Which 'servants of these men' were the Athenians forced to honour? We know of only one, and that is Alexander's comrade and friend Hephaestion, who died in 324. Like Achilles mourning for Patroclus in Homer's *Iliad*, on which Alexander was schooled, so Alexander mourned his friend. He gave him a magnificent funeral and instituted a heroic cult to him (Diod. 17.115.6, Plut. *Alexander* 72.2, Arr. 7.14.7). This cult is significant: Hephaestion was accorded semi-divine honours, and Hyperides must be singling him out here. Alexander's wish that Hephaestion receive heroic honours probably influenced the Greeks to discuss recognising Alexander's divinity for political reasons: see further G.L. Cawkwell, 'The Deification of Alexander the Great: A Note', *Ventures Into Greek History. Essays in Honour of N.G.L. Hammond*, ed. Ian Worthington (Oxford: 1994), 293-306.

The more terrible . . . deserved by those who died: Hyperides' misrepresentation and exaggeration are perhaps understandable. His speech was delivered when the Lamian War was taking a down-turn for the Greeks with Antipater's escape from Lamia and his successful return to Macedon (see 14 with commentary). Hyperides needed to exhort the Athenians and to depict the Macedonians as irreverently as he could. One way was to exploit his audience's pious indignation at the expectations of Alexander and the lengths to which the Greeks had been forced to go (ἀναγκάζομαι is used twice) with their embassies to the king pleading against the Exiles Decree and in the process pandering to his divinity: see Introduction, pp. 8-9.

κρίνοιμεν: See note on νομίζοιμεν in 20.

(23) **For no campaign . . . describe in words:** There is no question of the courage of the Greeks who rose in revolt against Macedon; however, the battles which they fought in no way outnumbered all the defeats of previous armies over the course of several hundred years! Indeed, the exaggeration is so great that the text may even be corrupt, and many previous editors have attempted to emend it (cf. the *apparatus criticus* of Colin, *ad loc.*). Hyperides refers to the siege of Lamia, to which Antipater had fled (cf. 12), which took place in the winter of 323/2 (Diod. 18.12.3-4, Plut. *Demosthenes* 27.1, *Phocion* 23.4-5, Polyaenus 4.4.2). Winter was not the normal campaigning season, but a siege cannot be interrupted and is a daily process, so the Greek force had to endure the severe cold and weather conditions in that part of Greece.

A phrase such as 'hard to describe in words' was a common rhetorical trick, allowing listeners (and readers) to conjure up their own images, which could be more vivid and dramatic than anything the speakers gave.

(24) **Leosthenes exhorted the citizens . . . sacrifice of life:** Leosthenes is again named specifically in the speech and his greatness as a commander stated. However, in keeping with the nature of an *epitaphios,* the sacrifice of those who died under him for a noble cause is also praised. Hyperides does not merely relate the circumstances of their death but states that in dying nobly for freedom, the ideal which all Greeks cherished the utmost, the soldiers gained everlasting life (cf. 27-29).

In place of an ephemeral body . . . individual courage: Cf. 16, 19, 28-29 and 43-44 (reference to the everlasting reputation of those who died). The use of the word autonomy stresses the great ideal of freedom (*eleutheria*) for all Greeks, which must be preserved even at the cost of human life: see commentary on 10. Hyperides elaborates on this ideal in the next section.

(25) **For there cannot . . . trust in the laws:** The Greek *polis* (city-state) was founded on individual autonomy. Each *polis* was more like a state than a city since each had its own territory and governed itself; each had its own citizenship, laws, coinage, and tried to be self-sufficient. The *polis* system arose owing to the geography of Greece and the Greeks' strong sense of individualism which led to a feeling of xenophobia for all others. This accounts for the numerous wars between the *poleis* which characterised Greek history and the importance attached to freedom (on this, see commentary on 10).

The rule of the law was common in *poleis*, and in Athens, for example, those jurors annually selected took a dicastic oath to uphold and vote in accordance with the laws: this oath is quoted in the commentary on Hyperides 5.1. In Athens, then, the *demos* (the political mass of the citizenry) was sovereign in that it administered all policy and was responsible for the maintenance of law, on which a state was founded; cf. Dinarchus 1.6 with commentary, on the Areopagus which originally was 'guardian of the laws' (*AP* 4.4, 8.4). Thus, for example, at 3.80.6 Herodotus says: 'The sovereignty of the people has, firstly, the fairest name of all – equality before the laws', and *isonomia* ('equality before the laws') became a political catchword in classical Athens.

The League of Corinth of 337 imposed by Philip II on Greece allowed the *poleis* their autonomy (Diod. 16.89.2; M.N. Tod, *Greek Historical Inscriptions* 2 [Oxford: 1948], no. 177; cf. T.T.B. Ryder, *Koine Eirene* (Oxford: 1965), 102-105 and 150-162). However, the limits on military alliances, and decrees such as that of Alexander ordering all Greek states (excluding Thebes) to receive back their exiles in 324 (Diod. 18.8.4), show that individual autonomy was really a thing of the past. On the other hand, because of the constant warfare between various *poleis* in the days before Philip, the Greeks were often financially exhausted. The Macedonian hegemony of Greece allowed the Greeks a period of peace and thus prosperity, which they had not enjoyed for decades: see Introduction, pp. 16-18.

A negative is necessary at the start of this section given the point which Hyperides is making. Therefore, I agree with Kenyon who prints οὐδὲν. The genitive case is necessary for αὐτονομία since it follows the preposition ἄνευ.

(26) **These men undertook hardships . . . others might live well:** A reference to those who fought against Macedon in the first year of the Lamian War, and especially those who maintained their winter vigil outside Lamia: see 23 with commentary. Ironically, their sacrifice did not result in others living well: when Antipater crushed the revolt the Athenians were severely punished. In addition to paying a large war indemnity, a Macedonian garrison was established in Athens and the democracy was overthrown and replaced by a Macedonian-backed oligarchy (Diod. 18.18.4-5).

The phrase πόνους πόνων διαδόχους has a ring to it and looks like a tragic quotation. However, it is not found in Aeschylus, Sophocles, Euripides or the remains of the minor tragedians. Since the orators frequently quote from the tragedians, and Euripides especially was fond of this type of expression, Hyperides may well be twisting, for example, Euripides,

Andromache 802: κακὸν κακῷ διάδοχον. However, it is odd for an orator to use a poetic tag without any acknowledgement, and the phrase in question may even be from a lost play of Euripides. Given that the present speech is an *epitaphios*, Hyperides may have felt that the poetic ornamentation was quite fitting since he was not afraid of innovation in his speeches (cf. Introduction, pp. 31 and 35-36).

(27-29) Fathers have become famous . . . for their bravery: Cf. 24. Although Leosthenes take centre stage in this speech, Hyperides cannot diminish the actions and achievements of those who also died in the war. He attempts to show that they did not die in vain for the cause of Greek freedom, and that their actions have contributed directly to their own personal glory and reputation, as well as that of their families. Stirring stuff indeed.

Hyperides' use of τάξις ('order of battle') makes the phrase he uses for eternal life ('everlasting battle array') a military metaphor. It is in keeping with the way the men died while exhorting his listeners to take pride in their demise and strength from their current situation: they died nobly, standing steadfast in their ranks, and so they will stand in the next life. This transition is likened by Hyperides not only to a rebirth but also to the passing from childhood from adulthood: in dying for freedom, these men moved from childhood to manhood, and their noble actions have guaranteed their reputation forever. Lysias in his funeral speech also says that the valour of those who died for this ideal has earned them immortality (2.79-81), as does Pericles in his alleged funeral speech (Thucydides 2.43), and Demosthenes in his (60.32).

(30-33) For on what occasion . . . younger men: Hyperides continues with his eulogy on the soldiers who served under Leosthenes, who will be remembered and admired at all times by all ages in the city. The appeals here echo those used by Lysias in his *epitaphios* (for example, 74), and may well have been common to this genre.

The papyrus is broken in sections 31, 32 and 33, but it seems that Hyperides rhetorically lists the three age groups of adult citizens. Further restorations in Jensen and other editors, mostly due to Blass, are highly speculative. It is wiser in this instance to translate only what can be seen with some confidence on the papyrus.

The reference to the state's legal provisions for surviving children is common in funeral orations; cf. those attributed to Pericles (Thucydides 2.44.3, 2.46.1) and Socrates (Plato, *Menexenus* 246d-247e, 249a). See 42, where the law concerning war orphans is cited. Note by contrast Hyperides 5.21, accusing Demosthenes of being the reverse of the great men referred to here and thus the archetypal bad role model.

(34) There are two reasons . . . Macedonians: The end of the first year of the Lamian War, roughly the time when Hyperides delivered this speech, did not bring freedom from Macedonian rule. The patriotic and glorious deeds of the Athenians' ancestors, especially when defeating an enemy power or fighting on behalf of their democracy, are frequent topoi in Greek oratory (cf. 37 with commentary, on Miltiades and Themistocles). The Athenians enjoyed hearing about these exploits, and they seem to have been often related by the Athenians' elders (cf. Dinarchus 1.25, 72 and 75). Naturally, any defeat of the 'oppressive' Macedonians would have been long remembered and highly praised, however this was not the case. Hyperides is right to applaud the bravery of those who defied Macedon on Alexander's death, but he was quite wrong to say that they brought freedom for Greece.

But if this sort of recollection ... brave men: The reference to Leosthenes and those who died with him neatly ends this long part of the speech.

The future participles ἀκουσόντων and ἐγκωμιάσοντος are needed here since Hyperides refers to a type of speech which has yet to be delivered.

(35-40) In this part of the speech, as in other *epitaphioi*, we have reference to the great deeds of the Athenians' and Greeks' ancestors. We also return to Leosthenes the individual as Hyperides compares his exploits with events from past history. Thus, whereas the heroes of the Trojan War championed the rights of one woman (35), Leosthenes championed all Greek women (36). Whereas Militades and Themistocles masterminded the great defeats of the Persians, who threatened Greek freedom, in the fifth century (37), Leosthenes apparently prevented an equally foreign foe – Macedon – which threatened Greek freedom from invading Greece in the first place and defeated it in its own land (38). And, whereas Harmodius and Aristogeiton in the late sixth century allegedly brought down the rule of the Pisistratid tyrants at Athens, Leosthenes (equally allegedly) brought down the Macedonian tyrants who ruled all of Greece (39). No wonder the courage and bravery of these men are to be praised and admired (40)!

(35) **It is clear ... these men in Hades:** In ancient Greece Hades was not thought of as a place to which the dead went (such as hell or heaven in Christian belief), but the person, the god of the underworld, hence ἐν Ἅιδου, in the 'House of Hades'. Moreover, Hades cannot be likened to a being such as Satan; he merely punishes wrongdoers, and thus he cannot be characterised as 'evil'.

Would we not expect ... Europe and Asia: There is some similarity with Isocrates, *Panegyricus* 83-84, and the Trojan War was a favourite historical topos of the orators.

Hyperides' analogy does not withstand historical scrutiny, and the rhetorical exaggeration is probably because of the occasion of the speech. According to tradition, the Greeks *en masse*, led by Agamemnon of Mycenae, waged war against the Trojans to retrieve the kidnapped Helen, wife of Menelaus of Sparta. The war, which is traditionally dated to the late twelfth century BC, lasted for ten years, and Troy was destroyed. The Trojan War is recounted in Homer's *Iliad*, and the return and adventures of the Greek hero Odysseus to his native Ithaca are told in Homer's *Odyssey*. The heroes of the war are called demigods at Homer, *Iliad* 12.23, and some received semi-divine status on their deaths, for example the Trojan Hector, killed by Achilles, who had a heroic cult at Troy and Thebes (Pausanias 9.18.5).

Hyperides suggests that Leosthenes and the Athenians alone excelled the combined Greek effort in the Trojan War since the Greek force merely destroyed one city (Troy) but the former brought down the empire established by Philip II and Alexander the Great and ended Macedonian rule. This is nonsense. For one thing, Athens was supported by many other Greek states at all times in the Lamian War; for another, the Greeks lost the war, and the Macedonian control of the empire remained intact. Hyperides' listeners would have been well aware that at the end of the first year of the Lamian War Macedonian power, though shaken by the defeats of Antipater at

Thermopylae and Leonnatus at Lamia (see 12-14 with commentary), had not been 'brought down completely'. Again, we see Hyperides guilty of rhetorical exaggeration, in keeping with the style of an *epitaphios*, for effect.

(36)   **They came to the defence . . . all Greek women:** The reference is to the Greeks' war against Troy over Helen, wife of Menelaus of Sparta: see 35 with commentary. On the championing and protection of Greek women by Leosthenes and his men, see 20 with commentary.

(37)   τῶν δὲ μετ' ἐκείνους: Sauppe introduced δέ, thus making a new sentence begin at this point. In spite of the anacoluthon (τῶν δὲ . . . διαπεπραγμένων, λέγω δὴ . . . ἐποίησαν, ὧν οὗτος . . . ἐποίησεν), in which there is no main sentence with the initial genitive plural, but it is instead picked up by the genitive plural ὧν, this formulation makes much better sense than the alternative, which is to begin the new sentence at λέγω. Those who were 'born after the Homeric heroes, but did things worthy of their valour' are the heroes of the Persian wars, not the present dead. This view is shared by Jensen and Burtt, not by Kenyon or Colin.

And those who were born after them . . . lives glorious: The patriotic deeds of the Athenians' ancestors are frequent topoi in Greek oratory, and those men who contributed to the rise of Athens in the days of the Persian Wars (490, 480-478) and the formation of the Delian League, which grew into a fifth-century Athenian empire, are amongst the most common. The following list is by no means exhaustive (for discussion see the relevant commentary sections in Dinarchus 1, listed below, who also makes much use of topoi). Thus, we see numerous allusions to the days of the Persian Wars (Din. 1.37), the restoration of Theban democracy in 379/8 (Din. 1.38-40), the exploits of Timotheus and Conon (Din. 1.14 and 75), the deeds of the sixth-century 'tyrannicides' Harmodius and Aristogeiton (Din. 1.101; cf. Hyp. 6.39 below), and the restoration of Athenian democracy in 403 (Din. 1.25). At the same time, the Persian war period in Greek history was deliberately exploited in epideictic oratory for patriotic effect.

Miltiades was the hero of the battle of Marathon in 490. In that year, the Persian king Darius invaded Greece as part of a grand design to conquer the Greeks (Herodotus 6.94; see 6.94-124 for the campaign). The Persian fleet laid waste some towns along its route, including Eretria on the island of Euboea (Herodotus 6.96-101). Athens was next, and in panic the people mobilised an army and requested help from the Spartans, who declined under questionable circumstances (Herodotus 6.102-103). The Persians landed at Marathon in eastern Attica, and the Athenians, supported by a small force of 1,000 Plataeans, faced them. There is no question that the 'invincible' Persian army was expected to win. However, owing to serious strategic errors on its part, such as landing in swampy ground which rendered the cavalry useless, and the brilliance of the Athenian general Miltiades, the Persians were defeated. The battle of Marathon was Athens' coming of age as a military power, and a victorious Miltiades dedicated spoils from it at Olympia, including his helmet, which can be seen in the Museum today with his name inscribed on it. Those Athenians who died in the battle were held in such honour that they were buried on the site, rather than their bodies transported to Athens, and a memorial set up over them (Thucydides 2.34.5, quoted in the introduction to the commentary above). On the battle see Herodotus 6.105-117, and on the period see, for example, N.G.L. Hammond, *A History of Greece*[3] (Oxford: 1986), 212-218.

Themistocles' policy of strengthening the Athenian navy laid the foundation for Athens' fifth century empire, which rested on its navy. Themistocles was also responsible for the rebuilding of the city walls and the building of those at the Piraeus (Thucydides 1.89.3 ff., *AP* 23.3-4, Plut. *Themistocles* 19.1 ff.). However, it is really for his role in defeating the Persians at the battle of Salamis in 480 that Themistocles is best remembered. In 481 the Persian king Xerxes (Darius having died some years previously) invaded Greece with the aim of total conquest (Herodotus 7.138). After he forced his way through Thermopylae (see 12 with commentary), the Greek fleet assembled at the Bay of Salamis in September 480. When the Persians sacked Athens (Herodotus 8.51-54) the Greeks were in panic and wanted to disperse immediately, but Themistocles sent a slave to Xerxes with the news that the Greek fleet would soon sail off and that he would aid the Persian cause (Herodotus 8.70-75, Plut. *Themistocles* 12). The Persians immediately sailed against the Greeks, and under Themistocles' direction the Persian fleet, despite being triple in size to the Greeks, was virtually annihilated. Salamis was a turning point in the war, for the Persians ceased their plan of conquest by sea and Xerxes himself fled back to Persia with only a fraction of his original army (Herodotus 8.113-120).

On the battle of Salamis see Herodotus 6.41-95, and on the period see, for example, Hammond, *History of Greece*[3], 237-244. On Themistocles see also *PA* 6669 and Davies, *APF*, 211-220, especially 214-217.

Dinarchus also refers to the exploits of Themistocles, and links him to another leader at this time, Aristides (see 1.37 with commentary). Whereas Dinarchus refers to the glorious past in order to contrast it with Demosthenes' disreputable deeds and venality, Hyperides uses the period of the Persian Wars (in 12 he refers to the battle of Thermopylae, which took place a short time before Salamis) for a quite different reason. He uses that period, when Greece faced a foreign enemy which threatened its freedom and autonomy, as an analogy to the present war against the Macedonians, who also endangered the freedom of the Greeks: see commentary on 10, on the ideal of freedom (*eleutheria*). So too do some of the other surviving funeral speeches; cf. Lysias (2.21-44) and Socrates (Plato, *Menexenus* 239d-241c). At the same time, in keeping with the nature of an *epitaphios*, Hyperides selects individuals who were directly responsible for Athens' greatness and argues that even they cannot match Leosthenes' achievements and worth.

(38) **Leosthenes excelled them . . . in their land:** A reference to Leosthenes' exploits at Thermopylae (see 12 with commentary), which prevented Antipater from marching further into Greece, and to his earlier battle in Boeotia (see 11 with commentary), at which he defeated a combined Boeotian and Euboean army. Although this section is technically inaccurate since Boeotia was in Greece, the fact that it had remained pro-Macedonian on Alexander's death indicates the contempt which the other Greeks felt for it.

As Colin, 303, says, Hyperides' use of ἀνδρείᾳ καὶ φρονήσει ('bravery and forethought') neatly shows Leosthenes' characteristic merits.

(39) **I think also . . . whole of Greece:** As so often in oratory we have historical inaccuracies since the orators were not concerned with accuracy but with the rhetorical presentation of arguments. Perhaps also this is to be expected even more in the present speech given Hyperides' aim of justifying and praising the deaths of Leosthenes and the other soldiers. In 546 Athens fell under the rule of the tyrant Pisistratus, and benefitted economically, culturally, and

commercially (*AP* 14-19, Plut. *Solon* 29). He died in 528/7, and power passed to his two sons, Hippias and Hipparchus (*AP* 17-18). Their rule was eventually characterised by problems especially in foreign affairs, and in 514 Harmodius and Aristogeiton murdered Hipparchus (Herodotus 5.55 ff., Thucydides 6.54-9, *AP* 18, [Plato] *Hipparchus* 229c1 ff., Diod. 10.17). That action did not bring an end to the tyranny as Hippias ruled for a further four years. In 510 a leading family, the Alcmeonidae, then in exile from Athens, influenced the Delphic oracle to persuade the Spartans to expel him (Herodotus 6.123, *AP* 19.4-6), thereby bringing an end to the tyranny. Nonetheless, Harmodius and Aristogeiton were still recognised as tyrannicides, and they and the period became not only the ideal of democracy but also a popular topos employed by the orators – Dinarchus also refers to Harmodius and Aristogeiton at 1.101 (see commentary *ad loc.*). Leosthenes and his men are likened to Harmodius and Aristogeiton in resisting despotism. However, it is important to note that Harmodius and Aristogeiton did not bring down the Pisistratid tyranny nor did Leosthenes depose the Macedonian rulers of Greece. On Harmodius and Aristogeiton see *PA* 2232 and 1777, respectively; cf. Davies, *APF*, 473-474; on the murder of Hipparchus quoting modern bibliography, see P.J. Rhodes, *A Commentary on the Aristotelian Athenaion Politeia* (Oxford: 1981), 227-233. On the period of the Pisistratid tyranny, see, most conveniently, N.G.L. Hammond, *A History of Greece*[3] (Oxford: 1986), 179-185 and A. Andrewes, *The Greek Tyrants* (London: 1974), 100-115.

On the reference to Hades, see commentary on 35.

The papyrus is corrupt in the third line here and a precise reading is impossible. I follow that proposed by Kenyon, which seems to fit the sense required.

(40) **How fine and incredible . . . Greeks:** Again, reference is made to the nobility of fighting, and dying, for the common freedom of the Greeks (see commentary on 10), a theme which naturally runs through a speech such as an *epitaphios* which is a eulogy to the dead. Hyperides has magnified the achievements of Leosthenes and his men by his distortion of historical fact, and this line of argument brings to an end what appears to be the penultimate part of the speech.

The papyrus is broken in section 40. However, from the tone of section 41 it seems highly probable that Hyperides was moving towards the epilogue, or final part, of the speech.

(41-43) The tone indicates that this is likely to be the epilogue of the *epitaphios* as Hyperides moves to exhort his listeners and offer them some consolation in their grief. He recognises this is no easy task (41), but again resorts to the argument that the bravery of those who died needs to be praised, that they themselves have won eternal glory, and hence weeping is unnecessary (41-42). Moreover, given the cause for which they died they will be well treated by the god of Hades (43). This section of the speech which we have today does not come from the papyrus, but is quoted in an early fifth century A.D. anthology of quotations from poets and prose-writers compiled by Stobaeus.

(41) **Perhaps it is hard . . . left behind:** Cf. 27-29. There is a very real human and moving touch in this section, which probably occurs towards the end of the speech, as Hyperides acknowledges that those who lost loved ones in the first year of the war will be grief-stricken. Condolences are also found, as we might expect, in other funeral orations (cf. Thucydides 2.44, 2.45.2, Dem. 60.37, Plato, *Menexenus* 247d-248d). Hyperides is powerless to bring actual comfort, and he knows it; he can only exhort his listeners to be brave and to take courage from the actions of those who died. That he achieves this is a tribute to his great rhetorical skill.

(42) **For they have not suffered ... in every way:** Cf. 16, 19 and 27-29, on the everlasting glory acquired by those who died for the cause of freedom.

The negative οὐ of the manuscripts of Stobaeus seems to be required here, given the thrust of Hyperides' point; hence I follow Kenyon. Other editors change οὐ to εἰ with Leopardi (1835).

For those of them ... guardian of their children: Again, the importance attached to children (cf. 8) is noted by the law which orders the state to be responsible for raising war orphans and awarding them honours, as told by Aeschines at 3.154:

> ... the herald would come forward and place before you the orphans whose fathers had died in battle, young men clad in the panoply of war; and he would utter that proclamation so honourable and so incentive to valour: 'these young men, whose fathers showed themselves brave men and died in war, have been supported by the state until they have come of age; and now, clad thus in full armour by their fellow citizens, they are sent out with the prayers of the city to go each his way; and they are invited to seats of honour in the theatre.'

The reputation of those who died for a noble cause even though childless calls to mind the final words of the Theban general Epaminondas in 362. As he lay dying, says Diodorus (15.87.6), 'one [of his friends] said "You die childless, Epaminondas", and burst into tears. To this he replied, "No, by Zeus, on the contrary I leave behind two daughters, Leuctra and Mantineia, my victories"'. These two battles (in 371 and 362) earned Epaminondas an everlasting reputation.

(43) **But if, as we assume ... the immortal judge:** On the reference to Hades see commentary on 35. This passage echoes 21-22 to a large extent: since the statues and altars and temples to the gods were allegedly 'uncared for' and 'the honours of the gods were being subverted' because the Athenians were forced to worship Macedonians, then those men who died fighting against Macedonian rule, and so championed the gods, would be rewarded in the after-life.

It is generally assumed (cf. Colin, 279) that this is not quite the end of the speech, but very close to the end.

226

Select Index